THE EVOLUTION AND FUTURE OF MONEY IN CANADA: IMPLICATIONS FOR THE DIGITAL AGE

Legal And Regulatory Perspective

THE EVOLUTION AND FUTURE OF MONEY IN CANADA: IMPLICATIONS FOR THE DIGITAL AGE

Legal and Regulatory Perspective

BENJAMIN GEVA

UNIVERSITY OF TORONTO PRESS
Toronto Buffalo London

The Evolution and Future of Money in Canada: Implications for the Digital Age
(Legal and Regulatory Perspective)
©University of Toronto Press 2025
Irwin Law
An imprint of University of Toronto Press
Toronto Buffalo London
utppublishing.com
Printed in Canada

ISBN 978-1-4875-6930-3 (paper)   ISBN 978-1-4875-6932-7 (EPUB)
                                   ISBN 978-1-4875-6931-0 (PDF)

Library and Archives Canada Cataloguing in Publication

Title: The evolution and future of money in Canada : implications for the digital age : legal and regulatory perspective / Benjamin Geva.
Names: Geva, Benjamin, 1946– author
Description: Includes bibliographical references and index.
Identifiers: Canadiana (print) 20250228475 | Canadiana (ebook) 2025022853X | ISBN 9781487569303 (paper) | ISBN 9781487569327 (EPUB) | ISBN 9781487569310 (PDF)
Subjects: LCSH: Money – Law and legislation – Canada. | LCSH: Money – Technological innovations. | LCSH: Monetary policy – Canada. | LCSH: Money – Canada – History.
Classification: LCC KE5602 .G48 2025 | LCC KF6205 .G48 2025 kfmod | DDC 343.71/032–dc23

Cover design: Kristjan Buckingham
Cover image: Spiroview Inc/Shutterstock.com; Yalcin Sonat/Shutterstock.com

We wish to acknowledge the land on which the University of Toronto Press operates. This land is the traditional territory of the Wendat, the Anishnaabeg, the Haudenosaunee, the Métis, and the Mississaugas of the Credit First Nation.

University of Toronto Press acknowledges the financial support of the Government of Canada, the Canada Council for the Arts, and the Ontario Arts Council, an agency of the Government of Ontario, for its publishing activities.

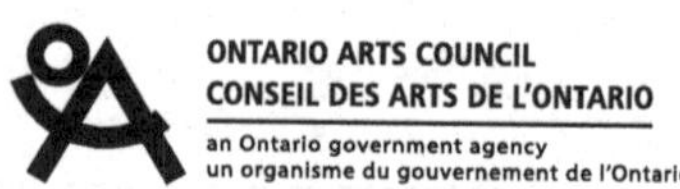

To Esther

SUMMARY TABLE OF CONTENTS

DETAILED TABLE OF CONTENTS

chapter eight
ENVISIONING A "HUB, SPOKES AND FELLOES" MONETARY SYSTEM:
WILL THE WOLF LIVE WITH THE LAMB?   *295*

ACKNOWLEDGMENTS

This is a slightly revised version of a study prepared for the consideration of the Department of Finance Canada and as such may not reflect its views. It is designed to guide policy makers both in choosing a policy path as well as in implementing it. As such it is both high-level and at times technical and of interest to both the public at large and specialists.

Parts of this study draw on previous work, some of which I published exclusively under my name, and others in which I was the lead author. I acknowledge with gratitude both the respective contributions to the joint work and the consent of my co-authors, Dorit Geva, Seraina Grünewald, Corinne Zellweger-Gutknecht, and Mohammed Muraj, for incorporating the joint work led by me into the study.

The published works are in particular:

- Benjamin Geva and Dorit Geva, "Non-state Community Virtual Currencies," c 11 in David Fox and Sara Green (eds), *Cryptocurrencies in Public and Private Law* (Oxford University Press, 2019) at 281;
- Benjamin Geva, "Cryptocurrencies and the Evolution of Banking, Money and Payments," in Chris Brummer (ed), *Cryptoassets: Legal, Regulatory and Monetary Perspective* (Oxford University Press, 2019) at 11;
- Benjamin Geva, Seraina Grünewald, and Corinne Zellweger-Gutknecht, "The E-banknote as a 'Banknote': A Monetary Law Interpreted" (2021) 41:4 *Oxford Journal of Legal Studies* 1119– 48;
- Benjamin Geva, "The Bearer Digital Coin: Optional Design and Legal Features" in Alessandro Palmieri and Giuseppe Versaci (eds), *European Legal Strategies for Payment Systems in the Open Banking Age*

(Sienna: Università di Siena - Dipartimento di Giurisprudenza - Studi «Pietro Rossi», 2023) at 227; and

- Benjamin Geva and Mohammed Muraj, "The Digitization of Money: Stablecoins and CBDC" (2024) 40 *Banking and Finance Law Review* 115

◆◆◆◆◆

- Appendix to chapter 4 was prepared by Ephraim Ajijola, an Osgoode Hall Law School of York University, Toronto doctoral student, who also provided research assistance and assisted me in writing chapter 4.
- For research assistance I am also grateful to Lisa Nguyen and Matthew Marks, both while JD students at Osgoode Hall Law School of York University, Toronto as well as to Maya Hyun Jee Élie, a student at Laval University in Quebec City. Matthew Marks also provided substantial editorial help.
- Funding provided by Department of Finance Canada, support by Osgoode Hall Law School, library support by Sharon Wang and her colleagues at Osgoode Law School Law Library, and feedback by Christopher Reid (at the time) policy analyst at the Department of Finance Canada, Financial Sector Policy Branch (subsequently succeeded by Geoff Solomon, policy advisor), and their team are acknowledged with gratitude. I also acknowledge with gratitude the consent of the Department of Finance Canada to the publication of this study and making it available to the public at large.
- Last but not least I thank the University of Toronto Press's wonderful team – particularly Josephine Mo, Barbara Porter, and Dale Clarry for their indispensable support, patience, and input.

ALL ERRORS AND MISUNDERSTANDINGS ARE MINE

Benjamin Geva
Toronto, Ontario
17 February 2025

SYNOPSIS

This study investigates how in a global context the concept of money in Canada has evolved in response to technological and institutional changes. It explores the impact of emerging digital technologies, such as digital assets, on how society and government regulators think about money.

The aim is to gain a better understanding of the evolving monetary regime in Canada from its inception up to the emerging digital age. This includes looking at digital assets such as value-referenced crypto-assets ("VRCA" also referred to as stablecoins) as a potential source of private money, the impact of digital assets on payment systems, and the role of government and central banks in shaping monetary regulation in response to the emergence of digital assets. In trying to set possible directions for the future, the study endeavours to observe and learn from history and examine to what extent if at all we gain insight to the future from the past. This applies to guiding policies and legal principles, doctrines, and rules.

The study is designed to inform policy development and analysis related to the ongoing financial sector legislative review focused on the digitalization of money. It builds on the voluminous literature – in Canada and elsewhere – and yet fills a gap in existing literature in integrating a legal perspective into a broad policy analysis addressing institutional and technological evolution.

◆◆◆◆◆

Each chapter addresses a distinct theme and has its own perspective. At the same time, borders among the various themes and perspectives are neither fixed nor rigid. Hence, overlaps are inevitable. With this in mind, what follows is a summary of each chapter.

Chapter 1 provides an extensive overview on the global evolution of money from barter to the digital era. It analyzes the concept of money, and presents the evolution of coins, banknotes, scriptural money, electronic money, and digital currencies. **Chapter 2** is a concise legal history of money in Canada. It discusses money and monetary arrangements in New France, the early period of the British takeover, the adoption of the dollar and the appearance of the banknote, the monetary system evolving as of Confederation, and finally, the Bank of Canada and the law governing the present monetary system. **Chapter 3** analyzes the legal features of currency notes (including banknotes). It provides a brief historical outline of the evolution of paper money in the West and goes on to discuss the discharge by payment in a convertible note and the legal nature of the inconvertible note. In this context it discusses whether a promissory note can be money and whether money can be a promissory note. **Chapter 4** discusses the digitalization of private money as reflected in the emergence of virtual currencies, particularly stablecoins. The focus of the chapter is the stablecoin. The chapter discusses legal aspects and risks involved in the purchase, holding, and storage of stablecoins. The chapter is followed by an Appendix consisting of an empirical study on features of cryptocurrencies circulating in Canada.

Chapter 5 discusses retail and wholesale Central Bank Digital Currencies (CBDCs). The perspective is that of legal and regulatory framework for implementation in Canada. The chapter addresses the emergence of CBDCs, as well as the Bank of Canada's power (if any) to issue and equip a retail CBDC with legal tender features under present laws. The chapter goes on to present the DBI – Digital Bearer Instrument – as the optimal retail CBDC and further provides parameters for selection. Following a discussion on the wholesale CBDC and the optimal architecture for issuance model, the chapter proposes for discussion a draft statute particularly addressing a CBDC selection procedure. **Chapter 6** discusses the nature of the digital coin (whether a virtual coin or CBDC) as an e-banknote. It addresses present law in Canada and asks whether the digital coin fulfills the function of a banknote. It further presents a United Nations Commission on International Trade Law (UNCITRAL) model law and American legislation addressing functional equivalence between possession and control as well as between delivery and transfer of control, and more specifically, the electronic promissory note. Addressing legislative options for Canada the chapter is followed by an Appendix proposing a text for an Electronic Promissory Notes Act.

Chapter 7 discusses non-state community currencies. Addressing basic questions such as "community" and "acceptance," it endeavours to focus on non-bank private currencies particularly in digital form. The chapter purports to demonstrate the convergence between the sociological and legal approaches and thus confirms the broad meaning of "money" covering community currency in general and in relation to cryptocurrencies in particular. The chapter concludes that the law is flexible so as to accord monetary status to anything accepted as money. As well, concerns with financial stability and the protection of the public justify some form of regulation of business activity in relation to digital community currencies.

Concluding **chapter 8** addresses the challenges faced by the current monetary system as the digital age keeps moving on and as a monetary system that has become centralized keeps moving toward more and more decentralization. The broad question is whether and how the current system can accommodate the new media and non-traditional issuers and remain operating harmoniously. With respect to new media the analysis builds on research conducted by the Bank of Canada on the co-existence in both Canada and the United States between government currency notes and private banknotes in periods in which concurrent use existed. The conclusion is that an optimal multi-medium harmonized national monetary system is feasible. Briefly stated, to meet the challenge posed by the ongoing evolution of the monetary system in Canada, uniformity of currency ought to be addressed. For its part, uniformity of currency consists of expression in the national unit of account, trading at par, uniform adherence to the national unit of account in prices, redeemability to government money on demand, acceptance at par, insurance against default, effective harmonized clearing, and clearing costs not being borne by users. A regime of effective regulation addressing non-bank issuers, and matters such as safety, security, and conformity with monetary policy, must be in place. Systems not denominated in Canadian dollars may operate and be tolerated. On their own they are unlikely to endanger Canadian monetary sovereignty. In the final analysis, in devising a legislative scheme implementing required steps to accommodate forthcoming changes, arguably, the leadership already held by the Bank of Canada in terms of currency issuance as well as the regulation of risk and monetary policy, ought to accord it a primary role.

chapter one

FROM BARTER TO DIGITAL: THE EVOLUTION OF MONEY

SYNOPSIS

Money is a crucial component of any exchange economy. Money is that which passes freely between members of society and is widely accepted in payment for goods and services, or in final discharge of debts. Inherently valuable objects were the first to be used as money. Subsequently, coins and banknotes came to serve as monetary objects due to their practicality and convenience. To facilitate payments and lending, commercial banks served as intermediaries, accepting cash deposits which could be used in non-cash payments, or lent out to others. Modern technology enhanced the ability of banks to perform payment and lending services, and various financial technology ("Fintech") companies began to offer financial products of their own. Legacy technologically powered financial products and services require intermediation. Digital currencies, on the other hand, can be used to make disintermediated payments, wherein digital "coins" pass directly from one party to another. This way, payments in digital currency resemble traditional cash payments, except that the former are carried out using digital ledger technologies.

SUMMARY OF CONTENTS

I. INTRODUCTION

In the modern economy, payments are typically made by means of transfers through bank accounts, and otherwise by the delivery of cash in the form of banknotes and coins. Funds available in bank accounts are also redeemable in banknotes and coins. As conduits of funds transfers, banks operate as intermediaries between payers and payees. They also distribute to their customers' banknotes, issued by the central bank, as well as coins. The recent emergence of digital currencies, facilitating payments outside of the banking system, as well as in items not created through banking operations, has put these fundamentals to the test, and has challenged the architectural premises of the present banking system.

This chapter deals with the evolution of money and the monetary system. **Part II** explores the meaning of "money." **Part III** addresses the evolution of coins and banknotes – the most distinct monetary objects in the current system, used in a disintermediated cash payment. **Part IV** discusses the evolution of the banking system so as to produce scriptural money and an intermediated payment system. **Part V** takes us to the cyber age. It addresses both electronic banking as a form of payment intermediation and the availability to the public of central bank balances as a challenge to payment intermediation. Digital currencies are discussed in **Part VI**, which goes on to examine the challenges they present to state-issued currency, payment intermediation, and the roles of banks in the payment systems. Concluding **Part VII** points at an irony: even as a challenge to banking, digital coins emerged as an outgrowth of an enhancement to banking. For their parts, centralized digital currencies may be linked to banking and the legacy monetary system. While changes of unknown scope and magnitude may be inevitable, banks, "banking," and payment intermediation are unlikely to disappear.

II. WHAT IS MONEY?

Money is said to be a medium of exchange, a store of value,[1] and a unit of account.[2] More specifically, it is a medium of exchange typically denominated in a unit of account. For quality, it either consists of or is backed by an object which

---

1   William Stanley Jevons, *Money and the Mechanism of Exchange* (Henry S King & Co, 1875) at 13, does not include this element in the definition. Indeed, money is a store of value only in the sense of being a "surplus" liquid resource available in one's hands for acquiring new commodities as may be needed and wished.

2   Nigel Dodd, *The Sociology of Money, Economic, Reason & Contemporary Society* (Continuum 1994) xv; for example, Geoffrey Ingham, *The Nature of Money* (Polity, 2004) at 198, "money"

excels in storing value. Otherwise, "[i]n order for money to function well as a medium of exchange, store of value, or unit of account, it must possess six characteristics: divisible, portable, acceptable, scarce, durable, and stable in value."[3] Fulfilling such functions, money is essential to the smooth operation of an exchange economy as well as to the accumulation of wealth which it allows. Money both facilitates the exchange and "acts as a measure … making things commensurable."[4] In contrast, money is not needed in a society consisting of self-sufficient economic units;[5] nor is it required in a utopian society in which products "are not exchanged, bought or sold" but rather are "stored in the communal warehouses, and are subsequently delivered to those who need them."[6] For an exchange economy, however, money is the lifeline.[7]

At present, in each country, including Canada, the monetary system is centralized. Coins and banknotes issued by the authority of the state, mostly by national central banks, are the standard monetary objects in all countries, so as to form "fiat money" and collectively be called "cash" or "currency." Credit posted in an account with a commercial bank ("bank") payable on demand gives rise to

---

is effectively something that "[r]egardless of its form and substance" answers the promise and description provided (and measured) by the unit of account.

3   Andrew T Hill, "Functions and Characteristics of Money" (Federal Reserve Bank of Philadelphia 2013), online: https://www.philadelphiafed.org/-./media/frbp/assets/institutional /education/lesson-plans/functions-and-characteristics-of-money-lesson.pdf, accessed 21 May 2024.

4   JAK Thomson (tr), *The Ethics of Aristotle: The Nicomachean Ethics* (Penguin, 1955) 154, in Aristotle's view, while "money is subject to the vagaries of the market just like other commodities … its purchasing power … is pretty constant," see also at 153–54, discussing in general the function of money in exchange of commodities. His account is said to be in line with that of Plato, see AR Burns, *Money and Monetary Policy in Early Times* (AM Kelley, 1965) at 457–58.

5   They can engage in a limited exchange through barter, which according to Aristotle is not "contrary to nature," see Aristotle, *The Politics* (TA Sinclair (tr), Penguin Books, 1962) at 42. Conversely, extensive commercial exchange depends on money, which according to him, "is justly regarded with disapproval, since it arises not from nature but from men's dealing with each other," see *ibid* at 46. See in general *ibid* at 38–46.

6   For this description of the communist method of production, see Nikolaĭ Bukharin and EA Preobrazhensky, *The ABC of Communism* (Eden Paul and Cedar Paul (trs), Penguin Books 1969) at 116–17. See also The Socialist Standard, "A World Without Money" (reproduced by Libom.org, The Socialist Party of Great Britain 1979), online: https://libcom.org/article /excerpts-world-without-money-les-amis-de-4-millions-de-jeunes-travailleurs, accessed 21 May 2024. The article states that money "is not a neutral instrument of measurement" so that it "will disappear." Ultimately, "In communist societies goods will be freely available and free of charge. The organisation of society to its very foundations will be without money."

7   See e.g., Adam Smith, *The Wealth of Nations: Books I-III* (Andrew Skinner (ed)) (Penguin, 1970) at 126–32, 135, 148. For the political economy of money in the context of its role in exchange economy, including an analysis of the position of both Adam Smith and Karl Marx as well as other leading thinkers, see Dodd, above note 2 at 1–23.

a debt owed by the bank to the depositor.[8] Such credit consists of currency deposited, transfers received, and credit extended. For their part, banks keep accounts either with each other, or more typically, with the central bank. Deposits held with commercial banks are "commercial bank money." Commercial banks' deposits held with the central bank, together with "fiat money" is "central bank money." Commercial bank money is redeemable on demand in banknotes and coins. Payments throughout the economy are carried out by the physical delivery of cash or transfers from one deposit account to another.

To enable them to repay on demand money deposited with them by members of the public, commercial banks keep money with the central bank (mostly by way of deposit and also by holding banknotes and coins). At the same time, commercial banks lend to members of the public out of money deposited with them. Money lent is typically redeposited and the entire sum on deposit is commercial bank money. Accordingly, under a fractional reserve system, central bank money available to commercial bank is in a lower sum than the sum of commercial bank money owed by them. The monetary system thus operates on the assumption that at any given time demand by the depositors for money on deposit with the bank will be satisfied by the amount of central bank money available to that commercial bank. A safety net consisting of the central bank acting as a "lender of last resort," public deposit insurance, and special bankruptcy or "resolution" framework, *together with a sophisticated network of prudential regulation and supervision*, are designed to remedy or even avoid a situation where this assumption does not work.

Economists take the narrow "monetary base" of a country to consist of the obligations of its central bank, both on banknotes it issues and on deposits it holds for commercial banks in their settlement (or reserve) accounts. The broader "money-supply" in the hands of the public is taken to consist of such banknotes issued by the central banks (plus coins for small change issued either by the central bank or the mint), together with demand deposits, held by the public in commercial banks. It is this "money supply" that reflects the purchasing power of a given society.[9]

Typically, if not universally, a modern state has an official or national currency as well as legal tender legislation. Generally speaking, having stated the official or national monetary unit of the country, a statute governing the

8 *Foley v Hill* (1848) 2 HLC 28, 9 ER 1002 (HL).
9 This is so since the essence of banking is lending the money on deposit, so that effectively both the depositors and borrowers can use it. For detailed economic perspective, see e.g., HH Binhammer and Peter S Sephton, *Money Banking, and the Canadian Financial System*, 8th ed (Nelson: Thomson Learning, 2001) at 197–220 (for discussion of banking and the creation of money) at 387–432 (for discussion of monetary controls and central banking).

currency, such as the *Currency Act* in Canada,[10] has two dimensions. First, all public accounts established or maintained in the country, any indictment or other legal proceedings, statutes and other legal pronouncements, as well as all contracts, transactions, instruments, and securities for money (unless otherwise agreed) are required to be expressed in that monetary unit. Second, the adoption and the compulsory use of media of exchange, that is, banknotes and coins denominated in the monetary unit are set out. In this context, money, that is, media of exchange, that a creditor is not privileged to refuse if it is tendered by a debtor in payment of their debt is "legal tender."[11] A more detailed elaboration on the scope and effects of legal tender banknotes and coins addresses the creditor's duty to accept (unless otherwise agreed), the acceptance by the creditor of full face value, and a legal recognition as a means of discharge from payment obligation.[12]

History has taught us that when an object is made "legal tender," is accepted as such and circulates, it becomes "money" even without its *a priori* formal designation as such.[13] A prominent example is the issuance by the United States of the first dollar banknotes ("Greenbacks") in 1862, in ostensible challenge to the Constitution that vested Congress with the power "to coin money."[14] The "Greenbacks" were paper bearer instruments transferable by mere delivery that carried no interest. Most important, they were not redeemable to coin or other specie, both being considered at the time as the "real" money. Nonetheless, they were made "legal tender in payment of all debts, public and private, within the United States. ... "[15] Over the years they have certainly become "money."[16]

The converse is however not true. An object may be "money" without being designated as an official currency or legal tender. Nor does money necessarily need to be issued by the government. Indeed, it was judicially acknowledged that "the regulation of the coin and currency of every State is a

10 See e.g., in Canada, *Currency Act*, RSC 1985, c C-52.

11 Arthur Nusbaum, *Money in the Law: National and International* (Foundation Press 1950) at 45 s 4.

12 See e.g., European Legal Tender Expert Group (ELTEG), "Report on the definition, scope and effects of legal tender of euro banknotes and coins" (ELTEG, 21 January 2009) at 4.

13 This is notwithstanding Nusbaum, above note 11 at 54–55 s 4, to the contrary, unless you read him to refer only to objects on which legal tender status is conferred but that nevertheless do not circulate, in which case I am not in disagreement with him.

14 US Const art I, § 8; see Thomas Wilson, *The Power "to Coin" Money: The Exercise of Monetary Powers by the Congress* (ME Sharp, 1991).

15 *An Act to Authorize the Issue of United States Notes, and for the Redemption or Funding thereof, and for Funding the Floating Debt of the United States*, Pub L No 37–33, § 1, 12 Stat 345 (1862).

16 This is in fact the theme of Ali Khan, "The Evolution of Money: A Story of Constitutional Nullification" (1999) 67 *U Cin L Rev* 393.

great prerogative right of the sovereign power. ... "[17] Nonetheless, I disagree with *Mann & Proctor* that the essential characteristics of "money," "must include a central bank or monetary authority responsible for the issue of the currency and including appropriate institutional provisions for its management through the conduct of monetary policy and the oversight of the payment system."[18] In an earlier edition[19] Mann's own definition was even narrower. Thereunder, "in law, the quality of money is to be attributed to all chattels which, issued by the authority of the law and denominated with reference to a unit of account, are meant to serve as universal means of exchange in the State of issue." In effect, this definition limits "money" to monetary objects issued by or under the authority of the state, *viz*, coins and banknotes. *Mann & Proctor*'s present definition is broader as it recognizes the existence of a national monetary system that goes beyond monetary objects and yet their present definition limits "money" to something issued under that system that in turn must be "national." Particularly, it appears to cover the broader "money-supply" in the hands of the public, consisting not only of banknotes issued by the central banks (plus coins for small change issued either by the central bank or the mint), but also the much larger amount of demand deposits, held by the public in commercial banks.

More in general, the meaning of "money" in law is context driven. For example, for the purpose of secured transactions, the Ontario *Personal Property Security Act* (PPSA) defines "money" to mean "a medium of exchange authorized or adopted by the Parliament of Canada as part of the currency of Canada or by a foreign government as part of its currency."[20] This appears to fit *Mann & Proctor*'s present definition. However, in section 22(1), side by side with other tangible types of personal property, "money" is listed by the PPSA as something in which physical possession may be taken, which reveals a statutory intention to limit "money" to something that meets Mann's earlier definition.

Critically, both Mann's earlier definition and *Mann & Proctor*'s present definition do not take into account, or more precisely, wrongly dismiss as "purely historical interest,"[21] the common law express recognition of the introduction of new monetary objects by mercantile or societal usage. The classic

---

17 *The Emperor of Austria v Day* (1861) 3 De G F&J 217 at 231, 45 ER 861at 867.

18 Charles Proctor, *Mann and Proctor on the Law of Money*, 8th ed (Oxford University Press, 2022) at 34–35 para 1.72.

19 FA Mann, The *Legal Aspects of Money*, 5th ed (Clarendon Press, 1992).

20 *Personal Property Security Act*, RSO 1990, c P.10, s 1(1).

21 Proctor, above note 18 at 19 para 1.30, by reference to (in fact plaintiff counsel's argument) in *Griffin v Thompson*, 43 US 244 (1844).

example is *Miller v Race* (1758),[22] where Lord Mansfield treated the banknote as something that by "the general consent of mankind" is "treated as money, as cash, in the ordinary course and transaction of business," so as to be "as much money, as guineas themselves are; or any other current coin, that is used in common payments, as money or cash."

On this point I am in full agreement with Khan, whose thesis is that:[23]

An official currency, though important, is not critical to the functioning of a monetary system. Even when the law authorizes a certain medium of exchange as official currency, the market continues to breed new substitutes because safety-conscious merchants prefer to deal in money substitutes rather than in official currency.

He goes on to highlight the predominance of the market, often with, but sometimes without, the help of the law, in determining what constitutes money:[24]

Money in the functional sense is not synonymous with legal tender or official currency. In a free economy, the market rather than the law dictates which form of money is used in commercial transactions. The law is still needed to recognize monetary conventions of the market and, sometimes, to clean up the mess the market leaves behind its monetary adventures. But rarely has the development of money been the pure artifact of governmental policy or political decision. Money is a living creature of the market and its form changes to facilitate commercial transactions in an ever more efficient, convenient, and safe manner. As such, most innovations in monetary practices are attributable to the decisions of the market.

Accordingly, by reference to its function as a universal medium of exchange, "money" is defined in a leading English case to be "that which passes freely from hand to hand throughout the community in final discharge of debts ... being accepted equally without reference to the character or credit of the person who offers it and without the intention of the person who receives it to consume it. ... "[25] This judicial definition is in line with an economist's perspective, according to which money is anything that is

---

22   (1758) 1 Burr 452, 97 ER 398, discussed in greater length in chapter 3.
23   Khan, above note 16 at 395.
24   *Ibid* at 396.
25   *Moss v Hancock* [1899] 2 QB 111 at 116. To the same effect see also *Reference Re Alberta Statutes* [1938] SCR 100 at 116, as well as *Johnson v State* 52 So 652 (Ala 1910) and *State v Finnegan* 103 NW 155 (Iowa 1905).

widely accepted in payment for goods, used as a medium of exchange, and expressed as the standard unit in which prices and debts are measured.[26]

This explains why credit to a bank account is characterized as "money." It is in this sense that Brandon J speaks in *The Brimnes, Tenax Steamship Co Ltd v The Brimnes (Owners)* (1973),[27] of payment in cash into a designated bank account as may be carried out by "any commercially recognized method of transferring funds, the result of which is to give the transferee the unconditional right to the immediate use of the funds transferred."[28] In this context, "unconditional" was broadly construed by the House of Lords in *The Chikuma* to mean "unfettered and unrestricted" and not merely "neither subject to the fulfilment of a condition precedent nor defeasible on failure to fulfil a condition subsequent."[29] Accordingly, payment into a bank account is carried out by having an unfettered and unrestricted right against their own bank to the immediate use of the funds conferred on the payee. In the process, bank credit is not assigned, but rather extinguishes in the payer's account and increases in the payee's account; the operation nevertheless results in the discharge of the payment obligation and as such the bank credit is "money."[30]

It should be pointed out that for something to be treated as money, it must be widely accepted as such within a relevant community. A bilateral agreement in a given case is unlikely to suffice. Furthermore, the issuance of something as money, even by a state, which is nevertheless not widely accepted as such, will not suffice to make that "something" into money.[31] The corollary is that even when it is not issued as money, or has been demonetized, something that circulates in a given community as money, is money.[32]

Despite its immense contribution to the facilitation of exchange, it may well be that as a uniform measure of value, "money" may not necessarily have been invented, or did not necessarily emerge, to improve

---

26 See e.g., Dennis H Robertson, *Money* (University of Chicago Press, 1962) at 2; *Personal Property Security Act (PPSA)* s 3.

27 [1973] 1 All ER 769, affd [1974] 3 All ER 88 (CA).

28 [1973] 1 All ER 769 (QB) 782 (Brandon J).

29 *A/S Awilco v Fulvia SpA Di Navigazione (The "Chikuma")* [1981] 1 Lloyd's Rep 371 at 375 (HL).

30 *Libyan Arab Foreign Bank v Banker's Trust Co* [1988] 1 Lloyd's Rep 259 at 273 (QB).

31 *Ottoman Bank of Nicosia v Chakarian* [1938] AC 260 (HL), where at 270 Lord Wright speaks of certain gold coins that ceased to circulate as legal tender and became commodities.

32 See e.g., Case 7/78 *R v Thompson* [1978] ECR 2247 at paras 27–28. The case was criticized on both its factual holding and adherence to the "Societal Theory of money" which they consider to be "inadequate" See Proctor, above note 18 at 32–33 paras 1.66–1.67. I disagree with the second ground.

commerce.[33] This is so notwithstanding the mythology to the contrary.[34] Rather, as a uniform measure of value, its roots may be traced to the practice of *wergeld*, "that of paying compensation primarily for the killing of a man but ... by extension [also] for injuries to himself or his family and household."[35] As well, the coin has roots in, and its use spread as a medium of taxing and spending by, the state.[36] Certainly, however, commerce and the exchange economy account for the improvement and further development of money.

As a generic term, "money" was said to be "any circulating medium in general use as the representative of value,"[37] or "anything that circulates as the ordinary medium of exchange in buying and selling property."[38] Accordingly, "money" is:

> Everything which by consent is made to represent property, and passes as such currently from hand to hand, whether it be the iron of the Spartans, the cowrie of the African, the gold and silver of the world, or the paper of modern Europe and America.[39]

Neither issuance by the state nor conformity to requirements as to form is thus an essential element in the definition of money.

III. COINS AND BANKNOTES

For its part, barter has two inherent drawbacks. They are the lack of an *a priori* measure of value, *viz*, a common denominator for the evaluation of goods,

---

33   RM Cook, "Speculations on the Origin of Coinage" (1958) 7 *Historia* 257 at 259–60.

34   Promoted by eminent thinkers such as Aristotle and Adam Smith, see e.g., Aristotle, *Politics*, above note 5 at 41–46 and Smith, above note 7 at 126–32. This mythology draws also other classical authors such as Herodotus and Xenophon. See e.g., Catherine Eagleton et al, *Money: A History*, 2d ed (British Museum Press, 2007) at 27–28.

35   Philip Greirson, *The Origins of Money* (The Athlone Press, 1977) at 19. Along similar lines in great detail, see the monumental work of David Graeber, *Debt: The First 5,000 Years* (Melville House. 2014). See also Karl Polanyi, "The Semantics of Money Uses," in George Dalton (ed), *Primitive, Archaic, and Modern Economies: Essays of Karl Polanyi* (Doubleday & Company, 1968) at 175.

36   See e.g., Christine Desan, "Coin Reconsidered: The Political Alchemy of Commodity Money" (2010) 11 Theoretical Inquiries in Law 361.

37   *Johnson v State* 52 So 652 (Ala 1910).

38   *State v Finnegan*, above note 25.

39   *Ibid*; *cf Rhodes v Lindly* 3 Ohio 51 (OH 1827), where payment "in good merchantable whisky" was held not to be payment in money presumably in the absence of proof as to its acceptability as such.

and the fact that "direct exchange can take place only when *double coincidence* of wants exists."[40] The existence of these two drawbacks explains why "money" was needed for an efficient economic exchange. Thus, in the prehistoric era, useful objects like weapons and rings, side by side with metals, were used as money.[41] Subsequently, in the pre-classical world, numerous objects served as "primitive money." Primitive money was "a unit or an object conforming to a reasonable degree to some standard of uniformity, which is employed for reckoning or for making a large proportion of the payments customary in the community concerned, and which is accepted in payment largely with the intention of employing it for making payments."[42] Primitive money was in fact a chattel with intrinsic utility and economic value, which in a given society served as a unit of account as well as a medium of exchange.[43]

In ancient Egypt, where economic exchange was predominantly done on a barter basis, various types of sticks or staves, copper objects, and gold served as a limited medium of exchange.[44] Barley and precious metals, particularly silver, were used as money in Babylonia and Assyria.[45] Sealed silver and copper ingots served this function in Cappadocia.[46] Sheep and weighed silver were the currency of the Hittite Empire.[47] The ancient Hebrews paid by livestock as well as by weighed silver.[48]

Weighed precious metals were to supersede cattle. In that process, metallic pieces were to be made of standard size and quality. Compared to oxen, metals "are durable and can be stored without any cost of maintenance." Particularly, precious metals were easy to hide. "Gold and silver, though not copper and iron [or lead], are also easily portable." Thus, "[t]he custom of making them into rings and spirals doubtless arose because people desired to carry their most precious possessions with them and therefore, placed them on their arms and legs." Last, there "was the homogeneity and divisibility of the metals" and the ability to make pieces of metal of any size that

---

40   Binhammer and Sephton, above note 9 at 14 (emphasis in the original).

41   Paul Einzig, *Primitive Money*, 2d ed (Pergamon Press, 1966) at 187–92.

42   *Ibid* at 317; see also George Dalton, "Primitive Money" (1965) 67 *American Anthropologist* 44.

43   For the existence of this stage of the evolution of money, see also AJ Toynbee, *A Study of History* (Oxford University Press, 1960) at 60.

44   *Ibid* at 193–202.

45   *Ibid* at 202–09.

46   *Ibid* at 209–10; see also Burns, above note 4 at 38.

47   Einzig, above note 41 at 210–11.

48   *Ibid* at 211–14. For a compilation of biblical authorities, see Leo Kadman and Arye Kindler, *Coins in Palestine Throughout the Ages* (La Da'ath Publishers, 1963) at 17 (in Hebrew); See also Y Grintz, "Banking Services as Mentioned in the Bible" (1981) 20:80 *Quarterly Banking Review* 83 (in Hebrew).

was desired.[49] Indeed, among all chattels, small fungible goods were the most suitable to be used as a medium of exchange. Fungible goods were mutually interchangeable; they could be replaced by equal quantities and qualities, and were estimated by weight, number, or measure.[50] Their individual identity, if it existed, was irrelevant. Small fungible goods, unlike oxen or sheep, were easily portable and could easily be hidden.

According to Jevons, an ideal "monetary object" is to possess five physical properties, *viz*, portability, indestructibility, homogeneity, divisibility, and cognizability.[51] Standardized metallic pieces were to meet all such requirements; compared to other small fungible chattels like corn, barley, or wheat, standardized metallic pieces are more durable and not depreciable. Specifically, gold neither tarnishes nor corrodes. The supply of precious metals was neither abundant nor scarce, and hence each piece could represent meaningful purchasing power while retaining a small size. It was true that, unlike grain or cattle, metallic pieces vary in size and quality; "[n]ature supplies no natural unit of the metals as she does of cattle."[52] However, metallic units might be carved out and made into standard size and quality, each representing a fixed value. Thus, by a process of elimination, precious metals, shaped into standard pieces, were destined to prevail as a universal medium of exchange.

The earliest coins were struck in Lydia (a city-state in Asia Minor) around 700 BCE.[53] During antiquity and the Middle Ages, having evolved from a commodity traded for its use-value into currency transferred in payment of debts,[54] the coin became the standard circulating object denoting a prescribed monetary value.[55] It was fundamentally a piece of metal fashioned into a prescribed shape, weight, and degree of fineness, stamped by the issuer under the authority of the sovereign with certain designs, marks, and devices.[56]

---

49   Burns, above note 4 at 28.

50   See in general, FH Lawson and Bernard Rudden, *Law of Property*, 3d ed (Oxford University Press, 2002) at 27.

51   To those five traits, he adds two non-physical properties, *viz* (i) utility and value, and (ii) stability of value. See Jevons, above note 1 at 31.

52   Burns, above note 4 at 28.

53   This is the conclusion, confirming the conventional wisdom on the matter, of the thorough study by Donald Kagan, "The Dates of the Earliest Coins" (1982) 86 *Journal of Archeology* 343.

54   For a comprehensive account see, e.g., Percy Gardner, *A History of Ancient Coinage 700–300 BC* (Ares Publishers, 1974).

55   Roughly speaking, antiquity comes to an end with the beginning of the Middle Ages, usually marked by the fall of Rome in 476 CE. The Middle Ages are commonly dated from the fifth century fall of the Western Roman Empire until the fall of the Eastern Roman Empire in the fifteenth century.

56   See in general definitions of "coin" in Daniel Greenberg (ed), *Jowitt's Dictionary of English Law*, 5th ed (Sweet & Maxwell, 2019) vol 1 at 470; "Coin in French, signifieth a corner, and

From its inception, and in theory[57] until the nineteenth century CE, the value of a coin, at least its ideal form, was primarily determined by reference to the weight of the precious metal it contained. At the same time, by definition, inasmuch as they are mere obligations to pay, banknotes are "fiat money," namely, of positive nominal value, notwithstanding the (relatively) worthless intrinsic value of the material of which they are made.[58]

Indeed, the aspiration for good-quality coins of which the nominal monetary value reflects the value of the materials from which they are made always existed. Nevertheless, throughout history, coins have been subject to an ongoing debasement, namely to a process under which an increasing gap is created between their higher nominal value and the value of the materials of which they were made. Debasement facilitated an uncontrolled growth in the quantity of money, leading to the reduction in its price, and a corresponding increase in the price level of all other goods. In a nutshell,[59] this was in part the result of the lack of availability of gold in an amount sufficient to satisfy demand or need for liquidity at a given time and place. As well, production costs precluded the efficient manufacturing of small change that as a result had constantly been debased, leading to a corresponding debasement of the high-denominated coins.[60] To this, one can add the sheer greed of rulers who had a monopoly on currency issuance of which production costs consisted not only of the minting cost, called the "brassage," but also of a tax paid to the sovereign, called "seigniorage" or "net seigniorage."[61] Finally, whether it was for the need of the economy or for personal gain, the ruler needed to attract gold for the production of coins. This could be done by returning to suppliers of gold coins of monetary value higher than that of the actual gold

---

from thence hath its name. ... " See Matthew Hale, *The History of the Pleas of the Crown* 1st American ed (Robert H Small, 1947) vol 1, 187 note 2.

57   For an unequivocal legitimization of the king's power to control the metallic content of a coin irrespective of its denomination see *Le Case de Mixt Moneys* (1605) Davis 18, 80 ER 507.

58   See Glossary in Thomas J Sargent and François Velde, *The Big Problem of Small Change* (Princeton University Press, 2002) at 375, the term is not conceptually different from "token money" referring to a coin not having the intrinsic value for which it is current, see 376.

59   For more details, see Benjamin Geva, *The Payment Order of Antiquity and the Middle Ages: A Legal History* (Hart Publishing, 2011) at 17–25.

60   This is the theme of Sargent and Velde, above note 58.

61   For these terms see e.g., John B Martin, "Seigneuriage and Mint Charges" (1884) 5 *Journal of The Institute of Bankers* 171 at 174. For a discussion on profits in one context, see e.g., P Spufford, *Monetary Problems and Policies in the Burgundian Netherlands 1443–1496* (EJ Brill, 1970) at 130–46. For seigniorage and other mint costs see also Frederic C Lane and Reinhold C Mueller, *Money and Banking in Medieval and Renaissance Venice, Vol 1: Coins and Money of Account* (John Hopkins University Press, 1985) at 16–23, 493–530.

they had provided.[62] Ultimately, in England, at the turn of the seventeenth century, *Le Case de Mixt Moneys* (1605)[63] recognized that sterling currency is usually associated with a coin of high metallic quality.[64] Nonetheless, the court held, the king has the prerogative "to give value to base metal by his stamp ... just as he may give estimation to a mean person and confer an honour on him."[65] Stated otherwise, in setting the extrinsic quality, that is, nominal value, for a coin, the king is not bound by its intrinsic quality.[66]

To address the deficiencies the coin-based monetary systems transformed in a few stages. First, during the seventeenth century CE, the banknote appeared as an obligation to pay coins or specie.[67] Originally, the obligor thereon was a goldsmith, the predecessor of the deposit bank in England.[68] Ultimately, in the course of the eighteenth century, following the establishment of the Bank of England in 1694,[69] the promise to pay on banknotes circulating as money became that of the central bank.[70]

Second, in the course of the nineteenth century, the coin reflecting a fraction of the unit of account became a token, that is, a piece of metal of a value lower than that which it denotes. The division of the basic unit of account into fixed token denominations at equal abstract sub-units[71] is called by economists the "standard formula."[72] Thereunder, the prescribed sum of such token

---

62   See in general, JL Bolton, *The Medieval English Economy 1150–1500* (JM Dent, 1980) at 297–98, 73–5.

63   (1605) Davis 18, 80 ER 507, above note 57. The case is extensively discussed e.g., by David Fox, "Case of Mixt Monies (1604)" in David Fox and Wolfgang Ernst (eds), *Money in the Western Legal Tradition: Middle Ages to Bretton Woods* (Oxford University Press, 2016) at 224.

64   *Ibid*, Davis at 23, 25; ER at 511, 513.

65   *Ibid*, Davis at 25, ER at 513.

66   *Ibid.*

67   See a detailed discussion on paper money in chapter 3.

68   James M Holden, *The History of Negotiable Instruments in English Law* (Gaunt & Sons 1993) at 70–73; A Feavearyear, *The Pound Sterling – A History of English Money*, 2d ed (Morgan Victor ed) (Clarendon Press, 1963) at 107–08.

69   *Bank of England Act, 1694* (UK), 5 & 6 Will & Mary, c 20, s XIX.

70   *Bank of England Act, 1708* (UK), 7 Ann, c 30, s 66, forfeited the private note-issuing power of banking firms. Subsequently, under *Country Bankers Act, 1826* (UK), 7 Geo IV, c 46, the note-issue power was restored to non-London banks. Ultimately, this power was severely curtailed and subsequently disappeared following the passage of the *Bank Charter Act, 1844* (UK), 7 & 8 Vict, c 32; see Holden, above note 68 at 87–94, 195–96.

71   E.g., one dollar for one hundred pennies (each of one cent), twenty nickels (each of five cents), ten dimes (each of ten cents), or four quarters (each of twenty-five cents).

72   See Sargent and Velde, above note 58 at 5 (as well as the Preface at XVII), specifically drawing on Carlo M Cipolla, *Money, Prices, and Civilization in the Mediterranean World, Fifth to Seventh Century* (Gordian Press, 1956) at 27. The triumph of the standard formula in the course of the nineteenth century is set out by Sargent and Velde, *ibid* at 306–19.

denominations is convertible at a fixed exchange rate to each other denomination and to the basic unit, regardless of their own metallic composition.[73]

Third, in the first third of the twentieth century CE, convertibility of banknotes ceased to exist; that is, the obligation to pay *in specie* embodied in a banknote became unenforceable;[74] technically, it was replaced by an obligation to pay other banknotes of the same denominated value. Thus, at present, banknotes and coins express abstract obligations; they are tokens convertible to other, albeit of the same type, tokens. Fourth, during the second half of the twentieth century, even the measurement of national unit of account by reference to a specified quantity of a given precious metal was abolished.[75] The external value of any national unit of account is now the price in which it is traded in international financial markets by reference to another national unit of account. In turn, the internal value of the national unit of account is assessed by reference to the price level in the economy, as responding to the monetary policy of the central bank in indirectly controlling the quantity of money supply through setting the key rate(s).[76]

For almost 3,000 years gold has dominated the monetary scene, first in the form of the material from which a coin is made, and later, through the holding by banks of gold reserve backing their obligations on banknotes. Heavily relying on Austrian economic theory, Saifedean Ammous explains the inherent advantages of gold to serve as money as follows.[77] To begin with,

---

73 That is, one hundred pennies, twenty nickels, ten dimes, or four quarters are convertible to one dollar. Two nickels are converted to a dime, etc. Each such conversion is irrespective of the metallic content of the sub-unit denominations (that is, the penny, nickel, dime, or quarter). The "standard formula" preceded the cessation of convertibility (discussed in the immediately following paragraph); yet, as it is understood today, the "standard formula" does not rule out (nor does it require) that the basic unit, e.g., the dollar, be convertible or at least anchored to the value of a specified quantity of a given precious metal.

74 In England, abolition of convertibility goes back to the *Gold Standard Act, 1925* (UK), 15 & 16 Geo 5, c 29; abolition was strengthened in the *Gold Standard (Amendment) Act, 1931* (UK), 21 & 22 Geo 5, c 46; see Holden, above note 68 at 279.

75 The "cutoff" date is 15 August 1971. On that day the US ceased to maintain the purchasing power of the US dollar in terms of a specified amount of gold. Thereby it effectively abolished the gold (or any other commodity) standard as the measurement for the international monetary system. Until then, all currencies had been measured by reference to the US dollar, which is turn, had been assessed in gold. See Rosa María Lastra, *Legal Foundations of International Monetary Stability* (Oxford University Press, 2006) at 362–63.

76 See e.g., William Coleman, "Monetary Policy, Accountability and Legitimacy: A Review of the Issues in Canada" (1991) 24 *Canadian Journal of Political Science* 711; Benjamin Friedman, "The Future of Monetary Policy: The Central Bank as an Army with Only a Signal Corps?" (1999) 2 *International Finance* at 261.

77 The ensuing discussion summarizes portions the first three chapters of Saifedean Ammous, *The Bitcoin Standard: The Decentralized Alternative to Central Banking* (Wiley, 2018).

there are two distinct quantities related to the supply of every good. The stock, namely existing supply, and the flow, namely the extra production that will be made in the next time period. The higher the ratio of the stock to the flow, the more likely a good will maintain its value over time and thus be more saleable across time. Accordingly, for a good to be money, there must be a mechanism to restrain the production of new units, so as to reduce its flow, and thereby to maintain the value of the existing units. A good of which supply is hard to increase can serve as "hard money." Conversely, a good of which supply is easy to increase can serve as "easy money."

Highlighting its durability and resistance to corrosion, Ammous explains the monetary role of gold throughout history in its consistent low rate of supply, that is, its flow. The high-stock-to-flow ratio of gold makes it the commodity with the lowest *price elasticity of supply*, which is defined as the percentage increase in quantity supplied over the percentage increase in price.

If people choose a hard money as a store of value, their purchasing to store it would increase demand for it, causing a rise in its price, which would incentivize producers to increase its supply. Nonetheless, because the flow is small compared to the existing supply, even a large increase in the new production is unlikely to depress the price significantly. Anything that is successfully used as money will have some mechanism that restricts the new flow of the good into the market, maintaining its value over time. Costly production of such a good is one such mechanism.

According to Ammous, two unique physical characteristics differentiate gold from other commodities. First, it is chemically stable, that is, virtually indestructible. Second, gold is impossible to synthesize from other materials and can only be extracted from its unrefined ore, which is extremely rare in the planet. The only way to increase the supply of gold is by mining gold from the earth. This is an expensive, toxic, and uncertain process – which ensures the low growth of its quantity, hence its high-stock-to-flow ratio.

It is against this background that we can understand the evolution of the gold coin to the ideal monetary object. However, as discussed, what could mainly be described as frictions in less than perfect markets, led the search for alternatives such as banknotes and scriptural money. At the same time, at their inception, obligations by banks to pay on banknotes were denominated in gold. At an idealized model, they were all backed by actual gold held by the bank, which among other things, solved the problem of low denomination, since there was no need to manufacture coins with value less than production cost. Globally, a model along these lines existed between 1871 and (and at least nominally) 1921 or so, in an era dominated by "the gold standard" during which the standard unit of account was based on a fixed quantity of gold. In the words of Polanyi, the adherence to the "gold standard" during that period reflected universal belief, that for better or worse, "banknotes have value because they represent gold."[78]

Ammous is of the view that the system failed because gold came to be under the control of large banks and big governments that abused their power to issue fiduciary moneys and later got to the point where not only convertibility but also any form of backing ceased to exist.[79] My own explanation to the fall of "the gold standard" and the ultimate demise of the dependence on gold is more benevolent and less dogmatic: societal needs, whether in conducting wars, development, or building a welfare state could not have been satisfied by the amount of gold, both available, and to be extracted. Whether a more amicable divorce between gold and money could have been achieved is in any event another question, not to be discussed here.

As well, Ammous appears to overlook that in a period of enhanced economic activity demand to gold increases so as to give a creditor systemic advantage over their debtor. This happens due to the continuous rise in the price of gold, caused by the increased demand to it. In turn, this leads to the fall of price of all other goods (paid in gold), so that a creditor would get in repayment of a debt, a higher purchasing power, compared to the one the creditor gave earlier, with the same amount of gold, upon lending it to the debtor.[80]

IV. SCRIPTURAL MONEY

Far-reaching enhancements in the banking system generated not only banknotes but also non-cash payments in the form of "scriptural money." The latter included money lent by the bank. True, banking institutions existed in Mesopotamia, ancient Greece, Rome, Greco-Roman Egypt,[81] and of course medieval Europe.[82] In fact, so far as I can tell, the term "bank money" was first used in connection with banking in Venice during the late Middle Ages.[83]

---

78   Karl Polanyi, *The Great Transformation: The Political and Economic Origins of Our Time* (2d Beacon Paperback ed, Beacon Press, 2001) at 26. Polanyi views the "gold standard" as one of the pillars of what he calls "The Hundred Years' Peace" of the nineteenth century world order, *ibid* at 3–32. Personally, and without diminishing my admiration to his monumental scholarship, I beg to differ on this characterization of the period that led to the First World War that was marked by social unrest, but this is off the point.

79   Ammous, *The Bitcoin Standard*, above note 77 at 41–72. The sad thing is that he may be right in assessing that it was war that gave the original impetus to high government cost.

80   Jacob Goldstein, *Money: The True Story of a Made-Up Thing* (Hachette Books, 2020) at 105.

81   Geva, above note 59 at 116–57.

82   *Ibid* at 352–69.

83   Reinhard Mueller, "The Role of Bank Money in Venice, 1300–1500" (1979) 3 *Studi Veneziani* at 47.

As well, State Banks flourished in post-medieval Europe, as for example, in Amsterdam[84] and Sweden.[85] However, the present monetary system was born in post-medieval *England*. Its roots are in the institutional transformation of the goldsmiths' system and the establishment of the Bank of England that followed.[86]

At their inception, banks were depositaries of money for safe-keeping. Inherent deficiencies in and inefficiencies in cash payment precipitated their use as conduits for non-cash payments. Thus, payment in cash is by the physical delivery from one person (payer) to another (payee). This is a face-to-face process which does not require intermediaries. More specifically, "payment" is "a bilateral act which requires the [payee] to accept the [payer]'s act of tender";[87] and is completed on the passage of possession in the money[88] when the payee takes delivery, thereby manifesting the acceptance of the tender.[89]

From the beginning, payment in cash had flaws, and under some circumstances was impractical. Particularly, this is due to costs and risks associated with the storage, carriage, and transportation of cash. Other concerns have been scarcity of cash and the inevitably cumbersome process of handling and paying with cash large sums of money. In a nutshell, an effective solution has been in the form of payment made to the payee, under the payer's instructions, by an intermediary who typically owed money to the payer.[90] Such payment would discharge both the payer's debt to the payee and the intermediary's debt to the payer. An optimal intermediary was a deposit-taker, that is, a banker, being a debtor to all depositors. When a payee preferred payment into their account with another banker (rather than in cash) the two bankers, that of the payer and that of the payee, settled periodically by paying the balance due for customers' payments going in both directions. Bankers kept funds with each other and ultimately with a central counterparty. Over the centuries, both national and global non-cash payment systems so evolved.

---

84   JG van Dillen, "The Bank of Amsterdam" in JG van Dillen (ed), *History of the Principal Public Banks* (Frank Cass & Co, 1964) at 86.

85   EF Heckscher, "The Bank of Sweden" in van Dillen, *ibid* at 161.

86   See e.g., Richard D Richards, *The Early History of Banking in England* (AM Kelley, 1965). For a succinct summary, see William Holdsworth, *A History of English Law* (Sweet & Maxwell, 1966) vol 8, at 185, 92.

87   David Fox, *Property Rights in Money* (Oxford University Press, 2008) at 28.

88   Hence, contract alone cannot transfer the legal title to money, *ibid* at 87.

89   *Ibid* at 79–86, 87–95.

90   Alternatively, having paid the payee, an intermediary who did not owe money to the payer, became owed by the payer.

At the heart of such a system stands the commercial bank. Bankers figured out that they did not need to keep in hand all deposited cash. The essence of commercial banking has thus become the taking of deposits (or other repayable funds) from the public by the banker and lending these deposits in the banker's own name.[91] Money so lent may also be deposited to bank accounts so that lending has only increased the amount of deposits for safekeeping and inter-account payments. Deposit taking and lending, as well as making and receiving payments, has defined the essence of commercial banking. Linked to these functions is the provision of inter-account payment services.[92]

Commercial banking (banking) has thus emerged as a form of financial intermediation between savers (depositors) and borrowers,[93] in a process in which new money has been created. The banker (or bank)[94] received coined money from savers.[95] Such coined money was either deposited to savers' accounts or receipted to them in the form of circulating notes. Coined money on deposit was partly lent to borrowers either in the form of credit to borrowers' accounts or in circulating notes. In this environment, payment intermediation in the form of non-cash payment services evolved as an outgrowth of deposit taking or, more in general, of maintaining deposit accounts for customers, whether the original depositors or the borrowers who deposited the proceeds of the loan.[96] This business model, thus premised

---

91   See e.g., definition of "credit institution" in Regulation (EU) No 575/2013 of 26 June 2013 on prudential requirements for credit institutions and investment firms and amending Regulation (EU) No 648/2012 [2013] OJ L176/1, art 4(1)(1), online: http://eur-lex.europa.eu /legal-content/EN/TXT/?uri=celex:32013R0575, accessed 27 May 2024.

92   Edwin Green, *Banking: An Illustrated History* (Rizzoli, 1989) 11; for a similar judicial discussion on the characteristics of banking see Lord Denning's judgment in *United Dominion Trust v Kirkwood* [1966] 2 QB 431 at 445–47 (CA).

93   For an insight into the process, though well into the later Medieval period, see e.g., Abbot Payson Usher, *The Early History of Deposit Banking in Mediterranean Europe*, vol 1 (Harvard University Press, 1943) particularly at 3–25.

94   Grammatically, "banker" is the professional individual, while "bank" is the institution. Until incorporation, there was no real difference, and this study will use the two terms interchangeably. Note also that "commercial banking," "banking," and "deposit banking" are, generally speaking, synonyms, and unless indicated otherwise are used in this study interchangeably.

95   "Coined money" is broadly used here to include specie.

96   See e.g., Meir Kohn, "Early Deposit Banking" (1999) Department of Economics Darmouth College Working Paper 99-03, online: http://sites.dartmouth.edu/mkohn/files/2017/03/99-03. pdf, accessed 27 May 2024; see also James McAndrews and William Roberds, "Payment Intermediation and the Origins of Banking" (1999) Federal Reserve Bank of Atlanta Working Paper 99–11, online: https://www.frbatlanta.org/research/publications/wp/1999/11.aspx, accessed 27 May 2024. Both studies cover the Middle Ages and overlook antiquity.

on fractional reserve, has been workable as long as not all depositors and note holders required payment in coin from the banker at the same time. In normal circumstances, it sufficed for a banker to keep at hand enough coined money to satisfy reasonable demand. Monitoring depositors' payment activity in accounts facilitated lending decision-making and led to specialization in advancing information-intensive non-traded loans, which became a principal niche for a profitable commercial banking business as well as effective financial intermediation for the economy as a whole. In the process, both the banknote and the credit to the bank account, being promises by banks to pay money, have become forms of money; being created against the fractional reserve of the coined money, its quantity by definition has been larger than that of the reserve.

While quantitatively consisting of the higher portion of the money supply, whose other and smaller component consists of banknotes and coins, "bank money" is in fact a multiplier of central bank money and is redeemable by banknotes and coins.

Against this background, the modern banking system, facilitating the emergence of the present monetary system, was born in post-Medieval England. Its roots are in the institutional transformation of the goldsmiths' system and the establishment of the Bank of England that followed.[97]

The process involved (1) the transformation of the business of individual goldsmiths into that of commercial or deposit bankers who accepted deposits, and lent out of them, including by discounting bills of exchange. As bankers they also facilitated depositors' cheque payments out of and into the deposits; (2) the existence of a tight network of all such goldsmiths ready to extend credit to each other, so as to allow for reciprocal correspondent banking services. Such services have facilitated interbank debt clearing and settlement, originally on a bilateral and later on a multilateral basis, leading to the establishment of a clearing house. This allowed risk reduction, enhanced efficiency, and the generation of common services that brought upon further development;[98] (3) the establishment of the Bank of England, originally as a lender to the government and then, having adopted goldsmiths' practices, gradually evolving in the subsequent two centuries into a modern central bank. As such, it maintains settlement accounts for deposit bankers (being

97   See e.g., Richards, above note 86 at 185–92.
98   See in detail, Stephen Quinn, "Balances and goldsmith-bankers: the co-ordination and control of inter-banker debt clearing in seventeenth-century London" in David Mitchell (ed), *Goldsmiths, Silversmiths and Bankers: Innovation and the Transfer of Skill, 1550 to 1750* (Alan Sutton Publishing and Centre for Metropolitan History, 1995) at 53.

the successors of goldsmiths) so as to facilitate interbank final settlement as well as to become a lender of last resort;[99] and (4) the issuance of banknotes, first as circulating obligations of goldsmiths evidencing either deposits or loans, then as paper money issued by the goldsmiths, and ultimately, as paper money, "legal tender," exclusively issued by the Bank of England.[100]

Both correspondent banking and customer payment activity required intensive monitoring by the goldsmith-bankers. In turn, this facilitated credit decision-making and led to specialization in advancing information-intensive non-traded loans. Such lending became a principal niche for a profitable commercial banking business as well as effective financial intermediation for the economy as a whole. In providing such loans, as well as in issuing banknotes and discounting bills of exchange, the goldsmith-bankers came to provide a reliable source of liquidity to the economy.

For its part, in departing from the model of the earlier Continental public bank, the Bank of England complemented private commercial banks without competing with or endeavouring to substitute for them. Rather, by being their bank and maintaining accounts for them,[101] it was able to furnish them with a source of liquidity so as to be a lender of last resort. As well, it provided them with the efficiency of multilateral settlement in reserve accounts held with it. In both ways, it gradually became, as a "central bank," an integral part of the private bank network.[102]

The banknote was issued first by the goldsmith-banker,[103] originally possibly as a "warehouse receipt" for deposited coins, and subsequently against

---

99   See HV Bowen, "The Bank of England During the Long Eighteenth Century 1694–1820" in Richard Roberts and David Kynaston (eds), *The Bank of England: Money, Power, and Influence 1694–1994* (Clarendon Press, 1995). See also Richard D Richards, "The First Fifty Years of the Bank of England (1694–1744)" in van Dillen, above note 84 at 201; Richard Roberts, "The Bank of England and the City" in Richard Roberts and David Kynaston (eds) *The Bank of England: Money, Power, and Influence 1694–1994* (Clarendon Press, 1995) at 152, 153. For its origins see also James E Thorold Rogers, *The First Nine Years of the Bank of England* (Clarendon Press, 1887).

100 Notes of the Bank of England were made legal tender in England and Wales for all payments (except for by the Bank itself) over five pounds by s 6 of the *Bank of England Act 1833* (UK), 3 & 4 Will IV, c 98.

101 While certainly there was rivalry, the fact is that "many goldsmiths opened accounts with the Bank within a few months of its creation," Holden, above note 68 at 93.

102 See e.g., Ben Norman, Rachel Shaw, and George Speight, "The History of Interbank Settlement Arrangements: Exploring Central Banks' Role in the Payment System" (2011) Bank of England Working Paper No 412, online: https://www.ecb.europa.eu/home/pdf/research /Working_Paper_412.pdf, accessed 27 May 2024.

103 See e.g., Richards, *Early History*, above note 86 at 40–43; Holden, above note 68; Feavearyear, above note 68 at 107–08; J Keith Horsefield, "The 'Stop of the Exchequer' Re-visited" (1982) 35 *Economic History Review* 511 at 523; *Tassell and Lee v Lewis* (1695) 1 Ld Raym 743 at 744; 91 ER 1397 at 1398.

a fractional reserve of coins or metal.[104] The power to issue banknotes was taken over by the Bank of England,[105] with convertibility ultimately ceasing to exist altogether in the course of the twentieth century.[106] Using funds on deposit at the central bank, commercial banks buy banknotes from the central bank and sell them for use to the public, against funds held by their customers on deposit with them. As they are exchanged out of and back into deposits "according to customer payment habits," as a form of cash, banknotes (together with coins), are not the principal form of money, a role now preserved to money deposited in banks.[107]

The integration of banks into a banking network, consisting of commercial banks multilaterally clearing in a clearinghouse,[108] and settling on the books of the central bank, which is an integral part of this network, has led to a fundamental albeit subtle change in the mode of the creation of money through "banking." Thus, deposits made to commercial banks are not typically in the form of specie or commodity money anymore. Rather, they are primarily created by lending or transferring funds into customers' deposit accounts. For its part, an addition to a bank's liquid assets is not typically made in the form of specie or commodity money, but rather in the form of an increase in the sum credited to that bank's own account; at least for a large bank such increase is in the credit to its account with the central bank.[109] Other than by receiving an interbank payment, liquidity designed to meet

104 Notes were issued by banks either against deposit of specie, that is, precious metal or coins, or against the negotiation, and hence in discount, of bills of exchange, as well as of promissory notes, see Adam Smith, *The Wealth of Nations* (Edwin Cannan (ed.), University of Chicago Press, 1976) vol 1 at 504; George Tucker, *The Theory of Money & Banks Investigated* (AM Kelly, 1964) at 161, 164.

105 See e.g., Holden, above note 68 at 92.

106 Convertibility was abolished for good in the United Kingdom under the *Gold Standard (Amendment) Act 1931* (UK), 21 & 22 Geo V, c 46.

107 Joseph Huber, "The Chicago Plan (100% Reserve) and Plain Sovereign Money" (Academia, 2015), online: http://www.academia.edu/31071041/The_Chicago_Plan_100_Reserve_and_Plain_Sovereign_Money, accessed 27 May 2024.

108 For the origins and early history of the London Clearing House see e.g., William Howarth, *Our Clearing System and Clearing Houses* (Effingham Wilson, 1884); see also Phillip W Matthews, *The Bankers' Clearing House: What it Is and What it Does* (Pitman & Sons, 1921). For a modern perspective on the scope of operation of a clearing house, see e.g., Herbert L Baer, Virginia G France, and James T Moser, "What Does a Clearinghouse Do?" (Spring 1995) 1 *Derivatives Quarterly* 39; see also James T Moser, "What is multilateral clearing and who cares?" (1994) Federal Reserve Bank of Chicago, Chicago Fed Letter no 87.

109 See Michael McLeay, Amar Radia, and Ryland Thomas, "Money creation in the modern economy" (*Bank of England*, Quarterly Bulletin 2014 Q1), online: https://www.bankofengland.co.uk/quarterly-bulletin/2014/q1/money-creation-in-the-modern-economy, accessed 27 May 2024.

deposit obligations is obtained, at least by a large commercial bank, in the form of credit posted to its account with the central bank, through borrowing in an interbank market, selling government securities, or as a last resort, borrowing from the central bank.

At the same time, non-cash payment activity continues to be primarily carried out over deposit accounts held in commercial banks. Monitoring depositors' payment activity in accounts continues to facilitate credit decision-making; it leads to specialization in advancing information-intensive non-traded loans, so as to continue to be a principal niche for a profitable commercial banking business, as well as an effective financial intermediation for the economy as a whole.[110] This must be true also in an era where credit information may be available from other sources such as a credit bureau.

The architecture, instruments, and institutions of the English system spread globally. At present, commercial banks take deposits from the public, lend into customers' deposit accounts, and provide payment services in conjunction with deposit accounts. In each country, at least all major commercial banks clear multilaterally and settle over deposit accounts they hold with the central bank.[111] They also maintain correspondent relationships[112] with local small banks as well as with cross-border or overseas large banks, so as to create a global network over which in principle non-cash payments can be made by any account holder to another in any currency. Moreover, as a rule, paper money in the form of banknotes is issued in each country by its central bank.

Banknotes, together with coins for small change, constitute cash (or currency). Payment in cash is typically made face to face, without any intermediation. Noncash payments, whether face to face or between distant parties, require intermediation. Where a payer and payee hold their respective accounts with the same bank a noncash payment is carried out by that bank debiting the payer's account and crediting the payee's account. Where a payer and payee hold their respective accounts at two banks which are correspondents a noncash payment involves debiting the payer's account by the payer's bank, crediting the payee's account by the payee's bank, and either

---

110 MS Goodfriend, "Money, Credit, Banking, and Payment System Policy" in David B Humphrey (ed), *The US Payment System: Efficiency, Risk and the Role of the Federal Reserve* (Kluwer Academic Publishers, 1990) at 247, 252–57.

111 Committee on Payment and Settlement Systems, *Core Principles for Systemically Important Payment Systems* (Bank for International Settlements 2001) 34–36, online: https://www.bis.org/cpmi/publ/d43.pdf, accessed 27 May 2024.

112 See in general, Committee on Payments and Market Infrastructures, *Correspondent Banking* (Bank for International Settlements, 2016), online: https://www.bis.org/cpmi/publ/d147.pdf, accessed 27 May 2024.

debiting the account of the payer's bank by the payee's bank or crediting the account of the payee's bank by the payer's bank. In a domestic payment system, at least all major banks hold their accounts with the central bank so that the interbank component of payment between two such banks is carried out as part of the multilateral interbank settlement on the books of the central bank. Otherwise, a noncash payment requires a chain of settlements on correspondent accounts, with or without settlement on the books of the central bank, or alternatively, one settlement between correspondent banks followed by another settlement on the books of a central bank.

To take a simple hypothetical example for the latter, the interbank component of a noncash payment in Australian currency from a customer of Bank A in Canada to a customer of Bank B in Australia, assuming that the two are non-correspondent major banks, is carried out by Bank A using its correspondent, another Australian major bank, which in turn, settles with Bank B on the books of the central bank of Australia.

Three principal features characterize payment services facilitated by the modern banking system. First, value held on deposit with participating banks, namely, "bank money" or more specifically, "commercial-bank money" (or even "ledger money"), is denominated in and is redeemable to fiat money (or banknotes), that is, an official currency or "legal tender." Second, such value is in the form of a claim in an account maintained with a bank. Typically, this is an asset account; however, payment may be made by means of a credit card, in which case payment is carried from the payer's credit account rather than asset account having a positive balance in bank money. Also, in such a case, payment results in an increase in the sum of bank money available to the payee in the payee's asset account – while the payer becomes obligated to reimburse the payer's bank, typically (if not exclusively) in bank money (originating from the payer's asset account). Third, claims against the central bank, that is, claims to "central-bank money," are available both to holders of fiat money/banknotes and the banks.[113] The latter multilaterally settle their reciprocal claims on the books of the central bank. Obligations on bank deposits payable on demand are referred to as "scriptural money," being a category covering both commercial and central bank money.[114] In principle, the sum of commercial bank money is a derivative of the sum of central bank money; the former manipulated by the

---

113 For the distinction between "commercial-bank money" and "central-bank money" see Mark Manning, Eriend Nier, and Jochen Schanz (eds), *The Economics of Large-value Payments and Settlement: Theory and Policy Issues for Central Banks* (Oxford University Press, 2009) at 4.

114 For this term see: Antonio Sáinz de Vicuña, "An Institutional Theory of Money" in Mario Giovanoli and Diego Devos (eds), *International Monetary and Financial Law: The Global Crisis* (Oxford University Press, 2010) at 517, 527.

central bank's power to set interest rates through the sale of government securities to banks and/or lending to banks, primarily with the view of achieving price stability.[115] Gold reserves, which may be assets of a central bank, do not play any explicit role in the creation of the money supply.[116]

The non-cash payment system is then premised on the use of "scriptural money." Its architecture is *centralized*. Thereunder, a bank maintains deposit accounts for customers (who thus keep with it commercial bank money). For its part, a large bank may also maintain deposit accounts (in commercial bank money) for correspondent banks. Finally, the central bank maintains settlement (deposit) accounts at least for large banks (which thus hold with it central bank money).[117] As a whole, the system can be visualized as a pyramid at whose head or apex stands the central bank with which at least large banks hold accounts, and possibly with small banks holding accounts with large banks. Individual and corporate customers are at the bottom or base of the pyramid holding their accounts in banks (whether large or small).[118]

V. THE COMING OF THE CYBER AGE

a. The Advent of Electronic Banking and e-Money

Historically, payment instructions accessing bank money were either oral or, more typically, in writing. Use of telecommunication, first the telegraph and

---

115 See e.g., Michael McLeay, Amar Radia, and Ryland Thomas, "Money in the modern economy: an introduction" (*Bank of England*, Quarterly Bulletin 2014 Q1) at 4, online: https://www.bankofengland.co.uk/quarterly-bulletin/2014/q1/money-in-the-modern-economy-an-introduction; McLeay et al, "Money creation," above note 109 at 14; see also B Friedman, "The Future of Monetary Policy: The Central Bank as an Army with Only a Signal Corps?" (1999) 2(3) *International Finance* 261. For an overview see also Warren Coats, "Econ 101: The Value of Money" (*Warren's Space*, 6 June 2022), online: https://wcoats.blog/2022/06/06/econ-101-the-value-of-money%EF%BF%BC/#content, accessed 27 May 2024.

116 For their function, see e.g., Ronan Manly, "Why the World's Central Banks hold Gold – In their Own Words" (*Bullionstar*, 20 March 2018), online: https://www.bullionstar.com/blogs/ronan-manly/worlds-central-banks-hold-gold-words/, accessed 27 May 2024.

117 On moving away from this tiering structure see e.g., Evangelos Benos, Gerardo Ferrara and Pedro Gurrola-Perez, "The impact of de-tiering in the United Kingdom's large-value payment system" (2017) Bank of England, Working Paper No 676, online: https://www.bankofengland.co.uk/working-paper/2017/the-impact-of-de-tiering-in-the-united-kingdoms-large-value-payment-system, accessed 27 May 2024.

118 See e.g., E Gerald Corrigan, "Luncheon Address: Perspectives on Payment System Risk Reduction" in Humphrey, above note 110 at 129–30; see also Hans J Blommestein and Bruce J Summers, "Banking and the Payment System" in Bruce J Summers (ed) *The Payment System: Design, Management and Supervision* (International Monetary Fund, 1994) at 15, 27; and Bruce J Summers, "The Payment System in a Market Economy" in Summers, *ibid* at 1–5.

then the transatlantic cable, goes back to mid-nineteenth century.[119] However, the watershed of electronic banking, where payments are processed as well as transmitted electronically, is a development of the second part of the twentieth century. Once it became possible to transmit instructions from a computer or computer terminal, the electronic funds transfer was born. Telecommunication in the electronic age was originally on cable or wire;[120] subsequently the wireless option became available,[121] and ultimately, instructions could be transmitted over the internet.[122]

Security in electronic funds transfer has been implemented by the physical protection of network components[123] and more recently by the introduction of tamper-resistant access devices and cryptographic data protection. Broadly speaking, "cryptography" (literally: secret writing) denotes "a method of storing and transmitting data in a particular form so that only those for whom it is intended can read and process it."[124] Strictly speaking, the term points at a specific method to that end, under which "complexity ... is injected into data so that only those who possess a key ... can remove the complexity ... and understand the intended message, while those without the key will not be able to retrieve the hidden message in a timely manner." The "process of applying cryptography to a message so that only its intended readers can understand it" is called "encryption"; the reverse, namely the "process of using a ... key to recover the intended message from its encrypted form," is called "decryption." Where the sender and receiver of a cryptographic message "share the same key data or mutually deducible key data," encryption is "symmetric."

119　See Douglas W Arner, Janos N Barberis, and Ross B Buckley, "The Evolution of Fintech: A New Post-Crisis Paradigm?" University of Hong Kong Faculty of Law Research Paper No. 2015/047, 4, online: https://papers.ssrn.com/sol3/papers.cfm?abstract_id=2676553, accessed 27 May 2024.

120　For an early discussion on the subject see Israel Sendrovic, "Technology and the Payment System" in Summers, above note 118 at 178.

121　See Gianni Bonaiuti, "Economic Issues on M-Payments and Bitcoin in Gabriella Gimigliano (ed.), *Bitcoin and Mobile Payments Constructing a European Union Framework* (Palgrave MacMillan, 2016) at 27.

122　See Committee on Payment and Settlement Systems, *Innovations in retail payments* (Bank for International Settlement, 2012), online: https://www.bis.org/cpmi/publ/d102.pdf, accessed 27 May 2024; see also Committee on Payment and Settlement Systems, *Survey of developments in electronic money and internet and mobile payments* (Bank for International Settlement, 2004), online: https://www.bis.org/cpmi/publ/d62.pdf, accessed 27 May 2024.

123　Gideon Samid, *Tethered Money: Managing Digital Currency Transactions* (Academic Press, 2015) at 80–81.

124　See definition of "cryptography" in Kathleen Richards, "Definition: Cryptography" (*TechTarget*, 2024), online: http://searchsoftwarequality.techtarget.com/definition/cryptography, accessed 27 May 2024.

Otherwise, where they do not share the same key data, encryption is said to be "asymmetric." Either way secrecy is achieved by means of the application of mathematical theories. Cryptographic complexity addresses factors relating to the decryption of the message and its result.[125] Security is enhanced by the use of random data[126] to generate keys, since "patterns could be recognized [and] could aid in a brute-force attack."[127] Looking ahead, security will be enhanced by the use of "quantum data," namely, data "marked" by merely being observed so as to alert the ultimate (designated) recipient to the fact that communication had been intercepted.[128]

Developments exploiting such technological achievements have not been limited to communication. It became also possible to "load" monetary value (that is, value denominated in an official or, in fact, any unit of account) on a tamper-resistant stored-value device such as a card or personal computer. In such a case, the value became known as "electronic money" or "e-money." The majority of e-money schemes have involved "balance-based" products. In such products, devices store and manipulate a numeric ledger, with transactions performed as debits or credits to a balance. Accordingly, this type of e-money is a monetary balance or value recorded electronically on and is available from a stored-value product (SVP), such as a chips card, a hard drive in a personal computer, or a server.[129] Such a record, accessible from the device without resort to the bank's computer system, can be viewed as a decentralized bank account.[130] E-money is said to "differ ... from so-called *access products*, which are products that allow consumers to use electronic means of

---

125 For definition of "cryptographic complexity" (as well as "cryptographic equivocation"), see Samid, above note 123 at 139–40 (Glossary).

126 For the superior protection of randomness premised on "a cipher which use[s] no mathematical complexity but instead call[s] for large amounts of randomness" see e.g., Carsten Stöcker and Gideon Samid, "Randomness: The Fix for Today's Broken Security" (*Medium*, 9 November 2017), online: https://medium.com/@cstoecker/randomness-the-fix-for-todays-broken-security-39ea7dc3a89b, accessed 27 May 2024.

127 Committee on Payment and Settlement Systems and The Group of Computer Experts of the central banks of the Group of Ten countries, *Security of electronic money* (Bank for International Settlement, 1996) 16, online: https://www.bis.org/cpmi/publ/d18.pdf, accessed 27 May 2024. A brute-force attack occurs when "An outsider could try to discover the plaintext by testing all possible decryption keys," *ibid* at 58.

128 Samid, *Tethered Money*, above note 123 at 106.

129 Committee on Payment and Settlement Systems et al, *Security*, above note 127 particularly at 5; see also information on "electronic money" in Wikipedia, "Electronic Money," online: https://web.archive.org/web/20170330071015/https://en.wikipedia.org/wiki/Electronic_money, archived website, accessed 27 May 2024.

130 Alan L Tyree, "The Legal Nature of Electronic Money" (1999) 10 *Journal of Banking and Finance Law and Practice* at 273, 276.

communication to access otherwise conventional payment services" in and out bank accounts.[131]

A minority of e-money products may still operate on devices that store electronic "notes" (sometimes called coins or tokens) that are uniquely identified by a serial number and are associated with a fixed, unchangeable denomination. In such a "note-based" model, transactions are performed by transferring notes from one device to another, and the balance of funds stored on a device is thus the sum of the denominations of all notes on the device. However, as in the "balance-based" products, transferability is typically restricted, and consumer cardholders may usually make payments only to merchants who may clear these payments or deposit the accumulated balances exclusively through their acquiring banks.[132] Such a product provides the link between traditional value-transfer systems to innovative circulating digital coins discussed in Part VI.

Under a variant of a "balance-based" e-money product, monetary value is not loaded on the device; rather, it is available from a master account, belonging to the issuer or someone acting on the issuer's behalf.[133] As in the case of e-money, monetary value is not available from the payer-debtor's own bank account.[134] However, such prepaid value is in a bank account, even if not that of the payer. Its use entails communication to the issuer and requires the cardholder to access a bank account (even if not theirs). From this perspective, a prepaid product device is more of a variant of an access device rather than of an SVP.

According to Crawford, e-money is truly "money" when it may circulate from one person to another, that is, from one SVP to another, without being "cleared" or intermediated by the issuer.[135] This seems to me to be true for both "balance-based" and "note-based" e-money products. However, upon reflection, e-money, in all its manifestations, is ultimately a variant of "bank

---

131 Committee on Payment and Settlement Systems, *Implications for Central Banks of the development of electronic Money* (Bank for International Settlement, 1996) at 1, emphasis in the original, online: https://www.bis.org/publ/bisp01.pdf, accessed 27 May 2024.

132 Committee on Payment and Settlement Systems et al, *Security*, above note 127 particularly at 5.

133 For the view that this is in fact e-money in the true sense see Nadia F Piffaretti, *A Theoretical Approach to Electronic Money* (1998) University of Fribourg Faculty of Economic and Social Sciences Working Paper no 302, online: https://ssrn.com/abstract=70793.

134 Unfortunately, the confusion between these two types of payment products is rampant. For a definition of "e-money" that does not include the prepaid product, see Ben Fung, Miguel Molico, and Gerald Stuber, "Electronic Money and Payments: Recent Developments and Issues" (2014) Bank of Canada Discussion Paper 2014-2, online: http://www.bankofcanada.ca/wp-content/uploads/2014/04/dp2014-2.pdf, accessed 27 May 2024.

135 Bradley Crawford, "Is Electronic Money Really Money?" (1997) 12 *Banking and Finance Law Review* 399.

money"[136] – or at least an obligation to pay in commercial bank money.[137] In part, this is because it originates from and in principle is backed by from a deposit in a bank. Moreover, while it is transferred from one person to another without intermediation, e-money does not circulate further.

Thus, whether e-money is purchased in cash or by means of a debit to the purchaser's bank account, the issuer has its own bank account credited with the amount sold to the purchaser. Where the e-money is purchased from a bank the account credited is the reserve account of the selling bank. In turn, e-money received by the payee is forwarded to the payee's bank which credits the payee's account with the amount of payment and forwards the e-money itself for redemption against the value previously credited to the seller's account. For their part, the payee may not circulate the e-money; to obtain its value the payee must deposit it. In the final analysis, even where pre-paid value or e-money is not issued by a bank, a scheme must facilitate the purchase and prompt redemption through banks.

"Electronic banking" enhanced payment services in several other ways. First, it introduced electronic processing to paper-based instruments such as cheques.[138] Second, it facilitated new as well as variations of existing products.[139] Third, new players, such as money transmitters,[140] payment institutions,[141] or

---

136   I am thus not persuaded by the classification of Committee on Payments and Market Infrastructures, *Digital Currencies* (Bank for International Settlement, 2015) at 6, online: https://www.bis.org/cpmi/publ/d137.pdf, accessed 27 May 2024, under which e-money is lumped with digital currencies as "E-money (broad sense)" so as to be contrasted with commercial bank money.

137   Nor am I persuaded on this point by Dan Awrey, *Beyond Banks: Technology, Regulation and the Future of Money* (Princeton and Oxford: Princeton University Press, 2024) who argues throughout this book that such an obligation is another category of "money."

138   See in general e.g., Benjamin Geva, "Is Death of the Paper Cheque Upon Us? The Electronic Presentment and Deposit of Cheques in Canada" (2014) 30 *Banking and Finance Law Review* 113; see also Benjamin Geva, "From Paper to Electronic Order: The Digitalization of the Check in the USA" (2015) 4 *Penn State Journal of Law and International Affairs* 96.

139   Such as preauthorized debits ("PADs") replacing the delivery of a series of post-dated cheques; the debit card complementing the credit card and to a large extent substituting both cash and cheques; preauthorized credits ("PAPs") substituting paycheques.

140   See e.g., s 102(14) of National Conference of Commissioners on Uniform State Laws, "Uniform Money Services Act (UMSA)" (Uniform Law Commission, 2004), online: https://www.uniformlaws.org/committees/community-home?communitykey=cf8b649a-114c-4bc9-8937-c4ee17148a1b, accessed 27 May 2024, under which "Money transmission" is defined to mean "selling or issuing payment instruments, stored value, or receiving money or monetary value for transmission. ... "

141   Defined in art 4(4) of Directive (EU) 2015/2366 of 25 November 2015 on payment services in the internal market, amending Directives 2002/65/EC, 2009/110/EC, and 2013/36/EU and Regulation (EU) No 1093/2010, and repealing Directive 2007/64/EC [2015] OJ L337/35, online: http://eur-lex.europa.eu/legal-content/EN/TXT/?uri=celex:32015L2366, accessed 27 May 2024, to mean: "a legal person that has been granted authorisation in accordance with Article 11 to provide and execute

e-money institutions[142] entered the scene as end-payment institutions in a payment transaction, facilitating domestic and international payments in small amounts to parties who do not have bank accounts. Fourth, the power balance in the partnership between financial institutions and telecommunication carriers has shifted, allowing the latter a greater voice and share in the payment market.[143] Fifth, in facilitating instant communication, electronic banking allowed the use of risk reduction methods as well as instant authorization leading to an immediate final credit to the payee's account way ahead of the interbank settlement; such may be the case in domestic large value wholesale payment systems,[144] and in retail fast payments networks.[145] This is also the case in a typical credit card payment, even when it is carried out internationally.[146]

Electronic banking facilitated branchless banking to the detriment of banks with a large branch network.[147] As well, the possible impact of electronic banking on monetary policy has been fiercely debated.[148] At the same time, none of the various facets of electronic banking has affected the architecture of the payment system even as it expanded its scope and globalized it. No wonder, the law governing wireless instructions is the same as the one governing wire orders.[149]

---

payment services throughout the [European] Union." The term does not include credit institution (bank), electronic money institution, or post office giro institutions. See art 1(1).

142 Defined under Article 2(1) of Council Directive 2009/110/EC of 16 September 2009 on the taking up, pursuit, and prudential supervision of the business of electronic money institutions amending Directives 2005/60/EC and 2006/48/EC repealing Directive 2000/46/EC [2009] OJ L267/7, online: http://eurlex.europa.eu/legal-content/EN/TXT/?uri=CELEX%3A32009L0110, accessed 27 May 2024, to mean: "a person that has been granted authorisation under Title II to issue electronic money."

143 See e.g., document issued by the Canadian Bankers Association, "Canadian NFC Mobile Payments: Reference Model" (Version 1.03, Canadian Bankers Association, 14 May 2012), online: https://cba.ca/Assets/CBA/Documents/Files/Article%20Category/PDF /msc_20120514_mobile_en.pdf, accessed 28 May 2024.

144 See e.g., the large value wholesale payment system in Canada where finality of payment is guaranteed by the central bank prior to the completion of settlement, CPSS, *Core Principles*, above note 111 at 30.

145 See e.g., Committee on Payments and Market Infrastructures, *Fast payments –Enhancing the speed and availability of retail payments* (Bank for International Settlements, 2016), online: https://www.bis.org/cpmi/publ/d154.pdf, accessed 28 May 2024.

146 For the legal nature of the credit card payment see in general, Benjamin Geva, 'The Processor and the Contractual Matrix in a Card Scheme: How Privity Fell and Resurrected in *Aldo v. Moneris*" (October 2013) 32(5) *National Banking Law Review* 73.

147 Hanno Beck, "Banking is essential, banks are not. The future of financial intermediation in the age of the Internet" (2001) 3 *Netnomics* 7.

148 See e.g., Benjamin J Cohen, "Electronic money: New day or false dawn?" (2001) 8 *Review of International Political Economy* 197.

149 See e.g., Benjamin Geva, "The Wireless Wire: Do M-Payments and *UNCITRAL* Model Law on International Credit Transfers Match?" (2011) 27 *Banking and Finance Law Review* 249.

For their part, money transmitters, payment institutions as well as e-money institutions have been using banks as intermediaries in the transfers in which they participate at either end of the transaction.[150] Thus, they increased rather than decreased payment intermediation. Furthermore, not treating such institutions as deposit takers hinges on a "benevolent" strict view of "deposit taking," so as to exclude the delivery of money for a specific purpose.[151] True, a payment instruction issued from a digital device such as a mobile phone rather than from a computer terminal or computer is often said to result in a mobile payment. When the payment scheme is operated over mobile devices it is even described as involving "mobile money." However, in substance, payment orders initiated from a digital or mobile device is a specie of an electronic funds transfer.[152] For its part "mobile money" is a form of "e-money." It is therefore confusing to treat such developments as reflecting a "digitization of state-issue currenc[y]" even in connection with an online (e-commerce) transaction.[153] Ultimately, efficiency is bound either to turn payment institutions into banks or for banks take over payment institutions, either directly or as subsidiaries, so as to eliminate this unnecessary layer of intermediation. The issue for banks is the adoption of a different level of service rather than the elimination of banks as an essential component in linking between payers and payees.

The broader question however is whether "electronic banking" has not been superseded by "Fintech," "snatching" money and payments from the banking system. Fintech refers to the use of technology by information technology (IT) firms[154] to deliver financial solutions directly to purchasers of financial products such as payment services.[155] Technology designed to deliver financial solutions

---

150 See e.g., Committee on Payment and Settlement Services and The World Bank, *General principles for international remittance services* (Bank for International Settlements and The World Bank, 2007), online: https://www.bis.org/cpmi/publ/d76.pdf, accessed 28 May 2024.

151 For a critical analysis see e.g., Benjamin Geva and Muharem Kianief, "Reimagining E-Money: Its Conceptual Unity with Other Retail Payment Systems" (2005) 3 *Current Developments in Monetary and Financial Law* 669 at 677–79.

152 Whether from (or into) an asset account, credit line, or stored-value – as the case may be.

153 Notwithstanding Joshua S Gans and Hanna Halaburda, "Some Economics of Private Digital Currency" (2013) Bank of Canada Working Paper 2013–38, online: http://www.bankofcanada.ca/wp-content/uploads/2013/11/wp2013-38.pdf, accessed 28 May 2024.

154 Generally speaking, IT "deals with the technology part of any information system, and as such deals with hardware, servers, operating systems and software etc," see e.g., Olivia, "Difference Between Information Systems and Information Technology" (*DifferenceBetween.com*, 23 April 2011), online: http://www.differencebetween.com/difference-between-information-systems-and-vs-information-technology/, accessed 28 May 2024.

155 A broader definition under which Fintech refers to the use of technology to deliver financial solutions will encompass the use of technology by banks such as in electronic banking, and hence is unhelpful for the purposes of this paper.

is, however, available also to banks whether directly or indirectly by purchase from IT firms. Alternatively, IT firms may become banks and compete with existing banks on equal footing. It is not that "banking" survives while banks die;[156] rather, as an economic model banking has adopted new technologies to be used by old and new types of institutions. Whether and to what extent this remains true in light of subsequent developments is discussed further below.

b. Availability of Central Bank Account Balances and Their Equivalents to the Public

In reviewing the present architecture of the payment system prior to the Fintech era Goodfriend opined that " … although valuing deposits at par and holding fractional reserves is efficient for individual banks, it had the potential for generating destabilizing systemwide bank runs." In his view this risk is, however, "remedied efficiently by central bank monetary policy,"[157] as well as by other payment system policies.[158] Conversely, reviving and building on old ideas, a recent set of proposals will make central bank money deposits available to the public either directly or indirectly.[159] A typical rationale, premised on new technological developments, is that:

> Central banking evolved at a time when service provision in local branches was integral to providing banking services. In that world it made sense for the central bank to "wholesale" its core exchange settlement and liquidity support services to banks which would then "retail" them to individuals and businesses via their branches, passbooks and cheque accounts. It was impracticable for central banks' services to be provided to individuals.

At the same time, the rationale goes on, "[m]odern technology enables us to extend some core central banking services to individuals and businesses."[160] As a matter of history, the argument is doubtful, as post-Medieval

---

156 As claimed by "clever consultants" according to *The Economist*, "Unresolved" (vol 428 issue 9108, *The Economist*, 2018) at 23.

157 Goodfriend, above note 110 at 248.

158 *Ibid* at 261.

159 Unfortunately, it has become common to treat such a proposal as relating to central bank digital currency. See e.g., Michael D Bordo and Andrew T Levin, "Central Bank Digital Currency and the Future of Monetary Policy" (2017) National Bureau of Economic Research Working Paper 23711, online: http://www.nber.org/papers/w23711, accessed 28 May 2024. Digital currencies (in the true sense of the term) are discussed in Part V below.

160 Nick Gruen, "Central Banking For All: A Modest Proposal for Radical Change" (Nesta, 2014) at 7, online: https://media.nesta.org.uk/documents/central_banking_for_all.pdf, accessed 28 May 2024.

public banks "retailed" their services to the public. Even so, it is true that with the increase in the size and geographical scope of the bank customer base, a centralized system is workable only in an enhanced technological environment. Under one thoughtful view, reform in that direction will democratize money.[161] Hence, banking-centralization proposals merit consideration.

One proposal premised on this rationale is the provision of payment services to the public exclusively by a designated government agency that will take deposits from the public but will have restricted investment powers so as to be able to invest only in safe assets such as super-collateralized real estate mortgages. Under that proposal, payment transactions will be carried out over deposit accounts with respect to which the liability of the depositary (the government agency) is effectively secured by investment in high quality assets. On this basis, such deposits will benefit from unlimited guarantee of the central bank. Under that proposal, commercial banks will be able to lend to customers and sell them investment products but be precluded from providing payment services.[162]

However, one may reasonably suppose that in upsetting the delicate balance between the roles of the public and private sectors in the monetary and payment systems, this proposal will be perceived as going too far (or in fact, nowhere). Certainly, in monopolizing payment services in the hands of a government agency, the proposal will stifle competition and give no incentive to innovate. Furthermore, the proposal is not persuasive in mandating a central bank guarantee on the top of the requirement to invest deposited funds in safe assets. I therefore doubt that in a capitalist economy this proposal will persuade policy makers. At the same time, unclothing it from these objectionable elements, the proposal is reminiscent of an earlier idea, that of "narrow banking"; thereunder payment transactions are carried out over bank deposits of which the proceeds are invested in safe asset (and not lending).[163] "Narrow banking" does not require the superimposition of a central bank guarantee

---

161 Saule T Omarova, "The People's Ledger: How to Democratize Money and Finance the Economy" (2021) 74 *Vanderbilt Law Review* 1231. The author endeavours to offer a blueprint for a comprehensive restructuring of the central bank balance sheet as the basis for redesigning the core architecture of modern finance.

162 Gruen, above note 160 *passim*. In the United Kingdom, he designates the National Savings and Investments (NS&I) as the appropriate governmental agency. At the moment, the NS&I accepts deposits from the public (up to prescribed ceilings) and places them in savings accounts from which payment services cannot be provided. In Gruen's words, "what is being proposed is to allow super-collateralised loans to be treated as part of the monetary system rather than the financial system," *ibid* at 9.

163 The term is said to be coined by Robert Litan, *What Should Banks Do?* (Brookings Institution, 2005). Litan discusses "narrow banking" at 6, 169–78, 186–87. See also Patrizio Lainà,

and in fact does not alter the traditional roles of commercial banks as deposit takers, providers of payment services, and lenders (albeit not out of deposits).

Under another proposal the central bank will open accounts and offer payment services directly to the public. This proposal is, however, said to impose "a large administrative burden" on the central bank that "could distract it from its other functions in [regulating] and managing monetary policy." It is further acknowledged that under the proposal the central bank, "a state-owned enterprise," would undertake pure market functions, in which it "would have no commercial incentive to innovate [payment] services."[164]

To meet these objections, under a variant, it is proposed that public access to scriptural central bank money or its equivalent will be indirect.[165] There are two alternative approaches to such a variant. One is premised on "full reserve banking"[166] while the other is of "plain sovereign money."[167] Briefly stated, under the former, the entire quantity of commercial bank money, namely, the total amount of demand deposits with banks, is to be backed by reserve of central bank money held by commercial banks on deposit with the central bank.[168]

Under the latter, that of "plain sovereign money,"[169] the distinction between the two types of scriptural money will be abolished; what will exist is only one category of scriptural money, being central bank, and thus

"Proposals for Full-Reserve Banking: A Historical Survey from David Ricardo to Martin Wolf" (2015) 4(2) *Economic Thought* 1 at 12.

164 Ben Dyson and Graham Hodgson, "Digital Cash: Why Central Banks Should Start Issuing Electronic Money" (Positive Money, 2016) at 15, online: http://positivemoney.org/wp-content/uploads/2016/01/Digital_Cash_WebPrintReady_20160113.pdf, accessed 28 May 2024.

165 *Ibid* at 16.

166 See e.g., Jaromir Benes and Michael Kumhof, "The Chicago Plan Revisited" (2012) International Monetary Fund, Working Paper WP/12/202, online: https://www.imf.org/external/pubs/ft/wp/2012/wp12202.pdf, accessed 28 May 2024; William R. Allen, "Irving Fisher and the 100 Percent Reserve Proposal" (1993) 36 *Journal of Law and Economics* 703.

167 See e.g., Huber, above note 107; Phillipe Bacchetta, "The Sovereign Money Initiative in Switzerland: An Economic Assessment" (Vollgeld, 27 June 2017), online: https://people.unil.ch/philippebacchetta/files/2017/06/Vollgeld_5.pdf, accessed 28 May 2024. For a blueprint see Ben Dyson, Graham Hodgson, and Frank van Lerven, "Sovereign Money: An Introduction" (Positive Money 2016), online: http://positivemoney.org/wp-content/uploads/2016/12/SovereignMoney-AnIntroduction-20161214.pdf, accessed 28 May 2024.

168 There are at least two variants as to the rules which will govern the conduct of monetary policy under such a regime, particularly as to the role of discretion by the central bank. For a summary see Huber, above note 107 at 3.

169 Beware of inconsistent use of terminology. Andrew Jackson, *Sovereign Money: Paving the Way for a Sustainable Recovery* (Ben Dyson (ed), Positive Money 2013), online: https://www.datocms-assets.com/132494/1717793629-sovereign-money-final-web.pdf, accessed 11 August 2024, uses the term to denote central bank money distributed directly to business to fund infrastructure projects.

commercial-bank-default risk-free, money.[170] It will be available to members of the public in accounts on the books of the central bank. Unless operated by the central bank itself, as discussed above, such accounts will be operated through and managed by commercial banks,[171] possibly in "transaction accounts."[172] The latter will be distinguished from "investment accounts," also managed by commercial banks. Funds in investment accounts will be invested in designated collections of assets, each of a broadly similar risk profile.

Commercial banks will not be able to lend out of transaction accounts and will thus lose their ability to create commercial bank money. Lending will rather be carried out of investment funds (possibly as well as from long-term borrowing from the public) except that it will not create additional money or purchasing power.[173] Thus, loans to third parties, out of funds on deposit in an investment account, will be outstanding prior to the maturity of the investment, during a period in which the money will not be available to the investment account holder.

Investment account holders will select the level of risk of the investment and will bear an agreed upon part of the risk of non-payment on the due date. Not being available to them prior to that, sovereign money owed to them will not serve as commercial bank money. Rather, prior to maturity on the investment account, sovereign money deposited in them will be lent by the bank and thus will exclusively be used by borrowers from the bank.[174] Thus, banking will fully reclaim its function as an intermediator between savers and borrowers.

Under both approaches commercial banks will cease to create money by lending into customers' deposits. Money creation will rather be under

----

170 However, it does not make sense to me to have a hybrid system under which *scriptural* money is available to the public in both commercial and central bank money as I read Dyson and Hodgson, "Digital Cash," above note 164 at 28–30 to suggest.

171 For a precedent from Sri Lanka, albeit for investors' securities accounts operated by intermediaries on the books of the central bank, see *Payment & Settlement Systems Act* no 28 (2005) c 2, ss 6–10, online: https://www.cbsl.gov.lk/sites/default/files/cbslweb_documents/laws/acts/en/Payment_setttlement_sys_act.pdf, accessed 28 May 2024.

172 For these two options see Bordo and Levin, above note 159.

173 Where required to meet demand further, lending may be done by the creation of new money by the central bank to be lent to banks and other lending institutions for the purposes of relending it to borrowers in the real economy. See Dyson, Hodgson, and van Lerven, above note 168 at 36.

174 Legally, of course, on maturity of the investment account the bank will be liable to depositors and investors regardless of possible default by borrowers, in which case it will be up to the bank to find sovereign money from other sources to fund its liability to depositors and investors.

the exclusive power of the central bank.[175] On their part, commercial banks will be limited to either (1) issue its "replication" or "shadow," but not expand its quantity (under the full reserve banking alternative), or (2) be restrained altogether from issuing it at all (under the plain sovereign money alternative).[176] They will, however, be able to lend and provide payment services.

An analysis of the pros and cons of each alternative, vis-à-vis each other as well as by reference to the current fractional reserve regime, is beyond the scope of this study as well as of the competence of this author. At the same time, in relation to the topic at hand, under both alternatives, banks will continue to accept deposits, make loans (albeit not out of demand deposits), and provide payment services. For sure, they may face competition from "payment institutions" that do not provide "investment accounts" services as well as lenders providing "investment accounts" but not "payment accounts." However, it is reasonable to expect that such competitors will be regulated, respectively on the payment, saving, and lending sides, so it will be possible for banks to leverage the combined services they give to their advantage. For example, as it is now, monitoring the payment activity of a customer will help a bank in making its lending decision regarding that customer. Hence, a reform under any of these lines will not change the role of commercial banks in the payment system.

However, what may change is the legal underpinning of the bank's liability for money deposited in the payments or transactions account. At the moment, a bank is liable to a depositor on a simple debt since the money deposited belongs to the bank, which can use it as it wishes.[177] Conversely,

<hr />

175 In connection with sovereign money see e.g., Dyson, Hodgson, and van Lerven, above note 167 at 28–37. One proposal for full reserve banking is for the central bank to act as a "currency board" in issuing new money only against a basket of available assets (of which gold is only one); see Warren Coats, "My Political Platform for the Nation – 2017" (*Warren's Space*, 31 December 2016), online: https://wcoats.wordpress.com/2016/12/31/my-political-platform-for-the-nation-2017/, accessed 28 May 2024 (see section on Monetary and Financial Policies); Warren Coats, "The Case for a Real SDR Currency Board" (2011) 22(2) *Central Banking Journal* 31.

176 For the view that "both logically and according to the International Accounting Standards, sovereign money cannot be considered to be a debt of the state. Instead, sovereign money conforms to the classification of equity," see Ben Dyson and Graham Hodgson, "Accounting for Sovereign Money: Why State-Issued Money is Not 'Debt'" (Positive Money, 2016) at 9: online: http://positivemoney.org/wp-content/uploads/2016/03/AccountingForSovereignMoney_20160309.pdf, accessed 28 May 2024.

177 The *locus classicus* for this proposition is *Foley*, above note 8.

under a "full reserve banking" scheme, under one option, the bank's obligation may be conceptualized by analogy to that of a securities intermediary that under Article 8 of the *Uniform Commercial Code* in the United States[178] as well as under the *Uniform Securities Transactions Act* in Canada.[179] According to this legislation, under the "indirect holding" regime, a securities intermediary is liable to an investor on a "securities entitlement" against which the securities intermediary must maintain 100 percent "financial asset."[180] At the same time, under a "plain sovereign money" regime the customers may be viewed as entitled from their banks under an "irregular deposit," which envisages a claim premised on an unidentified portion of a mixture of fungible assets (e.g., money) to which ownership is passed to the depositary from the various depositors.[181]

In the final analysis, technological feasibility does not necessarily lead to economic justification. For example, as pointed out at the beginning of this section, albeit ahead of Fintech, Goodfriend was on record highlighting the public's substantial efficiency gains of the fractional reserve at the cost of accepted risks, which are anyway mitigated by monetary policy, central bank lending, and deposit insurance.[182] To say the least, under the present system, banks are able to share with customers profit realized from lending out of demand deposits; the chance is that, in a regime under which scriptural central bank money is available to the public in any form, payment services will be more costly. Whether and to what extent gains in safety outweigh efficiency losses may be in the eyes of the beholder. This section should be taken as outlining banks' continued role and relative advantage in a central bank scriptural money environment rather than to be necessarily and unequivocally supporting such a regime.

---

178 See "Uniform Commercial Code (UCC) Article 8" (1994), ss 8-501–8-511, in conjunction with definitions in s 8-102, online: https://www.law.cornell.edu/ucc/8, accessed 28 May 2024.

179 See Uniform Law Conference of Canada, "Uniform Securities Transfer Act (USTA)" (2004), ss 106–16 in conjunction with definitions in s 1, online: https://ulcc-chlc.ca/ULCC/media /EN-Uniform-Acts/Uniform-Securities-Transfer-Act.pdf, accessed 28 May 2024.

180 See in general e.g., Benjamin Geva, "Securities Transfers in the Indirect Holding System – Law Reform in Canada in the Footsteps of UCC Article 8" (2007) 18 *Journal of Banking and Financial Law and Practice* 72–77.

181 In general, for the irregular deposit, see Robert W Lee, *The Elements of Roman Law with a Translation of the Institutes of Justinian*, 4th ed (Sweet & Maxwell, 1956) at 295; see also Reinhard Zimmermann, *The Law of Obligations – Roman Foundations of the Civilian Tradition* (Juta, 1990) at 215–19.

182 Goodfriend, above note 110 at 261. Bank regulation could be added to the listed items.

VI. DIGITAL CURRENCIES

The innovations discussed above concerned accessing accounts and transacting digitally, expressing value on the screen of a digital device, storing value in an SVP so as to give rise of e-money, and making central bank money or its equivalent available to the public. All have not changed the nature of an interbank transfer as a transfer of scriptural money in the form of a balance of monetary value. Nor have they changed the role of the bank as a payment intermediary. More to the point, it has not changed the concept of "money" itself.

This does not appear to be the case with the emergence of digital currencies. Very much like an electronic payment instruction, a digital coin consists of encrypted data expressed in strings of bits. However, as "an entity that amounts to a string of bits," a digital coin's string has a numerical value as well as a unique identity.[183] Like physical coins and banknotes, digital coins are not paid out of bank accounts, so their payment does not appear to require intermediation. And yet exactly as is the case with respect to electronic funds transfers, they are paid with over the cyber space.

The ensuing discussion excludes currencies not linked to the real economy[184] and is limited to coins that could be liquefied and redeemed, so as to be available for use in real trading, as well as for purchase of goods and services. Payment by such digital coins has the potential of bypassing both the bank account and the centralized multilateral interbank settlement.

A digital currency may be issued either privately, in which case it is "virtual currency," or by a central bank, in which case it is CBDC (Central Bank Digital Currency).[185] A virtual currency may have its own unit of account,

---

183 Samid, *Tethered Money*, above note 123 at 105–06.

184 Such as: (1) closed/"in-game only" schemes, in which a link to the real economy or fiat currency hardly exists; (2) schemes with unidirectional flow, under which the currency may originally be purchased with a fiat currency but may not be converted back to it, such as Facebook Credits, and even; (3) schemes with a bidirectional flow, envisaging conversion in both directions, albeit usually not used in entirely open loops throughout the entire economy, such as air miles in frequent flyer programs.

See European Central Bank and Eurosystem, *Virtual Currency Schemes* (European Central Bank 2012) at 12–15, online: https://www.ecb.europa.eu/pub/pdf/other/virtualcurrencyschemes201210en.pdf, accessed 28 May 2024; for an explanation as to why such a currency will not "migrate" to the real economy, see e.g., Gans and Halaburda, above note 153.

185 For the latter, see e.g., Committee on Payments and Market Infrastructures, *Central Bank Digital Currencies* (Bank for International Settlements 2018), online: https://www.bis.org/cpmi/publ/d174.pdf, accessed 28 May 2024; see also Norges Bank, *Central Bank Digital Currencies* (Norges Bank Papers no 1 2018), online: https://www.norges-bank.no/conten-

fluctuating by reference to the value of an official unit of account. In such a case, the virtual currency is *self-anchored*. It is in fact unanchored to any unit of fiat currency or commodity. Alternatively, a virtual currency may be a *"claim-check"* or *stablecoin* that is denominated in, namely pegged to, or claimed at par with, either an official currency's unit of account (as well as a basket of such currencies) or in the value of a specified amount of a designated commodity, whether or not it is backed by a reserve of such currency or commodity.[186] A CBDC is naturally denominated in the unit of account of the official currency. Either way, a scheme in which coins are issued, transferred, and redeemed under a centralized protocol is said to be centralized.[187] A digital currency that is issued, transferred, and redeemed over a *distributed ledger* is decentralized. Finally, a digital currency issued by a centralized operator and yet transferable over a distributed ledger (or otherwise under a decentralized protocol), is hybrid.[188]

The distributed ledger underlying decentralization is an asset database that can be shared across a network of multiple sites, geographies, or institutions.[189] Blockchain is an underlying technology, requiring the internet to support and maintain its peer-to-peer network, which enables digital implementation of a distributed ledger. Being a computerized ledger on a

---

tassets/166efadb3d73419c8c50f9471be26402/nbpapers-1-2018-centralbankdigitalcurrencies.pdf?v=18052018121950, accessed 28 May 2024.

186 See e.g., Amnon Samid, *Tethered Money*, above note 123 at 14–16 and Financial Stability Board, "Regulation, Supervision and Oversight of 'Global Stablecoin' Arrangements" (Financial Stability Board, October 2020) [FSB, Regulation], online (pdf): www.fsb.org/wp-content/uploads/P131020-3.pdf, accessed 25 July 2024. The assertion that denomination in its own unit of account appears to be an element in the definition of "virtual currency" (that is, privately issued digital currency) as in] Dong He et al, "Virtual Currencies and Beyond: Initial Considerations" (SDN/16/3, International Monetary Fund 2016) at 7: online: www.imf.org/external/pubs/ft/sdn/2016/sdn1603.pdf, accessed 28 May 2024, is thus inaccurate.

187 I am using this term here in a different sense than Liam Pak Nian and David Lee Kuo Chuen in David Lee Kuo Chuen (ed), *Handbook of Digital Currency: Bitcoin, Innovation, Financial Instruments and Big Data* (Elsevier, 2015) at 7, who use it to denote "closed system[s] with transactions within specific entities" in such items as loyalty points or air miles.

188 For this tripartite classification, see Dong He et al, above note 186 at 8 (where a third criterion is added *viz*, "mechanisms to implement and enforce internal rules on the use and circulation of the currency").

189 UK Government Chief Scientific Adviser, "Distributed Ledger Technology: beyond block chain" (UK Government Office for Science 2016) at 17– 8, online: https://www.gov.uk/government/uploads/system/uploads/attachment_data/file/492972/gs-16-1-distributed-ledger-technology.pdf, accessed 28 May 2024.

distributed network, it generates a single version of the record on each computer and in essence is:[190]

> A type of a database that takes a number of records and puts them in a block. ... Each block is then "chained" to the next block, using a cryptographic signature. This allows block chains to be used like a ledger, which can be shared and corroborated by anyone with the appropriate permissions.

Accuracy of the ledger is corroborated under a method determined under the rules adhered to by participants. Record security and visibility to authorized users is ensured by cryptography.

A *"cryptocurrency"* denotes a digital currency in which encryption techniques are used to regulate the generation of units of currency and verify the execution of payment transactions[191] on a decentralized network. Cryptography is thus used in cryptocurrencies to express and protect the value of the coins (the sequence of the bits), to prevent counterfeiting and fraudulent transactions, as well as to perform the validation and execution of transactions records via a distributed ledger, such as the blockchain. Each block contains a cryptographic hash[192] or algorithm that links it to the previous block along with a timestamp for the transactions from that block. The

190 *Ibid* at 17; see also e.g., Committee on Payments and Market Infrastructures, *Distributed Ledger Technology in Payment, Clearing, and Settlement – An Analytical Framework* (Bank for International Settlements 2017), online: http://www.bis.org/cpmi/publ/d157.pdf, accessed 28 May 2024; see also David Mills et al, "Distributed ledger technology in payments, clearing and settlement" (Finance and Economics Discussion Series 2016-095, Board of Governors of The Federal Reserve System 2016), online: https://www.federalreserve.gov/econresdata/feds/2016/files/2016095pap.pdf, accessed 28 May 2024; Robleh Ali, John Barrdear, Roger Clews, and James Southgate, "Innovations in payment technologies and the emergence of digital currencies" (*Bank of England*, Quarterly Bulletin 2014 Q3) at 262; for a lawyer's perspective see e.g., Muharem Kianieff, *Blockchain Technology and The Law: Opportunities and Risks* (Routledge, 2019).

191 This definition slightly modifies the one from "Basic Cryptocurrency Starter Guide" (*Medium*, 18 September 2017), online: https://medium.com/@Wolfofcrypto/basic-cryptocurrency-starter-guide-8f2071ea85de, accessed 28 May 2024, particularly, I replace "transfer of funds" by the "execution of payment transactions" to point at payment by the transmission of "coins" rather than "generic value" in the forms of funds.

192 "Hashing" was defined to be "a cryptographic technique to generate a unique code to represent [a] document which keeps the contents of that document confidential [so as] to verify that [it] exists and has not been tampered with." See Financial Conduct Authority, "Discussion Paper on distributed ledger technology" (Discussion Paper DP 17/3, Financial Conduct Authority 2017) at 18, online: https://www.fca.org.uk/publication/discussion/dp17-03.pdf, accessed 28 May 2024.

network allows online payments to be sent directly from one party to another without going through a bank or any other centralized counterparty.[193]

Having not been born in a vacuum,[194] the pioneering digital cash scheme, and the most prominent one so far, is Bitcoin.[195] Being "the first and still the most popular cryptocurrency," it "began life as a techno-anarchist project to create an online version of cash, a way for people to transact without the possibility of interference from malicious governments or banks."[196] It is a virtual,[197] self-anchored[198] cryptocurrency, for which scarcity is by design,[199] and a peer-to-peer decentralized system.[200] In his seminal paper,[201] its mythological founder Satoshi Nakamoto defined Bitcoin as an "electronic

<hr>

193 See e.g., Nian and Chuen, above note 187 at 5, 8.

194 For the pre-Bitcoin digital cash history of the "techno-libertarian" project see Goldstein, above note 80 at 189–212.

195 In the broader context of subsequent "plenty of alternatives" see e.g., Andreas Hanl, "Some Insights into the Development of Cryptocurrencies" (MAGKS Joint Discussion Paper Series in Economics No 04-2018, Philipps-University Marburg School of Business and Economics 2018).

196 *The Economist*, "Show Me the Money," 428 *The Economist* 2018 (issue 9107) at 12.

197 See e.g., definition in s 102(23) of the National Conference of Commissioners of Uniform State Laws, "Regulation of Virtual Currency Businesses Act" (Uniform Law Commission 2017), online: https://www.uniformlaws.org/committees/community-home?CommunityKey=e 104aaa8-c10f-45a7-a34a-0423c2106778, accessed 28 May 2024, under which "[v]irtual currency" is "a digital representation of value that is used as a medium of exchange, a unit of account, or a store of value; and is not legal tender. … " "Legal tender" is defined in s 102(8) as "the medium of exchange or unit of value, including the coin or paper money of the United States, issued by the United States or by another government."

198 Namely, its value is not pegged to that of a financial asset or commodity.

199 David Fox, "Cryptocurrencies in the Common Law of Property," in David Fox and Sarah Green (eds), *Cryptocurrencies in Public and Private Law* (Oxford University Press, 2019) at 147 para 6.26.

200 See e.g., Stuart Hoegner, "What is Bitcoin?" in Stuart Hoegner et al, *The Law of Bitcoin* (iUniverse 2015) at 1; Neil Guthrie, "The End of Cash? Bitcoin, the Regulators and the Courts" (2014) 29 *Banking and Finance Law Review* 355; for its mechanics, see Jonathan Levin, "Bitcoin: New Plumbing for Financial Services" (*Coindesk*, 29 November 2014), online: http:// www.coindesk.com/bitcoin-new-plumbing-financial-services/, accessed 28 May 2024; see also Nicholas Wenker, "Online Currencies, Real-World Chaos: The Struggle to Regulate the Rise of Bitcoin" (2015) 19 *Texas Rev L & Politics* 145; Jacob Hamburger, "Bitcoins vs. State Money Transmission Laws: Protecting Consumers or Hindering Innovation?" (2015) 11 *J L Economics & Policy* 229. See also Wikipedia, "Bitcoin," online: https://en.wikipedia.org/wiki/Bitcoin, accessed 28 May 2024; Andrey Sergeenkov, "What is Bitcoin?" (*Coindesk*, 26 January 2022), online: http://www.coindesk.com/information/what-is-bitcoin/, accessed 28 May 2024; Benjamin Wallace, "The Rise and Fall of Bitcoin" (*Wired*, 23 November 2011), online: http://www. wired.com/2011/11/mf_bitcoin/, accessed 28 May 2024; and *The Economist*, "The Great Chain of Being Sure About Things" (*The Economist*, 31 October 2015); see also ECB, *Virtual Currency Schemes*, above note 184 at 21–24; see also Bitcoin Wiki, "How Bitcoin Works," online: https:// en.bitcoin.it/wiki/How_bitcoin_works, accessed 28 May 2024.

201 Satoshi Nakamoto, "Bitcoin: A Peer-to-Peer Electronic Cash System" (Bitcoin.org, 2008) at 2, online: https://bitcoin.org/bitcoin.pdf, accessed 28 May 2024.

coin" consisting of a "chain of digital signatures" transferable from the payer to the payee "by digitally signing a hash of the previous transaction and the public key of the next owner and adding them to the end of the coin." Premised on distributed ledger technology (DLT), Bitcoin was born out of an ambition to create government-independent, censorship-resistant money.

The Bitcoin network consists of independent nodes, each operated by a "miner." Miners then bundle each proposed payment with others and create a new block for the blockchain. The new block is hashed and, together with other data, is rehashed. The data is repeatedly fed through a cryptographic "hash" function. The hash is put into the header of the proposed block and becomes the basis for a mathematical puzzle. The "miners" compete to reach a solution for it, and the first to come up with the right solution, as accepted by the majority of miners who submitted "proof of work,"[202] is rewarded with newly "minted" bitcoins. The mathematical puzzle is hard to solve, but once found, it is easy for the network to confirm that the answer is correct.[203] Nodes accept the block, whose header contains the hash of the previous block's header, by adding it to the chain that stretches back to the first Bitcoin block (the genesis block), containing the first transaction in the Bitcoin network. This construction is designed to make the Bitcoin blockchain tamperproof; if one tries to fake a transaction by changing a block that had already been stored in the blockchain, that block's hash would be different and ought to be apparent to all as having been tampered with. The "coin" thus carries with it its entire history so that each payment becomes part of its code.

According to Fox, "[s]tripped to its elements, [a crypto] coin consists of a string of data, manifested as a readable sequence of characters, which has been generated by a transaction on the system."[204] A Bitcoin "coin" is thus in the form of an unspent transaction output (UTXO),[205] being a data structured on the blockchain. It reflects the output of an earlier transaction received and is accessed from the payer's wallet. Where the payer does not use up the entire UTXO, payment is effected by splitting the outgoing payer's UTXO into two UTXOs: one in the sum of payment going to the payee's

---

202 "Proof of work" is defined to require "that the decentralized participants that validate blocks show that they have invested significant computing power in doing so." See E Napoletano, "Proof of Work Explained" (Benjamin Curry (ed), *Forbes Advisor*, 29 December 2023).

203 See e.g., Sara Green in Fox and Green, above note 199 at 1–5 paras 1.01-010.

204 Fox in Fox and Green, above note 199 at 143 para 6.13.

205 The term is explained for e.g., in Delton Rhodes, "What's a UTXO? A Guide to Unspent Transaction Output (UTXO)" (*Komodo*, 31 August 2023), online: https://komodoplatform.com/whats-utxo, accessed 8 May 2024.

wallet and the second in the amount of the UTXO balance returning to the payer's wallet.[206]

Payments are thus made from one Bitcoin *wallet* to another. Each such wallet is a computer file or a software program which has an email address serving as a public key. The wallet stores the private key (in effect the passcode) that controls the bitcoin.[207] What is transferred is the UTXO, described as "monetary fluid" representing the bitcoin sum accessed from the payer's wallet and originating from *all* Bitcoin "coins" accessed from that wallet.[208] Stated otherwise, a payer is unable to designate and set aside for payment any particular bitcoin. In effect, payment can be made in any sum available from the wallet, and regardless, at the end of the process, new bitcoins become associated with the payee's wallet, while those still associated with the payer's wallet may have changed their value and hence their identity. Transaction output is thus said to differ from transaction input, if only due to the diversified chain of provenance of input (from the payer's wallet). It would have been more accurate to speak of a Bitcoin payment resulting in a "coin" being *transformed* rather than *transferred*, except that each resulting "coin" carries with it identities of its predecessors as well as the impact of its subsequent partial use. Transaction information is stored on the blockchain and is present on every network node. At the same time, access to the "coins" and the value attached to them is limited to the one in control of the keys as well as the physical device or cloud having the wallet. If the device is lost, the use of the bitcoins remains available to the owner only where the wallet has been backed up, and where they have not been spent by the one in possession of the device and knowledge of the passcode.[209]

---

206 This is e.g., Nakamoto, above note 201; see also Stuart Hoegner, "What is Bitcoin?", above note 200 at 1; Guthrie, above note 200; for its mechanics, see Levin, above note 200; see also Wenker, above note 200, Hamburger, above note 200,Wikipedia, "Bitcoin," above note 200), Sergeenkov, above note 200, Wallace, above note 200; *The Economist*, "The Great Chain of Being Sure About Things," above note 200. See also Bitcoin Wiki, "How Bitcoin Works," above note 201.

207 Conventionally, "Bitcoin" (capitalized) refers to the technology and network whereas "bitcoins" (lowercase) refers to the currency, units, and "coins."

208 A participant may have indefinite numbers of such wallets. In any event, note that what is described in the text is the direct holding of bitcoins. Alternatively, in an indirect holding system, a participant keeps bitcoins with an intermediary. See Ryan J Straus and Matthew J Cleary, "The United States" in Hoegner et al, above note 200.

209 For Bitcoin mechanics, see Levin, above note 200. For more technical information, see e.g., "What Happens to Bitcoin Wallet/Bitcoins if PC is Stolen?" (*StackExchange*, 2015), online: https://bitcoin. stackexchange.com/questions/39101/what-happens-to-bitcoin-wallet-bitcoins-if-pc-is-stolen, accessed 28 May 2024; "Where are the User's Bitcoins Actually Stored?" (*StackExchange*, 2011),

It is argued that developers of cryptocurrencies "simply migrated the cryptographic tools used to safeguard communication and applied them to safeguard digital currency;" hence the vulnerability to erosive cryptographic intractability from which Bitcoin suffers, which is on the top of its vulnerability to potential leadership corruption.[210] Also, its operation, whether in facilitating payments, preventing double spending, or issuing new bitcoins, requires substantial computational energy and is thus said to be wasteful.[211] Bitcoin also suffers from poor scalability, as it can handle at most seven transactions per second.[212] By comparison, until recently, Visa and Mastercard cleared 2,000 transactions in a second,[213] or even a peak-volume of 10,000 transactions per second.[214] At present, Visa's actual transaction speed per second (TPS) is more than 65,000.[215]

online: https://bitcoin.stackexchange.com/questions/1600/where-are-the-users-bitcoins-actually-stored, accessed 28 May 2024.

210 Samid, *Tethered Money*, above note 123 at 26 and 101 for an argument against extrapolating cryptotools for transient communication to shielding digital currency. See 108–16 for details on the main bitcoin principles.

211 See details at e.g., Christopher Malmo, "Bitcoin is Unsustainable" (*Vice: Motherboard*, 29 June 2015), online: http://motherboard.vice.com/read/bitcoin-is-unsustainable, accessed 28 May 2024; see also e.g., John Quiggin, "Bitcoins are a waste of energy – literally" (*ABC News*, 5 October 2015), online: http://www.abc.net.au/news/2015-10-06/quiggin-bitcoins-are-a-waste-of-energy/6827940, accessed 28 May 2024.

212 See e.g., Bitcoin Wiki, "Scalability FAQ'" (*BitcoinWiki*), online: https://en.bitcoin.it/wiki/Scalability_FAQ#What_is_this_Transactions_Per_Second_.28TPS.29_limit.3, accessed 28 May 2024.

213 Saifedean Ammous, "Blockchain Technology: What is it good for?" (SSRN, 8 August 2016) at 2, online: https://papers.ssrn.com/sol3/papers.cfm?abstract_id=2832751, accessed 28 May 2024. More recently Visa's transaction speed per second (TPS) was increased to 65,000, online: https://www.visa.co.uk/dam/VCOM/download/corporate/media/visanet-technology/aboutvisafactsheet.pdf, accessed 31 July 2024.

214 Timothy B Lee, "Bitcoin needs to scale by a factor of 1000 to compete with visa. Here's how to do it" (*The Washington Post*, 17 November 2005), online: https://www.washingtonpost.com/news/the-switch/wp/2013/11/12/bitcoin-needs-to-scale-by-a-factor-of-1000-to-compete-with-visa-heres-how-to-do-it/?utm_term=.f6e09d78860d, accessed 28 May 2024.

215 See online: https://www.visa.co.uk/dam/VCOM/download/corporate/media/visanet-technology/aboutvisafactsheet.pdf, accessed 31 July 2024.
This remains higher than any cryptocurrency. By comparison, Bitcoin has seven TPS, online: https://en.wikipedia.org/wiki/Bitcoin_scalability_problem; Ethereum has fifteen TPS, online: https://info.etherscan.com/understanding-an-ethereum-transaction/> (though an upgrade to Ethereum known as "Proto-Danksharding" aiming to scale Ethereum to more than 100,000 TPS is underway, online: https://ethereum.org/en/roadmap/danksharding/); Solana maintains that it has capacity for 65,000 TPS, online: https://solana.com/news/network-performance-report-july-2023 although its average executed TPS is about 2,200, online: https://www.binance.com/en/square/post/2024-06-28-solana-s-average-tps-reaches-2200-with-over-80-transaction-success-rate-in-h1-2024-10085491122530; Ripple has capacity for 3,400 TPS but only process about 600 TPS, online: https://www.binance.com/en/square/post/979938295594; Litecoin has

Certainly, however, Bitcoin is driven not only by technological innovation but also by strong sentiments[216] against currency systems based on bank credit[217] and backed by government.[218] Its promoters cite its non-inflationary basis,[219] partly attributed to the limitation on the number of bitcoins to be generated by its protocol. Indeed, in general, Bitcoin's value is premised on its scarcity;[220] its specific value as a monetary asset, in fact "hard money," is the result of its high ratio of the stock to the flow.[221] In this sense it is a sort of "digital gold."[222] At the same time, in the long run, the finite number of bitcoins in existence may prove to adversely affect both prices and liquidity.[223] Furthermore, the current 21,000,000 cap is not engraved in stone and is thus subject to change.[224] Regardless, as a self-anchored digital currency, Bitcoin is a mathematical creature; being unsupported by the economic might of an issuer,[225] its principal weakness lies in the inherent instability of its value.[226] In the absence of any "objective rational[e] for any exchange value" Bitcoin is thus likened to "a game that triggered universal interest ... [but whose]

---

fifty-six TPS, online: https://www.forbes.com/advisor/au/investing/cryptocurrency/litecoin/; and Hedera has 10,000 TPS, online: https://hedera.com/hbar#:~:text=The%20Hedera%20 network%20achieves%2010%2C000,on%20network%20security%20or%20stability, all accessed 31 July 2024.

216 For an overview, citing the sources as immediately below, see European Central Bank and Eurosystem, above note 184 at 22–23.

217 Murray N Rothbard, *Economic Depressions: Their Cause and Cure* (Alabama: Ludwig von Mises Institute, 2009).

218 Friedrich A Hayek, *Denationalisation of Money*, 3d ed (London: The Institute for Economic Affairs, 1976).

219 European Central Bank and Eurosystem, above note 184.

220 As pointed out by Ammous, *The Bitcoin Standard*, above note 77 at 177, speaking of Bitcoin designer Nakamoto as the inventor of "digital scarcity"; for scarcity as the source for the value of a monetary asset see Karl Polanyi, above note 35 at 175, 197.

221 Ammous, *The Bitcoin Standard*, above note 77 at 5–6, 23, 155, 199–200.

222 Certainly I don't use this term here in the sense in which it is more commonly known, as in Aashika Jain, "What is Digital Gold?" (*Forbes Advisor*, 23 May 2024), online: https://www. forbes.com/advisor/in/investing/gold/what-is-digital-gold/, accessed 28 May 2024.

223 Samid, *Tethered Money*, above note 123 at 113.

224 Hoegner (ed), above note 200 at 1, 9 note 57.

225 Samid, *Tethered Money*, above note 123 at 14–16.

226 For a discussion on the nature of Bitcoin value, see e.g., William J Luther, "Is Bitcoin Intrinsically Worthless?" (2018) AIER Sound Money Project Working Paper No 2018-07, online https://papers.ssrn.com/sol3/papers.cfm?abstract_id=3000068, accessed 28 May 2024; but see Saifedean Ammous, "Can Bitcoin's Volatility be Tamed?" (2018) 24 *Journal of Structured Finance* 53, online: https://www.proquest.com/docview/2046624181?sourcetype=Scholarly%20 Journals, accessed 28 May 2024, who argues at 60 that "[s]hould the size of Bitcoin rise to a point where it constitutes a significant percentage of global monetary assets, demand variations for it will likely to become smaller in proportion to its size, and this volatility should decline."

infirmity is as intrinsic as Monopoly money." Last but not least, a competitor's self-anchored math-based currency may emerge and thereby lower the Bitcoin value. This casts a shadow on the acceptability of Bitcoin as a real substitute to fiat currency.[227]

It has specifically been suggested that to meet its unstable value, Bitcoin should be pegged in one way or another to the value of a specific fiat currency or commodity.[228] Albeit, this can be done only at a heavy ideological cost to its promoters, who highlight Bitcoin's independence from any outside control on both the quantity and the value.

Other than scalability and an unstable value, the principal hurdle for a universal acceptance of cryptocurrencies in general, and Bitcoin in particular, as the money of the future is that decentralization and the resulting absence of a trusted central counterparty may be more of a curse than a blessing.[229] In other words, efficiencies gained by cutting out intermediaries comes at a cost which outweighs the benefits.[230] According to Saifeadean Ammous, inefficiency is inherent in the blockchain technology in general and Bitcoin in particular:[231]

> Bitcoin has a blockchain not because it allows for faster cheaper transactions, but because it removes the need to trust in third party intermediation: transactions are cleared because nodes compete to verify them, yet no node needs to be trusted. It is unworkable for third party intermediaries to imagine they could improve their performance by employing a technology that sacrifices efficiency and speed precisely to remove third party intermediaries. For any currency controlled by a central party, it will

227 Samid, *Tethered Money*, above note 123 at 14–15 (for an illustration of instability), and 109–10 (for connection between self-anchoring and instability). The quotation is from 15.

228 *Ibid* at 114–21. Compare e.g., NationCoin, being a proposed Regulated and Sovereign Backed Cryptocurrency (RSBC). Its scheme envisages cryptocoins, which as in Bitcoin, will be created by and transacted over a blockchain. However, upon their creation, cryptocoins will be stored, and released to the public by a Digital Asset Reserve, as RSBC, at the fixed value of the national unit of account. Transactions are to be verified by "miners" who will be paid freshly minted cryptocoins. See Kartik Hegadekatti and Yatish S G, "Generation, Security and Distribution of NationCoins by a Sovereign Authority" (SSRN, 7 January 2017), online: https://papers.ssrn.com/sol3/papers.cfm?abstract_id=2888347, accessed 28 May 2024.

229 For an interesting historical study on the lessons from the misfortune of such absence see e.g., Isabel Schnabel and Hyun Song Shin, *Money and trust: lessons from the 1620 for money in the digital age* (Bank for International Settlements 2018), online: https://www.bis.org/publ/work698.pdf, accessed 28 May 2024.

230 A point highlighted Mark Carney, *Speech: The Future of Money* (Bank of England, 2 March 2018) at 6–9, online: https://www.bankofengland.co.uk/-/media/boe/files/speech/2018/the-future-of-money-speech-by-mark-carney.pdf?la=en&hash=A51E1C8E90BDD3D071A8D6B4F8C1566E7AC91418, accessed 28 May 2024.

231 Ammous, "Blockchain Technology," above note 213 at 2.

always be more efficient to record transactions centrally. Whether removing third party intermediation is a strong enough advantage to justify the increased inefficiency of distributed ledgers is a question that can only be answered over the coming years in the test of market acceptance of digital currencies. What can be clearly seen is that blockchain payment applications will have to be with the blockchain's own decentralized currency, and not with centrally-controlled currencies.

Elsewhere, Ammous explains that it is the high processing power threshold which prevents both hacking and the establishment of a central control. Both achievements secure neutrality and the full benefit of a decentralized structure for Bitcoin, but at the cost of a fixed supply of growth that cannot be made to adjust to satisfy a purely market-determined demand and hence results in price instability. At the same time, he observes, attempts in other currencies to bypass the expensive, inefficient, and wasteful Proof of Work (PoW), using other settlement mechanisms such as Proof of Stake,[232] consensus, or a trusted notary, compromise the neutrality of the system, enhance the control of the issuer, and/or require a third party verifier, all at the expense of the DLT premises. Hence, he concludes, Bitcoin could be no more than a store of value,[233] while other cryptocurrencies cannot fulfill any monetary feature.[234]

Ammous does not see the deflationary nature of Bitcoin as an impediment to its unit of account function. At the same time, having highlighted Bitcoin's inadequacy to serve as a medium of exchange for everyday transactions, he argues that Bitcoin may be "the best store of value humanity ever invented" so as to be capable of functioning as "a reserve currency" to be held by banks in cold storage.[235] Against the Bitcoin reserve, banks will perform payment

232 For the difference between proof of work and proof of stake see e.g., Mike Antolin, "Proof-of-Work vs Proof-of-Stake: What is the Difference?" (*CoinDesk*, 18 July 2022), online: https://www.coindesk.com/learn/proof-of-work-vs-proof-of-stake-what-is-the-difference/, accessed 28 May 2024.

233 Not everybody is in agreement. For considering Bitcoin to be an "imperfect store of value" due to its volatility see Aaron Kumar and Christie Smith, 'Crypto-currencies – An introduction to not-so-funny moneys' (2017) Reserve Bank of New Zealand Analytical Note Series AN2017/07 at 2, online: https://www.rbnz.govt.nz/-/media/ReserveBank/Files/Publications/Analytical%20notes/2017/an2017-07.pdf, accessed 28 May 2024.

234 Saifedean Ammous, "Can Cryptocurrencies Fulfill the Functions of Money?" (2016) Columbia University Center on Capitalism and Society Working Paper No 92, online: https://poseidon01.ssrn.com/delivery.php?ID=89803106806902001308410009400111511302400804906803, accessed 28 May 2024.

235 Ammous, *The Bitcoin Standard*, above note 77 at 198, 207, respectively; for predicting that Bitcoin will achieve gold parity so as to cause gold value to decrease, see e.g., Katrik Hegadekatti, "Blockchain Technology – An instrument of Economic Evolution?" (2017)

transactions by debiting payers' accounts and crediting those of the payees. With Bitcoin reserve banks will settle. However, other than eliminating the central bank, this model will mimic the role of banks in relation to payments in fiat currencies so that everyday Bitcoin transactions will be carried out "off-chain" in effect through banks or similar deposit taking institutions.[236]

Indeed, "a significant feature of digital currencies – and the primary driver of interest from retailers in accepting them in payment – is the promise of low transaction fees."[237]

At the same time, for their part:

Low transaction fees for digital currency payments are largely driven by a subsidy that is paid to transaction verifiers (miners) in the form of new currency. The size of this subsidy depends not only on the current price of the digital currency, but also on miners' beliefs about the future price of the digital currency. ... [T]his extra revenue allows miners to accept transaction fees that are considerably below the expected marginal cost of successfully verifying a block of transactions.[238]

However, in the long-run it may become impossible to sustain this subsidy:

Digital currencies with an ultimately fixed supply will ... be forced to compete with other payment systems on the basis of costs. With their higher marginal costs, digital currencies will struggle to compete with centralised systems unless the number of miners falls, allowing the remaining miners to realise economies of scale. A significant risk to digital currencies' sustained use as payment systems is therefore that they will not be able to compete on

---

Munich Personal RePEc Archive Paper No 82852, online: https://mpra.ub.uni-muenchen. de/82852/1/MPRA_paper_82852.pdf, accessed 28 May 2024. Not everybody is in agreement, see e.g., Tony Klein, Pham Thu Hien, and Thomas Walther, "Bitcoin Is Not the New Gold: A Comparison of Volatility, Correlation, and Portfolio Performance" (2018) 59 *International Review of Financial Analysis* 105.

236 For a more moderate hypothetical variation, under which currency issued under the Bitcoin standard will consist of Bitcoin, as well as fiduciary currencies issued by central banks and commercial bank money, both backed by Bitcoin, and in which central banks will continue to be lenders of last resort, see Warren E Weber, "A Bitcoin Standard: Lessons from the Gold Standard" (2016) Bank of Canada Staff Working Paper 2016-14, online: https://www. bankofcanada.ca/wp-content/uploads/2016/03/swp2016-14.pdf, accessed 28 May 2024.

237 Robleh Ali et al, "The Economics of Digital Currencies" (*Bank of England*, Quarterly Bulletin 2014 Q3) at 276, 281.

238 *Ibid.*

cost without degenerating ... to a monopoly miner, thereby defeating their original design goals and exposing them to risk of system-wide fraud.[239]

Aside from Ammous's vision, drawbacks in the utilization of decentralized digital currency schemes have led the way to the consideration of centralized digital currencies issued by trusted issuers such as either central banks or private issuers. In the ongoing fight against counterfeiters and fraudulent copiers centralized schemes are better positioned to apply superior defence measures in protecting the integrity of the database, as well as enhanced security procedures in both coin and identity verification upon redemption and in trade.[240] This is without mentioning the higher scalability of a centrally issued digital coin scheme. Two such technologies are set out below.

WingCash (now called "Open Payment Network") is a centralized system, allowing the issuer to determine the reserve requirement, under which a claim-check to fiat currency may be issued.[241] It has a multi-issuer platform using a centralized model, allowing for the ledger to replicate in multiple locations. Each claim-check is in the form of a unique web page with an immutably assigned web address (URL), typically cryptographically signed by the issuer. It is described as a digital bearer instrument with a fixed value which simulates a physical banknote. Each digital bearer instrument has a single "possession" attribute so that only the current holder can reassign "possession" to another entity. The ledger immediately records the update to the "possession" attribute to avoid the double-spending problem. As in the case of physical cash, the change of "possession" from one holder to another constitutes a payment. Therefore, the ledger keeps a record of the change of "possession" of each bearer instrument. Digital notes may be redeemed to fiat currency in the form of either physical cash or bank money. Among sixteen faster payments solutions,[242] WingCash's solution for digital Fednotes[243] came tied in first place.[244]

---

239 *Ibid.*

240 See e.g., Samid, *Tethered Money*, above note 123 at 92–94 and *cf ibid* at 125–27 as well as at 25, 98–100 albeit focusing on the advantage of paying with digital coins over that of paying in scriptural money which may expose account data to hackers.

241 For some information visit online: www.wingcash.com, accessed 29 May 2024.

242 Federal Reserve System "Strategies for Improving US Payment System" (Federal Reserve System, 26 January 2015), online: https://fedpaymentsimprovement.org/wp-content/uploads/strategies-improving-us-payment-system.pdf, accessed 28 May 2024.

243 For WingCash's proposal, see Bradley Wilkes et al, "National Digital Currency Platform Proposed for the Federal Reserve" (Wingcash 2017), online: https://web.archive.org/web/20170724173614/http://fasterpaymentsnetwork.com/#execsum archived link, accessed 29 May 2024. I am listed as one of the sixteen contributors to the solution proposal.

244 See Faster Payments Task Force, "The U.S. Path to Faster Payments Final Report Part Two: A Call for Action" (July 2017) at 13, online: https://fedpaymentsimprovement.org/wp-content

An alternative technology altogether underlying digital bearer instruments is that of BitMint. It facilitates a non-speculative and stable currency, consisting of randomized coins, each expressing a claim-check to a defined quantity of a specific commodity, including a fiat currency.[245] It "does not generate money per se; it generates a digital claim check for money (or any transactable valuable) held ready for instant redemption. The state of being redemption-ready renders the *BitMint* digital claim check into a de-facto transactable currency."[246] It may also be cascaded so as to be denominated in a unit of account anchored on the value of two or more fiat currencies, commodities, or indices.[247] BitMint coins are centrally minted while validation and transactions are decentralized, and are carried out directly between the payer and the payee. A mint generates coins from a quantum-randomness source, which makes the sequence of the bits that represent each coin identity and the sequence of the coin value function patternless. Not dependent on any intermediators, validation processes and payment transactions utilize the LeVeL-Paying-Field which does not suffer from flaws of blockchain.[248] It is quantum-resilient and, may be used as a CBDC or stablecoin.[249]

/uploads/faster-payments-task-force-final-report-part-two.pdf, accessed 28 May 2024.

245 For *BitMint* Money see online: https://www.bitmintcash.com/, accessed 24 May 2023). For the superior protection of randomness premised on "a cipher which use[s] no mathematical complexity but instead call[s] for large amounts of randomness," see e.g., Carsten Stöcker, "Randomness: 'The Fix for Today's Broken Security" (*Medium*, 9 November 2017), online: cstoecker.medium. com/randomness-the-fix-for-todays-broken-security-39ea7dc3a89b, accessed 25 July 2021. For *BitMint* being considered in China see "Q-Pay could mark the next sea change in finance Bank of Shanghai is testing BitMint's Q-Pay, a.k.a. 'pay like cash', which looks like a preamble to a new paradigm of digital money", DigFin, *Banking & Payments* magazine, 8 January 2019, online: https:// www.digfingroup.com/bitmint-q-pay, accessed 10 May 2023. For detailed information on BitMint (not to be confused with BitMinter) see also e.g., online: http://www.bitmint.com/, accessed 28 May 2024; "BitMint Overview" (*Startup Nation Central*, 16 February 2022), online: http://finder. startupnationcentral.org/company_page/bitmint/, accessed 28 May 2024, and sites and videos accessible through it; see also "BitMint: AI Powered Cyber Innovation" (*Medium*), online: https: //medium.com/@bitmintnews, accessed 28 May 2024, and associated articles.

246 BitMint, online: https://www.bitmintcash.com/, accessed 18 July 2024.

247 Samid, *Tethered Money*, above note 123 at 22.

248 Gideon Samid, "A LeVeL Paying Field: Cryptographic Solutions towards Social Accountability and Financial Inclusion" (Research Gate, February 2022), online: https://www. researchgate.net/publication/358479911_A_LeVeL_Paying_Field_Cryptographic_Solutions_ towards_Social_Accountability_and_Financial_Inclusion, accessed 28 May 2024.

249 For the two main technology archetypes, Quantum versus Crypto see Amnon Samid, "Automated Embedded Payment Systems" (2022) 12 *International Journal of Embedded Systems and Applications* 1, ss 2.2, 2.3, 2.4, online: https://www.researchgate.net/publication/367014225_ Automated_Embedded_Payment_Systems, accessed 28 May 2024.

BitMint money is generated through an economical *quantum mechanical process*,[250] which is energy-efficient and reduces waste. BitMint keeps a 100 percent reserve so that the purchasing commodity or fiat currency is always available for redemption on demand. BitMint was identified by Helmut Scherzer as "the only candidate qualifying as a universal digital representation of worldwide currencies."[251]

BitMint currency is protected by quantum physics, not dependent on erosive encryption, and claimed to be indefeasible by cyber threats.[252] It has a Validation Hierarchy under which coins are validated through subordinate nodes and may be tethered[253] so as to be "[m]oney with built-in limitation on its use"[254] such as where a coin is cryptographically linked to the rightful owner.[255]Tethering may also facilitate crypto-fusing contractual terms between a payer and a payee into the money, so as to disallow any use that is in breach of the contract. BitMint does not require the UTXO protocol for splitting coins; instead, it is executed independently by a users' phone application for any sum up to the sum of the coin. Payment is carried out by directly transmitting the bits that comprise the coin split to the payee's device under any communication method, without real time intervention of any remote server. BitMint money can be split off or amalgamated at any desired resolution[256] and can be paid continuously on a pay-as-you-go basis, e.g., as you pump gas into a car gas tank, rather than separately, e.g., upon the completion of the service. Users receive a coin to their device like a text message. As well, BitMint's Hard Wallet can validate and provide finality to off-line proximity payments.[257]

---

250   On this process, see e.g., "Introduction to Quantum Mechanics" (Wikipedia), online: https://en.wikipedia.org/wiki/Introduction_to_quantum_mechanics, accessed 28 May 2024.

251   Helmut Scherzer, "Chapter 36: On the Quest to the Ultimate Digital Money" in Claudia Linnhoff-Popien, Ralf Schneider, and Michael Zaddach (eds), *Digital Marketplaces Unleashed* (Springer, 2018) at 404.

252   For details, see Gideon Samid, "Bitcoin.BitMint: Reconciling Bitcoin with Central Banks" (BitMint LLC 2014), online: https://eprint.iacr.org/2014/244.pdf, accessed 28 May 2024. See also e.g., online: http://www.bitmint.com/bitcoin.htm, accessed 28 December 2017.

253   Samid, *Tethered Money*, above note 123 at 108.

254   *Ibid* at 140 (Glossary).

255   *Ibid* at 50, 100.

256   *Ibid* at 106–08 for details on randomized or entropic coins.

257   This is carried out by a "quick touch" by one device to another and applies even to a proximity payment in other than BitMinted coins: Gideon Samid, "BitMint Hard Wallet: Digital Payment without Network Communication: No Internet, yet Sustained Payment Regimen between Randomness-Verifiable Hard Wallets," *2020 IEEE International IOT, Electronics and Mechatronics Conference (IEMTRONICS)*, 2020 at 1–7, doi: 10.1109/IEMTRONICS51293.2020.9216456; Amnon Samid, "Automated Embedded Payment Systems," *International Journal of Embedded Systems and*

In the final analysis a centralized digital currency system is modelled on, or better, evolved out of, a "note-based" e-money scheme discussed in Part V. At the same time, due to technological advancements, a centralized digital currency system purports to overcome the restricted transferability under a "note-based" e-money scheme, which is limited to a single use of a coin in a typically (albeit not necessarily) small network. Rather, compared to the "note-based" e-money, not only that a centralized digital currency scheme typically has more features, a centralized digital currency system entails a higher if not unlimited circulation of coins among a larger if not unlimited number of participants. Regardless, since digital coins are to be bought with bank money and ultimately may be redeemed in bank money, a centralized digital currency scheme, while being bound to change means and methods of payment, will arguably not change the fundamentals with respect to the quantity of money and the role of banks in its creation and transmission.[258]

Notwithstanding the drawbacks set out earlier in this section, a few central bank decentralized or hybrid digital currency schemes, namely, use of the blockchain for settlement, have been floating.[259] In the United States, proposals have been made for Fedcoin, being a central bank-issued and centrally created cryptocurrency, to be available to the public at large.[260] Digital coins are to be centrally issued on a blockchain-style decentralized ledger, but with the central bank being in full control of quantity, timing, and fixed value in denominations of the national fiat currency unit of account. Effectively, transactions will be validated by an independent notary nominated

---

Applications (IJESA), Vol 12, No. 1/2/3/4, December 2022, at p. 10 online: https://www.researchgate.net/publication/367014225_, accessed 28 May 2024.

258 For a similar conclusion regarding (broadly and loosely defined) central bank digital currency, see Jack Meaning et al, "Broadening Narrow Money: Monetary Policy With a Central Bank Digital Currency" (2018) Bank of England Staff Working Paper no 724, online: https://www.bankofengland.co.uk/-/media/boe/files/working-paper/2018/broadening-narrow-money-monetary-policy-with-a-central-bank-digital-currency.pdf, accessed 28 May 2024.

259 See Morten Bech and Rodney Garratt, "Central bank cryptocurrencies" (*Bank for International Settlements Quarterly Review*, September 2017) at 55, online: https://www.bis.org/publ/qtrpdf/r_qt1709f.pdf, accessed 28 May 2024. See also Katrik Hegadekatti, "Towards Regional Monetary Unions through Blockchain Networks" (2017) Munich Personal RePEc Archive Paper No 82838, online: https://mpra.ub.uni-muenchen.de/82838/, accessed 28 May 2024; see also Heike Mai, "Why Would We Use Crypto Euros? Central bank-issued digital cash: a user perspective" (Deutsche Bank Reports, EU Monitor Global Financial Markets, 15 February 2018), online: https://www.dbresearch.com/PROD/RPS_EN-PROD/PROD0000000000462095.PDF, accessed 28 May 2024. For centralized, decentralized, and hybrid digital currency schemes see text at footnotes 186–87.

260 See e.g., Wendy McElroy, "Fedcoin: The U.S. Will Issue E-Currency That You Will Use" (*Bitcoin.com*, 12 January 2005), online: https://news.bitcoin.com/fedcoin-u-s-issue-e-currency/, accessed 28 May 2024.

by the central bank. A similar proposal was made in the United Kingdom for RSCoin.[261] Another proposal is for a NationCoin, being a Regulated and Sovereign Backed Cryptocurrency (RSBC). The scheme envisages cryptocoins, which as is in the case of Bitcoin, will be created by and transacted over a blockchain. Upon their creation, cryptocoins will be stored and released to the public by a Digital Asset Reserve, as RSBC, at the fixed value of the national unit of account. Transactions are to be verified by "miners" who will be paid freshly minted cryptocoins.[262]

As a proof of concept (PoC) both the Bank of Canada under the Jasper Project[263] and the Monetary Authority of Singapore under the Ubin Project[264] experiment with a DLT-based wholesale payment system premised on the use of a blockchain for interbank settlement in central bank money. For details including an assessment on the future role of blockchain technology in the evolution of financial infrastructure see chapter 5(V).

261   See George Danezis and Sarah Meiklejohn, *Centrally Banked Cryptocurrencies* (University College London, 2015), online: https://eprint.iacr.org/2015/502.pdf, accessed 28 May 2024, in part this article is too technical to the uninitiated in computer science and related subjects (including me). "RSCoin is the core of a system of scalable and auditable transactions, not a full product," which thus could be used as a basis for either a retail or wholesale product. Email message to the author from George Danezis dated 4 December 2017.

262   Hegadekatti and Yatish, above note 228.

263   See James Chapman et al, "Project Jasper: Are Distributed Wholesale Payment Systems Feasible Yet?" (Bank of Canada Financial System Review, June 2017), online: http://www. bankofcanada.ca/wp-content/uploads/2017/05/fsr-june-2017-chapman.pdf, accessed 28 May 2024. For the earlier stage of the project see Rod Garratt, "CAD-coin versus Fedcoin" (R3 Report May 2017), online: https://www.finextra.com/finextra-downloads/newsdocs/cad-coin-versus.pdf, accessed 28 May 2024. See also, Laura Shin, "Canada Has Been Experimenting With A Digital Fiat Currency Called CAD-COIN" (*Forbes*, 16 June 2016), online: http://www.forbes.com/sites/laurashin/2016/06/16/canada-has-been-experimenting-with-a-digital-fiat-currency-called-cad-coin/#536fabe91b0c, accessed 28 May 2024; Pete Rizzo, "Bank of Canada Demos Blockchain-Based Digital Dollar" (*CoinDesk.com*, 16 June 2016), online: http://www.coindesk.com/bank-canada-demos-blockchain-based-digital-dollar/, accessed 28 May 2024. See also Claire Brownell, "No cryptocurrency anytime soon, Bank of Canada says: 'We're very far off'" (*Financial Post*, 17 June 2016), online: http://business. financialpost.com/news/fp-street/no-cryptocurrency-anytime-soon-bank-of-canada-says-were-very-far-off, accessed 28 May 2024.

264   See Deloitte and Monetary Authority of Singapore, "The future is here – Project Ubin: SGD on Distributed Ledger" (Deloitte Consulting Ltd, 2017), online: http://www.mas.gov.sg/~/media/ProjectUbin/Project%20Ubin%20%20SGD%20on%20Distributed%20Ledger.pdf, accessed 28 May 2024.

VII.   CONCLUSION

In migrating "cryptographic tools used to safeguard communication and appl[ying] them to safeguard digital currency"[265] cryptocurrency developers effectively engineered payment disintermediation. They did so by means of tools that were originally fashioned to enhance payment intermediation through safeguarding interbank as well as customer-to-bank and bank-to-customer communication. Once issues of volatility, scalability, and deflation are resolved, cryptocurrencies have the potential to generate means of payment "offering much of the anonymity of cash while also allowing transactions at long distances" that can also "clear and settle quickly without an intermediary."[266] Ironically then, it is the evolution of a process in banking, enhancing payment intermediation, which could lead to the demise of banks as payment intermediaries. The result will not change even if centralized digital currencies are to supersede cryptocurrencies.

However, in my view, the chance is that the demise of both banks and payment intermediation will not happen, or at least not anytime soon. Certainly, we shall see some measure of payment disintermediation in the form of improved cryptocurrencies as well as centralized digital currencies. At the same time, banks have been fighting back to improve their own legacy systems. Thereby, they may successfully compete with digital currency payment services providers. For its part, a successful centralized digital currency system is likely to count on commercial banks buying and selling the currencies into and out of accounts maintained with them so as to become a universal "note-based" e-money scheme linked to banks and the legacy monetary system.

Regardless, it is hard to see banks, as both depositaries and lenders of money, disappear. Rather, they are likely to get themselves into the digital currency space and provide services as well as be in a position to cover risks that customers would prefer not to incur on their own. As well, there is a good chance that in competing with banks, IT firms that are issuers of digital currencies will become rather than supersede banks. And even if cryptoassets may one day reduce demand for central bank money, I doubt that the

---

265 Samid, *Tethered Money*, above note 123 at 26; see text at footnote 209.

266 Dong He, "Monetary Policy in the Digital Age" (June 2018) IMF Finance & Development 13, online: https://www.imf.org/en/Publications/fandd/issues/2018/06/central-bank-monetary-policy-and-cryptocurrencies-he, accessed 28 May 2024.

public will be ready to have control of the quantity of money surrendered to digital currency developers. Accordingly, changes to monetary policy will not be substantial even if the use of banks as payment intermediaries will be affected. This is true whether centralized digital currencies are to be traded with or issued by commercial banks, or whether central banks are to take over from the private sector the issue of digital currencies, whether under a centralized or decentralized scheme.

Possibly, both practicalities and anti-money laundering or anti-terrorist financing regulations may limit the size of payments to be made in digital currencies. Furthermore, the chance is that for a large payment, an RTGS system, with liquidity-saving mechanisms, settled between commercial banks on the books of a trusted central bank, will be preferred by participants over a large peer to peer digital cash payment between them.[267] For now, the scope and magnitude of future developments can only be speculated.

267 See e.g., Walter Engert and Ben SC Fung, "Central Bank Digital Currency: Motivations and Implications" (2017) Bank of Canada Staff Discussion Paper 2017-16 at 16–17, online: https://www.bankofcanada.ca/wp-content/uploads/2017/11/sdp2017-16.pdf, accessed 8 May 2024.

chapter two

MONEY IN CANADA: CONCISE LEGAL HISTORY[1]

SYNOPSIS

In New France, the use of agricultural commodities, card money, and other forms of paper money was widespread due to a shortage of coin. When New France was ceded to Britain, British coins circulated within the colonies and its currency was mandated as the uniform money of account. The dollar became the primary currency of account through the passage of the Currency Act in 1857. Around the same time, commercial banks were incorporated and issued convertible banknotes that circulated alongside the government-issued provincial convertible banknotes. Post-Confederation, the federal Government issued its own convertible Dominion Notes. The convertibility of Dominion Notes to gold was ultimately suspended in the early twentieth century. In 1934, the Bank of Canada was established. It was given the exclusive right to issue banknotes in Canada, and pre-existing banknotes began to be phased out. Initially, the Bank of Canada was required to maintain a gold reserve of not less than 25 percent of its notes and deposit liabilities. Over time this requirement was removed to allow Canada to pursue a robust currency and foreign exchange policy.

SUMMARY OF CONTENTS

---

1   For a brief outline see e.g., Pierre Duguay, "The quest for confidence: 400 years of money – from La Nouvelle France to Canada today" (Remarks to students and faculty of Laval University, 10 November 2008, online: https://www.bankofcanada.ca/2008/11/quest-confidence-400-years-money/, 28 July 2024.

<table>
<tr><td>VI. The Bank of Canada and the Law Governing the Present Monetary System</td><td>VII. Conclusion</td></tr>
</table>

I. INTRODUCTION

The official currency of Canada is the Canadian dollar (CAD). Its symbol is the dollar sign ($) and it is nicknamed the "loonie." Symbols such as CA$, Can$ and C$ are sometimes used to distinguish CAD from other dollar-denominated currencies.

Canadian dollar banknotes are issued by the Bank of Canada in five denominations: $5, $10, $20, $50, and $100. CAD is divided into 100 cents and its coins are issued by the Royal Canadian Mint in six denominations: 5¢, 10¢, 25¢, 50¢, $1, and $2.

CAD acts as the fifth most-held reserve currency in the world after the United States dollar (USD), the euro (EUR), British pound sterling (GBP), and the Japanese yen (JPY). The Canadian dollar, ranking as the sixth most traded currency globally, is also known as a commodity currency, due to Canada's rich natural resources and significant raw material exports.[2]

This chapter explores the legal history of money in Canada. **Part II** addresses the monetary arrangements in New France, roughly between 1608 and 1763. **Part III** discusses developments that occurred roughly during the first eighty years after the take-over by Great Britain. **Part IV** discusses key development roughly during the third-quarter of the nineteenth century, *viz* the introduction of the banknote and the triumph of the dollar as the currency of Canada. **Part V** examines the period between Confederation and the establishment of the Bank of Canada in 1935. **Part VI** addresses the establishment of the Bank of Canada and the history since then. Concluding **Part VII** highlights key recurring themes throughout the history, being the relationship between money and gold; multiplicity of currencies; uniformity of money; the respective role if any of government and private banks in making and distributing money; and finally, the role, if any, for non-bank private money.

2 See e.g., OANDA, "Canadian Dollar Currency" (OANDA FX Data Services), online: https://www.oanda.com/currency-converter/en/currencies/majors/cad/, accessed 28 July 2024.

II. NEW FRANCE

The monetary use of "wampum" – strings and belt fashioned from beads of white and purple mollusk shells – goes back to the early days of settlement.[3] With the establishment of the first colonial settlement in New France in 1608, the beaver pelt, and to a lesser extent wheat and moose skins, were used as media of exchange. As the colony expanded, coins from France came to be widely used, albeit until 1717, due to restricted supply, at a higher value than their nominal one.[4] Ratings of French coins were addressed in decrees dated 18 July 1654 and 7 October 1661.[5] Stamp of approval was also given to Spanish coins that circulated in New France even as French monetary units, *livres, sols and denier*, had been adopted on 20 March 1662 as money of account.[6]

According to McCullough, prior to 1662 there was very little coin in circulation in New France.[7] However, even with the infusion of coin upon the introduction of royal government and the arrival of troops in 1662–63, shortage of coined money persisted. In the middle of the seventeenth century this shortage led to the authorized widespread monetary use of agricultural commodities such as wheat, peas, Indian corn, and salt pork.[8] A typical temporary decree set a monetary value to a specified amount of an agricultural product and required the acceptance of the product at the set rate in payment to merchants and other creditors.[9]

A pressing need to pay soldiers precipitated the issue of card money in 1685 and 1686, as well as into the eighteenth century until the fall of New France. Initially, the cards were a mere financing tool and not a currency. Holders of the card money could convert them into bills of exchange following each year's infusion of funds from France. However, as the cards began

---

3   James Powell, *A History of the Canadian Dollar* (Bank of Canada 1999) at 1–2; for a detailed explanation see Nehemiah Vreeland, "Wampum: The Native Substitute for Currency in North America" (1910) 7 *The British Numismatic Journal* 341. See also Daniel Dematos, "Seashell Money in America" (The Tontine Coffee-House: A History of Finance, 13 December 2021), online: https://tontinecoffeehouse.com/2021/12/13/seashell-money-in-america/, accessed 16 March 2024.

4   Powell, *ibid* at 3.

5   See Adam Shortt (ed), *Documents relating to Canadian Currency, Exchange and Finance During the French Period* (Acland, 1925) Vol 1 at 2–4.

6   *Ibid* at 4–7.

7   AB McCullough, *Money and Exchange in Canada to 1900* (Dundurn Press, 1984) at 32.

8   Robert Chalmers, *A History of Currency in the British Colonies* (Eyre and Spottiswoode, 1893) at 175; McCullough, *ibid* at 33.

9   "Ordre De Prendre Le Ble En Paiement A Raison De 4 Livres Le Minot" Shortt, *Documents*, above note 5 vol 1 at 22–25.

circulating, confidence in the paper currency and its value in commerce grew, prompting fewer people to redeem them. It was this reduced pace of redemptions that encouraged bad behaviour. Combined with increased issuance, the reduced redemptions meant that the cards were increasingly a form of currency and no longer merely a debt obligation.[10]

Card money thus became paper money printed on playing cards, and redeemable in three months. Typically, the ordinance of issue attached a penalty for the refusal to accept the cards in payment.[11] Such card money was accepted by merchants and the public. Originally card money notes circulated freely at face value. Their value gradually depreciated as the government failed to meet its redemption obligation. Ultimately, toward the last quarter of the eighteenth century, their use discontinued.[12]

Coin scarcity also precipitated the monetary use of private notes ("bons"). These paper scrips were issued by merchants for use in payment of goods in the respective issuer's store but quickly began to change hands as money. The use of bons survived the fall of New France and in a way, together with brass and copper tokens, had periodically been used well into the 1930s.[13]

Against limits on the amount of card money that could be issued, the acceptability of "bons" even in the absence of legal support as well as metallic reserve, persuaded public authorities in New France to issue "ordonnances"/"ordinances" during the 1720s – that in effect were promises to pay card money on a later date and yet circulated on their own as money. In response to requests from the public, the government received permission from the king to reintroduce card money in March 1729. These cards would be redeemed each year for goods or bills of exchange payable in coin in France. Effectively being legal tender, the cards replaced the ordonnances. However, when the fund on which the card money was drawn dried up, new ordonnances, side by side with treasury notes in another form, payable in coin, called "acquits," were issued. Both types circulated as fiduciary money and in 1733 it was decreed that they must be accepted in payment on the

---

10   Daniel Dematos, "Quebec's Card Money" (The Tontine Coffee-House: A History of Finance, 20 March 2020), online: https://tontinecoffeehouse.com/2020/03/30/quebecs-card-money/, accessed 28 July 2024.

11   Shortt, *Documents*, above note 5, vol 1 at 69–71, 74–77.

12   Chalmers, above note 8, at 177–78; Powell, above note 3 at 4–9. The principal source on card money during that period is Emmanuel Bernier, "La pénétration de la monnaie de carte dans l'espace rural laurentien (1685-1743)" (Maîtrise en histoire: Mémoire, 2020).

13   Powell, above note 3 at 7, 92–93.

same footing as card money.[14] By the early 1750s, the distinction between card money and "acquits" had largely disappeared, and by 1757, the government had discontinued payments *in specie*.[15] With the increased military expenses a Royal Edict dated 15 October 1759[16] suspended their payment altogether. Ultimately, in the course of a long and complex process, obligations on such paper were honoured by France.[17]

III. THE BRITS ARE COMING

Under the 1763 Treaty of Paris[18] France ceded New France to Great Britain. Naturally the British takeover brought with it the circulation of British coins. It also brought with it the 1704 Proclamation of Queen Anne setting a fixed rate denominated in British monetary units to all "foreign coins" passing in the "several [British] Colonies and Plantations in America."[19] The role of British currency as a uniform money of account was enhanced by the *Uniform Currency Act, 1821*[20] purporting "to establish an [*sic*] uniform Currency through out this Province." Recognizing in Paragraph I that:

> [T]he several gold and silver coins current in this Province, have respectively a nominal legal value in pounds, shillings and pence, bearing the relative proportion of ten to nine, to the Sterling money of account in the United Kingdom of Great Britain and Ireland.

14   "Ordonnance Déclarant Monnaie Légale Les Ordonnances, Les Billets Et Les Acqutis" Shortt, *Documents*, above note 5, vol 2 at 634–38.

15   Powell, above note 3 at 8.

16   "Suspension Du Paiement Des Lettres De Change: 15 October, 1759," Shortt, *Documents*, above note 5, vol 2 at 928–33.

17   Sophie Imbeault, "La dette de la France : les papiers du Canada" (2013) 115 Cap-aux-Diamants 15 at 15, online: https://www.erudit.org/fr/revues/cd/2013-n115-cd0850/70079ac.pdf, accessed 28 July 2024; see also Powell, above note 3 at 10.

18   Text of treaty available at "Treaty of Paris 1763" (The Avalon Project: Documents in Law, History and Diplomacy, Yale Law School), online: https://avalon.law.yale.edu/18th_century/paris763.asp, accessed 1 August 2024.

19   According to Powell, above note 3 at 13, "Because the proclamation was ignored, the British Government converted it into legislation in 1707 with stiff penalties for those who did not comply." See *An Act for Ascertaining the Rates of Foreign Coins in Her Majesty's Plantations in America 1707* (UK), 6 Ann, c 57; rates are further provided by An Ordinance for Regulating and Establishing the Currency of the Province (14 September 1764) and ordinance of 15 May 1765; McCullough, above note 7 at 73.

20   Province of Upper Canada, *An Act to Establish a Uniform Currency Throughout this Province 182* (UK), 2 Geo IV, c 13.

Paragraph II of the Act required all valid debts incurred in the ordinary course of business to be expressed in "Provincial Currency, at five shillings to a dollar. ... " However, this is not to suggest that the value and hence the meaning of "dollar" had been universally accepted. The word "dollar" originates from the German word *thaler*, the name given to a silver coin first minted in Joachimsthal, Bohemia in 1519.[21] The Spanish dollar was minted in the Spanish Empire following a monetary reform in 1497 and was widely used as the first international currency because of its uniformity in standard and milling characteristics.[22] Spanish dollars had already been in circulation in New France, where weighing and appraisal for each individual coin had been required.[23]

In British North America two dollar-ratings competed. The Halifax rating used pounds, shillings, and pence (£, s., and d.) as the unit of account and valued one Spanish (or colonial Spanish) silver dollar weighing 420 grains (385 grains of pure silver 23) at *five shillings*, local currency. For its part, the competing York rating had originally been established in New York and was brought to Upper Canada by Loyalist immigrants. Thereunder, one Spanish dollar was valued at *eight shillings*. The Halifax rating was adopted in Nova Scotia in 1758,[24] which had been in British hands since the seventeenth century, that is, prior to the Treaty of Paris. It prevailed in Nova Scotia, and subsequently was adopted in 1796, in both Upper and Lower Canada.[25] However, the York rating remained in use in Upper Canada.[26] Hence, against the persistence of the use in the York rating, in rating "five shillings to a dollar,"[27] the *Uniform Currency Act, 1821* was meant to reinforce adherence to the Halifax rating.

---

21 Powell, above note 3 at 20.

22 Wikipedia, "Spanish dollar," online: https://en.wikipedia.org/wiki/Spanish_dollar, accessed 29 July 2024.

23 Powell, above note 3 at 4.

24 Province of Nova Scotia, *An Act for Establishing the rate of Spanish Dollars, and the interest of Money within this Province 1758* (UK), 32 Geo II, c 7. It was repealed around three years later, and no official record is available. See Horace A Flemming, "Halifax Currency" (Read before the NS Historical Society, May 1915), online: https://archives.gnb.ca/Exhibits/FortHavoc/html/HalifaxCurrency.aspx?culture=fr-CA, accessed 29 July 2024.

25 See e.g., Province of Lower Canada, *An Act for better regulating the Weight and Rates at which certain Coins shall pass Current in this Province, for preventing the falsifying, counterfeiting or impairing the same, and for repealing the Act or Ordinance therein mentioned 1796* (UK), 36 Geo III, c 5, para I, which may be the first enactment to confer a legal tender status to specified gold and silver coins.

26 Powell, above note 3 at 13–14.

27 *Ibid.*

The abortive United States invasion of 1812 triggered the issuance, not in excess of "two hundred and fifty thousand pounds currency," of Army Bills of Credit used to pay troops and buy provisions. Their circulation as money was backed by the order setting up their underlying scheme. They were denominated in dollars and payable, some with interest, "at the Rate of Exchange as fixed by Authority" in either cash or bills of exchange issued on London Treasury.[28]

An Ordinance Amending Ordinance on Fraudulent Copper & Brass Coins 1840[29] required that "any Copper or Brass Coin or Tokens" be "stamped with the nominal value thereof, and with the name" of its importer or manufacturer. At the same time, several gold[30] and silver[31] coins were expressly designated as "current and ... deemed to be legal tender" at specified rate in the *Gold & Silver Coin Rating Act* of 1836.[32] It was revised by *An Act to Regulate the Currency* of 1841,[33] which further made "the Pound Sterling as represented by the British Sovereign ... a legal tender for one pound four shillings and four pence, currency." Under Paragraph VII, the dollar was rated at *"five shillings and one penny,"* that is, slightly more than under the Halifax rating.

IV. TWO LANDMARKS: THE DOLLAR AND THE BANKNOTE

According to Powell, with "the prevalence and wide acceptance of Spanish silver dollars, it became increasingly difficult to maintain a currency system based on sterling."[34] To that end, *An Act to provide for the introduction of the Decimal System into the Currency* passed in 1851.[35] It was followed by the

28 Province of Lower Canada, *An Act to facilitate the circulation of Army Bills 1812* (53 Geo III, c 1); see (with a sample document) Powell, above note 3 at 14; for Treasury Notes in Nova Scotia and New Brunswick, see Powell, above note 3 at 15–16.

29 Province of Upper Canada, An Ordinance to amend and render permanent an Ordinance passed in the second year of Her Majesty's Reign, entitled, "An Ordinance to prevent the fraudulent manufacture, importation, or circulation of spurious Copper and Brass Coin" 1840 (3 Vict, c 8).

30 The British Guinea and Sovereign; and two types of the Eagle of the United States of America.

31 The British Crown, Half Crown, at three shillings, Shilling, at one shilling and three pence; and Sixpence; the Spanish Milled Dollar; and the Dollar of the United States of America.

32 Province of Lower Canada, *An Act to repeal and amend certain Acts of this Province, in relation to the Gold and Silver Coin made current by Law, and to make further provision respecting the rates at which certain Gold and Silver Coins shall pass current in this Province 1836* (UK), 6 Will IV, c 27.

33 Province of Canada, *An Act to Regulate the Currency of this Province 1841* (UK), 4 & 5 Vict, c 93.

34 Powell, above note 3 at 19.

35 Province of Canada, *An Act to provide for the introduction of the Decimal System into the Currency of this Province, and otherwise to amend the laws relative to the Currency 1851* (UK), 14 & 15 Vict, c 47.

Currency Act, 1853[36] that recognized British Pounds, Shillings & Pence and Dollars, mills & cents as alternative units of accounts. Effectively, this was the introduction of a decimal-based currency to Canada.[37] In setting the value of each such units by reference to gold, the 1853 statute is also taken to adopt the gold standard that persisted into the outbreak of the First World War in 1914.[38]

The position of the dollar as the currency of account prevailed under the *Currency Act 1857*.[39] The statute required all public accounts[40] to "be … rendered in dollars and cents" while merely giving the option to an accountant who so desires to "have a second column containing sums in pounds, shillings and pence, equivalent to the sums so slated in dollars and cents."

Paragraphs II and III of the *Act to amend the Currency Act of 1841*, passed in 1850,[41] authorized the Governor in Council to cause silver and gold coins to be struck for circulation as legal tender. In 1858, several sets of specially struck coins called proofs were prepared to celebrate Canada's new coinage.[42] However, coins used in Canada were minted in the United Kingdom until the establishment of a mint in Ottawa in 1908.[43]

Notes issued by banks in their course of business heralded the systematic issue of paper money.[44] In conjunction with experimentation throughout Europe, a system under which banks issued notes intended for circulation goes back to the post-Medieval goldsmith system in England. Goldsmiths, the forerunners of modern commercial banks, issued notes against either the deposit of coined money or by way of loans made out of such deposits. Holders of such notes used them to pay their creditors who either cashed them or paid them in discharge of their own debts.[45]

In the mid-nineteenth century, Tucker speaks of "two kinds of banks: banks of deposit and banks of circulation," with most banks belonging to

---

36 *An Act to Regulate the Currency 1853* (UK), 16 Vict, c 158 pt II.

37 Powell, above note 3 at 22–24.

38 *Ibid* at 33.

39 *An Act to require accounts rendered to the Provincial Government to be so rendered in dollars and cents 1857* (UK), 20 Vict, c 18.

40 Broadly stated to include "any party receiving aid from the Province, or otherwise accountable to the Government or Legislature thereof."

41 Province of Canada, *An Act to Amend the Currency Act of this Province 1850* (UK), 13 & 14 Vict, c 8.

42 Powell, above note 3 at 23.

43 *Ibid* at 24 footnote 35.

44 *Ibid* at 17–18.

45 See in general Benjamin Geva, *The Payment Order of Antiquity and the Middle Ages: A Legal History* (Hart, 2011) at 467–84.

the latter category[46] which "exclusively prevails in the United States" even as "borrowed from Great Britain."[47] Such banks "issue paper which performs the office of a circulating medium."[48] More specifically:[49]

> Their immediate and principal operations consist in discounting promissory notes and bills of exchange not yet due, that is, in lending money on the credit of these negotiable paper[s], after deducting or discounting the interest; and in receiving deposits of money for safe keeping. It is then by being banks of discount and of deposit, that they have become banks of circulation.

This happens in the following process:[50]

> [A]ny holder of a negotiable paper not due, who wishes it cashed, obtains a discount is offered either specie or the notes of the bank. Now as these notes are convertible into current coin at the pleasure of the holder, if the public have confidence in the solidity of the bank capital, and in the prudence and good faith of those who manage it … most persons will prefer the notes to specie. They are more easily carried or transmitted from place to place, are more readily secure from robbery, and are more readily counted. The same considerations which induce the original borrower to receive them from the bank, induce others to receive them from the bank and thus they obtain a general circulation.

Since at any time the holder is entitled to obtain payment in specie, it will be up to the bank's management to determine the amount of specie held available to meet obligations to note holders.

The injection of banknotes into the economy facilitated its expansion beyond the capacity of what could be achieved by means restricted to metallic money. After independence, the demand for circulating private banknotes in the United States only increased. This occurred against the background of a constitutional prohibition on states of the United States to emit "bills credit"[51] and a restriction of the power of Congress to effectively issue only

---

46   George Tucker, *The Theory of Money and Banks Investigated* (Charles C. Little and James Brown, 1839) at 145.

47   For note issuing as a banking function see e.g., *Shields v The Bank of England* [1901] 1 IR 172.

48   Tucker, above note 46 at 160.

49   *Ibid* at 161.

50   *Ibid* at 161–62.

51   US Const art I, § 10 which further precludes a state from coining money and making "any Thing but gold and silver Coin a Tender in Payment of Debts."

"coined money."[52] Overcoming these constitutional hurdles, state-chartered banks in the United States successfully issued banknotes "redeemable in constitutional coin."[53] This has been described as a triumph of market forces over the letter and spirit of the United States Constitution.[54]

No constitutional hurdles existed in Canada; and yet the emergence of circulating banknotes was part of the broader North American story underlined by the inadequacy of metallic currency to produce sufficient quantities of sound money and enhance economic growth.[55] Indeed, during the late eighteenth and into the early nineteenth centuries, Canada suffered from a persistent lack of coinage.[56] As indicated,[57] privately issued "bons" and publicly issued Army Bills supplemented the supply of means of payment.[58] In the years that followed the War of 1812, barter also became prominent with whiskey manifesting itself as a common medium of exchange.[59]

Having been envisaged as a bank of circulation, the Bank of Montreal was founded in 1817.[60] *The Act to incorporate the Bank of Montreal 1821*[61] authorized that bank to issue, as part of an indebtedness that shall not exceed

52   One of the powers given to Congress was "To coin Money, regulate the Value thereof, and of foreign Coin, and fix the Standard of Weights and Measures," US Const art I, § 8; see Thomas Wilson, *The Power "to Coin" Money: The Exercise of Monetary Powers by the Congress* (Armonk New York: ME Sharp, 1991).

53   See Ali Khan, "The Evolution of Money: A Story of Constitutional Nullification" (1999) 67 *University of Cincinnati Law Review* 393 at 413–17 (quote at 416).

54   In the language of Khan, *ibid* at 396, by reference to the overall process of the rise of paper dollars, "Law, most notably through the concept of promissory notes, provided the technical infrastructure to devise clever financing as well as to cloak and legitimize blatant deviations from the letter and spirit of the Constitution."

55   For a succinct overview see e.g., Muharem Kianieff, "Private Banknotes in Canada from 1867 (and before) to 1950" (2004) 30 *Queen's Law Journal* 400 at 407–12.

56   R Craig McIvor, *Canadian Monetary, Banking and Fiscal Development* (Macmillan, 1961) at 17.

57   Powell, above note 3 at 7, 92–93.

58   According to McIvor, above note 56 at 25, their withdrawal from circulation provided both an opportunity and a need for the establishment of banking institutions.

59   *Ibid* at 17.

60   *Ibid* at 25–26.

61   Province of Lower Canada, *An act for incorporating certain persons therein-named, under the name of "President, Directors and Company of the Bank of Montreal"* 1821 (UK), 1 Geo IV, c 25; citing Adam Shortt, "Currency and Banking, 1760–1841" in Adam Shortt and Arthur Doughty (eds), *Canada and its Provinces: A History of the Canadian People and their Institutions by One Hundred Associates* (Brook & Company, 1914) vol IV at 610; Powell, above note 3 at 17, footnote 27 states that "[t]he charter of the Bank of Montreal, which provided the model for other Canadian banks, was itself modelled on that of the First Bank of the United States, which was established in 1791 by Alexander Hamilton, the first US secretary of the Treasury."

three times the amount of the capital,[62] "[n]otes ... promising the payment of money [either] to any person or persons, his, her or their order ... [that] shall be assignable and negotiable by blank or other indorsement ... [or] payable to bearer, [that] shall be negotiable by delivery only."[63] Such notes "shall be payable in gold or silver coin, current by the laws of this Province."[64] This Act marks the introduction of bank paper money in Canada,[65] and in fact, the issuance of paper money not in connection with covering war expenses.

Into the middle of the nineteenth century new banks equipped with the power to issue notes were incorporated; their respective charters required convertibility and further restricted their liabilities by reference to their capital.[66] Notes were issued against the assets of a bank, at the head office, and in branches, with each head office and branch being obliged to redeem only notes issued by itself. No bond was required to back the notes redemption obligation. The monetary feature of these notes, that is, their own use as circulating money, has not been backed by legislation and has been established by their mere acceptance as such by the public. Shareholders were subject to double liability in case of the bank's failure. However, note holders had no preference over other creditors in terms of a lien on the bank's assets.[67] Strictly speaking, so far as the letter of the law is concerned, they were unsecured promises to pay money, in the form of current gold or silver coin, but not money itself.

In 1841, Lord Sydenham, Governor General of the new United Province of Canada, proposed the establishment of a provincial bank that would issue up to £1 million in provincial paper currency denominated in dollars,

62   *The Act to incorporate the Bank of Montreal 1821, ibid*; ninth point in para IX. Directors are to be personally liable for any excess.

63   *Ibid*; eleventh point in para IX.

64   *Ibid*; para X.

65   But *cf* Powell, above note 3 at 17, footnote 26, pointing at the existence of banknotes denominated in pounds and shillings, issued in 1792 by the Canadian Banking Corporation; except that "[i]t is not clear ... whether this bank ever opened business." Powell goes on to note that "[t]he success of the Bank of Montreal led to the incorporation of additional banks in Upper and Lower Canada as well as in the Atlantic provinces, all of which issued their own bank notes." *ibid*.

66   According to Powell, above note 3 at 18, "Banks committed themselves to maintain convertibility and, under their charters, restricted their total liabilities to a given multiple of their capital." But see Ben Fung, Scott Hendry, and Warren E Weber, "Canadian Bank Notes and Dominion Notes: Lessons for Digital Currencies" (2017) Bank of Canada Staff Working Paper 2017-5 at 6, online: https://www.bankofcanada.ca/2017/02/staff-working-paper-2017-5/, accessed 5 July 2024: "In general, note issues were limited to the amount of the bank's paid in capital plus specie plus government securities, but they were not subject to specie reserve requirements."

67   Powell, above note 3 at 17–18; Fung, *ibid* at 6.

one-quarter of which would be backed by gold; the remainder would be fiduciary issue backed by government securities. The proposal would further prohibit the issue of notes by the chartered bank. The proposal, which effectively would establish a central bank, was studied by a parliamentary select committee on banking and currency, but was ultimately rejected "because of widespread opposition, particularly from a strong bank lobby."[68]

Within twenty years, with the collapse of a few banks, followed by another failed attempt to introduce provincial paper money, circumstances had changed. Stripped of cash, the Province passed *An Act to provide for the issue of Provincial Notes 1866*. Its section 1 authorized the issuance of legal tender provincial notes, partly backed by gold, and payable on demand in gold in either Toronto or Montreal.[69] In section 2 the Act further authorized "[t]he Governor in Council [to] enter into arrangements with all or any of the Chartered Banks of this Province for the surrender" against compensation "of their power to issue notes." In fact, "only the Bank of Montreal, the government's fiscal agent, took up the offer." Once it agreed to act in that capacity, "all of its note issues were overprinted to indicate government issue until newly designed provincial notes were received."[70]

V. CONFEDERATION

Establishing Confederation, the *British North America Act, 1867*[71] conferred in section 91 on the Parliament of Canada exclusive legislative power in relation to "Matters coming within [enumerated] Classes of Subjects." They include "Currency and Coinage"; "Banking, Incorporation of Banks, and the Issue of Paper Money"; "Bills of Exchange and Promissory Notes"; and "Legal Tender."[72]

Full and exclusive competence relating to money and the monetary system was thus given to the federal Parliament.[73] Listed powers included not only currency, coinage, paper money, and legal tender, each of which dealing exclusively with money. Rather, they also included scriptural money insofar as it falls under banking. Furthermore, listed powers also included banknotes

---

68 Powell, above note 3 at 21–22.

69 *An Act to Provide for the Issue of Provincial Notes 1866* (UK), 29 & 30 Vict, c 30.

70 Powell, above note 3 at 24–26 (the quote is at 26).

71 *Constitution Act, 1867* (UK), 30 & 31 Vict, c 3; reprinted in RSC 1985, Appendix II, No 5.

72 *Ibid* at ss 91(14), 91(15), 91(18), and 91(20), respectively.

73 Emilio S Binavince and H Scott Fairley, "Banking and the Constitution: Untested Limits of Federal Jurisdiction" (1986) 65 *Canadian Bar Review* 228 at 333–37, albeit focusing on the banking jurisdiction.

and other currency notes insofar as they are promissory notes. In line with the prevailing understanding at that time, currency was linked to coinage and paper money to banking. Nonetheless, over the years, currency has not been limited to coinage and paper money has not been restricted to banking.

Indeed, shortly after the adoption of the *British North America Act, 1867,* the *Dominion Notes Act, 1868*[74] passed. In section 8 it empowered "the Governor in Council [to] authorize the issue of Dominion Notes to an amount not exceeding that Provincial Notes redeemed." Such notes were stated in section 8 to "be redeemable, in specie on presentation at offices to be established at Montreal, Toronto, Halifax[75] and St. John" as well as to "be a legal tender." Under section 13, "specie" was defined to mean "coin current by law of that one of the Provinces in which any Provincial or Dominion note is made payable, at the rates and subject to the provisions of the law in that behalf, or Bullion of equal value according to its weight and fineness."

In the footsteps of their predecessors, the provincial notes, Dominion Notes were partly backed by gold. Over time, as of the *Dominion Act, 1871,*[76] the size of the authorized note issue was increased. By 1913 the first $30 million had a 25 percent gold backing. Issues in excess of $30 million had to be fully gold-backed.[77] In section 1 the *Dominion Notes Act, 1868* further authorized the making of arrangements "with all or any of the Chartered Banks ... for the surrender ... of their power to issue notes" against compensation.

Another monetary statute which passed shortly after Confederation was the *Uniform Currency Act, 1871.*[78] Its section 2 provided that "The denominations of money in the currency of Canada, shall be dollars, cents, and mills ... ," thereby confirming the law stated in the *Currency Act, 1857.*[79] Specifically, the *Uniform Currency Act, 1871* aimed in section 1 to establish that "the currency of the Province of Nova Scotia shall be the same as that of the [other] Provinces," thereby eliminating the small difference between the rating under the 1841 *Currency Act* and the Halifax rating.[80] In section 3 the statute fixed the standard value of Canada currency by reference to the UK sovereign. The provision went on to set the dollar as the money of account in

74   *An Act to enable Banks in any part of Canada to use Note of the Dominion instead of issuing Notes of their own,* SC 1868, c 46.

75   For which a special rate was set under the aforesaid s 8.

76   *An Act to amend the Act 31 Victoria, Chapter 46, and to regulate the issue of Dominion Notes,* SC 1870, c 10.

77   Powell, above note 3 at 27.

78   *An Act to establish one Uniform Currency for the Dominion of Canada,* SC 1971, c 4.

79   *Ibid,* s 2; *Currency Act, 1857,* above note 39.

80   *Ibid,* s 1.

Canada, requiring its use in all public and private accounts, as well as in any indictment or legal proceeding, so that "all sums ... shall be understood to be in such currency, unless some other is clearly expressed, or must, from the circumstances of the case, have been intended by the parties."

Confederation heralded a stream of banking legislation some of which concerned banknotes.[81] As indicated, both the 1866 provincial note and the 1868 Dominion Note pieces of legislation encouraged banks to surrender their note issue power. Given the failure to incentivize banks other than the Bank of Montreal, incentives were cancelled in May 1870 and the Bank of Montreal resumed issuing its own notes in 1871.[82]

A statute passed in 1871[83] limited the amount of notes to be issued for the unimpaired capital of each bank, addressed denominations, and required banks to receive their notes in payment at par at any of their offices regardless of where the notes were payable.[84] Section 14 required banks to hold "as nearly as may be practicable" half of their cash reserves in Dominion Notes. Section 58 fastens on shareholders liability for paying off "debts and liabilities" of an insolvent bank, potentially very early in the insolvency proceeding. The *Bank Act* of 1880 accorded note holders a first charge on the assets of a suspended bank.[85]

The *Bank Act, 1890*[86] provided in section 51 that each bank "may issue and re-issue notes payable to bearer on demand and intended for circulation" in denominations of "no less than five dollars" and only in a multiple of five dollars. A bank was precluded from pledging, assigning, or hypothecating its notes.[87] Payment on the notes was to be secured by a first charge on the assets of the bank, ahead of that securing payment owed to the Government of Canada as well Provincial governments "in trust or otherwise."[88] Under section 55, each bank was required to make arrangements necessary to ensure the circulation at par in any and every part of Canada of all notes issued or re-issued by it and intended for circulation. Under section 54(7) holders of the notes of suspended banks would be paid interest at the rate of 6 percent

81 JD Falconbridge, *The Law of Banks and Banking*, 4th ed (Canada Law Book, 1929) at 131–36; see also Fung, above note 66 at 6–7.
82 *An Act respecting Banks and Banking*, SC 1870, c 11; Fung, above note 66 at 9.
83 *An Act relating to Banks and Banking*, SC 1871, c 5.
84 *Ibid*, ss 8–9.
85 *An Act to amend "An Act relating to Banks and Banking" and to continue for a limited time the charters of certain banks to which the said act applies*, SC 1880 vol 1, c 22, s 12(1).
86 *An Act respecting Banks and Banking*, SC 1890, c 31.
87 *Ibid*, s 52.
88 *Ibid*, s 53.

(changed to 5 per cent in 1900)[89] from when the bank suspended until the first day at which they were made payable.

A key component of that piece of legislation was the establishment under section 54 of the Bank Circulation Redemption Fund for notes of suspended banks. Each bank was required to contribute 5 per cent of its previous twelve months circulation. Where this did not suffice to cover the entire amount of default of that bank surviving banks were required to make the difference, albeit subject to an annual ceiling for each surviving bank of 1 percent of its previous twelve months circulation.

Subsequently, for each bank, note issue was allowed to expand during the moving of the crops[90] as well as against gold or Dominion Notes deposited in a newly established central gold reserve.[91]

The *Currency Act, 1910*[92] reconfirmed the dollarized denominations of money in the currency of Canada and reset the standard for gold and silver coin. As well, it (1) required that usually "[a]ll coins of the currency of Canada … " be coined in Ottawa,[93] (2) authorized "[t]he Minister of Finance … from time to time [to] issue out of the Consolidated Revenue Fund such sums as may be necessary for the purchase of bullion in order to provide supplies of coin for the public service," and (3) set a range of amounts respectively to be accepted in legal tender in gold, silver, and bronze coins, albeit, even as it clarifies that "[n]othing in this Act shall prevent any paper currency which under any Act or otherwise is a legal tender from being a legal tender."[94]

Section 15(1) of that statute required "[a]ll public accounts throughout Canada" to be kept, as well as "any statement as to money or money value, in any indictment or legal proceeding," to be stated "in the currency of Canada," namely, per section 2, "dollars, cents and mills." Section 15(2) followed suit in presuming the money of account of each contract, instrument, or transaction to be in the currency of Canada. Similar presumption is given in section 16 to sums mentioned in statutory provisions.[95] For their parts, under section 19, Dominion Notes, and unless provided otherwise by statute, banknotes, were to be issued, re-issued, or redeemed in the currency of Canada.

---

89   *The Bank Act Amendment Act*, SC 1900, c 26, s 11.

90   *An Act to amend the Bank Act*, SC 1908, c 7.

91   *An Act respecting Banks and Banking*, SC 1913, c 9.

92   *An Act respecting the Currency*, SC 1910, c 14.

93   *Ibid*, s 5.

94   *Ibid*, s 8. The quote is of s 8(3). See also s 11 as to the legal tender status of certain coins of certain provinces and of Canada prior to that Act.

95   *Ibid*, ss 17–18 address money of payment in the provinces of Nova Scotia, Prince Edward Island, and British Columbia.

Other provisions addressed the powers of the Governor in Council to provide for matters such as dimensions, designs, and other features of coins,[96] as well as procedures for the examination and testing of coins.[97]

The power to issue Dominion Notes and their legal tender status, as well as the treatment of remaining circulating Provincial Notes as "notes of the Dominion of Canada," were confirmed in the *Dominion Notes Act, 1914*.[98] Notes were stated to be "redeemable in gold."[99] Section 2(d) defined "gold" to be "gold coins which are a legal tender in Canada, and ... gold bullion in bars, each bar bearing either the stamp of the Royal Mint in the United Kingdom or of the branch thereof in Canada or ... Australia" or in a coinage mint in the United States, "certifying its weight and fineness at a valuation of one dollar in the currency of Canada for every 23.33 grains fine gold content. ... " Under section 5:

> The Minister of Finance shall always hold as security for redemption. fifty million dollars, issued and outstanding at any one time, an amount equal to not less than twenty-five per centum of the amount of such notes in gold.
>
> As security for the redemption of Dominion note issued in excess of fifty million dollars, the Minister shall hold an amount in gold equal to such excess.

Under section 6 the Governor in Council was authorized to borrow money to meet demand for redemption for which the security under section 5 would not suffice. Subsequently, the security under section 5 was stated to be waived for the issues of Dominion Notes issued for the purposes of the Canadian Northern Railway Company and Grand Trunk Pacific Railway Company.[100] Otherwise, the regime of gold backing, as opposed to gold redemption, survived until the collapse of the gold standard in 1931.

As the First World War broke out, an Order in Council of 3 August 1914[101] recommended that "the Government authorize the chartered banks of Canada to make payment in bank notes instead of in gold or Dominion notes until further official announcement in that behalf." This was interpreted to confer on banknotes a legal tender feature.[102] The Order went on to recommend an increase of permissible banknote issue against securities "as may be

---

96   *Ibid*, s 21.
97   *Ibid*, s 22.
98   *An Act respecting Dominion Notes*, SC 1915 (4th Sess), c 4.
99   *Ibid*, ss 3, 4, 10.
100 *An Act respecting certain issues of Dominion Notes*, SC 1915 (5th Sess), c 4.
101 PC 1914-2033 (1914) C Gaz vol 48 issue 6 at 466.
102 Powell, above note 3 at 37.

deposited by the banks and approved by the Minister of Finance." A second Order in Council, issued on 10 August 1914, suspended the redemption of Dominion Notes into gold.[103]

Both Orders in Council were subsequently "upgraded" into legislation as "*An Act to Conserve the Commercial and Financial Interests of Canada*" ("the *Finance Act*"), which received royal assent on 22 August 1914.[104] Under section 3 of the *Finance Act*, the Dominion Notes gold redemption suspension regime was stated to last only temporarily until 15 September 1914. However, under section 4 of the Act, in case of emergency, the Governor in Council was empowered "by proclamation published in The Canada Gazette" to authorize: (1) the making of advances to the chartered banks by the issue of Dominion Notes;[105] (2) the banks to issue excess circulation; (3) the banks to pay in bank notes; and (4) the postponement of the payment of all or any debts, liabilities and obligations. Furthermore, the Governor in Council was empowered by proclamation to "suspend the redemption in gold of dominion notes." Section 4(3) went on to provide that:

> A tender by a bank of its notes in payment of any of its liabilities ... shall be a sufficient and valid tender, and the payment at such time by a bank of any of its liabilities with its notes shall be as sufficient and valid a payment as if the same had been made in specie or Dominion notes: Provided in either case the total amount of the notes of the bank in circulation at that time, including in case of tender the amount tendered, does not exceed the amount of notes of the bank issuable

The provision thus conferred on banknotes a legal tender status,[106] except that interestingly, it placed on the payee the risk of violation by the paying bank. As well, strictly speaking, the provision did not go as far as requiring a creditor to accept bank notes from their non-bank debtor.

Under the power under the aforesaid section 4 of the *Finance Act, 1914* a proclamation was made on 3d September 1914[107] to, *inter alia*, extend the Gold Suspension Order in view of the war.

---

103 This Order could not be found in the *Gazette* (prior to 1947 only selected Orders in Council were published) and yet it is referred to in both the 3 September proclamation and the *Finance Act, 1914*.

104 *An Act to Conserve the Commercial and Financial Interests of Canada*, SC 1915 (4th Sess), c 3.

105 Effectively, this "gave the government the power to act as a lender of last resort to the banking system – one of the powers of a modern central bank." Powell, above note 3 at 38.

106 *Finance Act, 1914*, above note 104, s 4(3); Kianieff, above note 55 at 429.

107 Proclamation, 3 September 1914 (1914) C Gaz vol 48 issue 10 at 763–64.

For its part, the *Finance Act* of 1914 was extended in 1919[108] and revised in 1923.[109] Section 13 of the 1923 revision effectively provided for an automatic return to the gold standard after three years from 30 June 1923, unless the government took steps to the contrary.[110] Upon expiration of the three-year cap on the Gold Suspension Order triggered by the 1923 Act, the gold standard was automatically restored in Canada on 1 July 1926.[111] The Gold Suspension Order was thus in effect between April 1914 and June 1926.

Having reverted to the gold standard in July 1926 on the basis of the *Finance Act Supplementation Act* of 1923,[112] Canada again suspended the gold standard under 19 October 1931 Order in Council,[113] which remained in effect until 1 March 1932. Specifically, the 1931 Order in Council prohibited the export of gold from Canada with the implication that trade and commercial transactions were facilitated strictly on the strength of Dominion Notes backed by gold holdings. Nonetheless, the Order empowered the minister to approve gold export licences for banks as occasions may demand.

Following the expiration of the Order of 19 October 1931 on 1 March 1932 and in the absence of any statute to the contrary, gold export, and by extension the gold standard, returned to Canada at least on paper on 2 March 1932. Notwithstanding this return to gold standard and gold redemption, the *Gold Export Act*[114] was passed on 13 May 1932 vesting the Governor in Council with wide powers to prohibit the export of gold in all shapes and forms from Canada as may be necessary. In the same vein, *An Act to amend the Dominion Notes Act* (assented 30 March 1933)[115] provided that Dominion Notes shall be redeemable in gold, except that the Governor in Council "may from time to time, and for such period or periods as he may deem desirable" suspend this redeemability. Even so, it would appear that after the expiration of the Order of 19 October 1931, gold redemption existed only on paper. As glimpsed from the 1933 journals of the House of Commons of Canada, "letters, telegrams and other orders issued to Assistant Receivers General since

---

108 *An Act to provide for the Continuance in Force of a certain Proclamation made under The Finance Act, 1914, and to authorize the prohibition of the export of Gold*, SC 1919, c 21.

109 *An Act to supplement The Finance Act, 1914*, SC 1923, c 48.

110 Powell, above note 3 at 40.

111 See, Federal Reserve Board, "Foreign Banking and Business Conditions: Canada's Return to the Gold Standard" (July 1926) Federal Reserve Bulletin 534, online: https://fraser.stlouisfed.org/title/federal-reserve-bulletin-62/july-1926-20655/fulltext, accessed 1 August 2024.

112 *Finance Act Supplementation Act, 1923*, above note 109.

113 PC 1931-2617 (1931) C Gaz vol 65 issue 17 at 1042.

114 *An Act respecting the Export of Gold*, SC 1932, c 33.

115 *An Act to amend the Dominion Notes Act*, SC 1933, c 12.

21 September 1931 instructing them not to pay out gold for Dominion Notes on presentation."[116]

Finally, on 10 April 1933, an Order in Council was made formally suspending the return to gold redemption of Dominion Notes and gold export.[117] Thus, the last phase of gold standard only lasted from 2 March 1932 to April 1933, and with the weight of fines and imprisonment and moral suasion on the basis of national interest, gold export and gold redemption of Dominion Notes effectively ended in Canada.

VI. THE BANK OF CANADA AND THE LAW GOVERNING THE PRESENT MONETARY SYSTEM

The Bank of Canada, of which the establishment followed the recommendation of the Macmillan Commission[118], was incorporated under the *Bank of Canada Act, 1934*.[119] Its Preamble highlights the desirability:

> [T]o establish a central bank in Canada to regulate credit and currency in the best interests of the economic life of the nation, to control and protect the external value of the national monetary unit and to mitigate by its influence fluctuations in the general level of production, trade, prices and employment, so far as may be possible within the scope of monetary action, and generally to promote the economic and financial welfare of the Dominion.

The regulation of currency, in the broader context of the protection of the external value of the national monetary unit and other economic sources of measurements, was thus supposed to be a primary objective for the establishment of the Bank of Canada. While the regulation of currency is not necessarily the right to issue of currency, never mind the exclusive right to do so, Parliament implemented this power by conferring on the Bank of Canada the exclusive right to issue banknotes.

By no means was the nationalization of the banknote issuance power central in the debate leading to the establishment of the Bank of Canada as

---

116   Canada, *Journals of The Senate of Canada*, 17-4, no 71 (25 April 1933) at 214.

117   This Order could not be found in the *Gazette* (prior to 1947 only selected Orders in Council were published) and yet it is referred to in the *Report of the Royal Commission on Banking and Currency in Canada* (Ottawa: Privy Council Office, 1933) at 22 para 47 [MacMillan Commission]; see also James Holladay, "The Currency of Canada" (1934) 24 *The American Economic Review* 266 at 269.

118   MacMillan Commission, *ibid* at 81 para 293.

119   *An Act to Incorporate the Bank of Canada*, SC 1934, c 43.

a central bank.[120] Nonetheless, the point was not glossed over. Banks vehemently opposed to the loss of their issuance power. They warned against the dire results of the loss of revenue[121] as well as the closure of branches in small communities where unissued notes served as cash reserves.[122] The Macmillan Commission was not persuaded. It was of the view that the exclusive right to issue legal tender notes enabled the central bank to discharge its essential functions such as the regulation of credit and currency, keeping cash reserves for commercial banks, mobilizing gold reserves, managing the national debt, controlling exchange rates, and advising the federal Government. Accordingly, it opined, side by side with being a financial adviser to the government, holding its accounts and carrying out on its behalf all major financial transactions, a central bank "should have the sole right to issue legal tender notes" for its "full and satisfactory working" as such.[123] The present validity of this reasoning is addressed in this study in chapter 8.

Participants in the debate at the House of Commons were generally supportive of the establishment of the Bank of Canada as well as conferring on it the exclusive power to issue currency notes.[124] There seems, however, to be more skepticism in the Senate where greater attention was given to the losses incurred by commercial banks,[125] except that an acknowledgement of such losses was not necessarily seen as something to be avoided.[126]

Be that as it may, the *Bank of Canada Act, 1934*[127] passed. Its section 24(1) conferred on the Bank of Canada "the sole right to issue notes payable to

120 For this debate in the broader context of the establishment of the Bank of Canada see e.g., George S Watts, "The Origins and Background of Central Banking in Canada" (1972) *Bank of Canada Review* 15 reprinted as chapter 1 in George S Watts, *The Bank of Canada: Origins and Early History*, Thomas K Rymes (ed) (Carleton University Press, 1993); see also Michael D Bordo and Angela Redish, "Why Did the Bank of Canada Emerge in 1935?" (1987) 47 *Journal of Economic History* 405. For a succinct summary see Kianieff, above note 55 at 435–42.

121 Royal Commission on Banking and Currency in Canada, *Final Hearings at Ottawa: 14 September 1933* (King's Printer, 1933) at 23; Kianieff, above note 55 at 439.

122 *Final Hearings, ibid* at 22.

123 MacMillan Commission, above note 117 at 65 para 218; see also *ibid* at para 16.

124 Canada, Parliament, *House of Commons Debates*, 17th Parl, 5th Sess, vol 1 (29 January 1934) at 33 (Hon WL Mackenzie King); Canada, Parliament, *House of Commons Debates*, 17th Parl, 5th Sess, vol 1 (1 February 1934) at 167 (Hon Archibald Carmichael); Canada, Parliament, *House of Commons Debates*, 17th Parl, 5th Sess, vol 1 (22 February 1934) at 823–30 (Hon Edgar Rhodes) at 830–31 (Hon WL Mackenzie King) at 831–33 (Hon George Coote) at 833–36 (Hon James Woodsworth); Canada, Parliament, *House of Commons Debates*, 17th Parl, 5th Sess, vol 2 (8 March 1934) at 1283–85 (Hon WL Mackenzie King).

125 Canada, Parliament, *Debates of The Senate*, 17th Parl, 5th Sess, vol 1 (31 January 1934) at 24, 601 (Hon Joseph Casgrain).

126 *Ibid* at 35–37 (Hon Frank Black).

127 *Bank of Canada Act, 1934*, above note 119.

bearer on demand and intended for circulation in Canada" and went on to provide that "[s]uch notes shall be legal tender and shall be the first charge upon the assets of the Bank [of Canada]." Section 24(3) set out signature requirements and conferred on the Governor in Council the power to determine "from time to time" the denomination. Under section 24(4), "[t]he form and material of the notes shall be subject to approval by the Minister," except that "notes in either the English or the French language shall be available as required." Subject to the Governor in Council's power of suspension, redemption was stated in section 25(1) to be in gold upon demand made at the head office of the Bank of Canada "but only in the form of bars containing approximately four hundred ounces of fine gold." Section 25(2) conferred on the Governor in Council the power to suspend the operation of section 25(1) "from time to time and for such period as he may deem desirable.

In fact, the gold redemption scheme under the aforesaid section 25(1) never saw the light of the day. Thus, under P.C. Order 573 dated 7 March 1935 the Bank of Canada was authorized to commence business on 11 March 1935.[128] A day earlier, pursuant to the powers granted the Governor in Council under the aforesaid section 25(2), P.C. Order 574 was issued suspending for one year, as of 10 March 1935, the operation of section 25(1) of the *Bank of Canada Act*.[129] Going forward, the Governor in Council issued yearly orders for suspension of the gold for legal tender regime established under section 25(1) of the 1934 *Bank of Canada Act*. For example, by P.C. Order 756 issued on 17 February 1949, the aforesaid section 25(1) was suspended for a year with the order indicating that the provision had been suspended in 1948 by P.C. Order 678 dated 20 February 1948.[130] Eventually, and as the regime clearly served no useful or strategic purpose, with section 25 of the original 1934 *Bank of Canada Act* ultimately becoming section 22 in the 1952 revision,[131] the regime was finally abolished in 1966 under section 13 of the *Bank of Canada Amendment Act* assented on 23 March 1967.[132]The scheme providing for the convertibility of legal tender to gold under the aforesaid section 25(1), particularly its suspension and eventual repeal, was judicially noted by the Supreme Court of Canada in *Bank of Canada v Bank of Montreal*.[133]

---

128 PC 1935-573 (1935) C Gaz vol 68 issue 37, 1967.
129 PC 1935-574 (1935) C Gaz vol 68 issue 37, 1968.
130 PC 1949-756 (1949) C Gaz II vol 83 issue 5, 472.
131 *Bank of Canada Act*, RSC 1952, c 13.
132 *An Act to amend the Bank of Canada Act*, SC 1967, c 88.
133 [1978] 1 SCR 1148 at 1167.

Dominion Notes continued in circulation until 1935 when the Bank of Canada began operation. At that point the *Dominion Notes Act* was repealed[134] and the Bank of Canada assumed liability for the outstanding Dominion Notes.[135]

The *Bank and Banking Act* of 1934[136] had introduced the phasing out of banknotes issued by commercial banks. Under section 61(2), starting from "the amount of the unimpaired paid-up capital of the bank on the said day on which the Bank of Canada is authorized to commence business," the maximum amount of notes of a bank in circulation at any time, was to be reduced by 5 percent each year until 1941, then by 10 percent, so that "until Parliament further enacts, the amount of notes of a bank in circulation shall not exceed twenty-five per centum of the amount of the unimpaired paid-up capital of the bank."

The *Bank and Banking Act, 1944*[137] ended the era of the legislative authorization of commercial banks to issue notes intended for circulation. Subject to exceptions set out below, section 60(1) prohibited banks from issuing or re-issuing "notes ... payable to bearer on demand and intended for circulation." However, under section 61(a), and yet within limits, each of ten named banks[138] was allowed to "issue or re-issue outside Canada ... in any British Dominion, colony or possession, its notes payable to bearer on demand and intended for circulation in such [territory]." Also within limits, under section 61(1)(b), each of these banks was allowed to "issue or re-issue in Canada ... notes payable to bearer on demand and intended for circulation in Canada," except that this power was said to expire at the end of opening of the following calendar year. Particularly, under section 61(5), "the total amount of the notes of a bank issued for circulation outside of Canada and outstanding at any time [was required] not [to] exceed an amount equal to ten per centum of the amount of the unimpaired paid-up capital of the bank." To the same end, section 61(6) stated that:

The total amount of the notes of a bank issued for circulation in Canada outstanding at any time in the year [1944], shall not exceed an amount equal

---

134 *An Act to amend the Dominion Notes Act*, SC 1934, c 34.

135 *Ibid*, s 25(3), (4). See Statistics Canada, *Canada Year Book 1974: An annual review of economic, social and political developments in Canada* (Information Canada, 1974) at 726 para 19.1.2.

136 *The Bank Act*, SC 1934, c 24.

137 *An Act respecting Banks and Banking*, SC 1944, c 30.

138 Bank of Montreal; The Bank of Nova Scotia; The Bank of Toronto; La Banque Provinciale du Canada; The Canadian Bank of Commerce; The Royal Bank of Canada; The Dominion Bank; Banque Canadienne Nationale; Imperial Bank of Canada; and Barclays Bank (Canada).

to thirty-five per centum of the amount of the unimpaired paid up capital of the bank, and shall not, on and after the first day of January [1945] exceed an amount equal to twenty-five per centum of the amount of the unimpaired paid up capital of the bank.

Regardless, under section 60(2), no bank was allowed to issue notes during any period of suspension. For its part, section 63 precluded a bank from pledging, assigning, or hypothecating its notes and further provided that "no advance or loan made on the security of the notes of the bank shall be recoverable from the bank or its assets." Obligatory redemption of banknotes issued outside of Canada was provided by section 73 of the *Bank Act, 1967.*[139]

No further provisions addressing commercial banks' power to issue notes intended for circulation were passed. In January 1950 the chartered banks' liability for their notes issued for circulation in Canada as then remained outstanding was transferred to the Bank of Canada in return for payment of a like sum to the Bank of Canada.[140]

Section 26 of the *Bank of Canada Act, 1934* required the Bank to maintain a reserve consisting of gold coin and bullion strictly owned by the Bank in an amount not less than 25 percent of its notes and deposit liabilities ("Gold Reserve"). The Gold Reserve requirement was not affected and thus was preserved by the 1936[141] and 1938[142] *Acts to Amend the Bank of Canada Act.*

Meanwhile, on 5 July 1935, the *Exchange Fund Act*[143] was passed wherein the minister was empowered under sections 3–6 *inter alia* to:

(i)   Transfer the credit difference between the value and market price of gold in the Bank's reserve to a special account held by the minister;
(ii) invest such difference in gold, foreign exchange, or book balances of designated New York or London banks; and
(iii) resell such gold or investment.

As part of Canada's responses to the Second World War, an Order in Council was issued on 15 September 1939[144] creating *inter alia* the Foreign Exchange Control Board for wartime foreign exchange management. Further, in the interest of "the security, defence, peace, order and welfare of Canada," two Orders in Council were issued on 30 April 1940, to wit:

---

139   *An Act respecting Banks and Banking,* SC 1967, c 87.
140   Statistics Canada, *Year Book 1974,* above note 135 at 726 para 19.1.2.
141   *Bank of Canada Amendment Act,* SC 1936, c 22.
142   *Bank of Canada Act Amendment Act,* SC 1938, c 42.
143   SC 1935, c 60.
144   PC 1939-2716 (1939) C Gaz vol 73 issue 13 at 915.

(i)   Order in Council Authorizing the Issue and Sale to the Bank of Canada of $325,000,000 of Treasury Securities" for the purpose of funding the special account to facilitate the buying of gold from the Bank as well as foreign exchange from Canadian residents;[145] and

(ii)   the Exchange Fund Order[146] which contained details of the types of securities to be issued to the Bank.

It was necessary to issue securities to the Bank so that the Bank could in turn make sufficient funds available in the special account for the gold and foreign exchange purchase. Notably, section 7 of the 1935 *Exchange Fund Act*[147] empowers the minister to apply funds in the special account to purchase Dominion of Canada guaranteed securities. In this regard and considering that gold purchase would have occasioned an infraction of section 26 of the *Bank of Canada Act*, the governor, in Item 5 of the Exchange Fund Order,[148] temporarily suspended the operation of the Gold Reserve requirement pursuant to his powers under section 26(3) of the *Bank of Canada Act*.

Under that provision no suspension could continue for period longer than one year unless sanctioned by Parliament. Nonetheless, this limit did not apply to P.C. 1734 and the supplementary Exchange Fund Order[149] because they were issued pursuant to the powers conferred on the Governor in Council under the *War Measures Act, 1914*.[150] In section 3, the latter statute vested the governor with wide powers to "make from time to time such orders and regulations, as he may by reason of real or apprehended war, invasion or insurrection deem necessary or advisable for the security, defence, peace, order and welfare of Canada." Under section 6 of that Act, such provisions "shall only be in force during war, invasion, or insurrection, real or apprehended." Thus, the 1940 Exchange Fund Order, which came into force on 1 May 1940, remained in force throughout the duration of the Second World War, which ended in 1945.

---

145   PC Order 1734 does not appear to have been published in the *Gazette* (prior to 1947 only selected Orders in Council were published), the relevant parts of the Order are available in Board of Governors of The Federal Reserve System, "Canadian Financial Measures" (July 1940) 26:7 *Federal Reserve Bulletin* 677 at 677–78.

146   *Ibid* at 677.

147   SC 1935, c 60, above note 143.

148   Board of Governors of The Federal Reserve System, "Canadian Financial Measures," above note 145 at 677.

149   *Ibid*.

150   RSC 1927, c 206.

To keep the Gold Reserve suspension in place after the Second World War, the *Foreign Exchange Control Act, 1946*[151] provided in section 70(2) that "[n]otwithstanding anything contained in Section [26] of the *Bank of Canada Act*, they shall not, unless the Governor in Council otherwise provides, be required to maintain a minimum or fixed reserve ratio of gold or foreign exchange to its liabilities." Thereby, the Gold Reserve suspension received the parliamentary sanction required under section 26(3) of the *Bank of Canada Act* for it to continue for more than one year.

To further advance Canada's interest and solidify gains made under the *Exchange Fund Act*,[152] the *Foreign Exchange Control Act*[153] was passed on 5 July 1946, essentially to replace the *Exchange Fund Act* and provide expanded provisions on the operational ambits of the *Exchange Fund Act*.[154] For example, the *Foreign Exchange Control Act, 1946* in sections 5 to 9 described the special account as "Exchange Fund Account" with more elaborate provisions on application and governance. With a view to achieving an even more robust currency and foreign exchange policy, the *Foreign Exchange Control Act* was repealed by the *Currency, Mint and Exchange Fund Act*,[155] assented to on 4 July 1952. As demanded by policy, flexibility, and economic realities, the mandatory Gold Reserve requirement was removed, "unless the Governor in Council otherwise prescribes," by virtue of section 25 thereof. Specifically, apart from the one-year restriction on Gold Reserve suspension imposed by section 26(3) of the 1934 *Bank Act*,[156] the fact that gold, with its large physical storage requirement, is not interest yielding eventually made the Gold Reserve unattractive to Canadian authorities. Consequently, in amending *the Bank of Canada Act* in 1954,[157] the Gold Reserve requirement was made subject to section 25 of the *Currency, Mint and Exchange Fund Act* of 1952, which had obviated the Gold Reserve requirement "unless the Governor in Council otherwise prescribes." Safe to conclude that the combined effect of section 25 of the *Currency, Mint and Exchange Fund Act* of 1952 and section 10 of the *Bank of Canada Amendment Act, 1954* ended the Gold Reserve requirement in the absence of any contrary prescription by the Governor in Council. Whatever remained of the Gold Reserve requirement was finally removed from

151 SC 1946, c 53.
152 SC 1935, c 60, above note 143.
153 SC 1946, c 53, above note 151.
154 SC 1935, c 60, above note 143.
155 SC 1952, c 40.
156 SC 1934, c 24, above note 136.
157 *An Act to Amend the Bank of Canada Act*, SC 1953–54, c 33, s 10.

Canadian central banking as the Bank of Canada Acts contained in the 1970[158] and 1985[159] Revised Statutes of Canada made no mention of Gold Reserve provisions.

At present, under section 3(1) of the *Currency Act*,[160] "[t]he monetary unit of Canada is the dollar." The dollar must be taken to be "the currency of Canada" under which coins and notes are to be issued.[161] Subject to limitations as to what denominations can be used in payment of various sizes, under section 8(1), "a tender of payment of money is a legal tender if made" in coins and notes "that are current." Current coins and notes are those respectively issued by Royal Canadian Mint and the Bank of Canada.[162] The Governor in Council's power to authorize the issue, characteristics, and design of circulating coins is governed by sections 6.4–6.6 of the *Royal Canadian Mint Act*.[163] For its part, under section 25(1) of the *Bank of Canada Act*,[164] the Bank of Canada "has the sole right to issue notes and those notes shall be a first charge on the assets of the Bank." "Notes" are defined in section 1 to mean "notes intended for circulation in Canada." Under section 25(6), "Notes of the Bank of Canada are neither promissory notes nor bills of exchange within the meaning of the *Bills of Exchange Act*."[165] Section 25 goes on to require the Bank of Canada to make adequate arrangements for the issue into and removal of circulation notes. It further provides that denominations shall be set, printed, and signed or otherwise executed as the Governor in Council by regulation determines. Form and material of the notes shall be subject to the minister's approval, "but each note shall be printed in both the English and French languages,"[166] that is, on that point there is no discretion.

Sections 12–16 of the *Currency Act*[167] provide for, and regulate the use of, the Canadian dollar, being the "currency of Canada," as the national money of account, whether on its own, or by reference to foreign currencies. Here are the principal provisions:

12 All public accounts established or maintained in Canada shall be in the currency of Canada, and any reference to money or monetary value

---

158 *Bank of Canada Act*, RSC 1970, c B-2.

159 *Bank of Canada Act*, RSC 1985, c B-2.

160 *Currency Act*, RSC 1985, c C-52.

161 Respectively, under ss 7(1), 7.1 of the *Currency Act, ibid*.

162 See *ibid*, ss 7, 7.1.

163 RSC 1985, c R-9.

164 RSC 1985, c B-2, above note 159.

165 *Ibid*, s 25(6).

166 *Ibid*, s 25(4).

167 RSC 1985, c C-52, above note 160.

in any indictment or other legal proceedings shall be stated in the currency of Canada.

13(1) Every contract, sale, payment, bill, note, instrument and security for money and every transaction, dealing, matter and thing relating to money or involving the payment of or the liability to pay money shall be made, executed, entered into, done or carried out in the currency of Canada, unless it is made, executed, entered into, done or carried out in

  (a) the currency of a country other than Canada; or

  (b) a unit of account that is defined in terms of the currencies of two or more countries.

14 Any sum mentioned in dollars and cents in the *Constitution Acts, 1867 to 1982* and in any Act of Parliament shall, unless it is otherwise expressed, be construed as being a sum in the currency of Canada.

15 Notwithstanding any other law, where any law of Canada or any treaty, convention, contract or agreement to which Canada is a party makes reference to

  (a) a currency of a country other than Canada,

  (b) a unit of account that is defined in terms of currencies of two or more countries,

  (c) gold, or

  (d) a combination of any of the things mentioned in paragraphs (a) to (c), the Governor in Council may make regulations specifying, or specifying the means or method of ascertaining, determining or calculating, the equivalent dollar value of that currency, unit of account, gold or combination thereof.

16 For the purposes of the administration, application and operation of the laws relating to the customs, the Governor in Council may make regulations specifying, or specifying the means or method of ascertaining, determining or calculating, the equivalent dollar value of currencies of countries other than Canada for a day or any other period or generally.

Part II of the *Currency Act*[168] establishes the Exchange Fund Account of which the purpose is stated in section 17(2) to be:

  (a) to aid in the control and protection of the external value of the monetary unit of Canada; and

  (b) to provide a source of liquidity for the Government of Canada.

---

168 *Ibid.*

Under section 17(1) the Exchange Fund Account is in the name of the minister. Section 17.1 confers on the minister a power which "[t]he Minister may not delegate" to "establish a policy concerning the investment of the assets held in the Exchange Fund Account."

Finally, in contrast to the banknote, but in line with the treatment of the topic elsewhere, "scriptural money," as opposed to its transfer which falls outside the present study,[169] has never been regulated in Canada by statute. As anywhere else, credit posted in an account with a commercial bank payable on demand gives rise to a debt owed by the bank to the depositor.[170] Such credit consists of currency deposited, transfers received, and credit extended. For their part, commercial banks keep accounts either with each other, or more typically, with the central bank. Deposits held with commercial banks are "commercial bank money." Commercial banks' deposits held with the central bank, together with "fiat money," is "central bank money." Commercial bank money is redeemable on demand in banknotes and coins.

Commercial banks lend out of their deposits. By owing both the depositors and borrowers, they create money. Accordingly, as a rule, under a fractional reserve system, the amount of commercial bank money is larger than the amount of the amount of central bank money. This means that the system operates on the assumption that at any given time demand by customers – both the original depositors and borrowers – for banknotes and coins from their commercial bank will be satisfied by the amount of central bank money available to that commercial bank. A safety net consisting of the central bank acting as a "lender of last resort," public deposit insurance, and special bankruptcy or "resolution" framework, together with a sophisticated network of prudential regulation and supervision, are designed to remedy or even avoid a situation. In principle, the sum of commercial bank money is a derivative of the sum of central bank money; the former manipulated by the central bank's power to set interest rates through the sale of government securities to banks and/or lending to banks, primarily with the view of achieving price stability.[171]

---

169 For which see in Canada particularly *Canadian Payments Act*, RSC 1985, c C-21.

170 *Foley v Hill* (1848) 2 HLC 28, 9 ER 1002 (HL).

171 See e.g., Michael McLeay, Amar Radia, and Ryland Thomas, "Money in the modern economy: an introduction" (*Bank of England*, Quarterly Bulletin 2014 Q1) at 4, online: https://www.bankofengland.co.uk/quarterly-bulletin/2014/q1/money-in-the-modern-economy-an-introduction, accessed 2 August 2024; Michael McLeay, Amar Radia, and Ryland Thomas, "Money creation in the modern economy" (*Bank of England*, Quarterly Bulletin 2014 Q1) at 14, online: https://www.bankofengland.co.uk/quarterly-bulletin/2014/q1/money-creation-in-the-modern-economy, accessed 27 May 2024; see also B Friedman, "The Future of Monetary Policy: The Central Bank

VII.   CONCLUSION

Key recurring themes throughout the monetary history of Canada have been the relationship between money and gold; multiplicity of currencies; uniformity of money; the respective role if any of government and private banks in making and distributing money; and finally, the role, if any, for non-bank private money. Until not long ago, fundamental issues underlying each of these themes seemed to have been settled. As will be seen in ensuing chapters, to some degree or another, the ongoing digital revolution has challenged the prevailing consensus around most of the above themes. Whether lessons learned from history can guide policy makers in the resolution of issues arising in the digital age will be assessed in chapter 8.

---

as an Army with Only a Signal Corps?" (1999) 2(3) *International Finance* 261; for an overview see also Warren Coats, "Econ 101: The Value of Money" (*Warren's Space*, 6 June 2022), online: https://wcoats.blog/2022/06/06/econ-101-the-value-of-money%EF%BF%BC/#content, accessed 27 May 2024.

chapter three

PAPER MONEY: CURRENCY AND BANKNOTES

SYNOPSIS

Banknotes are in the form of promissory notes payable to bearer on demand issued by banks that circulate in the discharge of debts. They go back to seventeenth century England where goldsmiths privately issued notes both as receipts to depositors of coins and as loans. Goldsmiths held their own deposits at the Bank of England that gradually took over the power to issue banknotes that were given legal tender status and over the years became inconvertible. The English banking and monetary system served as a model in Canada. Principal legal issues in relation to banknotes are the discharging effect of convertible banknotes and whether inconvertible banknotes are "promissory notes" governed by the Bills of Exchange Act. *On the second question Parliament of Canada departed from the common law position (still in force in the United Kingdom) and gave a negative answer. This, however, does not exclude principles of law governing negotiable instruments from applying to notes issued by the Bank of Canada.*

SUMMARY OF CONTENTS

I. INTRODUCTION

It goes without saying that paper money is more convenient to handle than coined money even if this is only so because it weighs less and thus is more easily carried. Since it lacks intrinsic value, to be accepted in a given society, its use must be supported by the strength of and/or confidence in its issuer. Today, paper money is issued predominantly, if not exclusively, by a central bank and is not convertible to precious metal. The confidence required for its acceptability is in the control of its amount under the monetary policy of the issuing central bank. Historically, when paper money consisted of a written enforceable obligation to pay in valuable metal, the confidence had to be placed in the ability of the issuer to honour its obligation. This covered both the issuer's reputation and resources.

In his monumental classic work on the wealth of nations, Adam Smith spoke very favourably of convertible paper money. In his view,

> The substitution of paper in the room of gold and silver money, replaces a very expensive instrument of commerce with one much less costly, and sometimes equally convenient. Circulation comes to be carried by a new wheel, which it costs less both to erect and to maintain than the old one.[1]

Having recognized that paper money may increase the money supplied, he was further cognizant of the fact that the power to issue paper money is not unlimited; that is, an issuer is to maintain a metallic reserve adequate to meet a reasonable demand for conversion; any additional paper would require 100 percent reserve.[2] However, he added, "[t]he whole paper money of every kind which can easily circulate in any country never can exceed the value of the gold and silver of which it supplies the place."[3]

---

1   Adam Smith, *The Wealth of Nations*, Edwin Cannan (ed) (University of Chicago Press, 1976) vol 1 at 309. As banknotes are less heavy than coins I am not sure why he says that, by comparison to metal, paper money is only "equally convenient" rather than "more convenient."

2   *Ibid* at 320, where Smith gives the following example: "suppose that all the paper of a particular bank which the circulation of the country can easily absorb and employ, amounts exactly to forty thousand pounds; and that for answering occasional demands, this bank is obliged to keep at all times in its coffers ten thousand pounds in gold and silver. Should this bank attempt to circulate forty-four thousand pounds ..." it "ought to keep at all times in its coffers, not eleven thousand pounds only, but fourteen thousand pounds."

3   *Ibid* at 318. I take Smith to mean that paper money does not increase monetary demand, but rather (together with anything else which is money, such as coins), satisfies it; Adam Smith's specific formulation on the point is, however, criticized by Henry Thornton, *An Enquiry into the Nature and Effects of the Paper Credit of Great Britain* (1802), Friedrich Hayek (ed) (AM Kelley, 1962) at 94–96, pointing out that having broadly defined paper money to include bills of

Adam Smith recognized that "[t]here are several different sorts of paper money"; at the same time, he acknowledged that "the circulating notes of banks and bankers are the species which is best known, and which seems best adapted" to substitute and "have the same currency as gold and silver money."[4] This has been confirmed by history; particularly with the global ascent of central banking, the banknote came to dominate. Over the years, throughout the world, banknotes have become predominantly, or even almost exclusively, inconvertible.[5]

In its form a banknote is a promissory note made by a bank, payable to bearer on demand, and intended to circulate as money.[6] This is true even where it is merely denominated in a specific sum of money without an express promise to pay it.[7] As a rule, it neither bears interest[8] nor states a due date, and certainly is never made payable to a particular person or order. It is transferrable from one person to another by delivery; as such the banknote is a negotiable instrument,[9] passing from hand to hand free from claims and defences. For its part, any instrument payable to bearer on demand that is intended to circulate as money, whether it is issued by a bank or another type of issuer, including the government, is a currency note. "Currency note" is thus a broader term, which includes but is not limited to the banknote, which nevertheless is the primary category of the currency note.

---

exchange payable in a future date, Adam Smith should have taken into account the different speed of circulation between such instruments and banknotes payable to bearer.

4   Smith, above note 1 at 310.

5   But *cf* banknotes payable in banknotes of another currency. Such are Scottish banknotes, payable in pound sterling, which are not legal tender, see, below note 41. Also banknotes in a domestic currency pegged to another (foreign) currency, which themselves may be legal tender, may (albeit not necessarily) be payable in (namely, redeemable to) the (foreign) currency to which the banknotes are pegged. See e.g., WL Coats, "The Central Bank of Bosnia and Herzegovina: Its History and Its Issues" in Mario I Blejer and Marko Škreb (eds), *Central Banking, Monetary Policies, and the Implications for Transition Economies* (Kluwer Academic Publishers, 1999) at 367, 395–96.

6   Jonathan M Phillips, Richard Hanke, and Ian Higgins (eds), *Byles on Bills of Exchange*, 30th ed (Sweet & Maxwell, 2020) at 394.

7   See e.g., *Banco de Portugal v Waterlow and Sons Ltd* [1932] AC 452 487 (HL).

8   As such its holder "makes haste to part with it" so that it circulates better than the interest bearing bill of exchange payable in a specific future date. See Thornton, above note 3 at 93.

9   See e.g., David AL Smout, *Chalmers on Bills of Exchange*, 13th ed (Stevens & Sons 1964) at 274; Arthur W Rogers, *Falconbridge on Banking and Bills of Exchange*, 7th ed (Canada Law Book, 1969) at 127; Charles Proctor, *Mann and Proctor on the Law of Money*, 8th ed (Oxford University Press, 2022) at 24–25; subsequent editions of *Chalmers* and *Falconbridge*, which are in fact successors rather than new editions of the above works, do not have parallel discussions; a leading case is *Banco de Portugal*, above note 7 at 483, 487 (and as to the promise, see also 478, 480).

Historically currency notes were issued either against full or fractional metallic reserve. Originally, they were convertible to specie. They were issued either by governments or commercial banks. At present, a banknote is usually issued by the central bank,[10] which is deemed to be liable on it; however, the banknote may be made by statute the obligation of the state itself.[11] Either way it is typically inconvertible.

In Canada, as discussed in more detail in chapter 2, prior to the establishment of a central bank in 1934, paper money consisted of both banknotes, intended for circulation and issued by the chartered banks, and Dominion Notes issued by the Government of Canada.[12] Coins and Dominion Notes, but not banknotes, constituted legal tender.[13] Dominion Notes and banknotes carried a payment promise.[14] Dominion Notes were "redeemable in gold," with "gold" being defined as "gold coins which are a legal tender in Canada" and "gold bullion in bars," each stamped by a minting authority in the United Kingdom, Canada, Australia, or the United States.[15] Banknotes

10   But *cf* the position in Hong Kong, where banknotes are issued by designated commercial banks against certificates of indebtedness denominated in foreign currency issued to those banks by a currency board against payment of the amount in the foreign currency. See Joseph Yam, "Review of Currency Board Arrangements in Hong Kong" (Monetary Authority of Hong Kong, 5 December 1998) at 30, online: https://www.hkma.gov.hk/media/eng/publication-and-research /reference-materials/monetary/rcbahke.pdf, accessed 7 June 2024.

11   For example, *Federal Reserve Act*, Pub L No 63-43, § 16(1), 38 Stat 251 at 265 (1913) (codified as amended at 12 USC § 226) provides that Federal Reserve notes "shall be the obligations of the United States. ... They shall be redeemed in lawful money on demand at the Treasury Department of the United States, in the city of Washington, District of Columbia, or at any Federal Reserve bank." They are legal tender under the *Coinage Act*, Pub L No 89-81, § 31, 79 Stat 254 (1965); the abolition of convertibility goes back to the *Gold Reserve Act*, Pub L No 73-87, § 6, 48 Stat 337, 340-341 (1934). Thereunder, "Except to the extent permitted in regulations ... no currency of the United States shall be redeemed in gold." Such regulations have not been issued; they may be issued by the secretary of the treasury and require approval by the president.

12   See Muharem Kianieff, "Private Banknotes in Canada from 1867 (and Before) to 1950" (2004) 30 *Queen's Law Journal* 400. For a concise history of the Canadian paper money, see *Bank of Canada v Bank of Montreal* (1977) [1978] 1 SCR 1148, 1166–68 (per Beetz J), 1156–57 (per Laskin CJC), 1977 CanLII 36 (SCC); for banknotes in Canada under present law, see Bradley Crawford et al, *The Law of Banking and Payment in Canada*, vol III (Canada Law Book, 2008) §35:10.30(2).

13   See John D Falconbridge, *Banking and Bills of Exchange*, 5th ed (Canada Law Book Company, 1935) at 141–42. I specifically cite an edition written at the time such notes were valid; *Bank Act*, RSC 1927, c 12, ss 61–74; *Dominion Notes Act*, RSC 1927, c 41; *Currency Act*, RSC 1927, c 40.

14   This was noted by Laskin CJC in *Bank of Canada v Bank of Montreal*, above note 12 at 1156–1157; Banknotes were "payable to bearer on demand," *Bank Act, ibid*, s 61; the form of Dominion Notes "shall be ... as the Minister [of Finance] directs," *Dominion Notes Act, ibid*, s 4.

15   *Dominion Notes Act, ibid*, ss 4(3), 2(b). An earlier Act provided that Dominion Notes were redeemable "*in specie*," that is, in coin or bullion, see *An Act Respecting Dominion Notes*, RSC 1906, c 27, ss 4(2), 2(a).

were payable in coin,[16] and under some circumstances in Dominion Notes.[17] At present notes intended for circulation are issued exclusively by the Bank of Canada and are not redeemable; rather, they are payable in, exchangeable with, or redeemable by other such banknotes.

This chapter is designed to illuminate the legal features of the banknote in historical perspective and is yet also of contemporary importance. First, the body of law governing private law aspects of the inconvertible banknote is still to be identified. More important, as will be explored in subsequent chapters, digital coins may be circulating e-notes; if so, ghosts from the past will haunt us, forcing the determination once for all the juridical nature of the banknote in general, and payment by convertible currency note in particular.

II. A BRIEF HISTORICAL OUTLINE: A GLOBAL PERSPECTIVE[18]

The invention of paper money is attributed to the Chinese. Marco Polo reported to Europe on this invention in the course of the thirteenth century; accordingly, Davies singles out paper money as the only possible exception to the lack of Chinese direct influence on Western monetary history.[19] This lack of direct Chinese influence, from which paper money is excepted, is attributed to the lack of contact between the two civilizations until the modern era.[20] Pursuant to Toynbee, the feasibility of paper money is thus "associated with the two Sinic inventions of paper and printing" that culminated in the issue of paper money by the Sung Government in 970 CE.[21]

There are variations on some details of this account of the Chinese paper money. Goldstein traces the origins of paper money to receipts issued by merchants around 995 CE in Sichuan capital Chengdu. The receipts were for deposited heavy iron coins, which ended up circulating in discharge of payment obligations. The use of such receipts inspired the issuance and use of merchants' IOU documents in payment transactions. In the course of the thirteenth century, Koublai Khan imposed paper money, originally

---

16   Like any other payment governed by the *Currency Act*, above note 13.

17   *Bank Act*, above note 13, s 71.

18   The specific Canadian perspective is addressed in chapter 2.

19   This lack of direct Chinese influence, from which paper money is excepted, is attributed to the lack of contact between the two civilizations until the modern era. Glyn Davies, *A History of Money From Ancient Times to the Present Day*, 3d ed (University of Wales Press, 2002) at 55–58, 178–84.

20   Glyn Davies, *A History of Money From Ancient Times to the Present Day*, 3d ed (University of Wales Press, 2002) at 55–58, 178–84.

21   AJ Toynbee, *A Study of History: Abridgement of Volumes VII–X by DC Somervell* (Oxford University Press, 1957) at 62.

redeemable, and subsequently wholly fiduciary. However, experimentation was brought to end by the middle of the fifteenth century following the reign of Hongwu Emperor, founder of the Ming Dynasty, who in the second half of the fourteenth century endeavoured to abolish economic reforms introduced by the Mongolians.[22]

According to Eagleton and Williams, during the Song dynasty (960–1279 CE), the facilitation of inter-regional trade and the heavy weight of iron coins in China prompted the private issue and countrywide circulation of short-term (time-limited) "certificates of accounts" or "exchange notes." In 1189 CE the Jin issued circulating official exchange certificates with no expiration date. During the Mongol Yuan dynasty (1206–1367 CE) paper money was used exclusively, as the circulation of gold, silver, and copper coins was prohibited. Paper money was successfully forced by the Mongols into Korea but not into Iran.[23] Nonetheless, Davies opines that "the most celebrated experiment, which brought knowledge of the Chinese system much closer to the West, was that in the kingdom of Persia in 1294." Its experiment in the city of Tabriz lasted only two months and was "a complete disaster." At the same time, this was "the first recorded instance of block printing outside China" of which the West possibly learned.[24]

In the western hemisphere the first publicly issued currency notes, intended to circulate as money, were issued toward the end of the seventeenth century by colonies in North America.[25] William Scott speaks of "bills of credit issued [by colonial governments] issued in a form suitable for circulation as money."[26] In part this was motivated by the need to inject liquidity into a system that starved for coined money that came from Europe. As well this was a means for governmental borrowing particularly to finance wars. Army Bills of Credit issued in Canada during the War of 1812 with the United States is a good example. For its part, the paper United States dollar was issued as an inconvertible currency note under the *Legal Tender Act* of February 1862[27] during the United States Civil War.[28]

22   Jacob Goldstein, *Money: The True Story of a Made-Up Thing* (Hachette Books, 2020) at 14–23.

23   Catherine Eagleton et al, *Money: A History*, 2d ed (British Museum Press, 2007) at 149–50. According to Marco Polo (as quoted, *ibid* at 149), worn out notes issued during the Mongol Yuan dynasty could be replaced by holders at the mint for new ones at a discount of 3 percent.

24   Davies, above note 19 at 183; see also 178–84 (for his own account of the Chinese history).

25   According to John Kenneth Galbraith, *Money Whence it Came, Where it Went* (Bantam Books, 1976) at 62, "The first issue of paper money was by the Massachusetts Bay Colony in 1690." For a recent learned study see Katie A. Moore, *Promise to Pay* (University of Chicago Press, 2024).

26   William A Scott, *Money and Banking*, 5th ed (Bell & Sons, 1915) at 152–53.

27   *Legal Tender Act*, Pub L No 37-33, 12 Stat 345 (1862).

28   Davies, above note 19 at 488.

Ultimately, the universal use of currency notes evolved as part of the enhancement of the banking system. In this context, the emergence of paper money in Europe goes back to tentative endeavours of the seventeenth century continental public banks.[29] Overall they were not banks of issue. Nevertheless, a few exceptions existed. For example, Neapolitan, Sicilian, and Genoese banks issued a transferable credit instrument, called *fede di credito*, which was akin to a certificate of deposit or bank draft. This document did not freely circulate; rather, it was transferred by delivery accompanied by the signature of the payee authenticated by a notary, which was an awkward procedure designed to prevent fraud.[30] For its part, the Bank of Amsterdam issued to depositors receipts transferable by endorsement and ultimately payable to bearer so as to be "only a short distance [from] the creation of bank-notes."[31]

Europe's first freely circulating banknotes were issued in the middle of the seventeenth century by the public bank in Sweden.[32] Its "notes were partly certified cheques" drawn on it, "partly a sort of certificates of deposits." However, the note-issue was "against the wishes of [its] leaders ... and had never acquired any importance."[33]

It is to the circulating banknote system that hit roots in England during the second half of the seventeenth century that we can trace our modern monetary system. At its inception the system involved the private issue of banknotes. Thus, in post-Medieval England, goldsmiths, the forerunners of modern commercial bankers, issued notes either against the deposit of coined money or by way of loans made out of such deposits. Holders of such

29   For these banks see JG van Dillen (ed), *History of the Principal Public Banks* (Frank Cass & Co, 1964).

30   Raymond De Roover, "New Interpretations of the History of Banking" in Julius Kirshner (ed), *Business, Banking, and Economic Thought in Late Medieval and Early Modern Europe: Selected Studies of Raymond De* Roover (University of Chicago Press, 1974) at 224–25. Since the issuer was the bank itself and not the customer, this was more of a bank draft or cashier's cheque than a certified cheque, as proposed by De Roover.

31   Peter Spufford, "Access to Credit and Capital in the Commercial Centres of Europe" in Karl Davids and Jan Lucassen (eds), *A Miracle Mirrored: The Dutch Republic in European Perspective* (Cambridge University Press, 1995) at 303, 307.

32   Eagleton et al, above note 23 at 179; for more detail, see I Wiséhn, "Sweden's Stockholm Banco and the first European banknotes" in Virginia H Hewitt (ed), *The Banker's Art: Studies in Paper Money* (British Museum Press, 1995) at 12.

33   EF Heckscher, "The Bank of Sweden" in van Dillen, above note 29 at 178. Nonetheless, these notes were "Europe's first freely circulating banknotes." See Eagleton et al, above note 23 at 179.

notes used them to pay their creditors who either cashed them or paid them in discharge of their own debts.[34]

Some designers of the Bank of England wanted notes issued by it to circulate as money.[35] However, neither the Act of Parliament nor the Charter conferred upon the Bank an explicit note issuing power.[36] Nonetheless, the Bank of England modelled its banking operations on those of the goldsmiths,[37] and shortly after its establishment, began to issue to depositors, "probably to a very considerable extent,"[38] notes payable to bearer, similar to those of the goldsmith.[39]

Once introduced, the Bank of England notes competed successfully with goldsmith notes and finally superseded them as paper money.[40] "That the new institution did provide circulating notes and did not become bankrupt is a matter of history."[41] At present in the United Kingdom, albeit exclusively against a full reserve with the Bank of England, only commercial banks in Scotland and Northern Ireland are endowed with the right to issue banknotes,[42] which are not equipped with a legal lender status. At the same time,

34 See in general Benjamin Geva, *The Payment Order of Antiquity and the Middle Ages: A Legal History* (Hart Publishing, 2011) at 467–84.

35 James M Holden, *The History of Negotiable Instruments in English Law* (Gaunt & Sons, 1993) at 88.

36 *Bank of England Act, 1694* (UK), 5 & 6 Will & Mary, c 20, s XIX, provided in s XXIX for the Bank's power to issue formal notes under seal. "These notes were used for making payments to the Exchequer from the Bank. The Exchequer then paid them out to the government's creditors, but they never seem to have become a popular form of currency," Holden, above note 35 at 89; the silence of the statute as to the bank's power to issue circulating notes is explained by Albert Feavearyear, *The Pound Sterling: A History of English Money* (EV Morgan (ed)), 2d ed (Clarendon Press, 1963), by the strong opposition to that power, and the promoters' scheme to defuse this opposition by avoiding attention to their intention as to make the Bank a bank of circulation and issue, and not merely a bank of deposit. See Feavearyear, *ibid* at 126.

37 William Holdsworth, *A History of English Law*, 2d ed (Sweet & Maxwell 1937), vol 8 at 188.

38 *Bank of England v Anderson* (1837) 3 Bing 589 at 654; 132 ER 538 at 562 (Tindal CJ).

39 Holden, above note 35 at 89–90. Originally, such notes were of two types. Notes of the first type contained a promise to pay the whole of a deposit, or some irregular sum. Notes of the second type contained a promise to pay a round sum. "The note for a round sum soon became popular and gradually ousted that for an irregular amount." *ibid* at 89; see in general Richard D Richards, *The Early History of Banking in England* (AM Kelley, 1965) at 153.

40 Holden, above note 35 at 92.

41 *Ibid* at 92.

42 Such banknotes may circulate also in England. See Holden, above note 35 at 278 note 3; non-circulating £1 million and £100 million banknotes issued by the Bank of England, called Giants and Titans, back the issues of Scottish and Northern Irish issuing banks, see Bank of England, "Scottish and Northern Ireland Banknotes" (*Bank of England*), online: https://www.bankofengland.co.uk/banknotes/scottish-and-northern-ireland-banknotes, accessed 9 June 2024; in Scotland, the issue of banknotes is regulated by the *Bank Notes (Scotland) Act, 1845* (UK), 8 & 9 Vict, c 38. Under its s 5, "[a]ll bank notes to be issued or re-issued in Scotland shall be expressed to be for payment of a sum in pounds sterling, without any fractional parts of a pound. ... " Scottish banknotes are not legal tender even in Scotland and are

after some judicial hesitation,[43] notes of the Bank of England were made legal tender by statute, the relevant provision being section 6 of the *Bank of England Act, 1833*.[44] Subsequently, payment in Bank of England notes was held to be as good as "payment … in gold"[45] so as to provide the giver with the comfort of an absolute discharge, as well as to furnish the taker with a default-free instrument. Convertibility ended after the First World War.[46] Today, Bank of England notes are legal tender in England and Wales under the *Currency and Bank Notes Act, 1954*.[47] While section 1(3) of that Act[48] provides that notes issued by the Bank of England "shall be payable" at the Bank, such payment can be made in the Bank's own notes.[49]

convertible to pound sterling. But *cf* Scottish Banknotes (Acceptability in United Kingdom) HC Bill (2008–2009) [16], online: http://www.publications.parliament.uk/pa/cm200809/cm-bills/016/09016.1-i.html, accessed 9 June 2024, under whose s 1, other than when forgery is suspected, "a business must not make any distinction between Scottish and other banknotes issued in the United Kingdom in terms of acceptability as payment for goods and services."; see HM Treasury, "Banknote issue arrangements in Scotland and Northern Ireland" (HM Treasury Consultation Document, July 2005), online: http://webarchive.nationalarchives.gov.uk/+/http://www.hm-treasury.gov.uk/consultations_and_legislation/banknote_issue_arrange-ments/banknote_issue_arrangements_index.Cfm, accessed 9 June 2024. For the legal nature of such banknotes, as promissory notes and otherwise, see *Clydesdale Bank v The Commission-ers for her Majesty's Revenue & Customs* [2019] UKFTT 0419 (TC).

43 In *Wright v Reed* (1790) 3 TR 554, 100 ER 729, Ashurt J thought that notes issued by the Bank of England "are money to *all* intents" (emphasis added). But Lord Kenyon CJ understood *Miller v Race* (1758) 1 Burr 452, 97 ER 398, to hold that these notes "are considered as money to many purposes." Buller J was inclined to support Ashurt J, but ultimately sided with the chief justice. Acknowledging that "banknotes pass in the world as cash," he nonetheless stressed that "[t]his Court has never yet determined that a tender of banknotes is at all events a good tender."; in *Ex parte Imeson* (1815) 2 Rose's Bkcy Cas 225, instruments payable in "Bank of England Notes" were held not to be payable in "money" within the meaning of a statute governing promissory notes.

44 (UK), 3 & 4 Will IV, c 98. More accurately, the statute made the Bank's notes legal tender in England and Wales for all payments (except for by the Bank itself) over five pounds. See Holden, above note 35 at 196.

45 *Currie v Misa* (1875) 10 LR Exch 153, 164 (Ex Ct); see also *The Guardians of the Poor of the Lichfield Union v Greene* (1857) 26 LJ Ex 140 at 142; 156 ER 1459 at 1461–62.

46 Holden, above note 35 at 279. Relevant statutes are the *Gold Standard Act, 1925* (UK), 15 & 16 Geo V, c 29; and *Gold Standard (Amendment) Act, 1931* (UK), 21 & 22 Geo V, c 46.

47 (UK) 2 & 3 Eliz II, c 12, s 1(2) that goes on to state that "such notes of denominations of less than five pounds shall be legal tender in Scotland and Northern Ireland." However, no such notes are currently in circulation; at present, the lowest denomination for a bank-note issued by the Bank of England is five pounds. See online: https://www.google.com/search?q=what+are+the+denominations+of+notes+issued+by+the+bank+of+england&ie=UTF-8&oe=UTF-8&hl=en-ca&client=safari, accessed 11 June 2024.

48 *Ibid*, s 1(3).

49 Proctor, above note 9 at 25 footnote 135.

The monetary nature of private convertible banknotes has been addressed in England in a few judgments delivered by Holt CJ followed by Lord Mansfield between late seventeenth and mid-eighteenth centuries.

In *Tassell and Lee v Lewis* (1695), Holt CJ acknowledged that "[t]he notes of goldsmiths ... are accounted among merchants as ready cash."[50] However, he went on to qualify this statement saying that as a matter of law, a "note is looked upon as ready money payable immediately"[51] and held that a creditor could refuse a tender of goldsmith's notes and insist on payment in metallic money.[52] The recognition of the banknote as a monetary object, subject to laws that govern coins goes to *Miller v Race* (1758)[53] where Lord Mansfield had the following to say on banknotes:[54]

> They are not goods, not securities, nor documents for debts, nor are so esteemed: but are treated as money, as cash, in the ordinary course and transaction of business, by the general consent of mankind; which gives them the credit and currency of money, to all intents and purposes. They are as much money, as guineas themselves are; or any other current coin, that is used in common payments, as money or cash.
>
> They pass by a will, which bequeaths all the testator's money or cash; and are never considered as securities for money, but as money itself. ... On payment of them, whenever a receipt is required, the receipts are always given as for money; not as for securities or notes.
>
> So on bankruptcies, they cannot be followed as identical and distinguishable from money: but are always considered as money or cash.

Being treated as "money" the banknote passes "in currency" freely from hand to hand, so that stolen money cannot be recovered from a taker in good faith and for value. Accordingly, an action to recover a banknote may lie against a finder, "but not after it has been paid away in currency."[55]

The codification of the law governing bills and notes by the *Bills of Exchange Act*, first in 1882 in the United Kingdom[56] and shortly thereafter in 1890 in Canada,[57] did not treat the currency note including the banknote as a

---

50   *Tassell and Lee v Lewis* (1695) 1 Ld Raym 743 at 744; 91 ER 1397 at 1398.

51   *Ibid.*

52   *Ibid.*

53   *Miller v Race*, above note 43.

54   *Ibid* at 457 (Burr), 401 (ER).

55   *Ibid* at 458 (Burr), 401 (ER).

56   *Bills of Exchange Act*, 1882 (UK), 45 & 46 Vict, c 61.

57   *An Act Relating to Bills of Exchange, Cheques, and Promissory Notes*, 1890 (UK), 53 Vict, c 33.

distinct category of negotiable instruments. Rather, being "an unconditional promise in writing made by one person to another person, signed by the maker, engaging to pay, on demand ... a sum certain in money ... to bearer," the currency note fell into the definition of "promissory note" under (present as well as former) section 176 in Canada. Prior to the establishment of the Bank of Canada, when "the issue of notes intended to circulate as money [was] the exclusive privilege of the Dominion government and of the Banks chartered under the Bank Act," Falconbridge made the following observations on the juridical nature of the banknote, which are taken to apply equally to currency notes issued by the government:[58]

> A bank note contains a contract which is ambulatory by reason of mere passing of it from hand to hand. It is also a thing which is in itself valued as money and currency. A material alteration will invalidate it, such an alteration including the alteration the number which does not in fact affect the contract or promise to pay.[59] But as a result of s. 145 of the Bills of Exchange Act, the alteration of a note, if it is not apparent, does not invalidate the note in the hands of a holder in due course so as to prevent his suing on it according to its original tenor.[60]
>
> Property in a banknote passes, like that in cash, by delivery; and the person taking it in good faith and for value is entitled to the property, although the note was stolen from a former owner.[61] The holder of a bank note is prima facie entitled to prompt payment from the bank.

If a promissory note embodies a promise to pay money and money is payable on a promissory note can the banknote be truly both? With respect

---

58 John Delatre Falconbridge, *The Law of Banks and Banking*, 4th ed (Canada Law Book, 1929) at 139.

59 *Suffel v Bank of England* (1882) 9 QBD 555, 567.

60 At present the corresponding provision in the *Bills of Exchange Act*, RSC 1985, c B-4 is s 144 stating that:

(1) Subject to subsection (2), where a bill or an acceptance is materially altered without the assent of all parties liable on the bill, the bill is voided, except as against a party who has himself made, authorized or assented to the alteration and subsequent endorsers.

(2) Where a bill has been materially altered, but the alteration is not apparent, and the bill is in the hands of a holder in due course, the holder may avail himself of the bill as if it had not been altered and may enforce payment of it according to its original tenor.

Elements which are stated to be "in particular" material alterations are stated in present s 145 (originally s 146) as to date, sum payable, time of payment, and place of payment. The list is, however, not exhaustive. For the application of provisions governing bills to notes see present (as well as former) s 186.

61 *Miller v Race*, above note 43 at 457–58 (Burr), 401 (ER).

to the convertible banknote, which is certainly promissory note, the question relates to its discharging effect as money. With respect to the non-convertible banknote, which is certainly money, the question is whether it is a promissory note subject to laws governing promissory notes. These two questions are discussed in turn in the following two parts of this chapter.

III. DISCHARGE BY PAYMENT IN A CONVERTIBLE BANKNOTE: CAN A PROMISSORY NOTE BE MONEY?

As long as a banknote contains a banker's enforceable obligation to pay "money" a question to be addressed is the availability to the payee/creditor of a recourse against the payer/debtor upon the default of the promising banker. Technically, the question is whether payment by banknote is absolute or conditional. In the former case the risk of banker's default falls on the payee/creditor. In the latter case the risk falls on the payer/debtor. The risk does not exist for inconvertible banknotes and effectively has not existed for banknotes issued by a body backed by the government, including a central bank.

Under the law of negotiable instruments, when a bill or note is given in payment, the payment may be either absolute – in full discharge of the debt – or conditional on the payment on the note. In each case, when the instrument is subsisting, rights on the transaction that gave rise to the instrument cannot be exercised. Upon dishonour, in the case of a conditional payment, the obligation on the underlying transaction revives, and the holder is free to exercise rights on both the transaction and the instrument.[62] Conversely, in case of absolute payment, the taking of the instrument is an absolute discharge of the underlying debt and the holder is left with remedies on the instrument alone. Stated otherwise, the conditional payment suspends rights on the underlying transactions[63] while the absolute payment discharges them altogether. Whether an instrument is taken in conditional or absolute payment of a debt depends on the intention of the parties. The default rule, that is, the presumed intention, is that of conditional payment.[64]

---

62 There is of course only one recovery, and yet, for example, a seller-holder may exercise vendor's lien on the sale and sue on the instrument for a price.

63 *Re Charge Card Services Ltd* (1988) 3 All ER 702 (CA); but *cf Currie*, above note 45 at 162–64, where Lush J endeavours, in my view unpersuasively, to distinguish between the conditional payment doctrine to an agreement to suspend remedies.

64 *Stedman v Gooch* (1793) 1 Esp 3 at 6; 170 ER 262 at 263 (Lord Kenyon); *Maillard v Duke of Argyle* (1863) 6 Man & G 40, 134 ER 801; see also *Gunn v Bolckow, Vaughan & Co* (1875) 10 LR Ch App 491 at 500–501 (Sir G Mellish LJ).

A question as to the scope of the conditional payment principle arises where the instrument issued in payment of a debt is one on which a third party, particularly a bank, and not the debtor, is the party liable on it. Does the conditional payment principle apply in this case as well? The drafters of the American Uniform Commercial Code (UCC) gave a negative answer. Having codified the conditional payment principle,[65] they carved an important exception to it. Thereunder, the conditional payment principle does not apply to payment by means of an instrument on which a bank is liable and on which there is no recourse against the debtor. Such instrument is the certified cheque or bank draft (or their equivalents); payment of a debt by it is presumed to be in an absolute discharge of the debt.[66]

In the absence of such a provision in Canada, I will endeavour to see if the common law roots of an absolute payment can be traced. Stated otherwise, having established the existence of the conditional payment principle, has the common law recognized an exception, as under the UCC, where the instrument taken in payment is one on which a bank is liable? Caselaw involving banknotes, or their predecessors, goldsmith notes, will now be examined.

In *Tassell and Lee* v *Lewis* (1695),[67] having recognized that "[t]he notes of goldsmiths (whether they be payable to order or to bearer) are always accounted among merchants as ready cash, and not as bills of exchange," Holt CJ went on to state that:

> The time of receiving money upon a goldsmith's note is ... immediately, or else it will be at the peril of him who has the note. He who delivers over the note will not be charged, if the goldsmith fail[s], as the drawer of a bill of exchange would be; but the receiver is supposed to give credit to the goldsmith, and the note is looked upon as ready money payable immediately; and if he does not like, he ought to refuse it; but having accepted it, it is at his peril. [But note, if the party to whom the note is delivered demands the money of the goldsmith in reasonable time, and he will not pay it, it will charge him who gave the note.]

Had it not been for the bracketed language Lord Holt CJ would have been taken to treat the goldsmith note as taken in absolute payment so as to preclude the payee-creditor (being "[he] who has the note" and "the re-

---

65 For its application under American common law prior to the UCC codification see e.g., cases cited by William Everett Britton, *Handbook on the Law of Bills and Notes*, 2d edn (West Publishing Co, 1961) at 638 footnote 1(a).

66 Uniform Commercial Code, s 3-802 (1978); Uniform Commercial Code, s 3-310 (2002).

67 *Tassell v Lewis*, above note 50 at 744 (Ld Raym), 1398 (ER).

ceiver") from recovering from the payer-debtor (being "he who delivers over the note"). This is, however, substantially qualified if not mostly reversed by the bracketed language; thereunder, upon the goldsmith's default recourse is available to the payee-creditor (being "the party to whom the note is delivered") against the payer-debtor (being the one "who gave the note") as long as the payee-creditor demanded payment from the defaulting goldsmith "in reasonable time." Stated otherwise, payment by goldsmith note is actually conditional, provided demand is made to the goldsmith in a timely manner. The option of circulating the goldsmith note – immediately, in reasonable time, or otherwise – was not addressed by Holt CJ.

In *Ward v Evans* (1702)[68] Holt CJ stated, in express defiance of the prevailing mercantile opinion,[69] that the acceptance of a goldsmith note "is not actual payment." This appears to confirm his earlier view and suggests that other than where a payee expressly elected to receive goldsmith notes instead of coined money,[70] Lord Holt viewed such acceptance as conditional payment so as to allow the payee-creditor to recover from the payer-debtor if the goldsmith fails. Nonetheless, in elaborating, he went on to address two distinct scenarios:[71]

> [First] taking a [goldsmith] note for goods sold [which] is a payment, because it was part of the original contract; [Second, taking] paper [which] is no payment where there is a precedent debt. For when such a note is given in payment, it is always intended to be taken under this condition, to be payment if the money be paid thereon in convenient time.

The distinction drawn in the first sentence is between payment made for a fresh contemporaneous consideration such as in exchange for goods and payment made in discharge of a past due debt. The acceptance of goldsmith notes is "payment," namely absolute payment, in the former case (present contemporaneous *quid pro quo*) but not in the latter (antecedent debt). Rather, as to the latter scenario, under the concluding sentence, a goldsmith note given "in payment" of an antecedent debt is "payment" only "if the money be *paid* thereon in convenient time," [emphasis added], presumably in response

---

68   (1702) 2 Ld Raym 928 at 930; 92 ER 120 at 121. Powell J delivered a concurring judgment.

69   That is, "notwithstanding the noise and cry, that it is the use of Lombard Street, as if the contrary opinion would blow up Lombard-Street." *ibid.*

70   A statement he explicitly made in another report of the same case: (1796) 12 Mod 521, 88 ER 1492.

71   See also another report of the same case: (1795) 3 Salk 118, 91 ER 726 at 727; two other reports address only the conditional payment option: [1738] Holt 120, 90 ER 965; (1795) 2 Salk 442, 91 ER 383 at 384.

to a timely demand for payment.[72] Recourse will be available to the payee/creditor against the payer/debtor only upon non-payment by the banker in response to a timely demand by the payee/creditor who holds the banknote.

Subsequent caselaw set the deadline for presentment to the goldsmith, beyond which risk of the goldsmith's default falls on the payee-holder-creditor (so as to turn the payment absolute) of an antecedent debt to the morning after the day of receipt.[73] In fact this was in line with Holt CJ's statements in other reports of *Ward v Evans*.[74] Arguably, this period meets Holt CJ's requirements as to acting "immediately,"[75] "in reasonable time"[76] and "in convenient time."[77] In any event, as discussed below, caselaw that ensued did not adhere to the strict next morning deadline and reverted to Holt CJ's more flexible "reasonable time" formulation.

Camidge v Allenby (1827)[78] was an action by a seller against the buyer for a pre-existing debt (that is, antecedent) arising from the past sale of corn. The buyer paid the debt by banknotes issued by a bank which, not to the knowledge of the parties, had already stopped payment. The action was dismissed albeit reasoning varied.

Justice Bayley was of the view that "[i]f the notes had been given to the [seller] at the time when the corn was sold, he could have had no remedy upon them against the [buyer]."[79] That is, the bad banknotes would have been paid in absolute payment against a contemporaneous consideration. This would have been so because "if [the seller] consented to receive the notes as money, they would have been taken by him at his peril."[80]

At the same time, he went on to say that:

> The rule as to all negotiable instruments is, that if they are taken in payment of a pre-existing debt, they operate as a discharge of that debt, *unless* the party who holds the instrument does all that the law requires to be done, in order to obtain payment of them.[81]

---

72   See James Steven Rogers, *The Early History of the Law of Bills and Notes* (Cambridge University Press, 1995) at 203.

73   *East India Co v Chitty* (1742) 2 Str 1175, 93 ER 1109; see *Manwaring v Harrison* (1722) 1 Str 508, 93 ER 666; see Holden, above note 35 at 110.

74   See [1738] Holt 120, 90 ER 965; (1795) 2 Salk 442, 91 ER 383 at 384.

75   *Tassell v Lewis*, above note 50 at 744 (Ld Raym), 1398 (ER).

76   *Ibid* at 743 (Ld Raym), 1398 (ER).

77   *Ward v Evans*, above note 69 at 930 (Ld Raym), 121 (ER).

78   (1827) 6 B&C 373, 108 ER 489.

79   *Ibid* at 381–82 (B&C), 492 (ER). In the facts of the case payment was made a few hours after the sale.

80   *Ibid* at 382 (B&C), 492 (ER).

81   *Ibid* at 382 (B&C), 492–93 (ER) (emphasis added).

Stated otherwise, once the holder "does all that the law requires to be done, in order to obtain payment of them" – *but does not get payment* – absolute discharge is lost and becomes conditional, so that the holder is able to have a recourse against the payer.

A simpler way to put it is to say that discharge for a banknote given for a pre-existing debt is *conditional* on payment by the bank in response to the holder's timely action. Stated otherwise, recourse from the payer/debtor is available to the payee/creditor only upon non-payment by the banker, notwithstanding the holder's timely action. Otherwise, in case of untimely action (followed by the banker's default), the holder bears the loss and has no recourse against the payer/debtor. As for the time and action, in Bayley J's view, a creditor holding instruments (not only banknotes) given in payment of a pre-existing debt "was not bound immediately to circulate them, or to send them into the bank for payment." Rather, "he was bound, within a reasonable time after he had received them, either to circulate them or to present them for payment," if only to allow the payer/debtor a chance to seek recourse against their own debtor, namely the banker. Upon the creditor/holder's failure to do so, recourse against the debtor/payer has been lost.[82]

Mentioning neither *Tassell v Lewis*[83] nor *Ward v Evans*[84] Bayley J effectively applied them while adding two clarifications. First, he clarified that Holt CJ's "condition" in *Ward v Evans*[85] as to actual timely payment must be taken to be in response to timely demand for payment.[86] Second, according to Bayley J, passing on the banknote in circulation, thereby obtaining actual payment for it, has the same effect as demanding payment from the issuing banker. That is, by making a timely demand for payment, or by circulating the banknote, the payee demonstrates lack of reliance on the banker's creditworthiness, so as to retain the right to recover from the payer upon the banker's default.[87]

The two other judges (Holroyd and Littledale JJ) repudiated altogether the distinction between payment for a pre-existing debt on one hand and for fresh consideration on the other. Having in effect agreed with Bayley J as to the seller's failure to comply with requirements under negotiable instruments law, Holroyd J thought, on the basis of *Miller v Race*,[88] that what

---

82 *Ibid* at 382 (B&C), 492–93 (ER).
83 *Tassell v Lewis*, above note 50.
84 *Ward v Evans*, above note 68.
85 *Ibid* at 930 (Ld Raym), 121 (ER).
86 *Camidge v Allenby*, above note 78 at 382 (B&C), 492–93 (ER).
87 Of course, in case of circulation recovery by the payee from the payer will be triggered only upon the payee becoming liable to their own payee.
88 *Miller v Race*, above note 43.

mattered was that the "notes were paid by the [buyer] and received by the [seller] as money" so as to "operate as payment." It is thus the delivery and receipt of the banknotes as "money" and not "negotiable instruments" that characterized the payment as *absolute*.[89] Littledale J agreed and added "that there is no guarantee implied by law in the party passing a note payable on demand to bearer, that the maker of the note is solvent at the time when it is so passed."[90]

Speaking for the court in *The Guardians of the Poor of the Lichfield Union v Greene* (1857)[91] Bramwell B cited *Miller v Race*[92] for the proposition that "a bank note is not to be considered, in all respects at least, as a bill of exchange or promissory note, payable at a distant date." Rather, he explained, banknotes are treated as money. He went on to consider *Camidge v Allenby* as containing "the existing law upon the subject" explaining that "In that case a distinction was taken between a payment by bank notes at the time of the sale or of the original transaction, and a payment by bank notes of a pre-existing debt." He nonetheless went on to acknowledge that in *Camidge v Allenby*[93] this was the opinion of Bayley J "whose opinion upon the subject is not expressed to be to the same extent as those of Holroyd J or Littledale J." Rather, both "seem to be of opinion that if country bank notes are paid and received as money in *any transaction* of *payment* and both parties be innocent, that it is payment."[94] There is no distinction between payment for a contemporaneous consideration and for a pre-existing debt; payment is absolute in each case.

At the same time, it is not entirely clear where things stand regarding the requirement of a quick action by the payee/holder/creditor to obtain payment either by presentment to the issuing bank or circulating the note. Assuming it doesn't matter if the note was paid for a pre-existing or contemporaneous debt, upon the default of the banker on the note, does a "diligent" creditor-holder have a recourse against the debtor who delivered the note?

Developments in the United States during the nineteenth century did not help to clarify matters.[95] Some cases adhered to the distinction between

89   *Camidge v Allenby*, above note 78 at 384 (B&C), 493 (ER).

90   *Ibid* at 385 (B&C), 494 (ER).

91   *Lichfield Union v Greene*, above note 45.

92   *Miller v Race*, above note 43.

93   *Camidge v Allenby*, above note 78.

94   *Lichfield Union v Greene*, above note 45 at 888–91 (H&N), 1461–62 (ER) (emphasis added).

95   For an exhaustive summary, against the background of the English precedents, on which the ensuing discussion draws, see James S. Rogers, "The New Old Law of Electronic Money" (2005) 58 *SMU L Rev* 1253 at 1287–1300.

contemporaneous and precedent debts and applied it to the payment by banknote.[96] However, it appears that not everybody was convinced by the logic of Lord Holt's distinction. As well, it is possible to speculate that the absence of any substitute in the form of central bank banknotes may have led some to aspire for a finality rule also for payment in paper. Be that as it may, some cases disregarded Lord Holt's distinction altogether, and opted for a final and absolute, namely unconditional and absolute, payment presumption. Among them, some held that this payment-finality presumption always applied.[97] Others created an exception with respect to banknotes of a bank that had failed by the time its banknotes were taken by the creditor.[98] In such a case of a failed bank, and only in such a case, the "conditional payment" principle was said to apply. For courts that did not adhere to Lord Holt's distinction, all of this was regardless of whether the note was taken for a precedent or a contemporaneous debt.[99] In the absence of a "conditional payment" principle, creditors taking banknotes had to rely exclusively on the creditworthiness of the banker liable on the instrument. At present, the "absolute payment" presumption, ultimately accorded by the American UCC to instruments on which a bank is liable,[100] is associated with payment instruments such as cashier's cheques, teller's cheques, and money orders, and not banknotes not to mention other currency notes.

Surely, where applied, the "conditional payment" principle accorded protection to a creditor receiving goldsmith notes. Nevertheless, even then protection was not full. To begin with, the contingency of a possible action against the debtor after payment in goldsmith's notes had been made rendered such notes less attractive to creditors than coined money. Only payment by coins led to a final and immediate discharge of the debt. Second, a debtor who had deposited their money with a goldsmith who later became insolvent might have lost a substantial sum of money upon this goldsmith's failure, so that, generally speaking, such a debtor was not a promising defendant in terms of their creditworthiness. Third, the creditor's remedy against the debtor was available only to the "diligent" creditor; it was lost where the creditor failed to make a timely demand for payment upon the goldsmith.

96   See e.g., *Corbit v Bank of Smyrna*, 2 Harr 235 (1837).

97   See e.g., *Scruggs v Gass*, 16 Tenn 175 (1835); see also *Lowrey v Murrell*, 2 Port 280 (1835).

98   The leading case is *Ontario Bank v Lightbody*, 13 Wend 101 (NY 1834).

99   In the United States, complication of the issue only progressed, as the line between precedent and contemporaneous debts became blurred. See e.g., *Hall v Stevens*, 22 NE 374 (NY 1889).

100 See above note 66. For the instruments listed in the ensuing text above, see UCC section 3-104.

Faced with the risk of a goldsmith's failure and not being adequately protected against it, a creditor could not be required to accept goldsmith notes as complete substitutes for coined money.

IV. THE INCONVERTIBLE BANKNOTE: CAN MONEY BE A PROMISSORY NOTE?

In Canada, the *Bills of Exchange Act*[101] is modelled on its English counterpart. Specifically, the definition it contains for a "promissory note" is cast in the image of its English precedent.[102] As well, similarly to England, banknotes circulating as money in Canada are issued by the central bank, being the Bank of Canada,[103] and are inconvertible[104] as well as have legal tender status.[105] Unsurprisingly, during the period they were stated to be payable to bearer on demand, the original position followed that which prevailed in England. It was thus thought that:

> [A] banknote, as regards its form and essential requirements, is simply the promissory note of a bank payable to bearer on demand, and its issue, transfer and discharge are governed by the provisions of the Bills of Exchange Act relating to a note payable to bearer on demand.[106]

Nonetheless, this proposition was not received well by courts in Canada. First, *Bank of Canada v Bank of Montreal* (1977)[107] challenged precedents supporting it[108] on the ground "that the banknotes they dealt with were the notes of [commercial] banks or were redeemable in gold or were not legal ten-

---

101 At present it is *Bills of Exchange Act*, RSC 1985, c B-4.

102 See s 176, *ibid*.

103 Under the *Bank of Canada Act*, SC 1934, c 43, s 24(1), in principle, "the sole right to issue notes payable to bearer on demand and intended for circulation in Canada" was vested in the Bank of Canada.

104 Under s 25 of the *Bank of Canada Act, ibid*, banknotes were convertible to gold, except that that the Governor in Council was authorized to suspend convertibility. Convertibility was abolished in 1966 (*An Act to Amend the Bank of Canada Act*, SC 1966-67, c 88, s 13), except that in fact it had never been practised, since the Governor in Council passed every year an Order in Council suspending convertibility for that year. For a brief historical account, see *Bank of Canada v Bank of Montreal*, above note 12 at 1167.

105 Under s 24(1) of the *Bank of Canada Act, ibid*.

106 See e.g., Arthur W Rogers, *Falconbridge*, above note 9 at 127.

107 *Bank of Canada v Bank of Montreal*, above note 12.

108 Such as *Suffell v Bank of England* (1882) 9 QBD 555 (CA); *Gillett v Bank of England* (1889) 6 TLR 9 (QBD); *Raphael v Bank of England* (1855) 17 CB 161, 139 ER 1030; *Hong Kong and Shanghai Banking Corp v Lo Lee Shi* [1928] AC 181 (PC); *The Queen v Brown* (1854) 8 NBR 13 (NBSC); and *Re Toronto Beaches Election, Ferguson v Murphy* (1943) CanLII 79 (Ont SC).

der."[109] As will be seen below, in the Supreme Court of Canada, the proposition was ultimately accepted, but not wholeheartedly, in fact by default, and not without a fight. Second, ultimately, the characterization of the banknote as a "promissory note" was specifically rejected by legislation. Thus, Parliament eliminated in 1967 the promissory language with respect to Bank of Canada notes intended for circulation.[110] Thereafter, in 1980 another amendment was passed, explicitly stating that a banknote issued by the Bank of Canada is not an instrument governed by the *Bills of Exchange Act*.[111] This is the present section 25(6) of the *Bank of Canada Act*,[112] stating that "[n]otes of the Bank are neither promissory notes nor bills of exchange within the meaning of the *Bills of Exchange Act*." The position in Canada is thus as under the UCC in the United States where under UCC section 3-102(a) Article 3 does not apply to money.

Objections to the characterization of the banknote as a "promissory note" under the *Bills of Exchange Act*, in England and elsewhere where similar legislation exists, will now be examined. Examination is undertaken with regard to such jurisdictions where they lack specific statutory provisions as in Canada. It will be carried out by reference to caselaw specifically dealing with inconvertible banknotes issued by a central bank which are legal tender.

Prior to *Bank of Canada v Bank of Montreal*, the legal nature of the inconvertible banknote was a focal point for the discussion by the House of

---

109 *Bank of Canada v Bank of Montreal*, above note 12 at 1175.

110 SC 1966-67, c 88, above note 104, s 12, amending the *Bank of Canada Act*, RSC 1952, c 13 (now RSC 1985, c B-2). The earlier provision (RSC 1952, c 13, s 21(1)) stated that "[o]n and after the day on which the Bank is authorized to commence business the Bank shall, except as provided in the Bank Act, have the sole right to issue notes *payable to bearer on demand* and intended for circulation in Canada and may, subject to Section 23, issue such notes to any amount; such notes shall be legal tender, and shall be the first charge upon the assets of the Bank." SC 1953-54, c 33, s 8, repealed this provision and substituted it with the following: "The Bank has the sole right to issue notes *payable to bearer on demand* and intended for circulation in Canada and such notes shall be a first charge upon the assets of the Bank." This was the statutory provision which governed *Bank of Canada v Bank of Montreal*, above note 12. Subsequently, the provision was repealed by SC 1966-67, c 88, s 12, and replaced by the following: "The Bank has the sole right to issue notes intended for circulation in Canada and those notes shall be a first charge on the assets of the Bank." Emphasis to the language of the 1952 and 1953 provisions is added. In the 1967 provision there is no corresponding language to that emphasized in those of 1952 and 1953. Similarly, Bank of Canada notes "payable to bearer on demand" and "intended for circulation in Canada" were legal tender under the *Currency, Mint and Exchange Fund Act*, RSC 1952, c 315, s 7(1)(c). The "payable bearer on demand" language was eliminated in *An Act to amend the Bank of Canada Act*, SC 1967-68, c 88, s 20(1)(c).

111 *Banks and Banking Law Revision Act*, SC 1980-83, c 40, s 49.

112 *Bank of Canada Act*, RSC 1985, c B-2.

Lords in *Banco de Portugal v Waterlow and Sons, Ltd* (1932).[113] The latter case involved a note that did not contain an explicit promise to pay.[114] It was an action by the Bank of Portugal against a firm of printers engaged by it to print a series of notes to be put into circulation in Portugal. Due to the printers' negligence, spurious notes[115] were put into circulation. The Bank of Portugal was forced to issue good notes in exchange for the spurious notes; any other course of action would have undermined public confidence in Portuguese paper currency.[116] The specific question to be determined was whether the Bank of Portugal was right in maintaining that the damage suffered by it was measured by the entire face value of the spurious notes.

In a 3:2 decision, the House of Lords held in the Bank of Portugal's favour. In determining the actual loss suffered by the Bank of Portugal, the Court had to assess the value of the Bank's engagement to the Bank itself. That is, the issue to be determined was the amount of loss suffered by the Bank by virtue of incurring liability on a banknote put into circulation. The judgments given reflect opposing views on the principal issue. Nevertheless, they seem to generate consensus as to the nature of the banknote in its holder's hands.

The majority judgments[117] were premised on the nature of the banknote as not merely a piece of paper. Rather, emphasis was put on the fact that banknotes circulate on the basis of the creditworthiness of their issuer. Such creditworthiness is maintained by public law restrictions designed to adjust their quantity to actual resources. In the normal course of events, nobody will receive from the issuing bank a banknote, except for valuable consideration.

Viscount Sankey LC thought that, irrespective of inconvertibility, "a bank of issue receives value for every note which it issues." This is so since in connection with "a managed currency" there is no "unlimited right to issue notes."[118] Lord Atkin was of a similar opinion: "In any civilized State [the central bank] will not be permitted to issue notes to an unlimited amount." Obligations embodied in paper money must correspond to possible resources: "the State will require that behind the promises to pay there stand solid resources in the form of gold and liquid securities." Accordingly, it "will im-

---

113 *Banco de Portugal*, above note 7.

114 The promise was read into the note anyway, *ibid* at 487 (Lord Atkin).

115 In general, a valid banknote is legitimately made from a genuine plate and bears genuine signatures of issuing officers. A banknote which either bears a forged signature or is not a legitimate impression from a genuine plate is spurious. See Bryan A Garner (ed), *Black's Law Dictionary*, 11th ed (Thomson Reuters, 2019) at 179.

116 *Banco de Portugal*, above note 7 at 471 (Viscount Sankey LC).

117 The majority consisted of Viscount Sankey LC, Lord Atkin, and Lord MacMillan.

118 *Banco de Portugal*, above note 7 at 477.

pose a positive restriction on the issue of notes beyond an amount which it considers necessary."[119] This is true where the note is payable in gold, and "has not [been] altered" by inconvertibility, except that, thereunder, the Bank's liability is to pay with its own notes on other legal tender, and not gold.[120] In the final analysis, by issuing its notes, the Bank, like a trader who issues a promise to pay a fixed sum, "issues a bit of its credit to that amount."[121]

The majority's conclusion is stated by Lord MacMillan:[122]

> [T]he Bank, being compelled to issue for nothing notes for which if it had issued them in ordinary course it would have received value corresponding to the purchasing power of the number of [monetary units] which they represented, has suffered loss to the extent of the face value of these notes.

On the other hand, the dissenting law lords[123] focused on the fact that the issuing bank's power to put paper money to circulation was unattached to specific gold reserves or collateral securities. Lord Warrington thought that, on every banknote, "the obligation incurred by the Bank is merely to pay in other currency which it has power to create." Accordingly, where the Bank elects to issue good notes in substitution of circulating spurious notes, "all it has to do is to take so many pieces of printed paper from its existing stock or to have further notes created should the existing stock be insufficient." Under such circumstances, "[i]n either case, the loss to the Bank is … confined to the expense of procuring the necessary paper and of printing the necessary number of notes."[124] Lord Russell spoke of a "windfall for the Bank" by the majority decision since no actual loss had been proven.[125]

The extremity of both positions was severely criticized. A more sensitive valuation of damages might have been called for.[126] Such valuation ought to have recognized that the gain to the holder to whom a replacement note is issued is not the same as the loss to the issuing bank. Indeed, for the former

---

119   *Ibid* at 487.
120   *Ibid* at 488.
121   *Ibid* at 489.
122   *Ibid* at 511.
123   These were Lord Warrington of Clyffe and Lord Russell of Killowen.
124   *Banco de Portugal*, above note 7 at 484.
125   *Ibid* at 502.
126   For an extensive critical discussion see e.g., Arthur Nussbaum, *Money in the Law National and International: A Comparative Study in the Borderline of Law and Economics* (Foundation Press, 1950) at 84–89, and sources cited there; see also J. Tillotson, "The Portuguese Bank Note Case: Legal, Economic and Financial Approaches to the Measure of Damages in Contract" (1994) 68 *Australian Law Journal* 93; for a favourable analysis, see Proctor, above note 9 at 29–31.

the gain is the face value of the instrument; for the latter, the loss is the result of the reduction in the amount of its future permissible issue,[127] as a matter of implementing its monetary policy,[128] for which it potentially stood to make a modest profit. "Hence, the inconvertible note in the hands of the bank has a potential value which is far below that of a circulating note and difficult to formulate in exact figures."[129] However, both parties navigated the litigation so as to avoid a middle course. This did not escape the attention of two law lords. Thus, in his dissent, Lord Russell explicitly stated that "[t]he Bank [made] no claim based on curtailment of their powers of issue."[130] Thus, in the absence of an argument on the curtailment of the Bank's powers of issue, the dissent assessed the loss to the Bank to be limited to printing and other incidental expenditure incurred by it upon the issue of replacement notes. For his part, speaking for the majority, Lord MacMillan lamented that the parties presented a choice between two extremes, with no middle course.[131] This limited choice might have pushed the majority to focus on the gain to the holder as the proper basis for assessing damages.

Much of the discussion evolved around the nature of the banknote as a promissory note. In his concurring majority judgment, Lord MacMillan understood the dissenting position to be that "[a] promissory note which is perpetually renewable has theoretically no value, because it is never payable."[132] He rejected this view altogether. Nevertheless, his theory on the nature of the banknote, which purported to refute the dissent, seems to reflect a universal consensus, not rejected at all by the dissent, on the nature of the holder's right on a banknote. Thus, "quite irrespective of convertibility":

> [A] note when issued by the Bank of Portugal becomes by the mere fact of its issue legal tender for the sum which it bears on its face. The issued note represents so much purchasing power in terms of commodities. It can be used by the holder of it to purchase at current prices any commodity in the market, including gold and securities. It can equally be used by the Bank to

---

127 Nussbaum, *ibid.*

128 Banknotes held by the public are part of the money supply, regulated by the central bank of the relevant country. Usually, compared to "commercial-bank money," the amount of banknotes and coins in circulation, responding to public demand, is small and thus, for simplicity, the amount of banknotes (and coins) in circulation is usually overlooked in the analysis of monetary policy.

129 Nussbaum, above note 127 at 86.

130 *Banco de Portugal*, above note 7 at 501.

131 *Ibid* at 507.

132 *Ibid* at 508.

purchase commodities, including gold and securities, or to discharge debts due by it. It must be accepted by the Bank in discharge of debts due to it.[133]

In fact, as already was pointed out, there was no disagreement among the law lords as to the nature of the issuing bank's engagement to the holder of a banknote in circulation. Speaking for the majority, Lord Atkin stated that, even without an express promise to pay stated in it, "[a] bank note is a promissory note issued by a bank payable on demand," so as to be read as if it contains a promise to pay.[134] This was also the opinion of the dissenting Lord Warrington, who regarded issued banknotes as "promissory notes payable to bearer on demand."[135] Both agreed that payment by the issuing bank may be made in other banknotes, in gold if convertibility was to be resumed, or in other currency if so decreed.[136]

No similar consensus on the characterization of the inconvertible banknote emerged from the subsequent decision of the Supreme Court of Canada in *Bank of Canada v Bank of Montreal*.[137] Rather, in that case, views varied as to the nature of the issuer's engagement and the holder's right on it. In connection with a fact situation occurring in 1959, the case dealt with a Bank of Canada note in its pre-1967 form, that is, a legal tender inconvertible banknote, expressly stated to be payable to bearer on demand, not yet excluded from the scope of the Canadian *Bills of Exchange Act*.[138]

The specific question dealt with in that case was whether the ex-holder of a Bank of Canada banknote destroyed by fire is entitled to obtain from the Bank of Canada a substitute banknote.[139] Indeed, by issuing a note in replacement, the issuing bank suffers no loss since, in theory, the destroyed note is deleted from the liabilities on its balance sheet, and the new note is printed under existing powers.[140] Perhaps as a matter of policy, the main issue is whether a central bank should be burdened with the duty to scrutinize claims for destroyed notes.[141] In any event, the question was determined primarily not as such, but rather as a derivative of a broader question, as to

---

133 *Ibid.*

134 *Ibid* at 487.

135 *Ibid* at 483.

136 *Ibid* at 483–84 (Lord Warrington), 488–89 (Lord Atkin).

137 *Bank of Canada v Bank of Montreal*, above note 12.

138 See above notes 105, 111 and text around them.

139 Relevant provisions of the Canadian *Bills of Exchange Act*, RSC 1970, c B-5 cited in the case were ss 10, 156, 157, and 176. They are now ss 9, 155, 156, and 176 (RSC 1985, c B-4). They correspond to the English *Bills of Exchange Act*, above note 55, ss 97(2), 69, 70, and 83.

140 FA Mann, "The Destroyed Banknote" (1977–78) 2 *Canada Business Law Journal* 471.

141 See Nussbaum, above note 127 at 82–83.

the characterization of a banknote. Thus, in the absence of specific provisions relating to destroyed banknotes, the principal issue was the application of the provisions in the *Bills of Exchange Act*[142] governing lost instruments. To fall under these provisions, the banknote must be a "promissory note" governed by the *Bills of Exchange Act*.[143]

In the Ontario Court of Appeal,[144] Brooke JA discussed the effect of the promissory language contained in the banknote. Taking into account inconvertibility to gold, he nevertheless held that "payment [of Bank of Canada notes] can be made in legal tender of money,"[145] that is, in coins or other banknotes.[146] Indeed, he acknowledged that a Bank of Canada note "has the additional characteristics of being a note intended for circulation ... and of being legal tender or money."[147] However, he preferred to stay in line with previous judicial and scholarly authority.[148] He thus held that notwithstanding such "special characteristics," the Bank of Canada note "is nevertheless essentially a promissory note within the meaning of the definition in the Bills of Exchange Act."[149]

A panel of the Supreme Court of Canada was evenly divided. Thus, in not dismissing the appeal, it affirmed it, albeit by default.[150] Supporting the conclusion of Brooke JA, Beetz J stressed that "with respect to negotiable instruments, form prevails over substance." Hence, the fact that "Parliament has decreed by statute that the notes of the Bank of Canada be in the form of promissory notes as defined by ... the *Bills of Exchange Act*" cannot be ignored."[151] On this basis, as well as on authority,[152] he had "no hesitation in agreeing ... that the ... bank-note under consideration is a promissory note."[153]

---

142 Now RSC 1985, c B-4, above note 101.

143 The relevant provisions are ss 69–70 (England) and 155–156 (then ss 156–157 of RSC 1970, c B-5 (Canada)), see above note 139. These provisions apply to promissory notes (and not only to bills of exchange) by virtue of s 89(1) in England and s 186(1) in Canada.

144 *Bank of Montreal v Bay Bus Terminal (North Bay) Ltd* [1972] OJ No 734, 30 DLR (3d) 24 (Ont CA).

145 *Ibid* at para 12.

146 This is "pursuant to the provisions of s. 7 of the Currency, Mint and Exchange Fund Act [above note 110]" *ibid*. Presently *Currency Act*, RSC 1985, c C-52, s 8.

147 *Bank of Montreal v Bay Bus Terminal*, above note 144 at para 7.

148 Authority is set out in the judgment, *ibid* at paras 8–9.

149 *Ibid* at para 11.

150 *Bank of Canada v Bank of Montreal*, above note 12. The judgment siding with the Court of Appeal was delivered by Beetz J, with whom Ritchie, Pigeon, and De Grandpré JJ concurred. The dissenting judgment was of Laskin CJC, with whom Martland, Judson and Dickson JJ concurred. In a 4:4 decision, the appeal was dismissed.

151 *Ibid* at 1169.

152 Set out *ibid* at 1170–76.

153 *Ibid* at 1176. Responding to the attempt to distinguish old authorities Beetz J stressed that many of the leading textbooks and treatises considering notes of central banks as promissory

A powerful dissent was given by Laskin CJC, who gave particular weight to the public nature of the statutory scheme governing the Bank of Canada notes in contrast with the private nature of the instruments governed by the *Bills of Exchange Act*.[154] In his opinion, a contention premised on literal interpretation and application of the *Bills of Exchange Act* overlooked this contrast.[155]

Chief Justice Laskin could not assign a great degree of importance to the promissory language contained in the Bank of Canada note. In his view, "the statutory declaration that the notes are legal tender, added to the fact that they have no convertibility into gold or anything else, is a more persuasive indication of their character than the inscription on [the notes] that they are payable to bearer on demand."[156] Thus:

> What is said to be an unconditional promise to pay a sum certain in money is itself money. The words on the face of the paper money, "will pay to the bearer on demand", cannot alter its character as money and turn it into a different document which calls for the payment of money.[157]

In contrast, "a promissory note, by definition, involves an unconditional promise to pay a sum certain in money, but it is not itself money."[158] Thus, he stated that the promissory note and the banknote are quite distinguishable:

> True, the obligation of a promissory note may be carried forward by a renewal note, but no matter how many renewals there be, or how many replacements under different terms, there is no liquidation of the debt until it is discharged, and this may be by money or money's worth or the debt may be forgiven. To say that a banknote of the kind involved here imports similar legal consequences, that a non-convertible bank note is paid off by the giving of a bank note of similar face value is to go around in a circle: legal tender is exchanged for legal tender; a different piece of paper, true, but indistinguishable in legal effect from the one surrendered for it.[159]

Regarding the promise contained in the Bank of Canada note as "sterile from the very beginning,"[160] he found *Banco de Portugal v Waterlow & Sons*,

---

notes "have been published or re-edited after the abandonment of convertibility and while such notes were legal tender." *Ibid* at 1176.

154 The two views are juxtapositioned by Guy David, "Money in Canadian Law" (1986) 65 *Canadian Bar Review* 192 at 207–08.

155 *Bank of Canada v Bank of Montreal*, above note 12 at 1152–56.

156 *Ibid* at 1156.

157 *Ibid* at 1154.

158 *Ibid* at 1156.

159 *Ibid* at 1156.

160 *Ibid* at 1157.

Ltd[161] to be "completely unpersuasive on the point in issue."[162] In his view, inasmuch as the liability on an inconvertible banknote can be satisfied by the tender of another banknote of the same nature and value, such liability is "unreal" and basically unenforceable:

> [A]ny holder who would sue in such a situation must surely have his claim rejected … and be required to pay costs, if not also to be told that he is engaged in a vexatious proceeding.[163]

Finally, Laskin CJC dismissed the reliance placed on the balance sheet treatment of banknotes by the Bank of Canada. As required by statute, banknotes appear on the liability side of the balance sheet and are "first charge upon the assets of the Bank."[164] Nevertheless, in his view, "a promissory note is not in any sense a charge upon the assets of the maker."[165] Furthermore, inasmuch as most assets of a central bank are government debts, realization is impossible.[166] In fact it is even expressly unpermitted, or at least severely restricted, by statute.[167]

---

161 *Banco de Portugal*, above note 7. See text around notes 116–21, above.

162 *Bank of Canada v Bank of Montreal*, above note 12 at 1157.

163 *Ibid* at 1158.

164 Section 21(1) of the *Bank of Canada Act*, RSC 1952, c 13 (now s 25(1), of the *Bank of Canada Act*, RSC 1985, above note 112).

165 *Bank of Canada v Bank of Montreal*, above note 12 at 1159. On that point, Laskin CJC may have gone too far, at least for a promissory note in general, as a matter of private law. Arguably, the theory of s 25(1) of the *Bank of Canada Act* is that the Bank's indebtedness on banknotes is secured by way of first charge on the assets of the Bank. This, indeed, can be quite consistent with indebtedness on a promissory note as well. However, Laskin CJC appears to be correct as to the banknote. Thus, according to Nussbaum, above note 127 at 79–80, the production of issued banknotes on the liability side of the balance sheet of a central bank is "for reasons of accounting." Furthermore, reserve requirements ought to be construed as public law instruments and "are ordinarily not generators of private rights."

166 *Bank of Montreal, ibid* at 1160. According to the most recent statutory standard form, being *Bank of Canada Act*, RSC 1985, c B-2, Schedule II (as repealed by *Financial Consumer Agency of Canada* Act, SC 2001, c 9, s 202), assets of the Bank of Canada fall into six categories: (1) gold coin and bullion; (2) deposits payable in foreign currency; (3) advances to the Government of Canada, to Provincial Governments, and to members of the Canadian Payments Association (depository financial institutions); (4) investments in Treasury Bills of Canada, other securities issued or guaranteed by Canada or a province, bonds and debentures issued by the Industrial Development Bank and other bills and investments; (5) Bank premises; and (6) all other assets. In practice, "[t]he Bank of Canada does not maintain reserves of gold in its own right, and an examination of its balance sheet reveals that its assets are comprised mainly of federal Government securities," see David, above note 154 at 199.

167 Under the *Bank of Canada Act* the liquidation of the Bank of Canada requires specific legislation and is exempted from the coverage of general insolvency or winding-up statutes. Originally this was provided for in SC 1934, c 43, s 41. Presently it is provided for in RSC 1985, c B-2, s 34 (RSC 1970, c B-2, s 30 at the time of the judgment).

Under those circumstances, he rejected the submission that "the pre-1967 notes of the Bank of Canada fall within the definition of a promissory note under s. 176(1) of the *Bills of Exchange Act*."[168]

Ultimately, having failed to reach a decision, the Supreme Court affirmed, albeit by default, the judgment of the Court of Appeal.[169] The view that the banknote is a promissory note thus narrowly prevailed. However, Laskin CJC's dissent proved to be too well-reasoned to be ignored. Indeed, by the time the Supreme Court gave its decision in *Bank of Canada v Bank of Montreal*, Parliament had already eliminated, in 1967, the promissory language from the banknote.[170] Yet, it may have been recognized that due to *Banco de Portugal v Waterlow and Sons, Ltd*,[171] even the deletion of the promissory language from the post-1967 banknotes in Canada could not ensure that Laskin CJC's view would be adopted with regard to the new form.[172] Parliament thus intervened. Effectively following Laskin CJC's view, Parliament provided in 1980 that Bank of Canada notes are not promissory notes under the *Bills of Exchange Act*.[173]

This created a rift between the laws of England and Canada as to the characterization of the banknote. The question that arises is whether Laskin CJC's position, as in fact adopted by the legislature, is convincing. Another aspect of the same question is whether retaining the characterization of banknotes as promissory notes is justified as a matter of principle.

There are two basic flaws in Laskin CJC's position. First, he overlooked the history of the banknote as the forerunner of the modern promissory note.[174] Second, there is nothing conceptually wrong in viewing a particular type of a promissory note, such as the banknote, as money, as long as such a promissory note is treated as money even though it contains a promise to pay money.

At the same time, the contrary view failed to respond to Laskin CJC's two main points. The first refers to the existence of a comprehensive statutory scheme governing banknotes issued by a central bank so that a negative implication as to the application of the *Bills of Exchange Act* may be inferred.

---

168   *Bank of Canada v Bank of Montreal*, above note 12 at 1153.

169   See text at and around note 151, above.

170   See text and notes 111–12, above.

171   *Banco de Portugal*, above note 7.

172   For that position in *Banco de Portugal* (with regard to the Portuguese banknotes) see above note 124 and the text that follows.

173   *Banks and Banking Law Revision Act*, SC 1980-83, c 40, s 49 (presently RSC 1985, c B-2, s 25(6)) discussed in text at notes 112–113, above.

174   See in general Geva, above note 34 at 543–47.

The second point is the inconvertibility of the banknote to the point of rendering the payment promise into an empty formula, quite "sterile" and "unreal."

Arguably then, neither of the two views in *Bank of Montreal*, that of Beetz J and Laskin CJC is completely persuasive. Nor did the statutory solution in Canada resolve all practical issues. To begin with, historically, the "currency" of coin underlay the "negotiability" of the banknote. Both concepts preceded the *Bills of Exchange Act*[175] and can exist independently of it.[176] Arguably, the denomination on a coin is a binding representation by its issuer as to its nominal purchasing power. The same can be said of the banknote. Hence, the promissory language is not any more required; nor is it a distinctive element of the banknote. Its characterization as a promissory note is merely reminiscent of its historical development. Indeed, way back in 1758, Lord Mansfield spoke of Bank of England notes as "*treated* as money, as cash, in the ordinary course and transaction of business";[177] yet, he immediately continued and said that "they *are* as much money, as guineas themselves are; or any other current coin, that is used in common payments, as money or cash."[178] Certainly today, practically speaking, Bank of England notes are even more "money" than any current coin. Undoubtedly, the character of banknotes as "money" has come to overshadow their qualities as "promissory notes" so as, possibly, to supersede such qualities altogether. Indeed, it is quite likely that points relating to the juridical nature of the banknote and not explicitly provided for by banknotes legislation may well be decided by analogy to principles governing promissory notes and now codified in the *Bills of Exchange Act*.[179]

Ultimately then, at present, *Bank of Montreal* aside, notes issued by the Bank of Canada are not governed by the *Bills of Exchange Act*[180] even if only because under section 25(6) of the *Bank of Canada Act*[181] they are "neither promissory notes nor bills of exchange within the meaning of the *Bills of Exchange Act*." However, it does not follow that the Bank of Canada Notes are not negotiable instruments. As discussed earlier, the negotiability of the

---

175 *Bills of Exchange Act*, 1882, above note 55. The leading case is *Miller v Race*, above note 43.

176 From this perspective, the view that "coins may be described as 'negotiable chattels'" (Holden, above note 35 at 259–60) may be tainted with anachronism, as it may erroneously be understood to imply that "negotiability" *encompasses* the coin, while in fact "negotiability" was *heralded* by the "currency" qualities of the coin.

177 *Miller v Race*, above note 43 at 457 (Burr), 401 (ER) (emphasis added).

178 *Ibid* (emphasis added).

179 RSC 1985, c B-4, above note 101.

180 *Ibid*.

181 1985, c B-2, above note 113, s 25(6).

banknote was recognized by caselaw that preceded the *Bill of Exchange Act*.[182] For its part, the *Bills of Exchange Act* does not restrict negotiability to instruments governed by it; it does not exclude the existence of negotiable instruments outside of it. To that end, it has never been argued that the exclusion of the Bank of Canada note from the *Bills of Exchange Act* was intended to strip that note from the qualities of negotiability. Historically, it was the currency of the coin that served as the basis of what came later to be the negotiability of the banknote.[183] Having been "treated as money, as cash, in the ordinary course and transaction of business, by the general consent of mankind," in the era of Lord Mansfield as well as today, so as not to be recovered after they have "been paid away in currency,"[184] banknotes are negotiable instruments even where they are not governed by the specific provisions of the *Bills of Exchange Act*.[185]

This raises the question as to which law governs the Bank of Canada note. Section 25(1) (in conjunction with definitions under section 2) of the *Bank of Canada Act*[186] designates the Bank of Canada as the entity that has the sole right to issue notes intended for circulation in Canada. The only legal feature referred to in that provision is that "those notes shall be a first charge on the asses of the Bank [of Canada]." In turn, sections 7.1 and 8(1)(b) of the *Currency Act*[187] confer on such notes the legal tender quality. No other feature is addressed by legislation. Taking into account the roots of the *Bills of Exchange Act*[188] in a broader context of the law of negotiable instruments, it is plausible to argue that general principles, whether or not they were codified, will govern the Bank of Canada note, so that the provisions of the *Bills of Exchange Act*[189] may be guiding albeit not automatically applicable.

However, whether this solution, based on the non-application of the *Bills of Exchange Act*,[190] leads to a result which in substance is different from that premised on the application of that Act to the Bank of Canada note, albeit with necessary modifications, is in the eyes of the beholder. The former, as applied in Canada under the *Bank of Canada Act*,[191] will not preclude the

---

182   RSC 1985, c B-4, above note 101.
183   *Cf* Holden, above note 35 treating the coin as a negotiable chattel.
184   *Miller v Race*, above note 43 at 457–58 (Burr), 401(ER).
185   RSC 1985, c B-4, above note 101.
186   RSC 1985, c B-2, above note 113.
187   RSC 1985, c C-52.
188   RSC 1985, c B-4, above note 101.
189   *Ibid.*
190   *Ibid.*
191   RSC 1985, c B-2, above note 113.

application of a principle codified by the Canadian *Bills of Exchange Act*.[192] For its part, the latter, as arguably applies in the United Kingdom for a Bank of England note, will not preclude the rejection of a provision from the UK *Bills of Exchange Act*[193] notwithstanding the application of that Act in general.

In the final analysis it is universally agreed that the inconvertible central bank's currency note, while being money, is also a negotiable instrument. This is true even if the currency note is not in the statutory form of a "promissory note." At the same time, whether or not it is in the statutory form of a promissory note, the distinctive nature of the currency note as money suggests that not all principles and rules applying to negotiable instruments necessarily govern it. The real controversy is the optimal mechanism to express this conclusion. Generally speaking, the choice is between two options. The first is the non-application to that instrument of the statute governing negotiable instruments while importing principles underlying that statute. The second is the application of that statute to the instrument while excluding provisions deemed unfitting to the monetary character of the instrument. Canada adhered to the first option while the United Kingdom appears to adopt to the second. As stated, in principle, both appear to lead to the same result, of the need to pick and choose, whether what principles to include (Canada) and what statutory provisions to exclude (United Kingdom). Accordingly, the importance of section 25(6) of the *Bank of Canada Act*, under which "Notes of the Bank are neither promissory notes nor bills of exchange within the meaning of the *Bills of Exchange Act*" – ought not to be exaggerated.

V. CONCLUSION: GOING FORWARD

It appears that the legal nature of the inconvertible central bank's currency note has been sufficiently clarified. As indicated, the inconvertible central bank's currency note may be treated as a "promissory note" governed by the *Bills of Exchange Act*[194] – subject to changes that its added feature as a currency note requires. Alternatively, per the contrary route as followed in Canada by Parliament, the central bank's currency note may be excluded from the scope of the *Bills of Exchange Act*, which does not preclude the application of the law negotiable instruments, in part through analogy with the *Bills of Exchange Act* that codified it, from providing a guidance as needed.

---

192   RSC 1985, c B-4, above note 101.
193   *Bills of Exchange Act, 1882*, above note 55.
194   RSC 1985, c B-4, above note 101.

However, clarity is lacking in the law that governs the convertible currency note. Certainly, the case for seeing it as a "promissory note" governed by the *Bills of Exchange Act*[195] is stronger than the case of the inconvertible currency note. In fact, so far, I have not encountered any position arguing to the contrary. At the same time, had *Bank of Canada v Bank of Montreal*[196] arisen in connection with a convertible banknote, the particular issue, that of a right for a replacement note for a lost or destroyed one, and the underlying policies against such a right, would have been the same as in the case itself.

More crucial is the lack of conclusiveness as to whether and when payment by convertible currency note is absolute or conditional. Prima facie, this is a question of mere historical importance as the only circulating currency notes in Canada nowadays are the inconvertible ones issued by the Bank of Canada. However, as will be discussed in subsequent chapters, digital coins may be circulating e-notes; if so, ghosts from the past will haunt us, forcing the determination once for all of the nature of payment by convertible currency note.

195 *Ibid.*
196 *Bank of Canada v Bank of Montreal*, above note 12.

chapter four

THE DIGITALIZATION OF PRIVATE MONEY: STABLECOINS AS VIRTUAL CURRENCIES

SYNOPSIS

Stablecoins are primarily used to facilitate crypto trading by enabling easy conversion of fiat currency to cryptocurrency and vice versa. However, there is a growing adoption of stablecoins for payment and remittance purposes. This trend owes largely to the perception that the prices of stablecoins are not volatile. Yet, like other cryptocurrencies, stablecoins have been and are subject to price volatility. As well, stablecoin arrangements can pose significant risk to the payment system with potential contagion to the financial system. The risks have raised regulatory concerns and relevant authorities across the world put forward various regulatory responses. While there is an overall consensus as to global standards, approaches to implementation vary. In Canada stablecoins and stablecoin arrangements regulation is largely embodied in two Canadian Securities Administrators (CSA) staff notices that mostly treat stablecoins as investment products and regulate issuers indirectly. One reaction circulating globally is the issuance of digital currency by central banks, otherwise known as "central bank digital currency" (CBDC). With its current design and use cases, CBDC shares some attributes with stablecoins. For its part, the Canadian stablecoin regulation is expected to evolve into a more comprehensive regulatory approach with more distinct and specific guidelines as well as enforcement mechanism applicable to each category of market participant. In the long run, it is anticipated that other regulators, particularly the Office of the Superintendent of Financial Institutions (OSFI) and possibly the Bank of Canada, will join the CSA in devising a comprehensive regulatory scheme.

SUMMARY OF CONTENTS

I. INTRODUCTION

In the continuing process of the digitalization of money, digital currencies have been adopted for payment purposes. Among them, stablecoins have emerged as a reliable means of payment, particularly in international payments[1] and ramp-on transactions in digital assets, as well as investment objects. The parity of stablecoins to fiat currency, specifically the benchmarked currency, appears to be crucial to the growing preference of and/or confidence in the adoption of stablecoins for cross-border payments. Eliminating the necessity of bank intermediation, payment by stablecoins reduces costs and may thus make inroads into retail payments.[2]

This chapter examines the legal features of stablecoins as well as the legal issues arising in the course of their use. It also examines some notable laws and/or regulatory steps taken or proposed to address them. **Part II** puts the discussion in perspective by setting out a uniform terminology addressing the differences among terms such as digital currency, virtual currency, cryptocurrency, and stablecoin. **Part III** discusses the monetary features of a stablecoin, its distribution and transfer mechanism as a payment system and emerging legal issues. **Part IV** presents stablecoin arrangement

---

1   Cameron MacDonald and Laura Zhao, "Stablecoins and Their Risks to Financial Stability" (2022) Bank of Canada Staff Discussion Paper 2022-20 at 6–7, online: https://www.bankof-canada.ca/wp-content/uploads/2022/11/sdp2022-20.pdf, accessed 18 July 2024.

2   But notably, Visa has a contrary take in relation to the adoption of stablecoin for payment purposes. Its report shows that more than 90 percent of stablecoin transactions are "bot" (robot) transactions, and that less than 10 percent of stablecoin transactions are "organic." This report has the potential effect of reducing the commercial case for further development of stablecoin technology and stablecoin arrangements. See Emily Nicolle, "More Than 90% of Stablecoin Transactions Aren't From Real Users, Study Finds" (*Bloomberg*, 5 May 2024), online: https://www.bloomberg.com/news/articles/2024-05-05/more-than-90-of-stablecoin-transactions-aren-t-real-study-finds, accessed 28 July 2024.

risks and regulatory concerns. It focuses on security, issuer's insolvency, systemic risk, lack of interoperability, and the need to comply with securities laws, anti-money laundering, and anti-terrorist financing laws. **Part V** outlines regulatory developments addressing stablecoin arrangement risks in Canada, as well as highlighting those of the United States and the European Union. **Part VI** presents the central bank digital currency (CBDC) as a potential solution to most risks of stablecoins and as such a plausible route in the continuing process of the digitalization of money. Chapter 5 of this study contains a more thorough discussion of CBDC. **Part VII** concludes by summarizing the chapter and proposing areas for legislation and regulation. A brief comparative summary of the cardinal features of each regulatory system, whether common or distinct, is provided. The chapter is followed by an **Appendix** setting out an overview of the Canadian stablecoin landscape and the impact, if any, of regulation on stablecoin arrangements.

II. TAXONOMY: DIGITAL CURRENCIES, CRYPTOCURRENCIES, AND STABLECOINS

Until not long ago, "money" in a national monetary system consisted exclusively of tangible banknotes and coins (cash) and bank credit (scriptural money) redeemable to cash. Emerging new technologies introduced new types of monetary objects and investment vehicles, including, most recently, digital assets, particularly on distributed ledger technologies.[3] As an instrument representing value,[4] the digital asset is a distinct token consisting of data in the form of a unique string of bits. "This string must have a numeric value and must have an identity."[5] Such tokens may be in the form of a "digital bearer" instrument, transferrable from one device to another in which case like physical coins and banknotes, they are not paid out of bank accounts,

---

3   Distributed ledger technology refers to "the processes and related technologies that enable nodes in a network (or arrangement) to securely propose, validate and record state changes (or updates) to a synchronized ledger that is distributed across the network's nodes." See Committee on Payments and Market Infrastructures, *Distributed Ledger Technology in Payment, Clearing and Settlement: An Analytical Framework* (Bank for International Settlements 2017), online: https://www.bis.org/cpmi/publ/d157.pdf, accessed 18 July 2024.

4   Practically, "with properties that suffice to attest to and transfer ownership" see Digital Dollar Foundation and Accenture, *The Digital Dollar Project: Exploring a US CBDC* (Accenture and The Digital Dollar Foundation 2020) at 10, online: static1.squarespace.com/static/5e16627eb901b656f-2c174ca/t/5ecfc542da96fb2d2d5b5f15/1590674759958/Digital-Dollar-Project-Whitepaper_vF.pdf, accessed 18 July 2024.

5   Gideon Samid, *Tethered Money: Managing Digital Currency Transactions* (Elsevier Academic Press, 2015) at 105.

so that their payment does not appear to require intermediation by banks or other financial intermediaries.[6] However, as is exactly the case with electronic funds transfers, transfers of digital assets between distant parties are conducted over the internet or otherwise electronically.[7]

Alternatively, tokens may embody rights in and claims to an asset, reserve, or project such that the tokens represent an issuer's liability so that they are not directly transferable peer to peer without third party intermediation. Rather, in a process that mimics a traditional funds transfer,[8]

> [P]ayment is put into effect by reducing the sender's token balance at their issuing institution and creating a new tokenised liability for the receiver that is issued by their institution. Meanwhile, there is a concurrent transfer of central bank money using a wholesale CBDC.[9]

Whether tokens are transferable peer to peer or via third party intermediation, through automation, tokenization could deliver gains by greatly speeding up settlement and could also increase efficiency by ensuring all parts of a transaction occur simultaneously, a process called "atomicity" or atomic settlement.[10]

This chapter addresses only the first model of tokenization, that of the digital bearer instrument transmitted from a payer to a payee, typically in a discharge of a debt. While there is no universal consensus on terminology,[11] the ensuing discussion follows that of the ECB[12] and IMF.[13] Thereunder, "stablecoin" is a subcategory of "virtual currency," the latter

---

6   Rodney Garratt and Hyun Song Shin, *Stablecoins Versus Tokenised Deposits: Implications. For The Singleness of Money* (Bulletin No 73, Bank for International Settlements 2023) at 2–4, online: https://www.bis.org/publ/bisbull73.pdf, accessed 18 July 2024.

7   Hence their operations raise similar issues such as mistaken payment and overpayment (not to be discussed here). See e.g., *B2C2 v Quoine Pte Ltd* [2019] SHC(I) 03, affd *Quoine Pte Ltd v B2C2 Ltd* [2020] SGCA(I) 02; *Copytrack Pte Ltd v Wall*, 2018 BCSC 1709.

8   *Libyan Arab Foreign Bank v Bankers Trust Co* [1988] 1 Lloyd's Rep 229 (QB) 273.

9   Garratt and Shin, above note 6 at 4–6.

10 See e.g., Aldasoro et al, *The Tokenisation Continuum* (Bulletin No 73, Bank for International Settlements 2023) at 3, online: https://www.bis.org/publ/bisbull72.pdf. This is particularly true for Delivery vs. Payment (DVP) transactions where the asset to be delivered is on the blockchain.

11 Benjamin Geva, "Disintermediating Electronic Payments: Digital Cash and Virtual Currencies" (2016) 31 *Journal of International Banking Law Review* 661 at 664–65.

12 See European Central Bank and Eurosystem, *Virtual Currency Schemes* (European Central Bank, 2012) at 25, online: www.ecb.europa.eu/pub/pdf/other/virtualcurrencyschemes201210en.pdf.

13 See Dong He et al, "Virtual Currencies and Beyond: Initial Considerations" (SDN/16/3, International Monetary Fund 2016) at 7, online: www.imf.org/external/pubs/ft/sdn/2016/sdn1603.pdf, accessed 1 November 2024.

being a subspecies of "digital currency." Accordingly, "virtual currencies" are privately issued digital currencies.[14] They are contrasted with CBDCs which are obligations of the central bank.[15] A virtual currency may have its own unit of account, fluctuating by reference to the value of an official unit of account. In such a case, the virtual currency is *self-anchored*.[16] It is in fact unanchored to any unit of fiat currency or commodity. Alternatively, a virtual currency may be a *"claim-check"* or *stablecoin* that is denominated in, namely pegged to, or claimed at par with, either an official currency's unit of account (as well as a basket of such currencies) or in the value of a specified amount of a designated commodity, whether or not it is backed by a reserve of such currency or commodity.[17] Since prices of goods and services are typically denominated in an official currency, particularly (if not only), "claim-checks" or stablecoins denominated in that currency are good candidates to become private money to be used in retail transactions.[18]

Compared to other digital currencies, especially in terms of trading volumes, stablecoins are currently used predominantly in crypto-asset transactions (including crypto-lending).[19] Otherwise, their use is particularly efficient in cross-border payments (including remittances) and, at least

---

14   See also Council Directive (EU) 2015/849 of 20 May 2015 on the prevention and use of the financial system for the purposes of money laundering or terrorist financing [2015] OJ L141/73; see also virtual currency legislation in the US, discussed below in Part V.

15   See e.g., Rosa Maria Lastra and Jason Grant Allen, *Virtual Currencies in the Eurosystem: Challenges Ahead* (Policy Department for Economic, Scientific and Quality of Life Policies 2018) at 39, speaking of "central bank virtual currencies," online: www.europarl.europa.eu/cmsdata/150541/DIW_FINAL%20publication.pdf, accessed 1 November 2024.

16   Samid, above note 5 at 14–6.

17   See e.g., Financial Stability Board, "Regulation, Supervision and Oversight of 'Global Stablecoin' Arrangements" (*Financial Stability Board*, 13 October 2020), online: www.fsb.org/wp-content/uploads/P131020-3.pdf, accessed 25 July 2024.

18   El Salvador's Bitcoin adoption is not a true exception since both the unit of account and the digital entity derived from Bitcoin is dollarized. See Benjamin Geva, "Focus on a Specific Case: Bitcoin as Legal Tender: What did El Salvador Get Wrong in Going CBDC?" (2022) International Law Association, Committee on International Monetary Law, Lisbon Conference at 2, online: https://www.ila-hq.org/en_GB/documents/int-monetary-law-mocomila-interim-report-2022, accessed 2 November 2024.

19   Crypto-lending is crypto trading activity which involves individual crypto-owners depositing their crypto-assets into liquidity pools established by crypto trading platforms. The deposited crypto-assets are loaned to crypto-borrowers who pay a borrowing rate on the loaned crypto-assets. The depositors are then able to earn a deposit rate on the deposited crypto-asset. See Sirio Aramonte et al, *DeFi lending: intermediation without information?* (Bulletin No 57, Bank for International Settlements 2022), online: https://www.bis.org/publ/bisbull57.pdf, accessed 23 July 2024.

as long as central banks do not issue digital coins of their own, are good substitute to cash also in domestic transactions.[20] As their use reduces the need for intermediation it lowers transaction costs and provides streamlined settlement. However, due to the lack of regulatory oversight regarding their issuance and structuring discussed further below, stablecoins present risks and thus are "unlikely to reap their potential as payment vehicles unless they are properly regulated."[21]

Notwithstanding statements to the contrary, stablecoins are neither necessarily cryptocurrencies[22] nor are they necessarily linked to the blockchain and decentralized finance.[23] Rather, "A stablecoin is a digital coin that operates on a technological infrastructure and its value is stable in relation to some other asset. The currency issuer operates a mechanism that maintains the stability of the currency's value."[24]

Stablecoins may be either algorithm-based or asset-linked. Stablecoins falling into the former category maintain a stable value via protocols that adjust quantity in response to change of demand. Since they are not collateralized with a reserve of assets (such as fiat currencies, other digital currencies, or commodities), algorithm-based stablecoins are the most fragile. This is so because they are maintained by algorithms that manipulate the supply of such algorithmic stablecoin in order to maintain its peg against its reference asset. As such, algorithmic stablecoins are susceptible to errors and limitations in their algorithm to respond to varied market conditions. At the same time, an asset-linked stablecoin purports to maintain a stable value by referencing a commodity, digital asset, fiat currency, or a basket of any

---

20   For a detailed account of their use, see MacDonald and Zhao, above note 1 at 6–10. See also Ryan Clements, "Cryptocurrency: Challenges to Conventional Governance" (2022) Expert Report to the Public Order Emergency Commission, online: https:// publicorderemergencycommission.ca/files/documents/Policy-Papers/Cryptocurrency -Challenges-to-Conventional-Governance-of-Financial-Transactions-Clements.pdf, accessed 2 November 2024.

21   Jeremy Kronick and Mark Zelmer, *Stablecoins: Sailing Without a Rudder* (Commentary No 637, CD Howe Institute 2023) at 2, online: https://www.cdhowe.org/sites/default/files/2023-02/ Commentary_637.pdf, accessed 2 November 2024. In fact, this is also the position of the Bank of England. See e.g., Lucy White, "Bank of England Official Says Stablecoin Use May Need Limits" (*Bloomberg*, 17 April 2023), online: https://www.bloomberg.com/news/articles/2023-04-17 /bank-of-england-official-says-stablecoin-use-may-need-limits, accessed 2 November 2024.

22   As claimed e.g., by Financial Stability Board, "Regulation, Supervision and Oversight," above note 17 at 5; see also Alejandro Garcia, Bena Lands, and Dennis Yanchus, "Stablecoin, Assessment Framework" (2021) Bank of Canada Staff Discussion Paper 2021-6 at 7, online: https:// www.bankofcanada.ca/wp-content/uploads/2021/04/sdp2021-6.pdf, accessed 23 July 2024.

23   As claimed by Kronick and Zelmer, above note 21 at 1–2; see also Clements, above note 20 at 3, 9.

24   Bank of Israel, "Principles for 'Stablecoin' Activity in Israel" (February 2023) at 3 (in Hebrew).

of the above.[25] When the backing asset is the one in which the stablecoin is denominated, the stablecoin is truly a claim-check to an item in the reserve backing it.[26]

Whether a stablecoin is or is not money, its issuer must operate similarly to a central bank functioning in a "currency board" arrangement, under which central bank money in the local currency is fully backed by hard foreign currency.[27] Accordingly, an indispensable component of any regulation addressing stablecoins as money consists of both reserve and issuer requirements. Reserve ought to be full and to consist of highly liquid assets if not of only the asset(s) to which the stablecoin's value is linked.[28] For enhanced benefit, they also ought to be segregated and not form part of the issuer's equity.[29] Issuer requirements ought to identify who can issue a stablecoin, and address a variety of topics pertaining to reserve custodian, issuers, qualifications of directors and principal shareholders, capital adequacy, and governance structure. Impairment of redemption or decline in confidence will be bound to lower the value of the currency and generate "coin run."[30]

Virtual currencies, including stablecoins, using the blockchain may not necessarily have their own dedicated blockchain. Rather, some are built on existing third party blockchain(s) as is the case with USDC, DAI, and Tether, which are some of the most popular stablecoins.[31] Asset-linked stablecoins using the blockchain, whether or not built on a dedicated blockchain, are

---

25 Kronick and Zelmer, above note 21 at 3. Meta's Diem (originally Libra, and since vacated) is an example for an on-chain stablecoin while Ethereum exemplifies the on-chain category.

26 Accordingly, for example, BitMint website goes on to state that "BitMint ... does not generate money per se; it generates a digital claim check for money (or any transactable valuable) held ready for instant redemption. The state of being redemption-ready renders the BitMint digital claim check into a de-facto transactable currency." See online: https://www.bitmintcash.com/, accessed 18 July 2024.

27 T Shu-Ki, "Legal Frameworks of Currency Board Regimes" (1999) Hong Kong Monetary Authority Quarterly Bulletin 81/1999 at 50.

28 Conversely, as we have recently seen in the Silicon Valley Bank failure, value of safe liquid interest bearing assets will decline upon a stiff rise of interest rates.

29 Garcia et al, above note 22 at 12.

30 Similar to "bank runs." See extensive discussion by MacDonald and Zhao, above note 1 at 12–16. In Canada OSFI has been attending to the task, see Office of the Superintendent of Financial Institutions, "OSFI launches consultation on fiat-referenced crypto-asset arrangements and activities" (*Government of Canada*, 17 April 2023, online: https://www.osfi-bsif.gc.ca/en/news/osfi-launches-consultation-fiat-referenced-crypto-asset-arrangements-activities, accessed 2 November 2024.

31 Most stablecoins are built on the Ethereum blockchain as ERC-20s, which stands for "Ethereum Request for Comment number 20." With ERC-20 crypto developers are able to design tokens capable of recognizing smart-contracts. The tokens are also compatible with other crypto protocols.

either off-chain or on-chain. Off-chain stablecoins are backed by fiat currency and/or high-quality liquid assets. They are "off-chain" because their reserve of assets is maintained and authenticated by an independent third-party outside of the main blockchain network. Tether and USDC are examples of off-chain stablecoins. On-chain stablecoins such as MakeDAO's DAI stablecoin, LUSD, and Dollar on Chain are backed by blockchains-based digital assets which are riskier and thus tend to be overcollateralized. They do not require an issuer or the service of a custodian to satisfy redemption claims. They are "on-chain" because they use smart contracts, that is, they "are carried out on a blockchain from start to finish where they are verified and recorded on a public distributed ledger that cannot be changed after they are validated."[32]

The set of rules governing the exchange or transmission of data between devices constitutes a protocol. A centralized protocol is controlled, updated, and supported by one person, entity, or group of persons. Conversely, a decentralized protocol "is not dependent upon a single person or group to carry out the essential managerial or entrepreneurial efforts"; that is, it is "not economically or operationally controlled or unilaterally changed by a single person, entity or group of persons or entities under common control."[33] In particular, protocols are intended to achieve reliability with regard to the distributed ledger technology and, to this end, establish a method of validation, requiring consensus on the blockchain network. In other words, the ledger's accuracy is corroborated in accordance with a method determined under rules adhered to by participants on the network.

Based on the aforesaid consensus protocol options for a blockchain network, a distinction is to be made among three types of digital currency schemes, namely, a decentralized scheme, a centralized scheme, and a hybrid scheme. In a "decentralized" scheme, the digital currency is issued, transferred, and redeemed over a decentralized distributed ledger. Conversely, under a "centralized" scheme, the digital currency is issued, transferred, and redeemed over a centralized ledger. Finally, a digital currency transferable under a decentralized protocol – such as (but not only) over a distributed ledger and yet issued centrally – is considered to operate in a "hybrid" scheme.[34]

---

32   Kronick and Zelmer, above note 21 at 3.

33   Hester M Peirce, "Token Safe Harbor Proposal 2.0" (*US Securities and Exchange Commission*, 13 April 2021), online: https://www.sec.gov/news/public-statement/peirce-statement-token-safe-harbor-proposal-2.0, accessed 26 July 2024.

34   Dong He et al, above note 13 at 8, where a third criterion – on top of issuance and transfer – is added, *viz* "mechanisms to implement and enforce internal rules on the use and circulation

Regardless of the protocol/consensus mechanism adopted, cryptocurrencies are built on blockchain networks. The Office of the Superintendent of Financial Institutions (OSFI) in Canada defines "cryptocurrencies" to be "digital assets that depend primarily on cryptography and distributed ledger or similar technology."[35] The focus of the definition on "distributed ledger" and "cryptography" captures the essence of cryptocurrencies as digital currencies in which encryption is used to regulate the generation of units of currency[36] and verify the execution of payment transactions.[37] The underlying protocol therefore uses cryptography to create, maintain, and support the transfers and transactions of the digital assets/cryptocurrencies (the sequence of the bits), to prevent counterfeiting and fraudulent transactions, and to perform validation, execution, and recording.[38] These functions may be conducted on a distributed ledger, such as a blockchain. In a blockchain, each block contains a cryptographic hash or algorithm that links it to the

of the currency." Binance, Coinbase, and Kraken are prime examples of centralized crypto exchanges while Bitcoin is the classic example for a decentralized cryptocurrency; see e.g., Aspris et al, "Decentralized Exchanges: The 'Wild West' of Cryptocurrency Trading" (21 July 2021) International Review of Financial Analysis, Forthcoming, online: http://dx.doi.org/10.2139/ssrn.3717330, accessed 2 November 2024; Dong He et al, above note 13 at 8–9 characterize Ripple as a hybrid scheme.

35 Office of the Superintendent of Financial Institutions, "Interim arrangements for the regulatory capital and liquidity treatment of cryptoasset exposures" (*Government of Canada*, 18 August 2022), online: https://www.osfi-bsif.gc.ca/Eng/fi-if/rg-ro/gdn-ort/adv-prv/Pages/crypto22.aspx. The definition is stated to be in the footsteps of that of the Financial Stability Board, except that under the latter, "the relevant digital assets must be 'private'"; Financial Stability Board, "Regulation, Supervision and Oversight," above note 17 at 5.

36 See for example, definition of "Cryptocurrency" under Mich Comp Laws § 750.411j (2024), online: https://www.legislature.mi.gov/Laws/MCL?objectName=MCL-750-411J, accessed 4 November 2024. This distinctive feature is unfortunately missing in UK Jurisdiction Taskforce, "Legal Statement on Cryptoassets and Smart Contracts" (*The LawTech Delivery Panel*, November 2019) at paras 24–34, online: https://perma.cc/8SKS-CAUS, accessed 4 November 2024, where the focus (particularly in para 28) appears to be on the control of the asset (rather than on its generation) by cryptographic means.

37 This definition slightly modifies that from The Wolf of Crypto, "Basic Cryptocurrency Starter Guide" (*Medium*, 18 September 2017), online: wolfofcrypto.medium.com/basic-cryptocurrency-starter-guide-8f2071ea85de, accessed 24 May 2023. Specifically, I replaced "transfer of funds" with the "execution of payment transactions" to highlight payment by the transmission of "coins" rather than "generic value" in the forms of funds. See also "Cryptocurrency," online: https://en.wikipedia.org/wiki/Cryptocurrency, accessed 24 May 2024, defining a cryptocurrency as "a medium of exchange wherein individual coin ownership records are stored in a ledger existing in a form of a computerized database using strong cryptography to secure transaction records, to *control the creation of additional coins*, and to verify the transfer of coin ownership."

38 With regard to Bitcoin, for example, record security and visibility to authorized users is ensured by cryptography.

previous block, along with a timestamp for the transactions from that block. The immutable nature of the network enables cryptocurrency to be dealt directly from one party to another without going through a trusted intermediary[39] such as a bank or any other account-holding centralized counterparty or intermediary.[40]

The immutability of the blockchain and open network access means that a transaction record of the blockchain network is publicly available. The public availability of transacting parties and a record undermines parties' privacy. Technological advances in quantum-resistant (or quantum safe)[41] algorithms[42] have shown significant progress in achieving network immutability without compromising the cash-like privacy of transacting parties. To that end, available in the arsenal are (1) quantum-resistant algorithms, which

39   In this context "intermediary" refers to a person acting like a banker linking participants over payment accounts. But *cf* the argument that network participants who validate/verify transactions on the blockchain network are intermediaries – albeit in a different sense. Crypto exchanges like Binance, Kraken, and Coinbase as well as crypto wallet providers like MetaMask Crypto Wallet, Coinbase Wallet Web3, and Gemini Crypto Wallet are considered cryptocurrency intermediaries. See Immaculate Dadiso Motsi-Omoijiade, "Financial Intermediation in Cryptocurrency Markets – Regulation, Gaps and Bridges" in David Lee Kuo Chen and Robert Deng (eds), *Handbook of Blockchain, Digital Finance, and Inclusion*, vol 1 (Elsevier, 2017) at 207–23; also, the network validators who also act function as network nodes and who are incentivized by coin mining rewards are considered "new centralized intermediaries." See Bank for International Settlements, *The Crypto Ecosystem: Key Elements and Risks – Report submitted to the G20 Finance Ministers and Central Bank Governors* (Bank for International Settlements 2023), online: https://www.bis.org/publ/othp72 .pdf, accessed 22 July 2024.

40   Not every decentralized system is associated with a cryptocurrency. For a visual demonstration of this point, see Dong He et al, above note 34 at 8, Figure 1. I do not adopt the taxonomy proposed in that figure.

41   Sometimes (confusingly in my opinion) characterized as "quantum-based," see e.g., Amnon Samid, "Gaining trust for self-referential CBDC (practical solutions)" (*The Paypers*, 9 January 2024), online: https://thepaypers.com/thought-leader-insights/gaining-trust-for-self-referential-cbdc-practical-solutions--1266139, accessed 25 June 2024.

42   See e.g., Quantum-Readiness Working Group, "Canadian National Quantum-Readiness: Best Practices and Guidelines" (Version 3, 12 June 2023), online: https://ised-isde.canada. ca/site/spectrum-management-telecommunications/sites/default/files/attachments/2023 /cfdir-quantum-readiness-best-practices-v03.pdf, accessed 28 July 2024; See also, Tammy Xu, "What are quantum-resistant algorithms – and why do we need them?" (*MIT Technology Review*, 14 September 2022), online: https://www.technologyreview.com/2022/09/14/1059400 /explainer-quantum-resistant-algorithms/, accessed 28 July 2024; for the two main technology archetypes – Quantum versus Crypto see Amnon Samid, "Automated Embedded Payment Systems" (2022) 12 *International Journal of Embedded Systems and Applications* 1, online: https://www.researchgate.net/publication/367014225_Automated_Embedded_Payment _Systems, accessed 28 May 2024.

are cryptographic algorithms designed to withstand breaches and/or attacks from classical and quantum computers,[43] (2) Pattern-Devoid-Cryptography,[44] and (3) LeVeL-Paying-Field[45] withstanding quantum and AI-Cryptanalytic attacks.[46]

A prominent example covering these grounds is the BitMint digital currency.[47] It is centrally issued and de-centrally transferred from one device to another without necessarily using the blockchain.[48] As such it is a type of a hybrid model.[49] Additionally, BitMint is developed as a tool for anti-money laundering which also preserves the privacy of transacting parties.[50]

43 National Security Agency, "Quantum Computing and Post-Quantum Cryptography" (*National Security Agency*, August 2021), online: https://media.defense.gov/2021/Aug/04/2002821837 /-1/-1/1/Quantum_FAQs_20210804.PDF, accessed 28 July 2024; generally speaking, Quantum computing uses specialized technology –including computer hardware and algorithms that take advantage of quantum mechanics – to solve complex problems that classical computers or supercomputers can't solve, or can't solve quickly enough. See e.g., Josh Schneider and Ian Smalley, "What is Quantum Computing?" (IBM, 5 August 2024), online: https://www.ibm. com/topics/quantum-computing, accessed 4 November 2024.

44 Gideon Samid, "Pattern Devoid Cryptography" in Sudhakar Radhakrishan and Carlos M. Travieso-González (eds), *Biometrics and Cryptography* (IntechOpen, 2023), online: https:// www.intechopen.com/chapters/88027, accessed 22 July 2024.

45 Gideon Samid, "A LeVeL Paying Field: Cryptographic Solutions towards Social Accountability and Financial Inclusion" (Research Gate, February 2022), online: https://www.researchgate .net/publication/358479911_A_LeVeL_Paying_Field_Cryptographic_Solutions_towards _Social_Accountability_and_Financial_Inclusion, accessed 28 May 2024.

46 A cryptanalytic attack occurs e.g., where a hacker endeavours to decipher a ciphertext to derive the plaintext. So as to deduce e.g., encryption key. See e.g., Ashish Kumar Kendhe and Himani Agrawal, "A Survey Report on Various Cryptanalysis Techniques" (2013) 3 *International Journal of Soft Computing and Engineering* 287, online: https://www.ijsce.org/wp -content/uploads/papers/v3i2/B1534053213.pdf, accessed July 28, 2024.

47 For BitMint Money see "BitMintMoney," online: https://www.bitmintcash.com/, accessed 18 July 2024; for the superior protection of randomness premised on "a cipher which use[s] no mathematical complexity but instead call[s] for large amounts of randomness," see e.g., Carsten Stöcker, "Randomness: The Fix for Today's Broken Security" (*Medium*, 9 November 2017), online: cstoecker.medium.com/randomness-the-fix-for-todays-broke n-security-39ea7dc3a89b, accessed 18 June 2024; for BitMint being considered in China see "Q-Pay could mark the next sea change in finance" (*DigFin*, 8 January 2019), online: https:// www.digfingroup.com/bitmint-q-pay, accessed 18 June 2024.

48 This is not to say that at least in principle a blockchain cannot become quantum safe. See e.g., LCX Team, "Quantum Resistance in Blockchain Explained" (*LCX*, 4 January 2024), online: https://www.lcx.com/quantum-resistance-in-blockchain-explained/, accessed July 22, 2024.

49 For this distinction, see text above at note 34.

50 BitMint, "Simplicity Rediscovered: A pragmatic approach for Digital Currency, tested and ready for practical exploitation" (*Reserve Bank of New Zealand*), online: https://www.rbnz. govt.nz/-/media/project/sites/rbnz/files/consultations/future-of-money/future-of-money--

III. STABLECOINS AS MONEY TRANSFERRED IN A "PAYMENT SYSTEM"

A monetary object is said to be a medium of exchange, a store of value,[51] and a unit of account.[52] As long as these three elements exist for a virtual currency, whether a given virtual currency is "money" depends on the level of its acceptability in a given segment of society or a community.[53] This could be determined, if not by statute and/or regulation, on a case-by-case basis by courts.[54]

So far, no Canadian case has found a cryptocurrency to be "money." For its part, *Re Quadriga Fintech Solutions Corp et al*[55] stands for the proposition that cryptocurrency owned by a bankrupt debtor is "property"[56] forming part of the estate divisible among the bankrupt's creditors. It further characterizes cryptocurrency claims in bankruptcy as liquidated claims, since they "can be easily ascertained 'as a matter of arithmetic.'" In turn, *Copytrack Pte Ltd v Wall*[57] was an action for the wrongful retention or conversion of cryptocurrency tokens mistakenly transferred. In the facts of the case, having been advised by the plaintiff of the error, the defendant nevertheless transferred the

-central-bank-digital-currency/13179031231_bitmint-digital-money-foundation_redacted.pdf, accessed 28 July 2024.

51   William Stanley Jevons, *Money and the Mechanism of Exchange* (Henry S King & Co, 1875) at 13, does not include this element in the definition. Indeed, money is a store of value only in the sense of being a "surplus" liquid resource available in one's hands for acquiring new commodities as may be needed and wished.

52   Nigel Dodd, *The Sociology of Money, Economic, Reason & Contemporary Society* (Continuum, 1994) at xv; for e.g., Geoffrey Ingham, *The Nature of Money* (Polity, 2004) at 198, "money" is effectively something that "[r]egardless of its form and substance" answers the promise and description provided (and measured) by the unit of account.

53   For the critical role of community acceptance of an object as money, see e.g., Christine Desan, "Coin Reconsidered: The Political Alchemy of Commodity Money" (2010) 11 *Theoretical Inquiries in Law* 361 at 368–70; by reference to digital currency, overlooked by those who define digital currencies as limited to cryptocurrencies see e.g., JS Nelson, "Cryptocommunity Currencies" (2020) 105 *Cornell Law Review* 909 at 913 footnote 22.16, 947–53.

54   *Cf* the standard required for proving the acquisition of negotiability by a document by mercantile usage: EP Ellinger, "Legal Problems of Modern Commercial Paper" (1990–91) 6 *Banking and Finance Law Review* 65 at 70.

55   *Re Quadriga Fintech Solutions Corp et al* (24 March 2020) Toronto, ONSC CV-19-627184-00CL (31-2560674), CV-19-627185-00CL (31-2560984), and CV-19-627186-00CL (31-2560986).

56   By comparison, other cases were more hesitant even to that, see *MMD v JAH*, 2019 ONSC 2208, 140; *Cicada 137 LLC v Medjedovic*, 2021 ONSC 8581, 6; *MW v NLMW*, 2021 BCSC 1273; *Kostrinsky v Nasri*, 2022 ONSC 2926; *Shair.com Global Digital Services Ltd v Arnold*, 2018 BCSC 1512; *Nelson v Gokturk*, 2021 BCSC 813. For a recent review see Jake Cabott, Jason Uswak, and Peter Horemans, "The legal treatment of cryptocurrency in Canada: recent developments" (*Lexology*, November 2022), online: https://www.lexology.com/library/detail .aspx?g=5c9b453e-2160-4afd-800d-2b01b4a5b609, accessed 5 November 2024.

57   *Copytrack*, above note 7.

tokens into a cryptocurrency trading account with cryptocurrency exchange. Later he agreed to return the tokens. However, the tokens were transferred out of the defendant's wallet into five different wallets by an unknown third party who unlawfully accessed the defendant's wallet without the defendant's knowledge or consent. The defendant's principal defence was that he no longer had control of the tokens and was therefore unable to return them. For their part, the plaintiff argued that cryptocurrencies are "goods" because they have the following characteristics:[58]

(a) They are capable of being possessed, stored, transferred, lost and stolen;

(b) They were, at the time the conversion and wrongful detention began, held in the [defendant's] Wallet;

(c) They are specifically identifiable and have been traced to five wallets in which they are currently being held; and

(d) They can be used as a medium of exchange, a store of value, and a unit of account, like funds or currency.

The first two characteristics are incorrect. As discussed, a cryptocurrency token is an intangible and as such even as it can be "controlled," it cannot be "possessed," possession being limited to tangible assets.[59] At the most, "control" is a functional equivalent for possession, but this conclusion cannot be taken for granted, that is, without an analysis leading to it.[60] Notwithstanding *Li v Li*,[61] particularly relied on by the plaintiff, conversion is an action premised on the denial of rights in "goods"[62] and as such is unavailable to a claimant to an intangible such as a cryptocurrency. Conversely, the last two characteristics are valid, except that the analogy between cryptocurrencies and "funds or currency" is unhelpful. Neither "funds" nor "currency" has a precise jurisprudential meaning; for its part, "funds" are intangible. In fact, the fourth and last characteristic supports the nature of the cryptocurrency token as money,[63] even as it is an intangible.

---

58   *Ibid* at 30.

59   The point is demonstrated e.g., in the *Personal Property Security Act*, RSO 1990, c P.10, s 22(1) under which perfection by possession can be attained only in a tangible collateral. Conversely, under s 22.2(1), "A security interest in electronic chattel paper may be perfected by control of the collateral."

60   For this conclusion expressed in a statute and possibly reached as a common law principle see discussion at the end of Part III.

61   2017 BCSC 1312. To that end see also, *Nelson v Gokturk*, above note 56.

62   See e.g., CHS Fifoot, *History and Sources of the Common Law: Tort and Contract* (Stevens & Sons, 1949; rep Greenwood 1970) at 109. In this context "goods" is broadly understood to include every tangible item.

63   Dodd, above note 52.

In the final analysis, leaving open the question as to whether a cryptocurrency token is a "good" [*sic*] or a digital form of currency,[64] the court allowed the action, ordering that the plaintiff be entitled to trace and recover the tokens "in whatever hands those ... tokens may be currently held."[65] Effectively then, the case can be rationalized only on the third characteristic, that grounded on traceability.

Nonetheless, for a stablecoin to function as money, a mechanism for payment by its transfer must be in place,[66] so as to be a "brought under existing payment services regulation."[67] Such a mechanism is an integral part of a "stablecoin arrangement" (SA), meaning "[a]n arrangement that combines a range of functions (and the related specific activities) to provide an instrument that purports to be used as a means of payment and/or store of value. ... "[68] In effect it is a "payment system." This view aligns with views expressed by the Committee on Payments and Market Infrastructures (CPMI) in its 2023 Report.[69] According to the CPMI, a properly designed and regulated SA has the potential to improve international payments. For their part, SAs give rise to risks requiring regulatory responses addressed immediately below.

---

64   *Copytrack*, above note 7 at 33.

65   *Ibid* at 37. In the facts of the case, the one in control of the tokens, was not a bona fide purchaser for value, so as to take the tokens free from the plaintiff's claim, even if they were "money." At the same time, this is a strange judgment, with little benefit to the plaintiff, since the person in control of the tokens was not a party to the litigation.

66   Garcia, above note 22 at 3, 7 (adding of a third function, i.e., the provision of financial services accessed using the coin).

67   Kronick and Zelme, above note 21 at 13–15, 17.

68   Financial Stability Board, "'Regulation, Supervision and Oversight,'" above note 17 at 5 (glossary).

69   Committee on Payments and Market Infrastructures, *Considerations for the use of stablecoin arrangements in cross-border payments* (Bank for International Settlements 2023), online: https://www.bis.org/cpmi/publ/d220.pdf, accessed 18 July 2024. The report relies on and/or proceeds on the assumption that the regulatory recommendations proffered in the CPMI, and International Organization of Securities Commissions IOSCO 2022 report (as well as other reports) have been observed. See CPMI and IOSCO, *Application of the Principles for Financial Market Infrastructures to stablecoin arrangements* (Bank for International Settlements and IOSCO, 2022), online: https://www.iosco.org/library/pubdocs/pdf/IOSCOPD707.pdf, accessed 19 July 2024. This CPMI and IOSCO guideline was released as an improvement to an October 2021 guidance of the same description.

IV. STABLECOIN ARRANGEMENT RISKS
AND DESIGNING REGULATORY RESPONSES

a. Crypto-asset Activities Risks

Compared to a non-cash payment over an interbank legacy payment system, payment by stablecoin does not require banking intermediation since it is not being made through bank accounts, and can be made from one person to another. As such it has a great potential for cost reduction. However, a comprehensive regulatory framework governing stablecoins is required to address security against hacking and counterfeiting, as well as consumer and investor's protection.[70] It is also required to address blockchain related problems as well as risks associated with the identity of the issuer, that as a rule, is not even required to be a regulated financial institution.

Notably, the wide use of a blockchain for payment and settlement is, however, problematic. First, so far, the settlement has been slower than existing legacy payment systems.[71] Second, unresolved disagreement among

---

70   To that end see e.g., European Commission, "Proposal for a Regulation of the European Parliament and of the Council on Markets in Crypto-assets, and amending Directive (EU) 2019/1937" COM(2020) at 593 final, online: https://eur-lex.europa.eu/legal-content/EN/TXT/?uri=CELEX%3A52020PC0593, accessed 5 November 2024.

71   For example, Visa's actual transaction speed per second (TPS) is more than 65,000. See Visa, "Fact Sheet: What You Need to Know About One of the World's Largest Payments Companies" (*Visa*), online: https://www.visa.co.uk/dam/VCOM/download/corporate/media/visanet-technology/aboutvisafactsheet.pdf, accessed 5 November 2024. It is currently faster that any cryptocurrency TPS; by comparison, Bitcoin has seven TPS, see "Bitcoin Scalability Problem" (*Wikipedia*, 3 October 2024), online: https://en.wikipedia.org/wiki/Bitcoin_scalability_problem, accessed 5 November 2024; Ethereum has fifteen TPS, see Raja Amir, "Understanding an Ethereum Transaction" (*Etherscan*, 8 August 2023), online: https://info.etherscan.com/understanding-an-ethereum-transactio n/, accessed 5 November 2024 (though an upgrade to Ethereum known as "Proto-Danksharding" aiming to scale Ethereum to more than 100,000 TPS is underway, see "Danksharding" (*Ethereum*, 24 July 2024), online: https://ethereum.org/en/roadmap/danksharding/, accessed 5 November 2024; Solana maintains that it has capacity for 65,000 TPS, see Solana Foundation, "Network Performance Report: July 2023" (*Solana*, 20 July 2023), online: https://solana.com/news/network-performance-report-jul y-2023, accessed 5 November 2024, although its average executed TPS is about 2,200, see Binance News, "Solana's Average TPS Reaches 2200 With Over 80% Transaction Success Rate in H1 2024"(*Binance Square*, 28 June 2024), online: https://www.binance. com/en/square/post/2024-06-28-solana-s-average-tps-reaches-2200-with-over-80-tra nsaction-success-rate-in-h1-2024-10085491122530, accessed 5 November 2024; Ripple has capacity for 3,400 TPS but only process about 600 TPS, see Coinstages, "XRP's Meteoric Rise: 3,400 TPS and a \$5 Price on the Horizon" (*Binance Square*, 6 December 2023), on-

developers or other actors such as miners may create "hard forks" namely, a bifurcation in a distributed ledger whereby separate and irreconcilable ledgers are created.[72] Specifically,[73] SAs may feature "probabilistic settlement," where a misalignment between legal finality and technical settlement may occur.[74] A misalignment occurs, for example, when legal finality is thought to have been achieved, but a "fork" causes technical settlement to be reversed. With probabilistic settlement, even if the relevant legal framework and the SA's rules and procedures have defined the point at which final settlement occurs, the possibility remains that forks emerge that could lead to a reversal of technical settlement of transactions. The probability for a given state of technical settlement to be conclusive increases as more transactions are added to the ledger. At the same time, the settlement risk implications of a fork increase with the number of transactions added to the ledger, as they are subject to a potential reversal.

Third, differences in design preclude blockchain interoperability. For their part, limited scalability and a lack of interoperability prevent network effects from taking root, and lead to a system of parallel blockchains which adds to governance, settlement, and legal finality risks.[75]

Fourth, in a payment by cryptocurrency over a blockchain, the transaction is exposed on the blockchain and thus compromises on privacy. This is so since the chain of custody of the cryptocurrency is written on a distributed ledger and is thus exposed. Verification of transfer requires identification of the payer's public key and transfer is publicized to the entire community. Conversely in a quantum-resistant currency,[76] the chain of custody, together with terms of use, can be written on the coin itself; it is not necessary to identify payer; and the bit sequence defines only the unique

---

line: https://www.binance.com/en/square/post/979938295594, accessed 5 November 2024; Litecoin has fifty-six TPS, see E Napoletano and Farran Powell, "What is Litecoin? How Does it Work?" (*Forbes*, 11 June 2024), online: https://www.forbes.com/advisor/au /investing/cryptocurrency/litecoin/, accessed 5 November 2024; Hedera-has 10,000 TPS, see "HBAR" (*Hedera*), online: https://hedera.com/hbar#:~:text=The%20Hedera%20network%20achieves%2010%2C000,on%20network%20security%20or%20stability, accessed 5 November 2024.

72 Financial Stability Board, "Decentralised financial technologies: Report on financial stability, regulatory and governance implications" (*FSB*, June 2019) at 23, online: https://www.fsb.org /wp-content/uploads/P060619.pdf, accessed 5 November 2024.

73 CPMI and IOSCO, *Stablecoin Arrangements*, above note 69 at para 3.4.3.

74 *Ibid* at para 3.4.5.

75 Frederic Boissay et al, *Blockchain scalability and the fragmentation of crypto* (Bulletin No 56, Bank for International Settlements 2022), online: https://www.bis.org/publ/bisbull56.pdf, accessed 18 July 2024.

76 Amnon Samid, above note 41.

identity of the coin, exactly like the serial number on a paper banknote.[77] This is because quantum technology money, by design, makes forgery, duplication, and/or counterfeiting almost impossible, and an issuer would be alerted of any such unauthorized attempt.[78] Thus, quantum-resistant currency or quantum money technology may be able to preserve parties' privacy without jeopardizing currency security.

Fifth, a payment by cryptocurrency over a blockchain requires online validation and can thus be performed from beginning to end only where internet is available. This feature poses a challenge to payment and settlement process. Conversely, considering quantum cryptography capabilities, for genuine freshly minted coins (and thus by definition unspent), BitMint's Hard Wallet can validate and provide finality to off-line proximity payments.[79]

Risks for financial stability are of great importance. The Bank for International Settlements (BIS) Committee on Payments and Market Infrastructures (CPMI) and the Board of the International Organization of Securities Commissions (IOSCO) addressed the topic. They identified four overarching considerations that an authority may take into account when it assesses the systemic importance of an SA within its jurisdiction, with such assessment being for the purpose of applying the Principles for Financial Market Infrastructures (PFMI) addressing financial stability:[80]

- The first consideration is the size of the SA, in terms of number of users as well as number and value of transactions and value of stablecoins in circulation;
- The second element is the nature and risk profile of the SA's activity. This takes into account type of users and transactions;
- The third factor is the interconnectedness and interdependencies of the SA with the real economy and financial system; and

---

77   See e.g., Gideon Samid, "A LeVeL Paying Field," above note 45.

78   Karol Bartkiewicz et al, "Experimental quantum forgery of quantum optical money" (2017) 3 NPJ Quantum Information, online: https://doi.org/10.1038/s41534-017-0010-x , accessed 10 August 2024.

79   This is carried out by a "quick touch" by one device to another and applies even to a proximity payment in other than BitMinted coins, Gideon Samid, "BitMint Hard Wallet: Digital Payment without Network Communication: No Internet, yet Sustained Payment Regimen between Randomness – Verifiable Hard Wallets" (IOT, Electronics and Mechatronics Conference, Institute of Electrical and Electronics Engineers 2020) at 1–7; BitMint, above note 26.

80   CPMI and IOSCO, *Stablecoin Arrangements*, above note 69 at para 2.1.3.

- The fourth and last factor to be considered is the substitutability of the SA[81], i.e., whether there are available alternatives to using the SA as a means of payment or settlement for time-critical services.[82]

For an SA of a fiat-backed stablecoin, one plausible systemic risk scenario is a spill-over from the default of a commercial bank holding the reserve against which stablecoins are issued so as to preclude their redemption. The other scenario is where stablecoins are used as instruments of finance. Their use as instruments of finance makes it easier for leverage to build up by the creation of collateral chains, that is, "multiple claims on the same underlying collateral."[83] The result "is not unlike fractional reserve banking, with collateral requirements replacing reserve requirements."[84] The absence of full reserve creates new money with a potential to have an impact on both monetary and financial stability. Indeed, as under a "currency board" regime, the full reserve of the reference asset is only of the "monetary base" and not of the full "monetary supply," which includes money lent.[85]

b. Designing Regulatory Framework for Crypto-asset Risks

Addressing crypto-asset activities risks, the Financial Stability Board (FSB) published on 11 October 2022 an invitation to the public to comment on the formulation of framework for the international regulation of such activities.[86] The core components requested for this framework are proposals for:

81 IOSCO had in March 2020 published a public report on "Global Stablecoin Initiatives" wherein it broadly considers regulatory issues that large-scale adoption of stablecoins may trigger. See IOSCO, "Global Stablecoin Initiatives Public Report" (OR01/2020, *IOSCO*, March 2020), online: https://www.iosco.org/library/pubdocs/pdf/IOSCOPD650.pdf, accessed 28 July 2024. The report annexed the preliminary analysis on applying PFMI to SA.

82 In May 2023, IOSCO also published consultation Report on "Policy Recommendations for Crypto and Digital Asset Markets," IOSCO also raised some issues relating to stablecoin adoption for consideration. See IOSCO, "Policy Recommendations for Crypto and Digital Assets Markets: Consultation Report" (CR01/2023, *IOSCO*, May 2023), online: https://www.iosco.org/library/pubdocs/pdf/IOSCOPD734.pdf, accessed 28 July 2024.

83 MacDonald, above note 1 at 2.

84 *Ibid* at 19, and in great detail, at 19–26.

85 At least in theory, resulting risks can be eliminated by precluding lending not backed by a full reserve.

86 Financial Stability Board, "International Regulation of Crypto-asset Activities: A Proposed Framework – Questions for Consultation" (*Financial Stability Board*, 11 October 2022), online: https://www.fsb.org/wp-content/uploads/P111022-2.pdf, accessed 28 July 2024. The public responses were published on 4 January. See "Public Responses to FSB's Pro-

- recommendations that promote the consistency and comprehensiveness of regulatory, supervisory, and oversight approaches to crypto-asset activities and markets and strengthen international cooperation, coordination and information sharing; and
- revised high-level recommendations for the regulation, supervision, and oversight of "global stablecoin" arrangements to address associated financial stability risks more effectively.[87]

In turn, as for the ultimate objective, the FSB stated that:

- An effective regulatory framework must ensure that crypto-asset activities are subject to comprehensive regulation, commensurate to the risks they pose, while harnessing potential benefits of the technology behind them.
- The regulatory framework should reflect the relevance of crypto-assets for financial stability and support proper market functioning.
- High regulatory standards are required in particular for stablecoins – that could be widely used as a means of payments and/or store of value, as they could pose significant risks to financial stability.
- Regulation should provide for adequate transparency, accountability, market integrity, investor and consumer protections, and AML/CFT defences across the crypto-asset ecosystem.[88]

Proposed recommendations to achieve such a framework are requested to be,

[G]rounded in the principle of "same activity, same risk, same regulation": where crypto-assets and intermediaries perform an equivalent economic function to one performed by instruments and intermediaries of the traditional financial sector, they should be subject to equivalent regulation. Regulation should also take account of novel features and specific risks of crypto-assets and address potential financial stability risks that could arise

---

posed Framework for International Regulation of Cryptoasset Activities" (*FSB*, 4 January 2023), online: https://www.fsb.org/2023/01/public-responses-to-fsbs-proposed-framewor k-for-international-regulation-of-crypto-asset-activities/, accessed 18 July 2024. The final report published in July 2023 is discussed further below.

87   Financial Stability Board, "International Regulation of Crypto-asset Activities,'" above note 86.

88   Financial Stability Board, "Regulation, Supervision and Oversight," above note 17 at 2.

from the growing interlinkages between the crypto-asset ecosystem and the traditional financial system.[89]

In a joint statement, the Office of the Superintendent of Financial Institutions (OSFI), the Financial Consumer Agency of Canada (FCAC), and the Canada Deposit Insurance Corporation (CDIC), expressed their adherence to the FSB's underlying principle of "same activity, same risk, same regulation."[90] Accordingly, the joint statement thus requires federal regulated entities to be aware of:

- applicable prudential regulation;
- the new and enhanced requirements under the *Financial Consumer Protection Framework*;[91] and
- crypto-assets' ineligibility for deposit insurance under the *Canada Deposit Insurance Corporation Act.*[92]

Expanding upon the October 2022 Report, the final FSB report was released in July 2023[93] with regulatory recommendations. Notably and in contrast to the October 2022 Report, the July 2023 Report recommends comprehensive regulation and supervision of the entire value chain of stablecoin arrangements.[94] Nonetheless, the Committee on Payments and Market Infrastructures (CPMI) and the Board of the International Organization of Securities Commissions (IOSCO) have pointed out that the Application of the Principles for Financial Market Infrastructures to stablecoin arrangements[95] should not apply to entities which merely accept or use stablecoins as a means of payment.[96] Such entities are non-SA FMIs. CPMI

---

89   *Ibid.*

90   Office of the Superintendent of Financial Institutions, "Statement to Entities Engaging in Crypto-asset Activities and Related Services" (*Government of Canada*, 16 November 2022), online: https://www.osfi-bsif.gc.ca/en/news/statement-entities-engaging-crypto-asset-activities-or-crypto-related-services, accessed 5 November 2024; see in general, Mohammed Muraj et al, "For Crypto, Canadian Federal Financial Regulators Support More of the 'Same'" (Torys, 30 November 2022), online: https://www.torys.com/our-latest-thinking/publications/2022/11/for-crypto-canadian-federal-financial-regulators-support-more-of-the-same, accessed 5 November 2024.

91   SOR/2021-181.

92   RSC 1985, c C-3.

93   Financial Stability Board, "High-level Recommendations for the Regulation, Supervision and Oversight of Global Stablecoin Arrangements (Final Report)" (*Financial Stability Board*, 17 July 2023), online: https://www.fsb.org/wp-content/uploads/P170723-3.pdf, accessed 18 July 2024.

94   *Ibid* at 4–5.

95   CPMI and IOSCO, *Stablecoin Arrangements*, above note 69. This CPMI and IOSCO guideline was released as an improvement to October 2021 guidance of the same description.

96   *Ibid* at paras 1.3.1, 1.3.3.

and IOSCO also recommend that other regulations should be applied where stablecoins are used for speculative or investment purposes, essentially pointing out that the guidance applies only to entities using stablecoins as a payment system.[97] CPMI and IOSCO urge regulatory authorities to clearly disclose the criteria used to determine the systemic importance of SAs. Authorities can then also discretionarily monitor the growth of SAs to determine their systemic importance. Regulatory authorities are also encouraged to foster cross-border cooperation among themselves.[98] Additionally, it is necessary to bear in mind that human intervention may be necessary in certain instances regarding the governance of SAs, and that such human interventions may be to tweak the smart or algorithmic governance of SA's to adapt to prevailing circumstance.[99]

In the 2022 Guidelines, CPMI and IOSCO expanded on the class of non-Financial Market Infrastructures (FMI) functions that may pose material risks to FMIs. Such functions include node operators and other service providers that may or may not be corporately related to the FMI.[100] The mention of node operators is particularly noteworthy. Neither miners nor node operators but rather validators are involved in SA. While most stablecoins are ERC-20s[101] built on third-party blockchains which rely on node operators, it is doubtful that the guideline is directed at host blockchain nodes which do not participate in the SA process. Hence, the mention of node operators in the 2022 Guidelines is odd.

In addition to transaction settlement on indicated value date, guidelines recommend preference for "intraday or real time" settlement as a way to mitigate settlement risk. In this regard, transaction settlement must be cognizable as final under relevant FMI structures and insolvency law.[102] Regarding transaction finality vis-à-vis probabilistic settlement, the guideline has called for an independent legal opinion on best approach.[103] Relatedly, CPMI and IOSCO urge SA issuers to put measures in place to address/prevent potential misalignment between legal state of transaction and the ledger state.[104] There is no specifically recommended measure, but

---

97   *Ibid* at para 1.3.3.
98   *Ibid* at para 2.1.4.
99   *Ibid* at para 3.2.6.
100 *Ibid* at para 3.3.3.
101 For ERC-20 see above, note 31.
102 CPMI and IOSCO, *Stablecoin Arrangements*, above note 69 at para 3.4.1.
103 *Ibid* at para 3.4.3.
104 *Ibid* at para 3.4.5. This is a newly introduced recommendation which appears to have been influenced by the recent crypto exchange failures.

it appears that such measure would require some form of loan loss provisioning. While this would be easy for bank SAs to deal with, it will be an uphill battle for non-bank SAs to deal with since loan loss provisioning is not envisaged as part of the business models of non-bank crypto issuers. Effectively, the guidance may have the effect of stifling the innovation in the market and making it less competitive.

Another type of risk identified is misuse for criminal activity. Specifically, similarly to money transfers, stablecoin transactions may be misused for money laundering and terrorist finance. Accordingly, businesses dealing in virtual currencies are subject to anti-money laundering and anti-terrorist financing control as if they were dealing in money.[105] This was pointed out by the FATF *Report to the G20 Finance Ministers and Central Bank Governors on So-called Stablecoins*.[106] The Report identified three money laundering/terrorist financing risks of stablecoins:

(i)   Anonymity;[107]
(ii) Global reach Layering, namely the ability of quickly exchanging between different virtual assets; and
(iii) Potential for mass-adoption

As well, the Report identified the following three residual money laundering/terrorist financing risks:

(i)   Risks from anonymous peer-to-peer transactions via an unhosted wallet (known also as cold storage or self-custody), that is, a crypto wallet that is not hosted on a crypto platform like an exchange, but rather allows users to store their crypto assets outside a crypto platform;
(ii) Risks from weak or non-existent Anti-Money Laundering/Counter Terrorist Financing regulation by some jurisdictions: and
(iii) Risks from so-called stablecoins having a decentralized governance structure.

---

105   See Clements, above note 20 at 20–22.

106   The Financial Action Task Force, "FATF Report to G20 on So-called Stablecoins" (*FAFT*, 7 June 2020), online: https://www.fatf-gafi.org/en/publications/virtualassets/documents/report-g20-so-called-stablecoins-june-2020.html, accessed 26 July 2024.

107   What is exposed on a distributed ledger (which may be accessible to the public at large) so as to compromise privacy is the payer's public key and not their own credentials so that customer identification information may be disguised and not be revealed at least directly. See "FATF Report," *ibid* at 8; Dong He et al, above note 13 at 9 thus speak of cryptocurrencies as "pseudo-anonymous."

In Canada, businesses dealing in virtual currencies must be registered as domestic or foreign "money services businesses" (MSB) with the Financial Transactions and Reports Analysis Centre of Canada (FINTRAC). The latter is Canada's financial intelligence unit pursuant to the *Proceeds of Crime (Money Laundering) and Terrorist Financing Act (PCMLTFA)*[108] and the regulations passed thereunder.[109] Dealing in virtual currency includes both virtual currency exchange and virtual currency transfer services. A non-resident business dealing in virtual currency must register as a foreign MSB if it directs its services to persons in Canada. Additionally, the requirements for all reporting entities under the PCMLTFA to report to FINTRAC receipts of $10,000 or more of cash in any twenty-four-hour period has been extended to receipts of the equivalent of $10,000 of virtual currency.

Potential investors must remain mindful of existing prohibitions on dealing in property owned or controlled by a designated person or providing financial or related services to or for the benefit of a designated person under Canadian sanctions and anti-terrorism financing laws.[110]

As an "evidence of indebtedness," and perhaps more so when it is purchased with an investment intent so as to be an "investment contract," a stablecoin may be seen as a "security"[111] so as to fall under the jurisdiction of a securities regulator.[112] Regardless, securities regulators in Canada also assert jurisdiction over the trading of cryptocurrencies, such as Bitcoin, that are ordinarily not considered to be securities. Such is the case where the Crypto Asset-Trading Platform (CTP) takes custody of the cryptocurrency

---

108 SC 2000, c 17.

109 See e.g., SOR/2022-76.

110 These include the *United Nations Act*, RSC 1985, c U-2; *Special Economic Measures Act*, SC 1992, c 17; *Freezing Assets of Corrupt Foreign Officials Act*, SC 2011, c 10; *Justice for Victims of Corrupt Foreign Officials Act*, SC 2017, c 21; and the *Criminal Code*, RSC 1985, c C-46.

111 See e.g., Ontario *Securities Act*, RSO 1990, c S5, s 1(1), defining "security" to include (e) "bond, debenture, note or other evidence of indebtedness" and (n) "any investment contract." For treating the investment intent as a predominant factor in characterizing an "investment contract" (in prong (n)) as "security," see *Pacific Coast Coin Exchange v Ontario Securities Commission*, 1977 CanLII 37. As for "bond, debenture, note or other evidence of indebtedness" in prong (e), see *Ontario Securities Commission v Tiffin et al* (2020) 150 OR (3d) 714, where even as the court recognized that "the words of legislation must always be read in context and harmoniously with the intention" (*ibid* at para 49) it interpreted prong (e) quite broadly (*ibid* at para 50);. On *Tiffin* and prong (e) see e.g., Christopher C Nicholls, *Securities Law*, 3d ed (Irwin Law, 2023) at 56–61.

112 See Clements, above note 20 at 7–14.

and then provides the user with a "contractual right" to the delayed, rather than immediate, delivery of the cryptocurrency.[113]

V. REGULATORY RESPONSES TO STABLECOIN ARRANGEMENT RISKS

a. CSA in Canada

In Canada, stablecoins and SA are the subject[114] of two Canadian Securities Administrators (CSA)[115] staff notices ("CSA Notices") designed to provide guidance to cryptoasset trading platforms (CPTs). They are:

(i) the Staff Notice 21-332 Crypto Asset Trading Platforms: Pre-Registration Undertakings – Changes to Enhance Canadian Investor Protection ("CSA First Notice");[116] and

(ii) CSA Staff Notice 21-333 Crypto Asset Trading Platforms: Terms and Conditions for Trading Value-Referenced Crypto Assets with Clients ("CSA Second Notice").[117]

---

113 See above, note 111; see also Canadian Securities Administrators, "CSA Staff Notice 21-327: Guidance on the Application of Securities Legislation to Entities Facilitating the Trading of Crypto Assets" (*Ontario Securities Commission*, 16 January 2020), online: https://www. osc.ca/en/securities-law/instruments-rules-policies/2/21-327/csa-staff-notice-21-327-guidanc e-application-securities-legislation-entities-facilitating-trading, accessed 7 November 2024; *Kik Interactive v AIG*, 2020 ONSC 8194 avoided addressing the question.

114 CSA Staff Notices are designed to guide as to their practices.

115 The CSA "is the umbrella organization of Canada's provincial and territorial securities regulators whose objective is to improve, coordinate and harmonize regulation of the Canadian capital markets." See CSA "About Us" (*CSA*), online: https://www.securities-administrators. ca/about/, accessed 20 July 2023.

116 CSA, "CSA Staff Notice 21-332 Crypto Asset Trading Platforms: Pre-Registration Undertakings – Changes to Enhance Canadian Investor Protection" (*Ontario Securities Commission*, 22 February 2023), online: https://www.osc.ca/en/securities-law/instruments-rules-policies/ 2/21-332/csa-staff-notice-21-332-crypto-asset-trading-platforms-pre-registration -undertakings-changes, accessed 7 November 2024.

117 CSA, "CSA Staff Notice 21-333 Crypto Asset Trading Platforms: Terms and Conditions for Trading Value-Referenced Crypto Assets with Clients" (Ontario Securities Commission, 5 October 2023), online: https://www.osc.ca/en/securities-law/instruments-rules-policies /2/21-333/csa-staff-notice-21-333-crypto-asset-trading-platforms-terms-and-conditions -trading-value, accessed 7 November 2024.

Staff Notice 21-333 set for compliance by CTPs with Staff Notice 21-332 and Staff Notice 21-333. CTPs are expected to stop dealing in or listing non-compliant stablecoins. The enforcement of the deadline would require CTPs to delist non-compliant VRCAs.

Binance, OKX, dYdX, and Paxos ended their operations in Canadian sequel to the issuance of Staff Notice 21-332; see Cointelegraph, "Binance Calls it Quits in Canada, Blames New Rules" (*Binance Square*, 12 May 2023), online: https://www.binance.com/en

The First Notice was issued in relation to crypto-assets generally but directed specifically at Crypto-Trading Platforms (CTPs). The Second Notice was issued specifically in relation to stablecoins, otherwise termed "Value-Referenced Crypto Assets." It was issued after the FSB's July 2023 Report and appears to adopt its recommendations.

Canadian Securities Administrators (CSA) are of the view that stablecoins, or stablecoin arrangements (SAs), may constitute securities and/or derivatives.[118] The CSA disfavours the term "stablecoin." This is so since "these types of assets can also experience volatility and there have been several instances over the past year where crypto-assets purported to be "stablecoins" did not maintain their "peg" on trading platforms."[119] Rather, the CSA prefers to refer to such instruments as "Value-Referenced Crypto Asset" (VRCA). It points out that "consumers may be misled into believing that VRCAs are risk-free, that their price will not deviate from its reference value (both in the normal markets and during difficult events) or that they have a direct claim on the reserve of assets." Accordingly, the CSA requires "transparency of [such] arrangements about their reserves of assets, the stabilization mechanisms of their value and their governance [which] are generally key issues that require appropriate regulation to protect VRCA holders."[120]

/square/post/518423, accessed 7 November 2024. The regulatory pressure on Binance is a little more than others considering that Binance is a CTP as well as a stablecoin issuer. Binance is the issue of Binance USD (BUSD). CTPs have struggled to comply with the CSA Notices on account of certain "technical issues." As such, the CSA extended compliance deadline to 31 October 2024. See CSA, "Canadian securities regulators provide update on interim approach to value-referenced crypto assets" (*CSA*, 17 April 2024), online: https://www.securities-administrators.ca/news/canadian-securities-regulators-provide-update-o n-interim-approach-to-value-referenced-crypto-assets/, accessed 8 August 2024.

118   CSA, "Staff Notice 21-332," above note 116 at 9–13. See also, Mohammed Muraj, Konata T Lake, and Glen R Johnson, "Stability and security: the CSA's characterization of stablecoins" (*Torys*, 9 March 2023), online: https://www.torys.com/en/our-latest-thinking/publications/2023/03/the-csas-characterization-of-stablecoins#:~:text=The%20CSA%20in%20 SN%2021,their%20peg%20on%20trading%20platforms, accessed 7 November 2024. The CSA's characterization of stablecoins as securities is challenged by the industry. See Claire Brownell, "Crypto industry pushes back on stricter stablecoin rules" (*The Logic*, 27 March 2023), online: https://thelogic.co/news/exclusive/crypto-industry-pushes-back-on-stricte r-stablecoin-rules/, accessed 7 November 2024. This view was also expressed in FSB, "Regulation, Supervision, Oversight (Final Report)," above note 17.

119   CSA, "Staff Notice 21-332," above note 116 at 10. For instance, "stablecoins" like Terra and Tether both failed to maintain their pegs in May 2022. Terra never recovered while Tether regained stability but has dropped below its peg on several other occasions since then. See FSB, "Regulation, Supervision, Oversight (Final Report)," above note 17.

120   CSA, "Staff Notice 21-332," above note 116 at 11. The industry "acknowledges these concerns … but argues treating stablecoins as securities is the wrong way to go about it." Rather, it proposes, that instead of asserting that stablecoins are securities or derivatives, the CSA

Per the CSA Notices, VRCAs are further categorized as "Fiat-Backed Crypto Assets" (FBCAs)[121] and non-FBCAs. As their names suggest, the former are backed by fiat currencies while the latter by other assets including a basket of fiat currencies. In turn, the CSA pronouncement expressed certain concerns about the risks inherent in stablecoin arrangements of both sub-categories. Paramount are the concerns that:

(i) FBCAs may not have adequate reserve assets with proper "stabilization mechanism" or that the referenced "fiat currency may not be in a segregated reserve account";[122]

(ii) the primary use of VRCAs "to facilitate the trading, borrowing and lending of other crypto assets" may lead to overleverage and maturity mismatch with potential stablecoin "run" and attendant risks to financial system;

(iii) ignorance or information gap among VCRA customers about reserve claims and redemption rights may exist; and

(iv) the occurrence of mismanagement of reserve custodianship and governance.[123]

The CSA highlights the concern that consumers may be misled into believing that stablecoins are risk-free. As a way to address this concern, CTPs are required "to conduct sufficient due diligence to ensure that applicable risks in respect of the VRCA are addressed." In particular, as part of the pre-conditions for the authorization to permit CTPs to offer VRCAs to Canadian clients, a CTP must ensure for each issuer that:[124]

- the VRCA is a fiat-backed crypto asset;[125]
- where distributions of the fiat-backed crypto asset are made in Canada, such distributions are made in compliance with applicable Canadian securities legislation;

---

and its members should work with [platforms] and other stakeholders to find ways of enhancing the existing product due diligence and disclosure requirements under the existing ... regulatory framework." See Brownell, above note 118 at 5.

121 CSA, "Staff Notice 21-333," above note 117 at 1.

122 CSA, "Staff Notice 21-332," above note 116 at 10.

123 *Ibid* at 11.

124 *Ibid* at 12–13.

125 In CSA, "Staff Notice 21-332," above note 116 at 13 the CSA indicates that it will consent to the trading of a "Value-Referenced Crypto Asset so long as it is fully-backed by an appropriate reserve." Nonetheless in CSA, "Staff Notice 21-333," above note 117 at 1 the CSA clarifies that this notice only applies to Fiat-Backed Crypto Assets (FBCA). As such, while Staff Notice 21-333, above note 117 applies only to FBCAs, Canadian regulators will consider other stablecoins so long as they are fully backed.

- the issuer of the fiat-backed crypto asset maintains a reserve of assets with a market value at least equal to the value of outstanding units of the fiat-backed crypto asset at the end of each day;
- the reserve of assets is comprised of highly liquid assets, such as cash or cash equivalents;
- the reserve of assets is held by a qualified custodian in favour of the fiat-backed crypto asset holders;
- the reserve of assets is segregated from assets of the issuer and the assets of each class of other crypto asset issued by the issuer;
- the reserve of assets is subject to a monthly attestation and an annual audit from an independent auditor, copies of which are made publicly accessible in a timely manner;
- the redemption rights of the VRCA holder, directly or indirectly, against the issuer of the fiat-backed crypto asset, or the reserve of assets, are clearly articulated in policies and procedures and publicly disclosed;
- the issuer of the fiat-backed crypto asset maintains a plan for recovery and to support an orderly wind-down in case of a crisis or failure by the issuer or an affiliate of the issuer;
- the issuer of the fiat-backed crypto asset maintains effective governance practices;
- key accurate information about the fiat-backed crypto asset is made publicly accessible in plain and non-technical language; and
- the CTP is not otherwise prohibited from allowing clients to enter into crypto contracts in respect of the fiat-backed crypto asset.

As well, the CSA points at the existence of greater risks in connection with algorithm-based VRCAs and has indicated that it will not consent to the offering of such instruments by CTPs.[126]

In response to the risks inherent in SA, authorities throughout the world are developing legal and regulatory responses. Having outlined the position in Canada, the ensuing discussion will outline major developments in the United States and the European Union, respectively.

b. The US GENIUS Act

A number of bills addressing stablecoins have been introduced for discussion at the United States Congress. For example:

---

126 CSA, "Staff Notice 21-332," above note 116 at 13.

- *Managed Stablecoins are Securities Act* of 2019 (HR 5197);[127]
- *Stablecoin Classification and Regulation Act* of 2020 (HR 8827);[128]
- *Bill to establish reporting requirements for persons who issue fiat currency-backed stablecoins, and for other purposes* (HR 8498);[129]
- *Stablecoin Transparency Act* (HR 7328);[130]
- *Payment Stablecoin Issuers and digital dollar Act 2023*;[131]
- *Clarity for Payment Stablecoins Act* of 2023 (HR 4766);[132] and
- *Stablecoin TRUST Act of 2022* (S 5340)[133]

The legislative responses to stablecoin regulation appear to have been fueled by the report of the President's Working Group on Financial Markets of 2021 which recommends full scale stablecoin laws and regulation.[134] Having been placed on the Union Calendar as recently as 5 July 2024, the *Bill for Clarity for payment Stablecoins Act* of 2023, the sixth in the list above, has gained traction. Having captured the essence of other stablecoin-related bills,[135] it served as a basis for the *Guiding and Establishing National Innovation*

127 Managed Stablecoins are Securities Act, HR 5197, 116 Cong (2019), online: https://www.congress.gov/116/bills/hr5197/BILLS-116hr5197ih.pdf, accessed 21 July 2024.

128 Stablecoin Classification and Regulation Act, HR 8827, 116 Cong (2020). https://www.congress.gov/116/bills/hr8827/BILLS-116hr8827ih.pdf, accessed 21 July 2024.

129 Bill to establish reporting requirements for persons who issue fiat currency backed stablecoins, and for other purposes, HR 8498, 117 Cong (2022), online: https://www.congress.gov/117/bills/hr8498/BILLS-117hr8498ih.pdf, accessed 21 July 2024.

130 *Stablecoin Transparency Act*, HR 7328, 117 Cong (2022), online: https://www.congress.gov/117/bills/hr7328/BILLS-117hr7328ih.pdf, accessed 8 August 2024.

131 United States HR Draft Bill, "To provide requirements for payment stablecoin issuers, research on a digital dollar, and for other purposes" (118 Cong 2023), ss 101(16), 201, online: https://docs.house.gov/meetings/BA/BA21/20230419/115753/BILLS-118pih-Toproviderequirementsforpaymentstablecoinissuersresearchonadigitaldollarandforotherpurposes.pdf, accessed 19 June 2024.

132 *Clarity for Payment Stablecoins Act*, HR 4766, 118 Cong (2023), online: https://www.congress.gov/118/bills/hr4766/BILLS-118hr4766rh.pdf, accessed 21 July 2024.

133 *Stablecoin TRUST Act*, S 5340, 117 Cong (2022), online: https://www.congress.gov/117/bills/s5340/BILLS-117s5340is.pdf, accessed 21 July 2024.

134 President's Working Group on Financial Markets, The Federal Deposit Insurance Corporation and the Office of the Comptroller of the Currency, "Report on Stablecoins" (November 2021), online: https://home.treasury.gov/system/files/136/StableCoinReport_Nov1_508.pdf, accessed 26 July 2024.

135 HR 4766, above note 133 ("US GENIUS Act"). Save for the *Payment Stablecoin Issuers and digital dollar Act 2023*, above note 132), other stablecoin-related Bills last recorded progress in 2019, 2020, and 2022. Efforts have been made to reconcile the *Payment Stablecoin Issuers and digital dollar Act 2023* and HR 4766, above note 132, to achieve a bipartisan bill. See "McHenry Delivers Opening Remarks at Markup of Stablecoin, ESG Legislation" (27 July 2023), online: https://financialservices.house.gov/news/documentsingle.aspx?DocumentID=408941, accessed 28 July 2024.

for US StableCoins (GENIUS) Act[136] approved in March 2025 by the US Senate Committee on Banking, Housing and Urban Affairs and is expected to be passed before the August 2025 break ("GENIUS Act").[137]

The Genius Act section 2(15) defines "payment stablecoin" to mean a digital asset:

(A) ... a digital asset –
    (i)   that is or is designed to be used as a means of payment or settlement; and
    (ii) the issuer of which –
        (I)   is obligated to convert, redeem, or repurchase for a fixed amount of monetary value, not including a digital asset denominated in a fixed amount of monetary value;
        (II)   represents that such issuer will maintain or creates the reason-able expectation that it will maintain a stable value relative to the value of a fixed amount of monetary value; or
        (III) has complied with the authorization requirements of this Act;
    and
B) that –
    (i)   is not a national currency;
    (ii) is not a deposit ...
    (iii) does not offer a payment of yield or interest; and
    (iv) is not a security ... other than a bond, note, evidence of indebtedness, or investment contract satisfying the conditions described in subparagraph (A).

Section 3 prohibits "any person other than a permitted payment stablecoin issuer to issue a payment stablecoin for use by any person in the United States." For its part, "a permitted payment stablecoin issuer" is defined in section 2(16) to be:

(A) a subsidiary of an insured depository institution[138] that has been approved to issue payment stablecoins under section 5;

---

136   Bill S 919, *Guiding and Establishing National Innovation for U.S. Stablecoins (GENIUS) Act of 23 2025, 1st Sess, 119th Congress, US, 2025* (Placed on Senate Legislative Calendar under General Orders No 33, 18 March 2025) [GENIUS].

137   The same Bill for Clarity for payment Stablecoins Act of 2023 is also the basis for Bill HR 2392, *Stablecoin Transparency and Accountability for Better Ledger Economy (STABLE) of 2025 Act*, 1st Sess, 119th Congress, US, 2025 (Placed on the Union Calendar No 68, 6 May 2025).

138   *GENUIS* above note 136, at s 2(16)(A).

(B) a Federal qualified nonbank payment stablecoin issuer[139] that has been approved to issue payment stablecoins under section 5; or

(C) a State qualified payment stablecoin issuer.[140]

Section 5 governs the approval process for institutions covered by subparagraphs (A) and (B).

Under section 4(a)(1)(A),

Permitted payment stablecoin issuers shall –

(A) maintain reserves backing the outstanding payment stablecoins of the permitted payment stablecoin issuer on an at least 1 to 1 basis, with reserves comprising –

(i) United States coins and currency (including Federal reserve notes) ... ;

(ii) funds held as demand deposits .... or insured shares at an insured depository institution ... subject to limitations established by the Corporation and the National Credit Union Administration, as applicable, to address safety and soundness risks of such insured depository institutions;

(iii) Treasury bills, notes or bonds ... with a remaining maturity of 93 days or less ... ;

(iv) repurchase agreements with the permitted payment stablecoin issuer acting as a seller of securities and with an overnight maturity that are backed by Treasury bills with a maturity of 93 days or less;

(v) reverse repurchase agreements ...

(vi) securities issued by an investment ...

(vii) any other similarly liquid asset approved by the primary Federal payment stablecoin regulator ... or

(viii) any reserve. ...

Section 4(a)(1) goes on to require issuers to publicly disclose their redemption policy, establish procedures for timely redemption, and publish a monthly composition of reserve. Section 4(a) further restricts reserve rehypothecation, requires the certification of the accuracy of monthly reports, and provides for capital, liquidity, and risk management requirements. Finally, the provision addresses the treatment under bank secrecy legislation and provides for limitation on activities.

Section 6 contains detailed provisions regarding supervision and enforcement while section 7 governs state qualified stablecoin issuers. Anti-money

139 *Ibid* at s 2(16)(B).
140 *Ibid* at s 2(16)(C).

laundering protections are provided for in section 8. Section 9 addresses the qualifications and obligations for engaging in the business of providing custodial or safekeeping services for the payment stablecoin reserve. Treatment of payment stablecoin issuers in insolvency proceedings and interoperability are respectively addressed in sections 10 and 11.

In turn, section 12 mandates the carrying out of a study of non-payment stablecoins "including endogenously collateralized payment stablecoins." Under section 12(b) an "endogenously collateralized stablecoin" is defined to mean any digital asset:

(1) in which its originator has represented will be converted, redeemed, or repurchased for a fixed amount of monetary value; and

(2) that relies solely on the value of another digital asset created or maintained by the same originator to maintain the fixed price.

Section 13 addresses Congressional oversight on rulemaking. Section 14 provides that powers of regulated financial institutions are not affected. In turn,, section 15 clarifies that payment stablecoins are not securities or commodities. On this count, in carving payment stablecoins out of the regulatory coverage of Securities and Exchange Commission as investment contracts the US GENIUS Act appears to take a different route than the one taken by regulators in Canada and the European Union. Reciprocity for payment stablecoins issues in overseas jurisdictions is dealt with in section 16.

c. EU MiCA (Markets in Crypto-assets) Regulation: A Partial Overview

i. Introduction

Regulation (EU) 2023/1114 of the European Parliament and of the Council of 31 May 2023 on markets in crypto-assets (EU MiCA or MiCA)[141] is a

---

141 Regulation (EU) 2023/1114 of 31 May 2023 on markets in crypto-assets, and amending Regulations (EU) No 1093/2010 and (EU) No 1095/2010 and Directives 2013/36/EU and (EU) 2019/1937 [2023] OJ L150/40 (EU MiCA), online: https://eur-lex.europa.eu/eli/reg/2023/1114/oj, accessed 29 July 2024.

Though already passed in the EU Parliament, it has been recommended that the "date of application of the EU MiCA should be deferred and/or staggered." This is to allow for the adoption of regulatory technical standards, implementing technical standards and delegated acts that are necessary to further specify certain elements of the Regulation. Nonetheless, Preamble Paragraph 119, Titles III (Asset Referenced Token – Authorization Requirements et al) and IV (E-Money Tokens – Authorization Requirements et al) entered into application from June 2024. As scheduled (European Securities Market Authority "MiCA Implementing Measures," online: https://www.esma.europa.eu/esmas-activities/

crypto regulation aimed at providing clear guidelines to stakeholders in the EU stablecoin ecosystem. Its detailed provisions reinforce compliance with existing EU rules for securities trading while also providing specific requirements for stablecoin market participants.

Under MiCA, crypto-assets are classified into:

(i)   "e-money tokens" - which are "crypto-assets that aim to stabilise their value by referencing only one official currency";

(ii) "asset-referenced tokens" - "which aim to stabilise their value by referencing another value or right, or combination thereof, including one or several official currencies; and

(iii) "crypto-assets other than asset-referenced tokens and e-money tokens, [which are] a wide variety of crypto-assets, including utility tokens."[142]

Thus, EU MiCA captures stablecoins under two distinct heads, namely, e-money tokens and asset referenced tokens. In terms of objectives in relation to stablecoins the EU MiCA seeks to address the fragmentation of the legal framework applicable to their issuance, ensure a proper functioning of markets while protecting customers, and preserve market integrity and financial stability.[143]

In terms of structure, the general principles and objectives of EU MiCA are stated in the paragraph 119 Preamble. The regulatory steps and procedures are provided in the Articles 1–149. Focusing on some salient provisions, the next paragraphs will consider EU MiCA's approach to regulating the two heads of stablecoins in relation to the identified risks and concerns.

ii. Crypto-asset White Paper Requirement

A hallmark of EU MiCA is the requirement fastened on an offeror to the public of all three categories of crypto-assets to publish "a crypto-asset white paper" informing "prospective retail holders of crypto-assets ... of the characteristics, functions and risks of the crypto-assets that they intend

---

digital-finance-and-innovation/markets-crypto-assets-regulation-mica, accessed 8 August 2024), EU MiCA has been fully applicable since 30 December 2024 (even as the process of finalizing measures is still ongoing). See John Salmon, Eoin O Connor et al, "The EUs markets in Crypto-Assets MiCA Regulation a Status update," 20 February 2025, online: https://www.hoganlovells.com/en/publications/the-eus-markets-in-crypto-assets-mica-regulation-a-status-update, accessed 21 February 2025.

142   EU MiCA, above note 139, Preamble para 18.

143   *Ibid*, Preamble para 112.

to purchase."[144] The requirement is stated to apply specifically to issuers of e-money tokens[145] as well as asset referenced tokens.[146]

With variations determined by whether crypto-asset white paper is for e-money tokens or assert-referenced tokens, stablecoin white papers are required to contain, among other things, detailed issuer information, rights and obligations, risks, environmental impact, lack of coverage or insurance warnings, orderly redemption rights,[147] and claims[148] as well as the custody[149] and investment[150] of the reserve asset. Nonetheless, unlike in connection with securities issuance, crypto-asset white papers do not have to be pre-approved before publication by an issuer.[151]

The requirement in Canada under the CSA Second Notice[152] for issuers to make certain information publicly available in relation to value referenced crypto-assets is in essence similar to the EU MiCA crypto-asset white paper requirements. Notably, the issuer information requirements in the CSA Notices are neither framed as "white paper" nor are the requirements as elaborate as those contained in EU MiCA. Also, unlike EU MiCA, which directly imposes the white paper requirements on the issuer, the CSA Notices indirectly place compliance burden of the issuer information requirements on CTPs.

---

144 *Ibid*, Preamble para 24. For details, see art 6 and Annex I.
145 *Ibid*, Preamble para 66, arts 48(1)(b) and 51.
146 *Ibid*, art 19.
147 Also, issuers of e-money tokens should ensure that holders of such tokens can exercise their right to redeem their tokens at any time and at par value against the currency referencing those tokens. See EU MiCA *ibid*, para 19. See also, art 49 for detailed provisions on redemption rights of e-money token holders.
148 *Ibid*, Preamble para 67, holders of e-money tokens should be provided with a claim against the issuer of the e-money tokens. Holders of e-money tokens should always be granted a right of redemption at par value for funds denominated in the official currency that the e-money token is referencing. The provisions of Council Directive 2009/110/EC of 16 September 2009 on the taking up, pursuit, and prudential supervision of the business of electronic money institutions amending Directives 2005/60/EC and 2006/48/EC and repealing Directive 2000/46/EC [2009] OJ L267/7, on the possibility of charging a fee in relation to redemption are not relevant in the context of e-money tokens.
149 For example, see EU MiCA, above note 139, art 37 on custody of reserve assets.
150 *Ibid*, art 36, spells out mandatory reserve assets and composition and management of such reserve of assets. As per Preamble para 70, *ibid*, where an issuer of e-money tokens invests the funds received in exchange for e-money tokens, such funds should be invested in assets denominated in the same official currency as the one that the e-money token is referencing in order to avoid cross-currency risks. Articles 38 and 54 provide guidelines on the investment of reserve assets for asset-referenced tokens and e-money tokens respectively.
151 *Ibid*, art 51(11).
152 *Ibid*, Appendix A(2) and (3).

iii. E-money Tokens – Issuer Requirements

In a bid to address issuer competence and protect holders' right of redemption, EU MiCA prescribes that only authorized credit institutions and electronic money institutions can issue e-money tokens.[153] This requirement seems to be in line with the "principles of 'same activities, same risks, same rules' and of technology neutrality."[154] Since an e-money token is considered by EU MiCA to be electronic money, and since credit institutions and electronic money[155] institutions are subject to regulatory scrutiny under applicable laws, EU authorities appear confident that restricting e-money token issuance to these entities would ensure adequate regulatory oversight, market confidence, and financial stability.[156] A similar approach seems to have been adopted under the US GENIUS Act which essentially limits persons who can be "permitted stablecoin issuers" to institution-categories subject to financial regulation.[157]

iv. Significant Asset-referenced Tokens and E-money Tokens

It is recognized that some asset-referenced tokens and e-money tokens with a "large customer base, a high market capitalization, or a large number of transactions" could be used by a large number of holders, in which case their use may trigger "specific challenges in terms of financial stability, monetary policy transmission or monetary sovereignty."[158] Such highly subscribed asset-referenced tokens and e-money tokens are classified[159] as "significant asset-referenced tokens and e-money tokens," and should be subject to more stringent requirements like "higher capital requirements, interoperability requirements and liquidity management policy." Issuers of significant e-money tokens have the additional requirement in relation to asset reserve, custody, and reserve investment.[160] Issuers may also indicate during application for

---

153 *Ibid*, Preamble para 19.

154 *Ibid*, Preamble para 9.

155 *Ibid*, Preamble para 66 lists requirements to be fulfilled by all issuers of e-money tokens.

156 *Ibid*, art 48 for detailed requirements for the offer to the public or admission to trading of e-money tokens.

157 HR 4766, above note 132, § 2(14)(A-C), (19), and § 3.

158 EU MiCA, above note 139, Preamble para 59.

159 *Ibid*, arts 43 and 56 for classification of asset-referenced tokens and e-money tokens as significant tokens.

160 *Ibid*, Preamble para 71. Issuers of significant e-money tokens are also subject to dual supervision-competent national authorities and the European Banking Authority (EBA), see para 103. The EBA is empowered in para 106 to amongst other things, carry out on-site inspections, take supervisory measures, and impose fines on issuers of significant e-money token and significant asset-referenced tokens.

an asset-referenced token or e-money token to be categorized as significant asset-referenced tokens.[161]

v. Cap on Trading and Exchange Volume of Asset-referenced Tokens

MiCA sets restrictions on the issuance of an asset-referenced token used widely as a means of exchange. Specifically, under Article 23(1), the issuer is required to stop issuing that asset-referenced token and submit a plan to ensuring reduction in the averages below those specified in the provision,

> Where, for an asset-referenced token, the estimated quarterly average number and average aggregate value of transactions per day associated to its uses as a means of exchange within a single currency area is higher than 1 million transactions and EUR 200 000 000, respectively

Among other things, this provision will ensure that tokens do not put unnecessary pressure on the Euro or the EU financial system.

vi. Interest Prohibition

Under MiCA stablecoins may not bear interest. Specifically, the Regulation prohibits e-money issuers as well as "crypto-asset service providers when they provide crypto-asset services related to e-money tokens" to pay interest to holders of e-money tokens. This includes "interest not related to the length of time that such holders hold those e-money tokens."[162] A similar prohibition applies to issuers of asset-referenced tokens and cryptoasset service providers when providing cryptoasset services related to asset-referenced tokens, except that in such a case the prohibited interest is only the one "related to the length of time during which such holders are holding those asset-referenced tokens."[163] For both types of tokens this prohibition is designed "to reduce the risk that [they] are used as store of value."[164] Presumably, this is designed to ensure that the EU crypto-asset market is not overtly exposed to over-leverage as well as credit and liquidity risk.

Notably, this prohibition would preserve the EU crypto market from the pricing mismatch period known as "crypto winter." This was a prolonged period in 2022 when crypto-asset prices were down more than 55 percent due to panic selling which had been triggered by rising interest rates. The

---

161 EU MiCA, above note 139, arts 44, 57.

162 *Ibid*, Preamble para 68. Prohibition is detailed in art 50.

163 *Ibid*, Preamble para 58. Prohibition is detailed in art 40.

164 *Ibid*, Preamble paras 58, 68.

significant drop in prices resulted in the mismatch of crypto-asset prices on the records of crypto dealers such as exchanges and lenders. Notable crypto bankruptcies such as FTX, Voyager Digital, Celsius Network, and Block-Fi have been attributed to the crypto winter of 2022, which underlined the over-leverage of crypto-assets held by those companies.[165] Another potential effect or design of this prohibition could also be to discourage the adoption of stablecoin for use other than as payment instrument.

vii. Own Funds Requirements

According to Preamble paragraph 53, in order "[t]o address the risks to the financial stability of the wider financial system, issuers of asset-referenced tokens should be subject to own funds requirements." In principle, "own funds" are "calculated as a percentage of the reserve of assets that back the value of the asset-referenced tokens." The requirement is initiated in paragraphs 44 and 53 of the Preamble and fully set out in Article 35. It does not apply to e-money token issuers, although paragraph 110 of the Preamble indicates that e-money tokens that become or set out as "significant e-money tokens would also be subject to own funds requirements." The own funds requirements and stress testing requirements in Preamble paragraph 110, Articles 35 and 45 are reminiscent of Basel's capital adequacy requirements for financial institutions.[166]

VI. CBDC VERSUS STABLECOINS

In recent years, against the background of the issuance of virtual currencies by private actors[167] and the decline in the use of banknotes,[168] a growing

---

165 Akanksha Jalan and Roman Matkovskyy, "Systemic risks in the cryptocurrency market: Evidence from the FTX collapse" (2023) 53 *Finance Research Letters* 103670.

166 The Basel Committee on Banking Supervision, "The Basel Framework" (Bank for International Settlement, 2024) especially arts 20.5–20.6, 20.31–20.4.1, and 53.45–53.47, online: https://www.bis.org/baselframework/BaselFramework.pdf, accessed 26 July 2024.

167 Prominent schemes include Bitcoin, Litecoin, Ether, and Ripple. Many are listed in "List of Cryptocurrencies" (*Wikipedia*, last edited 29 October 2024), online: https://en.wikipedia.org/wiki/List_of_cryptocurrencies, accessed 7 November 2024; see analysis by Saifedean Ammous, "Can Cryptocurrencies Fulfil the Functions of Money?" (2016) Columbia University, Center on Capitalism and Society Working Paper No 92, online: http://dx.doi.org/10.2139/ssrn.2832769, accessed 29 July 2024.

168 See e.g., Bank of Canada, "Contingency planning for a central bank digital currency" (*Bank of Canada*, February 2020), online: https://www.bankofcanada.ca/2020/02/contingency-planning-central-bank-digital-currency/#2-Public-policy-considerations, accessed 7 November 2024, albeit with respect to the first point, only by reference to the possible wide use of "digital currencies … issued by private sector entities … an alternative to the Canadian

number of central banks[169] have been investigating the possibility and implications of issuing a digital form of central bank money for use by the general public. Such digital currency is known as central bank digital currency (CBDC),[170] or retail CBDC (rCBDC).[171] While thus far only a handful of central

dollar as a method of payment, store of value and *unit of account*" (emphasis added), but even as a mere alternative scenario to the second one. See also Ledger Insights, "Bank of Canada plans 2023 CBDC consultation as it moves to development" (*Ledger Insights*, 13 December 2022), online: https://www.ledgerinsights.com/bank-of-canada-plans-2023-cbdc-consultation-as-it-moves-to-development/, accessed 7 November 2024.

169   See e.g., Anneke Kosse and Ilaria Mattei, *Gaining momentum – Results of the 2021 BIS survey on central bank digital currencies* (BIS Papers No 125, Bank for International Settlements 2022), online: https://www.bis.org/publ/bppdf/bispap125.pdf, accessed 7 November 2024; European Central Bank, "Report on a Digital Euro" (*European Central Bank*, October 2020), online: https://www.ecb.europa.eu/pub/pdf/other/Report_on_a_digital_euro~4d7268b458.en.pdf, accessed 7 November 2024. See also Bank of England, "Central Bank Digital Currency: Opportunities, Challenges and Design" (Discussion Paper, *Bank of England*, March 2020), online: https://www.bankofengland.co.uk/-/media/boe/files/paper/2020/central-bank-digital-currency-opportunities-challenges-and-design.pdf?la=en&hash=DFAD18646A77C00772AF1C5B18E63E71F68E4593, accessed 7 November 2024; Bank of Canada, "Contingency Planning," above note 166). At present, 103 central banks (excluding individual national central banks that are part of currency unions) have recently launched, piloted, experimented with, and/or researched retail central bank digital currency (CBDC), not including two that started issuing retail CBDC and then shut down the platforms (Ecuador and Finland). See Kiffmeister, "Jurisdictions Where Retail CBDC Is Being Explored" (Kiffmeister Chronicles, 12 August 2024), online: https://kiffmeister.com/2024/08/12/jurisdictions-where-retail-cbdc-is-being-explored/, accessed 7 November 2024.

170   Retail CBDCs differ from wholesale CBDCs in that the latter is used only among financial intermediaries while the former is used by the wider economy. See Bank for International Settlements, *Annual Economic Report 2021* (Bank for International Settlements 2021), online: https://www.bis.org/about/areport/areport2021.pdf, accessed 7 November 2024; see above note 6.

171   See e.g., Raphael Auer, Giulio Cornelli, and Jon Frost, "Taking Stock: Ongoing Retail CBDC Projects" (*BIS*, Quarterly Review March 2020), online: https://www.bis.org/publ/qtrpdf/r_qt2003z.htm, accessed 7 November 2024; Christian Barontini and Henry Holden, *Proceeding with Caution – A Survey on Central Bank Digital Currency* (BIS Papers No 101, Bank for International Settlements 2019), online: https://www.bis.org/publ/bppdf/bispap101.pdf, accessed 7 November 2024; Codruta Boar, Henry Holden, and Amber Wadsworth, *Impending Arrival – A Sequel to the Survey on Central Bank Digital Currency* (BIS Papers No 107, Bank For International Settlements 2020), online: https://www.bis.org/publ/bppdf/bispap107.pdf, accessed 7 November 2024; George Calle and Daniel Eidan, "Central Bank Digital Currency: An Innovation in Payments" (*R3*, April 2020), online: https://cointhinktank.com/upload/CBDC%20-%20an%20innovation%20in%20payments.pdf, accessed 7 November 2024; Central Bank Digital Currencies Working Group, "Key Aspects Around Central Bank Digital Currencies: Policy Report" (*CEMLA Fintech Forum*, May 2019), online: https://www.cemla.org/fintech/docs/2019-06-KeyAspectsAroundBankDigitalCurrencies.pdf, accessed 7 November 2024; Johannes Duong, "Overview of Central Bank Digital Currency – State of Play" (*SUERF*, Policy Note Issue No 158, 30 April 2020), online: https://www.suerf.org/policynotes/12575/overview-of-central-bank-digital-currency-state-of-play, accessed 7 November 2024.

banks stepped in,[172] according to a recent survey cited by SWIFT, 24 percent of central banks will introduce a CBDC within the next couple of years.[173]

In a way, the CBDC is a stablecoin issued by the central bank. However, the embodiment by it of a "claim" on the central bank setting it aside from virtual ("real") stablecoins. Thus, its use does not give rise to predominant stablecoin risks, discussed here in Part IV, such as systemic risk, lack of interoperability, and issuer's insolvency, or more in general, default risk. As well there is no ambiguity as to its character as money and not a security. Not surprisingly, the introduction of CBDC was predicted to be a "game changer," even if only for "encouraging banks to reduce their reliance on deposits."[174]

Even if the central bank's power to issue banknotes arguably covers their issuance in an electronic form,[175] the specific wording of the authorizing statute may limit the power to the paper format. Regardless, it may be desirable to have the power to issue e-banknotes explicitly anchored in a statute, if only because this is something that will directly affect the public at large and its implementation will require strong public support.

As in connection with stablecoins, the quantum-resistant currency, deploying quantum randomness premised on patternless cryptography, achieving network immutability without compromising the cash-like privacy of transacting parties, appears to be most suitable to serve as a CBDC. Particularly, this is due to the hack-proof security of such currency. As well, such currency can also be validated offline over a "hard wallet" and its chain of custody can be written on the coin itself so as not to identify the payer but only the identity of the coin. Finally, the quantum-resistant currency is easily scalable given that quantum computing has more computing power compared to classical computing. As already indicated, quantum-resistant

---

172 Excluding countries that adopted Bitcoin one way or another, these are the Bahamas and Nigeria. See *Bahamian Dollar Digital Currency Regulations*, 2021, SI No 88, online: https://cdn.centralbankbahamas.com/documents/2022-02-11-11-53-25-Bahamian-Dollar-Digital-Currency-Regulations-2021-Final-Gazetted.pdf, accessed 7 November 2024; see Central Bank of Nigeria, "Regulatory Guidelines on the eNaira" (25 October 2021), online: https://www.cbn.gov.ng/Out/2021/FPRD/eNairaCircularAndGuidelines%20FINAL.pdf , accessed 08 August 2024.

173 Zhiyuan Sun "SWIFT moves to next phase of CBDC testing after positive results" (*Cointelegraph*, 9 March 2023), online: https://cointelegraph.com/news/swift-moves-to-next-phase-of-cbdc-testing-after-positive-results, accessed 7 November 2024.

174 Cyril Monnet, *Digital Euro: An assessment of the first two ECB progress reports* (European Parliament 2023) at 19, online: https://www.europarl.europa.eu/RegData/etudes/IDAN/2023/741508/IPOL_IDA(2023)741508_EN.pd, accessed 7 November 2024.

175 As argued by Benjamin Geva, Seraina Grünewald, and Corinne Zellweger-Gutknecht "The E-banknote as a 'Banknote': A Monetary Law Interpreted" (2021) 41 *OJLS* 1119 at 1122–33. See chapter 5 of this study.

algorithms are cryptographic algorithms designed to withstand breaches and/or attacks from classical and quantum computers. Notably, BitMint's technology gives it the scalability to make payments from one device to another without the intermediation of any interbank transfer system.[176] The dominance of blockchain crypto-based solutions in some current proposals[177] ought thus to be re-thought.

Regardless of its design, CBDC will reduce the security cost involved in the distribution of paper banknotes. Also, holding e-cash in electronic wallets, compared to holding paper banknotes in physical ones, will have a similar effect. CBDC will further lead to a national e-banknotes payment system, or at least to the interoperability among the various bank systems.

On the negative side, CBDC may adversely have an impact on existing issuers of stablecoins and thus may discourage continuing innovation that is more likely to exist in a competitive environment such as that of stablecoin arrangements. This impact may, however, be reduced by decentralizing the payment system and encouraging competition among banks as to their service delivery. Having a new medium of payment is likely to lead to more innovation in new applications and systems to support the new medium and its benefits. Also on the negative side, acting as an instrument with the liquidity and anonymity of cash, but without the limitations on portability that come with physical cash, CBDC may increase criminality risks.[178] In turn, a system in which the chain of custody may be verified by court order will operate to counterbalance this risk.

In the final analysis, the reduced use of cash and the inadequacy of the stablecoin system as a comprehensive substitute, may present the CBDC as

---

176 See above, notes 47, 50, and 76–79 accompanying text.

177 See e.g., Federal Reserve Bank of Boston and Massachusetts Institute of Technology Digital Currency Initiative, "Project Hamilton Phase 1: A High Performance Payment Processing System Designed for Central Bank Digital Currencies" (*Federal Reserve Bank of Boston*, 3 February 2022) at 30, online: file:///C:/Users/bgeva/Downloads/Project-Hamilton-Phase-1 -Whitepaper.pdf, accessed 7 November 2024; Philipp Sandner, "The Digital Programmable Euro, Libra, and CBDC: Implications for European Banks" (*Medium*, 26 August 2020), online: https://philippsandner.medium.com/the-digital-programmable-euro-libra-an d-cbdc-implications-for-european-banks-316a8eb96d4e, accessed 13 November 2024. See also Jonas Gross, "The Digital Programmable Euro: Statement by the FinTech Council of the German Federal Ministry of Finance (Unofficial Translation" (*Medium*, 31 July 2020), online: https://jonasgross.medium.com/the-digital-programmable-euro-statement-b y-the-fintech-council-of-the-german-federal-ministry-of-14b85a951218, accessed 13 November 2024. See also Raphael Auer, Giulio Cornelli, and Jon Frost, "Rise of the Central Bank Digital Currencies: Drivers, Approaches and Technologies" (*BIS*, 24 August 2020, online: https:// www.bis.org/publ/work880.htm, accessed 8 November 2024.

178 Financial Action Task Force, "FATF Report to G20, above note 106 at 26.

an optimal method to the digitalization of cash.[179] For a CBDC wide-ranging discussion see chapter 5 of this study. In turn, chapter 8 addresses the option of a co-existence between CBDC and stablecoins.

VII. CONCLUSION

Stablecoins are claim-check digital currencies. Each is denominated in, that is, pegged to or claimed at par with, either an official currency's unit of account (as well as a basket of such currencies) or in the value of a specified quantity of a designated commodity. To maintain its nominal value, a stablecoin ought to be backed by a full reserve of liquid safe assets, the currency or commodity in which it is denominated. Stablecoins are mainly used in international transactions. They are mostly cryptocurrencies, but could be "quantum-resistant.[180] in which case there is a greater potential for enhanced features, such as security, off-line use, and privacy. Their emergence requires adaptation of payment laws as well as the establishment of a legal and regulatory framework governing their issuance, holding, transfer, and storage.

Primary risks raised by the use of stablecoins relate to value instability, insolvency, at least imperfect interoperability, and potential subjection to securities regulation laws, of which compliance may be costly. Some risks will be eliminated altogether, and others will be reduced once CBDC comes to the forefront. Issued by the central bank as an e-banknote it will supersede, at least in part, both privately issued stablecoins and the paper banknote. This is likely to be the case particularly if CBDC is issued in a bearer format that will promise to be secure and scalable, facilitate efficiency as well as along online validation as well as off-line validation, and ensure universal accessibility as well as privacy.

Risks of criminal use are bound to exist in digital currency systems, whether of stablecoins or CBDC, and may be stronger in the former. A system in which the chain of custody may be verified by court order will operate to counterbalance this risk.

At present, to reduce risks, stablecoins available for the public ought to be regulated in terms of issuer and system requirements as well as risks. As for CBDC, a specific legislative framework ought to reflect public support for it, eliminate any shade of doubt as to the central bank's power to issue it, and

---

179 But *cf* PYMNTS "CBDCs' Relevance Questioned After Canada Casts Skepticism" (*PYMNTS*, 11 August 2023), online: https://www.pymnts.com/cbdc/2023/cbdcs-relevance-questioned -after-canada-casts-skepticism/, accessed 8 November 2024.
180 For quantum-resistant currency, see above, notes 41–45.

to regulate its status as legal tender. Regardless, a comprehensive regulatory framework ought to govern its distribution and transfer.

Overall, as demonstrated in Part IV, there is a global consensus as to stablecoin and SA risks. At the same time, as demonstrated in Part V, there is no global consensus as to the best regulatory approach for encountering such risks. One prominent dividing line is between jurisdictions focusing on stablecoins as securities and others focusing on them as means of payment. Canada and the European Union fall into the first category while the United States into the other. A brief comparative summary of the cardinal features of each system, whether common or distinct, concludes this chapter.

While the CSA SA requirements are not as elaborately drafted as those of MiCA and the US GENIUS Act, it is clear that the CSA SA requirements are largely in consonance with the principal objectives of them. Nonetheless, a purposive read of the CSA Notices would show that the Canadian approach to SA regulation is one-dimensional and indirect. Specifically, MiCA and the US GENIUS Act have distinct provisions that are clearly and particularly directed at issuers,[181] CTPs,[182] and custodians[183] with distinct guidelines for each participant in the SA value chain. On the other hand, the CSA Notices seek to achieve compliance with CSA requirements for the whole Canadian SA value chain through enforcement measures directed at CTPs alone. Thus, stablecoin issuers and asset reserve custodians are indirectly regulated through CTPs. For example, Appendix A of the CSA Second Notice[184] lists preconditions for which a CTP would be permitted to allow its clients to deal in FBCAs.[185] The listed preconditions are mostly items that an issuer must fulfill or information solely available to issuers. Thus, issuer

---

181   For example, Title III (arts 16, 17, 18) of the EU MiCA, above note 139 is Application for Authorization clearly directed at different categories of issuers.

182   "Operation of trading platform for crypto-assets," reserve custody services are "Ancillary" Investment services and activities under Annex I of Directive (EU) 2014/65/EU of 15 May 2014 on markets in financial instruments and amending Directive 2002/92/EC and Directive 2011/61/EU [2014] OJ L173/349. These activities in connection with SAs and general crypto-assets are directly regulated in art 60 of the EU MiCA, above note 139. The US GENIUS Act does not contain guidelines for trading platforms as it's focused mainly on issuance and reserve custody. Also, the US GENIUS Act does not intend for "payment stablecoins," which are essentially considered a payment and settlement instrument, to be dealt for trading purposes or even considered securities and/or derivatives. See HR 4766, above note 133, § 13. Thus, obviating the need for trading platform guidance.

183   For example, EU MiCA, above note 139, arts 37, 75 provide clear guidance directed at reserve custodians. See also HR 4766, above note 132, §§ 8 and 12(b), on custody and customer protection.

184   CSA, "Staff Notice 21-333," above note 117 at 7–13.

185   *Ibid* at 2.

compliance is sought to be enforced by proxy through CTPs.[186] Accordingly, "if a CTP requests written consent from the CSA for its clients to enter into crypto contracts to buy or deposit a particular VRCA, the CTP is expected to conduct sufficient due diligence to ensure that applicable risks in respect of the issuance of the VRCA are addressed."[187] Rather than impose direct and distinct regulatory requirements on issuers, the First Notice, merely implores issuers "to address applicable risks" without any clear and specific guidance like those contained in EU MiCA and the US GENIUS Act.[188] For its part, rather than clearly demanding evidence of compliance with issue requirements from VCRA issuers, the Second Notice merely requires the issuer to file an undertaking which mirrors the preconditions imposed on the CTPs in Appendix A.[189] True, while the First Notice was directed only at CTPs, the Second Notice directly requires VCRA issuers to file a compliance undertaking.[190] Even so, it is the CTP, who, as part of Appendix A preconditions imposed on CTPs, bears the burden of confirming that the VCRA issuer has filed the Appendix B undertaking.[191]

Notwithstanding CSA's indirect approach to regulating VRCA issuers in Canada, it is clear that Canadian authorities seek to exercise some level of regulatory oversight on VRCA issuers as well as CTPs. Like the CSA Notices, MiCA regulates stablecoin issuers as well as CTPs, otherwise described as "crypto-asset service providers."[192] At the same time, for its part, unlike the CSA Notices and EU MiCA, the US GENIUS Act does not seek to regulate CTPs at all.

Treatment of custodial services varies. Like the EU MiCA, the US GENIUS Act seeks to bring stablecoin reserve assets "custodial or safekeeping services"[193] within its regulatory ambit. At the same time, with respect to reserve asset custody, the CSA Notices only prescribe periodic disclosures requirements[194] in relation to "details of the composition of the reserve of

---

186   See Clements, above note 20 at 12. On this score, CTPs are required to first seek and obtain approval, and for such approval to be granted the CTP is expected to ascertain that the VRCA meets the prescribed criteria for stablecoin arrangement acceptability under the CSA Notices.

187   CSA, "Staff Notice 21-332," above note 116 at 12.

188   *Ibid* at 13.

189   CSA, "Staff Notice 21-333," above note 117 at 14–22.

190   *Ibid*, Appendix B (Undertaking from VRCA Issuer).

191   *Ibid*, Item (5) Appendix A.

192   See for example, EU MiCA, above note 139 at Preamble para 21. MiCA seeks to regulate all stablecoin market participants, not just issuers and trading platforms.

193   HR 4766, above note 132, § 8.

194   CSA, "Staff Notice 21-332," above note 116 at 5–6.

asset."[195] Unlike the EU MiCA and the US GENIUS Act, the CSA Notices do not impose direct and/or distinct regulatory requirements relating to reserve asset custodians. The CSA Notices merely require that reserve asset custodians must be a "Qualified Custodian."[196] Under the EU MiCA, but unlike the CSA Notices, reserve custodian services are within the class of stablecoin market services regarded as "crypto assets related services and activities"[197] with clear guidance provided in relation to custodian custody of reserve asset.

As noted by the CSA, the CSA Notices represent an "interim approach" which requires "comprehensive framework."[198] Thus, in the footsteps of the US GENIUS Act and EU MiCA, the Canadian stablecoin regulation is also expected to evolve into a more comprehensive regulatory approach with more distinct and specific guidelines as well as enforcement mechanism applicable to each category of market participant. In the long run, it is anticipated that other regulators, particularly, OSFI, will join the CSA in devising a comprehensive regulatory scheme.

What is however missing from the regulatory schemes is the regulation of digital currencies used in payment as part of the monetary system. This aspect, particularly by reference to the powers of the Bank of Canada, including the possible co-existence between stablecoins and CBDC, will be addressed in chapter 8.

This chapter is followed by an Appendix providing an overview for the Canadian stablecoin landscape.

---

195 CSA, "Staff Notice 21-333," above note 117, Appendix B "Undertaking" at 17.
196 *Ibid*, Appendix B (3)(b)(ii). Notably, requiring reserve asset custodians to be "Qualified Custodians" would bring them under the purview of relevant Canadian laws and regulation.
197 EU MiCA, above note 139, Preamble para 6.
198 CSA, "Staff Notice 21-332," above note 116 at 13 and CSA, "Staff Notice 21-333," above note 117 at 4.

APPENDIX: Canadian Stablecoin Landscape[199]
Prepared by Ephraim Ajijola

a. Background

There are more than 9,000 active cryptocurrencies in circulation globally.[200] Bitcoin is the most dominant with more than 40 percent market capitalization.[201] Ethereum is second with more than 19 percent market capitalization.[202] This information holds true in Canada as well. As of 2022 in Canada, Bitcoin[203] leads the chart in terms of the most owned digital currency. Ether comes next, with Dogecoin, Bitcoin Cash, Litecoin, Binance Coin, Ripple, Stellar, Tether, USDC, Polkadot, Chainlink, Dai, and Monero also recording notable ownership among Canadians.[204]

Generally, the circulation of crypto is driven by two commercial activities, to wit: crypto investment trading; and payments. The major driver of crypto circulation in Canada is crypto investment trading with CTPs recording significant daily transaction volumes.

As of 2023, it is estimated that 10 percent of Canadians (about 3.9 million) own crypto-assets.[205] Notably, in terms of computing power, Canadian

---

199 The Appendix adopts doctrinal methodology to examine the various laws applicable to the Canadian stablecoin landscape. It then uses secondary research method to analyze how the Canadian stablecoin ecosystem is evolving around applicable laws and regulation. The outcome of this analysis forms the bulk of the Appendix.

200 Statista, "Number of cryptocurrencies worldwide from 2013 to November 2024" (*Statista*, November 2024), online: https://www.statista.com/statistics/863917/number-crypto -coins-tokens/, accessed 9 November 2024.

201 For cryptocurrency, market capitalization refers to the cumulative market value of the cryptocurrency in supply taking into account the most recent price of the cryptocurrency. See Maria Teresa Chimienti, Urszula Kochanska, and Andrea Pinna, "Understanding the crypto-asset phenomenon, its risks and measurement issues" (*European Central Bank*, 2019), online: https://www.ecb.europa.eu/press/economic-bulletin/articles/2019/html/ecb.ebart201905_03~c83aeaa44c .en.html, accessed 27 July 2024.

202 Statista, "Bitcoin (BTC), Ethereum (ETH) Dominance – Their Market Cap Relative to the Market Cap of All Other Cryptocurrencies in the World – on June 21, 2024" (*Statista*, June 2024), online: https://www.statista.com/statistics/1269302/crypto-market-share/, accessed 27 July 2024.

203 The dominance of Bitcoin seems understandable because other coins are termed and viewed as "altcoins" – a coinage for bitcoin alternatives.

204 Daniela Balutel, Christopher S Henry, and Doina Rusu, "Cryptoasset Ownership and Use in Canada: An Update for 2022" (2023) Bank of Canada Staff Discussion Paper 2023–14, online: https://www.bankofcanada.ca/wp-content/uploads/2023/07/sdp2023-14.pdf, accessed 26 July 2024.

205 Ontario Securities Commission, "Crypto Asset Survey 2023: Final Report" (*Ipsos*, 2023), online: https://www.osc.ca/sites/default/files/2023-12/inv-research_20231129_crypto-asset -survey-2023.pdf, accessed 28 July 2024.

cryptocurrency miners represent the fourth largest contribution to the blockchain.[206] Like other jurisdictions such as the United States (16 percent)' United Kingdom (13 percent), and Germany (13 percent), cryptocurrency adoption in Canada is budding, although, there was a 3 percent drop in 2023 compared to 2022 when about 13 percent (about five million) of Canadians were estimated to own crypto-assets.[207] This drop in crypto-ownership in Canada may be attributed to the regulatory tightening on the Canadian market for crypto-assets.[208] Of the 3.9 million crypto-owning Canadians, about 585,000 Canadians are estimated to own stablecoins.[209]

The circulation of stablecoins and indeed any virtual currency is largely dependent on regulation.[210] Canada is looking to enforce more regulatory measures in connection with stablecoins, which Canadian regulators prefer to describe as "value-referenced crypto-assets" (VRCA).[211] The ensuing discussion will consider the stablecoin landscape in Canada by reference to the applicable/anticipated regulation.

---

206 Christian Paas-Lang, "Crypto at a Crossroads: Some Provinces are Wary of the Technology's Vast Appetite for Electricity" (*CBC*, 18 March 2023), online: https://www.cbc.ca/news /politics/crypto-mining-electricity-provinces-, accessed 28 July 2024; see also Naomi Powell, "Crypto-miners Flood into Canada, Boosting the Hopes of Small Towns Looking for a Break" (*Financial Post*, 23 June 2020), online: https://financialpost.com/technology/blockchain /towns-hopeful-but-cautious-as-crypto-miners-flood-into-canada, accessed 28 July 2024.

207 Ontario Securities Commission, "OSC Survey Explores Canadians Crypto Ownership and Knowledge" (*OSC*, 19 October 2022), online: https://www.osc.ca/en/news-events/news /osc-survey-explores-canadians-crypto-ownership-and-knowledge, accessed 28 July 2024. Although, Statista puts the estimate at 13 percent for both 2023 and 2024. See Statista, "Share of respondents who indicated they either owned or used cryptocurrencies in 56 countries and territories worldwide from 2019 to 2024" (*Statista*, April 2024), online: https://www. statista.com/statistics/1202468/global-cryptocurrency-ownership/, accessed 29 July 2024.

208 See Part V general on Stablecoin regulation in Canada. For example, Binance and some other cryptocurrency trading platforms exited the Canadian crypto market on account of regulatory demands. See Crypto PM, "Binance Leaves Canada | Here's The Big Reason" (*Binance Square*, 12 May 2024), online: https://www.binance.com/en/square/post/518931, accessed 29 July 2024.

209 That's about 15 percent of the 3.9 million, see Statista, "Number of cryptocurrencies worldwide," above note 198.

210 Other minor factors are population size, GDP or national economy size, and population/certain demographic size, e.g., population of size of youth and mean. "Crypto owners are more likely than non-crypto owners to be men, age 25-44, employed full-time, to have attained high education levels, to own other kinds of investment products, to have high financial knowledge and to be self-directed investors." See Statista, "Number of cryptocurrencies worldwide," above note 198 at 6.

211 See Part V generally for Stablecoin regulation in Canada.

b. Canadian Stablecoin Landscape

Unlike the situation with respect to the United States dollar (USD), there are only a few known stablecoins pegged on a one-on-one basis against the Canadian dollar (CAD). They are QCAD,[212] CADT,[213] and CADC.[214] CAD pegged stablecoins are not widely sought after and mostly used as bridge or ramp-on for conversions between other stablecoins. Apart from the relatively small size of the Canadian GDP, the rarity of CAD pegged stablecoins is also due to the fact that the CAD is not held as a foreign exchange reserve currency of other countries. This implies that there is no significant trading request for CAD oriented crypto transactions or cross-border payments. At the same time, USD pegged stablecoins are used to facilitate crypto trading by customers as ramp-on from fiat currency to other regular virtual currencies and vice versa. USD pegged stablecoins are also mostly attractive and adopted for cross-border payments.

As of 2021, about 320 businesses[215] in Canada accept payment in crypto with more than half of those businesses being in Vancouver[216] and Toronto.[217] There are none in Quebec. It is recommended by Canadian authorities that crypto only be accessed and traded on CPTs approved by relevant Canadian regulators.[218] Indeed, within the Canadian cyberspace only authorized CTPs are available for access to Canadians. This means that Canadians would be unable to access unauthorized CTPs on their devices. Where CTP is not licensed to carry on business in Canada, such CTP, even if available within the Canadian cyberspace must withdraw their services from or decline to serve Canadian clients.[219] In spite of this cyberspace restriction, crypto enthusiasts are known to access unauthorized CTPs using virtual private net-

---

212   Issued by Canadian fintech firm Stablecorp.

213   CADT is issued by Blockchain Venture Capital Inc.

214   Issued by PayTrie AB Inc, a Canadian company.

215   Statista, "Businesses in the 15 Biggest Cities in Canada that Either Have a Cryptocurrency ATM or Offer Crypto as an In-Store Payment Method as of March 9, 2021" (*Statista*, March 2021), online: https://www.statista.com/statistics/1224707/firms-with-crypto-payment -solution-canada-city/, accessed 27 July 2024.

216   With more than one hundred businesses.

217   With more than seventy businesses.

218   Canadian Securities Administrators, "Crypto Trading Platforms Authorized to Do Business with Canadians" (*CSA*, 11 October 2024), online: https://www.securities-administrators.ca /crypto-trading-platforms-regulation-and-enforcement-actions/crypto-trading-platforms -authorized-to-do-business-with-canadians/, accessed 9 November 2024.

219   Some Canadian clients get through this barrier by not identifying themselves as Canadians.

work (VPN) services.[220] For example, "Binance," a CTP banned in Canada for regulatory non-compliance in May 2023, is still accessed by many Canadian crypto owners through VPNs.[221] The majority of the authorized CTPs in Canada do business only Canada[222] with the implication that coins listed thereon are indicative of the coins which are most popularly held in Canada. From an aggregation of Canadian CTPs, USD Coin (USDC), UST (TerraUSD), Tether (USDT), and Dai are the most sought after stablecoins in Canada[223] with about 1 percent of Canadians reported as owning stablecoins.[224] Also, 1 percent of Canadian digital currency owners use crypto for international money transfer,[225] and many hold the view that it is easier to make payments with stablecoins.[226]

220 Secure internet connection services with coded connection to internet networks. VPNs allow for the concealed bypass of (national) restriction or ban on internet networks by masking the user's IP address with the IP address of another count.

221 Barbara Shecter, "Binance's exit and Bank of Canada's digital loonie discussions: How they impact Canadian crypto" (*Financial Post*, 16 May 2024), online: https://financialpost.com /fp-finance/cryptocurrency/binance-exit-bank-of-canada-talks-digital-dollar-impact-crypto, accessed 27 July 2024.

222 For example, Wealthsimple, Newton, Bitbuy, Bitvo (Bitvo was acquired by Bitbuy); see WonderFi Technologies Inc, "Bitbuy Announces Acquisition of Bitvo Client Accounts and Bitvo. com" (*Newsfile*, 15 November 2023), online: https://www.newsfilecorp.com/release/187449 /Bitbuy-Announces-Acquisition-of-Bitvo-Client-Accounts-and-Bitvo, accessed 13 November 2024); Shakepay, Coinberry (Coinberry was acquired by Bitbuy), see Temur Durrani, "Kevin O'Leary-backed WonderFi to buy Coinberry" (*The Globe and Mail*, 18 April 2022), online: https://www.theglobeandmail.com/business/article-kevin-oleary-wonderfi-coinberry-crypto /?intcmp=gift_subscribed, accessed 13 November 2024. VirgoCX, Coinsquare, Netcoin, and NDAX serve only Canadians. ByteX, Coinbase, Coinsmart, Crypto.com, and Kraken serve Canada, the United States, and other countries with a more extensive coin listing.

223 For Wealthsimple, see "Available Crypto" (*Wealthsimple*), online: https://help.wealthsimple. com/hc/en-ca/articles/360058452093-Available-crypto, accessed 9 November 2024; for BitBuy, see "Buy a bit. Sell a bit" (*BitBuy*), online: https://bitbuy.ca/#coins, accessed 9 November 2024; for Newton see "Explore our Cryptocurrencies" (*Newton*), online: https://www.newton. co/prices, accessed 9 November 2024; for Coinsquare, see "An Introduction to our Supported Crypto" (*CoinSquare*), online: https://coinsquare.com/en-ca/coins/, accessed 9 November 2024; for Coinsmart, see "Our Cryptocurrencies" (*Coinsmart*), online : https://www.coins-mart.com/markets/, accessed 9 November 2024; for VirgoCX, see "Market," online: https:// virgocx.ca/page#/market/FIL_CAD, accessed 9 November 2024.

224 Balutel et al, above note 202 at 5.

225 Stephen Yun, "The Future of Digital Payments is Here" (*Payments Canada*, 2023) at 46, online: https://www.payments.ca/sites/default/files/PaymentsCanada_Canadian_Payment_Methods_and_Trends_Report_2023_En.pdf, accessed 27 July 2024. The low adoption of crypto for payments in Canada is driven by crypto knowledge gaps and general safety concerns. See OSC, "Crypto Asset Survey," above note 205 at 7.

226 Ipsos, *Financial Consumer Agency of Canada Survey of Stablecoin Users (Canada)* 2023 (Financial Consumer Agency of Canada 2024) at 9, online: https://publications.gc.ca/collections /collection_2024/acfc-fcac/FC5-90-2024-eng.pdf, accessed 27 July 2024.

Notably, each of these stablecoins is pegged against the US dollar and is Resident[227] as an ERC-20[228] token on the Ethereum network and on other blockchain networks. This means such stablecoins are not built on a dedicated blockchain network of their own. Tether in particular is known to exist as a token on multiple blockchains such as Ethereum, Algorand, Liquid Network, Avalanche, EOS, Liquid Network, Omni, Near, Polygon, Solana, Tron, Statemine, Tezos, Statemint, and on the Bitcoin Cash's Standard Ledger protocol.

c. Canadian Stablecoins Business Models

Stablecoins have been the basis of different business models in the Canadian landscape. The business models can be described in two broad categories, namely: (1) crypto trading; and (2) crypto-backed lending.[229]

In Canada, CTPs engage in crypto trading. They carry on business and are regulated at the federal level as Money Services Businesses (MSB) under the supervision of the Financial Transactions and Reports Analysis Centre of Canada (FINTRAC) with compliance requirements under the *Proceeds of Crime (Money Laundering) and Terrorist Financing Act* (PCMLTFA).[230] As of September 2023, there are about thirteen MSBs[231] granted exemptive relief to do business as CTPs with Canadians with ten[232] others in the pre-registration process to continue doing crypto business in Canada.

An exchange can be centralized or decentralized. Decentralized exchanges offer no intermediary services and users mostly engage in P2P transactions to

---

227 "Resident" is a blockchain term adopted to connote that a digital currency does not have a dedicated blockchain of its own and that such digital currency is built or developed on a host blockchain such as the Ethereum blockchain.

228 For ERC-20 see above, note 31.

229 This is a type of loan arrangement whereby the lender extends fiat currency loans to a borrower. As security or collateral for the loan, the borrower deposits crypto-assets with the lender. Crypto-backed lending is not to be confused with crypto lending. For crypto lending see, above note 19.

230 SC 2000, c 17. There are other province specific requirements with which MSBs have to comply. For example, British Columbia and Quebec have passed laws in this regard. See *Money-Services Businesses Act of Quebec*, CQLR c E-12.000001; see Bill 19, *Money Services Businesses Act*, 4th Sess, 42nd Parl, British Columbia, 2023 (assented to 11 May 2023), SBC 2023, c 19.

231 Canadian Securities Administrators, "Crypto Trading Platforms Authorized to Do Business with Canadians," above note 216.

232 Ontario Securities Commission, "Registered Crypto Asset Trading Platforms" (OSC, 11 October 2024), online: https://www.osc.ca/en/industry/registration-and-compliance/registered-crypto-asset-trading-platforms, accessed 9 November 2024.

consummate deals. Examples of decentralized exchanges are LocalBitcoins, Uniswap, Paxful, and PancakeSwap. Notably, LocalBitcoins closed shop some time in 2023 on account of low crypto trading volume caused by the 2023 crypto-winter.[233] On centralized exchanges, such as Binance, FTX, Coinbase, Kraken, Bitbuy, and Wealthsimple, there is an intermediary function/service rendered to facilitate transactions. Specifically, the intermediary identifies and matches buyers and sellers, and completes transactions on customers' behalf. So far, all exchanges authorized in Canada are centralized exchanges.[234]

Notwithstanding their description as "stable," VRCAs may be subject to speculative trading.[235] Panic trading in general crypto markets and the crypto winter have tested the stability of stablecoins. For example, the failure of Terra UST, which was the third largest digital currency, accentuated the doubt about the general price stability of stablecoins,[236] thus exposing stablecoins to increasingly speculative trading. While the failure of Terra UST is attributable to the fact that it is an algorithm-referenced stablecoin, fiat backed stablecoins, especially those that fail to maintain one-to-one backing to the reserve fiat currency, are also susceptible to speculative trading. For example, USDT (Tether) became the subject of increased speculative trading when it lost its one-to-one peg against the US dollar in 2022.[237] In June 2023, the trading price of Tether fluctuated in response to its falling US dollar peg.[238] Also, the fluctuation in the price of the underlying non-fiat-based reserve asset can render the price of such stablecoin unstable. On Canadian CTPs, stablecoins, especially USDC, USDT, and DAI are listed as available for trading with differing price per time. This means that Canadian customers

233 For the general effects of "crypto winter" see above, note 164.

234 Canadian Securities Administrators, "Crypto Trading Platforms Authorized to Do Business with Canadians," above note 216. Generally, for the difference between centralized and decentralized exchanges see, above, note 34.

235 Gordon Liao, Thomas Hadeed, and Ziming Zeng, "Beyond Speculation: Payment Stablecoins for Real-time Gross Settlements" (*SSRN*, 12 June 2023), online: https://ssrn.com/abstract=4476859, accessed 26 July 2024.

236 Antonio Briola et al, "Anatomy of a Stablecoin's failure: The Terra-Luna case" (2023) 51 *Finance Research Letters* 103358, online: https://www.sciencedirect.com/science/article/pii/S1544612322005359, accessed 8 August 2024.

237 Steven Ehrlich, "Tether Falls From Its $1 Price Peg Amid Market Turmoil Across Multiple Exchanges" (*Forbes*, 29 November 2022), online: https://www.forbes.com/sites/stevenehrlich/2022/11/10/tether-falls-from-its-1-peg-amid-market-turmoil/, accessed 26 July 2024.

238 Vicky Ge Huang, "Tether Loses Peg as Broader Crypto Market Sells Off" (*Wall Street Journal*, 15 June 2023), online: https://www.wsj.com/livecoverage/stock-market-today-dow-jones-06-15-2023/card/tether-loses-peg-as-broader-crypto-market-sells-off-lQuPmBFO6WbCxuFxJ371, accessed 9 November 2024. Although, Liao, above note 233, found evidence that stablecoins have not been used less for speculative trading.

can diversify their crypto portfolios by procuring stablecoins with CAD or by exchanging regular cryptos for stablecoins. In some cases, stablecoins are procured with fiat to enable customers to easily procure other regular virtual currencies. In essence, stablecoins enhance the liquidity of CTPs. Also, CTPs offer stablecoin-based margin or leverage products which are designed to enable customers to hedge against crypto volatility.[239]

CTPs and the general rise in the popularity virtual currencies also means that cross-border crypto payment remittance is on the rise. One percent of Canadians who own crypto reported using crypto for international money transfer.[240] CTPs play an important role in the adoption and/or facilitation of stablecoins for payment purposes, especially international payments. After a wallet-to-wallet transfer of stablecoins has been completed between transacting parties, a desirous stablecoin recipient is able to convert such stablecoin to fiat currency on a CTP. For example, a stablecoin owner can use the "spot trading" option available on most crypto exchanges to sell such stablecoin at the current market price.[241] While crypto payment remittances typically involve wallet to wallet, crypto owners or recipients are able to cash out or sell virtual currencies on CTPs. Transaction indices are indicative of the fact that stablecoins have increasingly become adopted for cross-border remittance. For example, Layer2 Financial Holdings Inc. (now known as "Rail"), a Canadian technology company adopted stablecoin to facilitate business-to-business (B2B) cross-border transactions.[242]

CTPs also offer crypto-lending products and services whereby customers offer their stablecoins for lending while charging periodic crypto interest payments.[243] Some CTPs offer crypto-lending as part of the many crypto products and services available on their platform while some only offer crypto-lending as a business model. For example, defunct crypto companies like Voyager

---

239 See for example, Binance stablecoin margin products. See Binance, "Margin Leveraged Crypto Trading on Spot" (*Binance*), online: https://www.binance.com/en/margin-trading, accessed 26 July 2024.

240 Yun, "The Future of Digital Payments is Here," above note 223 at 46. See also Stephen Yun and Ajoke Olorundare, "Rebound and Grow: Canadian Payment Methods and Trends 2022" (*Payments Canada*, 2022), online: https://payments.ca/sites/default/files/PaymentsCanada_Canadian_Payment_Methods_and_Trends_Report_2022_En_0.pdf, accessed 26 July 2024.

241 Dipen Pradhan, "Spot Trading In Crypto: What Are They, And How Do They Work?" (*Forbes*, 5 November 2024), online: https://www.forbes.com/advisor/in/investing/cryptocurrency/what-is-spot-trading-in-crypto/#:~:text=Spot%20trading%20in%20crypto%20involves,traders%20buy%20and%20sell%20instantly, accessed 9 November 2024.

242 Rail, "Use Cases" (*Rail*), online: https://layer2financial.com/payments-2/, accessed 9 November 2024.

243 For crypto-lending see above note 19.

and Celsius offered crypto-lending as the mainstay of their business model. Nonetheless, CTPs are prohibited from offering margin and leverage products/services in Canada.[244] In addition to the prohibition on crypto margin and leverage products, the CSA, as noted earlier,[245] has imposed additional regulatory requirements on CTPs in relation to stablecoins. In the absence of any regulatory transition and/or market deepening measures, it is anticipated that enforcement of the CSA Notices on VRCA would further reduce Canadian stablecoin trading volume, at least, temporarily.

With crypto-backed lending, some Canadian lenders are in the business of receiving virtual currency, especially stablecoins, as security for fiat currency advanced as loan to customers. Crypto-backed lending is typically provided by non-bank credit companies which are usually not required to comply with prudential regulatory and/or capital requirements that are otherwise mandatory for banks.[246] Crypto-backed lenders are subject to oversight by the Financial Consumer Agency of Canada[247] (FCAC) and Financial Transactions and Reports Analysis Centre of Canada[248] (FINTRAC). These regulators ensure that crypto lenders conform with Know Your Customer/product as well as anti-money laundering (AML) and counter-terrorist financing (CTF) requirements. Depending on the business model, crypto lenders may also be required to register as Money Services Business under FINTRAC requirements. Other laws and regulations that may apply apart from relevant provincial requirements are the *Proceeds of Crime (Money Laundering) and Terrorist Financing Act*[249] (PCMLTFA), *Criminal Interest Rate Regulations*,[250] and the *Retail Payment Activities Act*.[251] Provincial laws regarding personal property security apply generally to loan collaterals in Canada.[252] Such laws would

---

244 CSA, "Staff Notice 21-333," above note 117 at 7.

245 Generally for stablecoin regulation in Canada see Part V.

246 Rohan Arora et al, "Non-bank financial intermediation in Canada: a pulse check" (*Bank of Canada*, March 2021), online: https://www.bankofcanada.ca/2021/03/staff-analytical-note-2021-2/, accessed 29 July 2024.

247 OSFI, "Statement to entities engaging in crypto-asset activities or crypto-related services," above note 90.

248 Financial Transactions and Reports Analysis Centre of Canada, "FINTRAC's compliance guidance: Reporting large virtual currency transactions to FINTRAC" (*Government of Canada*, 1 June 2021, online: https://fintrac-canafe.canada.ca/guidance-directives/transaction-operation/lvctr/lvctr-eng, accessed 8 August 2024.

249 SC 2000, c 17. See ss 5, 9.

250 Pursuant to Canada's *Budget Implementation Act*, SC 2023, c 26, amending s 4600 of the *Criminal Code*, RSC 1985, c C-46.

251 SC 2021, c 23, s 177. See for example, ss 5, 20, and 23.

252 For example, Ontario's *Personal Property Security Act*, RSO 1990, c P.10; and the *Civil Code of Québec*, CQLR c CCQ-1991.

also apply to crypto-backed lending. Nonetheless, considering the nascency of crypto-assets generally, the applicable laws do not have provisions specifically designed for the taking and perfection of security interests over crypto-assets.[253]

In terms of market players, some crypto-backed lenders carrying on business in Canada include APX Lending, LEDN, and SALT Lending. As noted earlier,[254] stablecoins are perceived as securities in Canada. This means that the relationship/engagement of crypto-backed lenders and Canadian clients effectively brings them under the purview of the CSA Notices. This is so notwithstanding the fact that crypto-backed lenders are neither CTPs, nor are fiat funds advanced in connection with crypt-backed loans considered "margin, credit or leverage" under the CSA Notices.[255] Nonetheless, even though the CSA Notices are not directed at crypto-backed lenders, a purposive interpretation of the Notices would show that the primary intention is to protect "Canadian clients." For example, The First Notice provides that:

> The new commitments we are now requesting from unregistered CTPs relate to the following areas: enhanced commitments in relation to the custody and segregation of crypto assets held on behalf of Canadian clients; enhanced commitments to preclude the unregistered CTP from pledging, re-hypothecating or otherwise using crypto assets held on behalf of Canadian clients.[256]

There are also requirements and/or prohibitions in relation to the custody, segregation, re-hypothecation or other uses of crypto-assets held on behalf of Canadian clients which require that custodians must be engaged to hold 80 percent of the total value of stablecoins.[257] Also, the CSA Notices put significant emphasis on the "deposit" of VRCAs. In this sense, "deposit" captures arrangements or business models which requires Canadians to part ways with stablecoins on a temporary basis. In this regard, there is the

---

253 By way of comparison, in the United States, art 12 of Uniform Commercial Code (UCC) was promulgated in 2022 to cover commercial transactions involving "Electronic Controllable Records." By extension, art 9 of the UCC was updated so that security interests could be perfected in digital assets: https://higherlogicdownload.s3.amazonaws.com/UNIFORMLAWS/b7c515db-1895-4387-bb2d-ee99e58c0066/UploadedImages/Act_Infographics/2022_Amend-ements_to_UCC_Infographic_July_7_2022.png, visited 3 July 2025. For more on UCC Article 12 see chapter 6.

254 See Part V.

255 CSA, "Staff Notice 21-332," above note 116 at 7.

256 *Ibid* at 1.

257 *Ibid* at 4–7.

requirement to obtain the prior-written consent of the CSA before engaging in activities which involve taking deposit of VRCAs from Canadian clients.[258] This further brings crypto-backed lenders within the regulatory confines of the CSA.

Based on the foregoing, crypto-backed lenders would also be required to comply with the relevant requirements of the CSA Notices. Otherwise, the non-enforcement of such provisions on crypto-backed lenders would occasion a regulatory arbitrage capable of defeating the purpose and/or intention behind VCRA regulation in Canada. In reaction to the CSA Notices, some crypto-backed lenders are introducing "custodied loans"[259] to enable them to comply with the CSA prohibition on re-hypothecation or other uses of VCRAs held on behalf of Canadian clients. Others are withdrawing stablecoin collateralization from Canadian clients while others are leaving the Canadian market altogether.

d. MintChip: Use Case and Current Status

For a rounded discussion of the stablecoin-ecosystem, it is helpful, at this juncture, to discuss MintChip which, though not a stablecoin or cryptocurrency, is a notable development with similar crypto-attributes. MintChip is also not a CBDC.[260] Rather, it is an electronic money service that operates somewhat like a virtual wallet for cash.[261] Developed and announced in 2012 by the Royal Canadian Mint, MintChip is designed as a form of electronic payment system for transactions in fiat currency.[262] As such, MintChip is not a digital currency although, as demonstrated below, it shares certain features with digital currency.

By way of use case and technical details, MintChip allows electronic money to be transferred between users through smart devices within which MintChip microchips have been inserted. These microchips have been pro-

258 See e.g., *ibid* at 2, 12. See also CSA, "Staff Notice 21-333," above note 117 at 2, 3, and 12.

259 A Rapsey, "Ledn Launches Custodied Loans, Bringing A New Level Of Collateral Safeguards For All Customers" (*Ledn*, 6 December 2023, online: https://blog.ledn.io/en/ledn-custodied-loans, accessed 27 July 2024. With "custodied loans," the VCRA loan collateral will not be held by the lender so that such VCRAs do not form part of the pool of crypto-assets available for the lender's rehypothecation.

260 For discussion on "CBDC versus Stablecoins," see above Part VI.

261 See "The MintChip Challenge" (*Devpost*, 2012), online: https://mintchipchallenge.devpost.com/, accessed 29 July 2024.

262 Emily Jackson, "Royal Canadian Mint to create digital currency" (*Toronto Star*, 11 April 2012), https://www.thestar.com/business/royal-canadian-mint-to-create-digital-currency/article_7ca3ad4b-101c-529b-bc67-adf2149663b9.html, accessed 29 July 2024.

grammed to record digital value of Canadian dollars using account balances rather than blockchain or any distributed ledger technology. The microchips have unique ID which may be likened to cryptocurrency public address and private keys.[263] Thus, as between end-users or as between chip to chip, MintChip payment process is effectuated without any need for intermediation. This is different from the initial loading of a chip with funds which involves intermediation. This initial intermediation role is played by authorized brokers who act as liaison between chip holders' financial institution and the chip's account balance technology.

To use the service, a device bearing a MintChip microchip is loaded with currency equivalent by an authorized broker/dealer and then enabled to send and receive digital cash in both online and offline modes.[264] During transactions, the sending microchips, through the smart device, communicate using coded messages. Such coded messages cryptographically embody transaction details verifiable by the receiving MintChip microchip-enabled smart device. This is possible through the sending chip's unique ID – a feature similar to cryptocurrency keys.

MintChip launched with Canadian dollar as the chip's currency of operation but with the expectation to onboard other currencies like the US dollar and the British pounds at the launch of an ungraded version.[265] Nonetheless, before the anticipated upgrade, Nanopay Holdings Inc acquired MintChip in 2016 and the MintChip service has since been commercially launched for transaction processing by partnering with banks and retailers as well as for P2P payments for service integration in Canada.[266] It is expected that MintChip would be further deployed for backend operations of a Nanopay-owned bank to be called "Payments Bank"[267] upon successful banking licence application.[268]

---

263   The Canadian Press, "Royal Canadian Mint sells Mintchip digital payments platform to Toronto's nanoPay" (*CBC*, 13 January 2016), online: https://www.cbc.ca/news/science/mintchip-nanopay-1.3402059, accessed 29 July 2024.

264   Jackson, above note 260.

265   Roger Aitken, "Bitcoin-Like MintChip Acquired By Canada's nanoPay With Digital Cash Future Promise" (*Forbes*, 17 December 2020), online: https://www.forbes.com/sites/rogeraitken/2016/01/12/bitcoin-like-mintchip-acquired-by-canadas-nanopay-with-digital-cash-future-promise/, accessed 26 July 2024.

266   David George-Cosh, "Canada Puts Halt to MintChip Plans; Could Sell Digital Currency Program" (*The Wall Street Journal*, 4 April 2014), online: https://www.wsj.com/articles/BL-CDRTB-4452, accessed 26 July 2024.

267   See Notice (Nanopay Holdings Inc) (2020) C Gaz I, 1987.

268   Geoff Zochodne, "Firm that bought MintChip technology now seeking Canadian banking licence" (*Financial Post*, 4 August 2020), online: https://financialpost.com/news/fp-street/firm-that-bought-mintchip-technology-now-seeking-canadian-banking-licence, accessed 26 July 2024.

chapter five

RETAIL AND WHOLESALE CBDC: LEGAL AND REGULATORY FRAMEWORK FOR IMPLEMENTATION IN CANADA

SYNOPSIS

Currently, central bank money is only available to the public in the form of physical currency such as coins or banknotes. A Central Bank Digital Currency (CBDC) is a digital coin issued by a country's central bank. A CBDC that is made directly available to the public is called a retail CBDC (rCBDC). CBDC available for interbank transactions is wholesale CBDC (wCBDC). Arguably, optimal rCBDC is a ("token-based") quantum-resistant Digital Bearer Instrument (DBI). Under the Bank of Canada Act the Bank of Canada is likely to have the power to issue wCBDC as well as rCBDC in the form of a DBI. However, enacting a new and purpose-built piece of legislation would be the best way to implement rCBDC in Canada.

SUMMARY OF CONTENTS

I. INTRODUCTION

This chapter discusses the legal and regulatory framework for CBDC implementation in Canada. **Part II** sets out the emergence of CBDC in the context of the modern monetary and payments system. **Part III** analyzes the power to issue an account-based and Digital Bearer Instrument (DBI)-based CBDC. **Part IV** lists principal features to be considered in adopting the optimal design. **Part V** discusses the legal issues arising with respect to digital currency used in interbank payments (wCBDC) particularly in settlement of financial obligations. **Part VI** sets out alternative options for CBDC architecture and issuance models focusing on possible divisions of responsibilities between the central and commercial banks. Concluding **Part VII** presents for discussion a preliminary legislative proposal to govern the issue and regulation of the digital Canadian dollar by reference to the optimal design presented in the chapter.

II. THE EMERGENCE OF CBDC

a. Money and CBDC

At present, central bank money is available to the public only in the form of currency, mostly paper banknotes. In the context of a well supervised banking system, in which a safety net including deposit insurance is available, this scheme is not problematic. At the same time, with the advent of digital currencies, side by side with the declining role of cash in payment transactions, various proposals have been made to make central bank money available to the public other than in the form of tangible coins and banknotes. Such plans have been identified as Central Bank Digital Currency (CBDC).

In the form in which CBDC is available to the entire public CBDC is known as retail CBDC or rCBDC.[1] Otherwise, when it is available only to financial institutions or some of them it is a wholesale CBDC or wCBDC. Throughout this chapter, CBDC and rCBDC will be used interchangeably while wCBDC will specifically be noted.

The position of the present United States Administration to CBDC is negative. Upon taking over the presidency, in a clear departure from the

---

1   At present, 103 central banks (excluding individual national central banks that are part of currency unions) have recently launched, piloted, experimented with, and/or researched retail central bank digital currency (CBDC) not including two that started issuing retail CBDC and then shut down the platforms (Ecuador and Finland): Jurisdictions Where Retail CBDC Is Being Explored – Kiffmeister Chronicles" (Kiffmeister Chronicles, 12 August 2024), online: Kiffmeister Chronicles – Curated Fintech News, accessed 12 August 2024.

policies of his predecessor,[2] President Trump issued Executive Order 14178 of 23 January 2025 (EO)[3] effectively prohibiting the issuance of CBDC (other than when required by law). In Section 2(c) the EO defines CBDC to mean "a form of digital money or monetary value, denominated in the national unit of account, that is a direct liability of the central bank."

EO Section 1 highlights the Administration's policy "to support the responsible growth and use of digital assets, blockchain technology, and related technologies across all sectors of the economy, including by:

...

(v) taking measures to protect Americans from the risks of Central Bank Digital Currencies (CBDCs), which threaten the stability of the financial system, individual privacy, and the sovereignty of the United States, including by prohibiting the establishment, issuance, circulation, and use of a CBDC within the jurisdiction of the United States."

Without listing any such risks EO Section 5 goes on to provide that

(a) Except to the extent required by law, agencies are hereby prohibited from undertaking any action to establish, issue, or promote CBDCs within the jurisdiction of the United States or abroad.

(b) Except to the extent required by law, any ongoing plans or initiatives at any agency related to the creation of a CBDC within the jurisdiction of the United States shall be immediately terminated, and no further actions may be taken to develop or implement such plans or initiatives.

So far, worldwide, the United States is an outlier in its categorical rejection. In the absence of supportive arguments, that position can only be noted.

Pfister distinguishes among good, bad, and ugly motives for the issuance of rCBDC.[4] The good motives are the provision of a perfectly safe asset for making transactions as well as the preservation of some degree of privacy

2   See EO Section 3 revoking "Executive Order 14067 of March 9, 2022 (Ensuring Responsible Development of Digital Assets)" as well as rescinding "[a]ll policies, directives, and guidance issued pursuant to [it]," and directing to revoke "the Department of the Treasury's 'Framework for International Engagement on Digital Assets,' issued on July 7, 2022."

3   United States President, *Strengthening American Leadership in Digital Financial Technology* (Executive Order 14178), 90 Fed Reg 8647.

4   Christian Pfister, "Motives for a Retail Central Bank Digital Currency: The Good, the Bad, and the Ugly" 2023/4 *Revue Internationale des Services Financiers/International Journal for Financial Services* 28.

in transactions. As a counterargument to the first motive, he chagrins the inevitable disintermediation which will require policy makers to take measures to disincentivize or limit CBDC holding. As for the second, he observes that anonymity may not be fully achieved in CBDC payments. For their part, the bad motives "appeal to feelings such patriotism, familiarity or solidarity, but are debatable from an analytical point of view."[5] These are preserving the role of public money as the monetary anchor for the payment system; protecting the strategic autonomy of the national payments and monetary sovereignty; fostering innovation, efficiency, and competition in payments; supporting financial inclusion; and the enhancement of the international role of the currency. Finally, the ugly motives are those not explicitly stated; these are the support of public finance and the revenue and hence the power of central banks; "fear of missing out"; and use as a vehicle for mass surveillance.

A full discussion of these arguments is beyond the scope of the present study. I should, however, note that rCBDC may at least serve as a possible defence mechanism against the potential adverse impact of the multiplicity of virtual currencies including stablecoins on the uniformity of money and monetary policy.

Addressing CBDC design an IMF Working Paper states that:[6]

> [T]he design features contemplated by central banks can be plotted on four axes: (i) account-based v. token-based, (ii) wholesale v. retail, (iii) direct v. indirect, and (iv) centralized v. decentralized.

Most of these competing features can be addressed, at least at this stage, summarily. As already discussed, the wholesale versus retail distinction addresses the users: wholesale CBDC or wCBDC are to be used by banks in the interbank domain. Retail CBDC or rCBDC is to be used by the public at large. The direct versus indirect dichotomy addresses the distribution of the retail CBDC to the public at large, whether directly by the central bank, or through commercial banks. The centralized versus decentralized dichotomy addresses the mode of settlement.

As for the first axis, there is however confusion as to the meaning of "token" as distinguished from "account-based."[7] A common explanation goes as follows:

For legal purposes, if the CBDC is based on a current account contractual relationship, it can be classified as account-based, that is, a digital balance linked to specific users on the books of the central bank. Account-based CBDC would deploy conventional banking techniques (based on a contractual relationship between the central bank and the CBDC holder) in which transfers are done through debits and credits of accounts. If it is classified as token-based, it implies that a sui generis claim on the central bank is incorporated in an immaterial token, and the transfer of the token equals the transfer of the claim.[8]

Along these lines, a token-based coin is a bearer instrument like a banknote.[9] At the same time, an "account-based" currency is under a system in which members of the public at large have accounts with the central bank.[10] Accordingly, an account-based CBDC is an entry-based currency which requires payer identity verification, namely, that payers be recognized as the rightful owners of the claim they offer. It also requires that sufficient funds be identified to back the claim, and that the transfer be registered by all relevant parties. Conversely, token-based systems require the verification of the validity of the intangible object used to pay rather than the account information of participants.[11]

This explanation is criticized as overlooking the fact that a digital currency could be, and perhaps usually is, both account- and token-based, as prior to payment both parties' credentials and the validity of the intangible object

---

org/2020/08/token-or-account-based-a-digital-currency-can-be-both/, accessed 18 June 2024; see also, for the tokenization of deposit accounts, Rodney Garratt and Hyun Song Shin, *Stablecoins Versus Tokenised Deposits: Implications For The Singleness Of Money* (Bulletin No 73, Bank for International Settlements 2023), online: https://www.bis.org/publ/bisbull73.pdf, accessed 18 June 2024.

8   Gabriel Soderberg et al, *How Should Central Banks Explore Central Bank Digital Currency?* (Fintech Notes 2023/008, International Monetary Fund 2023), online: https://www.elibrary. imf.org/view/journals/063/2023/008/article-A001-en.xml, accessed 18 June 2024.

9   Reserve Bank of India, "Concept Note on Central Bank Digital Currency" (*Reserve Bank of India*, 7 October 2022), online: https://rbi.org.in/Scripts/PublicationReportDetails. aspx?UrlPage=&ID=1218, accessed 18 June 2024.

10   For discussion of account-based versus token-based approaches, see Bank of England, "Central Bank Digital Currency: Opportunities, Challenges and Design" (March 2020) Discussion Paper at 46–47, online: https://www.bankofengland.co.uk/-/media/boe/files/paper/2020/ central-bank-digital-currency-opportunities-challenges-and-design.pdf, accessed 12 August 2024.

11   Tobias Adrian and Tommaso Mancini Griffoli, *The Rise of Digital Money* (Fintech Notes 19/001, International Monetary Fund, 15 July 2019), online: https://www.imf.org/en /Publications/fintech-notes/Issues/2019/07/12/The-Rise-of-Digital-Money-47097\, accessed 20 June 2024.

of payment ought to be verified.[12] However, it seems to me that this criticism misses the point as it overlooks the centrality of the intangible object verification in the token-based systems and the absence of this element in the account-based system.

Regardless upon reflection, the distinction between account-based and tokenized currency proves to be too simplistic. For example, it fails to take into account the tokenization of deposits,[13] or perhaps more accurately, the tokenization of deposit claims, which demonstrates that an account-based system can also be tokenized. Indeed, a token was defined as "a sort of 'container' that can represent rights and creates the conditions for establishing the connection to the legal subjects."[14] There is nothing to preclude this "container" from representing claims under a bank deposit. Tokens are thus not exclusive to intangible object or virtual bearer instrument currencies. Being token-based does not distinguish such currencies from account-based currencies that can also be tokenized.

Rather, the unique feature of tokens as digital assets is their operability on a programmable platform on the basis of trustworthy technologies:[15]

> Ledgers record information about ownership. Traditional ledgers rely on two segregated components: the database layer stores records of assets, while the application layer incorporates centralised logic and governance rules into the system and manages the recording, updating and deletion of assets on the ledger. … In traditional ledger systems, trust in the accuracy of the records relies on trust in the ledger's operator. This trust is usually supported by institutional arrangements and legal frameworks that have evolved over time. … Advances in technology have produced a new type of "programmable ledger" that allows for the use of smart contracts and composability. Any transaction on such a ledger is done according to pre-agreed standards, whether in the form of fund transfers, locking of assets as collateral or other functions. … Transactions on a programmable platform require tradeable digital assets that are specific to that platform. They must comply with the platform's standards and the rules of its smart contracts. These digital assets are called tokens.

---

12   Garratt, "Token or Account," above note 7.

13   Rodney Garratt and Hyun Song Shin, *Stablecoins Versus Tokenised Deposits: Implications For The Singleness Of Money* (Bulletin No 73, Bank for International Settlements 2023), online: https://www.bis.org/publ/bisbull73.pdf, accessed 18 June 2024.

14   Thomas Nägele, *The Legal Nature Of Tokens Under Liechtenstein's TVTG* (DLT Media 2021).

15   Iñaki Aldasoro et al, *The Tokenisation Continuum* (Bulletin No 72, Bank for International Settlements 2023) at 2, online: https://www.bis.org/publ/bisbull72.pdf, accessed 18 June 2024.

Stated otherwise, in a legacy account-based system, the trust is put on the institution that maintains and operates the account. For its part, a bearer instruments legacy system may run without any oversight of a trusted intermediary. Conversely, on a programmable ledger, the trust is put on technology, requiring the financial claims to be transformed to "tradeable digital assets" meeting suitable specifications. Such tradeable digital assets are tokens. For their part:

> Tokens combine core and service layers ... which resemble the segregated database and application layers in traditional platforms. The core layer contains the information to uniquely identify and define the asset and its owner. The service layer specifies the rules and logic governing a token's use on the platform (eg in smart contracts).[16]

In the final analysis the correct distinction is between account-based and DBIs, with the latter being necessarily tokens. The former, i.e. claims on a bank deposit are typically not, and yet they may or may not be tokens. Accordingly, the "token-based" and "account-based" are not two mutually exclusive categories. Rather, the dichotomy is between the DBI and account-based rCBDCs.

b. Account-based rCBDC

Proposals for making central bank account balances available to the public at large were extensively discussed in chapter 1. Against this background, account-based rCBDC, on all its variations, is a new name to an old idea. While receiving an account-based CBDC will give the payee the added security of a central bank's obligation, there has rarely been an issue in receiving payment in commercial bank money on which the payee's bank is liable. And if there is a role to monetary objects in the implementation of monetary policy – that is, the supporting task of achieving the uniformity of money[17] – this role is not fulfilled by scriptural money.

Nonetheless, the Proposal for a Regulation of The European Parliament and of The Council on the establishment of the digital euro of June 2023[18]

---

16   *Ibid* at 2–3.

17   Corinne Zellweger-Gutknecht, Benjamin Geva, and Seraina Grünewald, "Digital Euro, Monetary Objects, and Price Stability" (2021) 7 *Journal of Financial Regulation* 284.

18   European Commission, "Proposal for a Regulation of the European Parliament and of the Council on the Establishment of the Digital Euro" COM (2023) 369 final, online: https://eur-lex.europa.eu/legal-content/EN/TXT/?uri=CELEX%3A52023PC0369, accessed 18 June 2024.

purports to establish the digital euro as an account-based product, so that payment with it will be carried out and into a "digital euro payment account," defined in Article 2(5) to mean:

> [A]n account held by one or more digital euro users with a payment service provider to access digital euro recorded in the digital euro settlement infrastructure or in an offline digital euro device and to initiate or receive digital euro payment transactions, whether offline or online, and irrespective of technology and data structure;

In selecting this route, the proposal appears, under the interpretation put forward below, to adopt an innovative way for the implementation of an account-based CBDC.

The Opinion of the European Central Bank of 31 October 2023 on the digital euro (CON/2023/34)[19] explains Article 2(5) as follows:

6.1   The ECB takes note that the proposed regulation sets out *the legal nature of the digital euro as a direct liability of a Eurosystem central bank toward digital euro users, while the contractual relationship for the provision of digital euro payment services is only between the PSPs distributing the digital euro and their clients* [emphasis added]. It is of crucial importance for maintaining the two-tiered monetary system, safeguarding financial stability and avoiding disintermediation of PSPs that PSPs remain fully responsible for the management of their relationships with their clients. ...

6.2   Based on the content of paragraph 6.1, the ECB understands that users will be and remain the only owners, or holders, of property interests in the rights represented by digital euros, even though users will only be able to access and use their holdings through a PSP. In other words, the PSP provides payment services enabling the user to hold and transfer the digital euros provided, but the underlying funds are a liability of the central bank. PSPs remain responsible and liable for ensuring the safety of the payment services they provide, also in relation to the digital euro.

This approach raises a question as to how an account run by a Payment Services Provider (PSP) can be a liability of a National Central Bank (NCB). Specifically, this is not an undertaking by the PSP to pay commercial bank money backed by a full reserve with the NCB. Nor is it an undertaking of

---

19   Opinion of the European Central Bank CON/2023/34 On the Digital Euro [2024] OJ C/2024/669, online: https://www.ecb.europa.eu/pub/pdf/legal/ecb.leg_con_2023_34.en.pdf, accessed 18 June 2024 (emphasis added); PSP stands for a Payment Services Provider, including a bank.

a PSP to provide its customer CBDC it holds with the NCB.[20] Rather, it is CBDC held directly by the customer at an account run by the PSP. The legal structure for achieving this has not been publicized by the European Central Bank (ECB) and may not have been worked out yet. In my view a possible mechanism is that of the assignment of rights. Thus, a CBDC obligation is issued by an NCB to a PSP. The PSP then assigns/transfers – effectively sells – the corresponding right to its customer – and credits it to a designated customer's account run by the PSP. The balance of this account is of the sum owed by the NCB (and not the PSP) through the successive assignments by the PSP to the customer. More specifically, the balance consists of the sum of the successive assignments by the PSP reduced by the withdrawals by the customer.

Further as to the role and basic features of the digital euro, under the press release that accompanied the Proposal states:[21]

> Like cash today, the digital euro would be available alongside existing national and international private means of payment, such as cards or applications. It would work like a digital wallet. People and businesses could pay with the digital euro anytime and anywhere in the euro area.
>
> Significantly, it would be available for payments both online and offline, i.e. payments could be made from device to device without an internet connection, from a remote area or underground car park. While online transactions would offer the same level of data privacy as existing digital means of payments, offline payments would ensure a high degree of privacy and data protection for users: they would allow users to make digital payments while disclosing less personal data than they do today when making card payments, just like when paying with cash, and the same as what they disclose when they take cash out of an ATM. Nobody would be able to see what people are paying for when using the digital euro offline.
>
> Banks and other payment service providers across the EU would distribute the digital euro to people and businesses. Basic digital euro services would be provided free of charge to individuals. To foster financial inclusion, individuals who do not have a bank account would be able to open and hold an account with a post office or another public entity, such as

---

20   Modeled on the "securities entitlement" to a securities under art 8 of the Uniform Commercial Code (UCC); NCB stands for a National Central Bank which is a euro issuer.

21   European Commission Press Release, "Single Currency Package: new proposals to support the use of cash and to propose a framework for a digital euro" (*European Commission*, 28 June 2023), online: https://ec.europa.eu/commission/presscorner/detail/en/ip_23_3501, accessed 18 June 2024.

a local authority. It would also be easy to use, including for persons with disabilities.

Merchants across the euro area would be required to accept the digital euro, except very small merchants who choose not to accept digital payments (as the cost to set up new infrastructure to accept payments in digital euro would be disproportionate).

Such a mechanism facilitates the use of an account-based CBDC while at the same time does not require the central bank to maintain, directly or indirectly, accounts to retail customers. However, as an account-based mechanism, it does not eliminate intermediation. Nor is it premised on the existence of a monetary object, even if intangible, such as a DBI, that operates to anchor uniformity of money with the view of safeguarding an efficient monetary policy and thus the maintenance of stable prices.

c.　"Digital Coins" and "Digital Currency" – What Are They?

As a token representing value,[22] the digital coin in a DBI-based system is a distinct entity consisting of data in the form of a unique string of bits: "This string must have a numeric value and must have an identity."[23] Like tangible coins and banknotes that physically move in payment from the hands of one person to those of another, a digital coin moves from the control of one person to that of another. As well, and again like tangible coins and banknotes, digital coins are not paid out of bank accounts, so their payment does not appear to require intermediation by banks. However, as is exactly the case with electronic funds transfers, unlike tangible banknotes and coins, digital coins are paid over the cyberspace. Each digital coin may take the form of a total unspent amount in a wallet[24] or, as will be seen below, a digital representation of what would otherwise be a distinct tangible banknote.

22　Practically, "with properties that suffice to attest to and transfer ownership," Digital Dollar Foundation and Accenture, *The Digital Dollar Project: Exploring a US CBDC* (2020) at 10, online: https://static1.squarespace.com/static/5e16627eb901b656f2c174ca/t/5ecfc542da96fb-2d2d5b5f15/1590674759958/Digital-Dollar-Project-Whitepaper_vF.pdf, accessed 18 June 2024 (where the quoted language is part of the definition itself).

23　Gideon Samid, *Tethered Money: Managing Digital Currency Transactions* (Academic Press, 2015) at 105.

24　Such a coin exists only as "an identifiable address with a balance." See Corinne Zellweger-Gutknecht, "Developing the Right Regulatory Regime for Cryptocurrencies and other Value Data" in David Fox and Sarah Green (eds), *Cryptocurrencies in Public and Private Law* (Oxford University Press, 2019) at 57, 86.

An assortment of digital coins or, more specifically, a system under which digital coins are issued, transferred, and redeemed, is a digital currency system. A privately issued digital currency may have its own unit of account, fluctuating by reference to the value of an official unit of account, in which case it is self-anchored. Alternatively, it may be a "claim-check" or stablecoin that is denominated in, pegged to, or claimed at par with either an official currency's unit of account or in the value of a specific commodity, whether or not it is backed by a reserve of such currency or commodity.[25]

Assuming that unlike the holding of physical cash the holding digital currency does not involve the risk of loss or theft – there are a few clear advantages to payment by digital coin over payment by means of account balance:[26]

- Payment in "bank money" is indirect, as it requires intermediation between the payer and payee by one or more banks. Conversely, payment in "cash" is typically made directly from payer to payee without any intermediation and is therefore less costly;
- Payment by digital coin does not require the surrender to the payee of the payer's account information and may be made directly – hence more secure than an inter-account transfer;
- Digital coin security focuses on the issuer rather than on numerous bank accounts used for payment in bank money and hence, by concentrating on one or few locations, it facilitates enhanced defence, and improves the safety of the financial system.

As mentioned, a digital currency is a system under which digital coins – being DBIs – are issued, transferred, and redeemed. All of the transactions are recorded in a digital ledger, that is, in a database or rather a set of information stored electronically in a file. While centralized ledgers are hosted by a central institution, distributed ledgers are shared across a network of multiple sites, geographies, or institutions.

Various underlying technologies enable the implementation of the ledgers. Depending on this, connectivity may be provided over the internet or by a telecommunications carrier. Therefore, a payment in digital currency made from one digital device to another may, but does not necessarily require, the intermediation of a dedicated electronic network. Blockchain, for example,

---

25   See e.g., Financial Stability Board, Regulation, "Supervision and Oversight of 'Global Stablecoin' Arrangements: Final Report and High-Level Recommendations" (*FSB*, 13 October 2020).

26   Samid, *Tethered Money*, above note 23 at 125–26.

requires the internet to support and maintain its distributed peer-to-peer network that generates a single version of the record on each participating computer. In essence, it is[27]

> [A] type of a database that takes a number of records and puts them in a block. ... Each block is then "chained" to the next block, using a cryptographic signature. This allows block chains to be used like a ledger, which can be shared and corroborated by anyone with the appropriate permissions.

The rules according to which a digital currency system operates constitute its protocol. A centralized protocol requires a central server, whereas a decentralized protocol runs without one and instcad makes users active participants in the operational process.[28] Protocols are in particular intended to achieve reliability with regard to the ledger and, to this end, establish a method of validation, often requiring consensus. In other words, the ledger's accuracy is corroborated in accordance with a method determined under rules adhered to by participants. Two such methods, algorithm-based cryptography and probability-based randomization, will be explained shortly.

A "cryptocurrency" is a digital currency in which encryption is used to regulate the generation of units of currency[29] and verify the execution of payment transactions.[30] The underlying protocol therefore uses cryptography to

27 UK Government Chief Scientific Adviser, "Distributed Ledger Technology: beyond block chain" (UK Government Office for Science 2016) at 17, online: https://www.gov.uk/government/uploads/system/uploads/attachment_data/file/492972/gs-16-1-distributed-ledger-technology.pdf, accessed 18 June 2024.

28 A centralized protocol may further necessitate the intermediation of either a central switch's operator or a custodian acting as a virtual storage facility or warehouse technician for the coins. In general, protocols (whether centralized or decentralized) do not depend on the intermediation of bank accounts and thus differ entirely from account-balance payment systems with centralized ledgers.

29 This distinctive feature is unfortunately missing in UK Jurisdiction Taskforce, "Legal Statement on Cryptoassets and Smart Contracts" (The LawTech Delivery Panel, November 2024) at paras 24–34, online: https://www.blockchain4europe.eu/wp-content/uploads/2021/05/6.6056_JO_Cryptocurrencies_Statement_FINAL_WEB_111119-1.pdf, accessed 18 June 2024, where the focus (particularly in para 28) appears to be on the control of the asset (rather than on its generation) by cryptographic means.

30 This definition slightly modifies that from The Wolf of Crypto, "Basic Cryptocurrency Starter Guide" (*Medium*, 18 September 2017), online: https://medium.com/@Wolfofcrypto/basic-cryptocurrency-starter-guide-8f2071ea85de, accessed 18 June 2024. Specifically, I replaced "transfer of funds" with the "execution of payment transactions" to highlight payment by the transmission of "coins" rather than "generic value" in the forms of funds; See also "Cryptocurrency" (*Wikipedia*), online: https://en.wikipedia.org/wiki/Cryptocurrency, accessed 18 June 2024, stating "[a] cryptocurrency, crypto-currency, or crypto is a digital asset designed to work as a medium of exchange ... using strong cryptography to secure transaction records, control the creation of additional coins, and verify the transfer of coin ownership."

express and protect the value of the coins (the sequence of the bits), to prevent counterfeiting and fraudulent transactions, and to perform validation, execution, and recording.[31] These functions are conducted on a distributed ledger, such as a blockchain. Thereon, each block contains a cryptographic hash or algorithm that links it to the previous block, along with a timestamp for the transactions from that block. The network allows online payments to be sent directly from one party to another without going through a bank or any other account-holding centralized counterparty.[32]

As already explained in chapter 4, the wide use of a blockchain for payment and settlement is problematic. For the completion of the discussion the analysis on this point will repeat here almost verbatim.

First, the settlement is slower than in existing payment systems. Second, unresolved disagreement among developers or other actors such as miners may create "hard forks" namely, a bifurcation in a distributed ledger whereby separate and irreconcilable ledgers are created.[33] Specifically,[34] blockchains may feature "probabilistic settlement," where a misalignment between legal finality and technical settlement may occur.[35] A misalignment occurs, for example, when legal finality is thought to have been achieved, but a "fork" causes technical settlement to be reversed. With probabilistic settlement, there is a possibility that forks emerge that could lead to a reversal of technical settlement of transactions. The probability for a given state of technical settlement to be conclusive increases as more transactions are added to the ledger. At the same time, the settlement risk implications of a fork increase with the number of transactions added to the ledger, as they are subject to a potential reversal.

Third, differences in design preclude blockchain interoperability. For their part, limited scalability and a lack of interoperability prevent network

31 With regard to Bitcoin, for example, record security and visibility to authorized users is ensured by cryptography.

32 Not every decentralized system is associated with a cryptocurrency. For a visual demonstration of this point, see Dong He et al, "Virtual Currencies and Beyond: Initial Considerations" (SDN/16/3, International Monetary Fund 2016) at 8, Figure 1. I do not adopt the taxonomy proposed in that figure.

33 Financial Stability Board, "Decentralised financial technologies: Report on financial stability, regulatory and governance implications" (FSB, June 2019) at 23, footnote 82, online: https://www.fsb.org/wp-content/uploads/P060619.pdf, accessed 18 June 2024.

34 Committee on Payments and Market Infrastructures (CPMI) & Board of the International Organization of Securities Commissions (IOSCO), *Consultative Report: Application of the Principles for Financial Market Infrastructures to Stablecoin Arrangements* (Bank for International Settlements & International Organization of Securities Commissions 2021) at para 3.4.5, online: https://www.bis.org/cpmi/publ/d198.pdf, accessed 18 June 2024.

35 *Ibid* at para 3.4.3.

effects from taking root, and lead to a system of parallel blockchains which adds to governance, settlement, and legal finality risks.[36]

Fourth, in a payment by cryptocurrency over a blockchain, the transaction is exposed on the blockchain and thus compromises on privacy. This is so since the chain of custody of the cryptocurrency is written on a distributed ledger and is thus exposed. Verification of transfer requires identification of the payer's public key and transfer is publicized to the entire community. Conversely in a quantum-based currency, the chain of custody, together with terms of use, can be written on the coin itself; it is not necessary to identify payer; and the bit sequence defines only the unique identity of the coin, exactly like a serial number on a paper banknote.[37]

Fifth, a payment by cryptocurrency over a blockchain requires online validation and can thus be performed from beginning to end only where internet is available. Conversely, for genuine freshly minted coins (and thus by definition unspent), BitMint's Hard Wallet can validate and provide finality to off-line proximity payments. This is carried out by a "quick touch" by one device to another and applies even to a proximity payment in other than BitMint's coins. As pointed out in chapter 4, as an emerging alternative to crypto-based currencies BitMint is a digital currency deploying quantum randomness.[38]

Regardless, Gideon Samid argues that the developers of cryptocurrencies "simply migrated the cryptographic tools used to safeguard communication and applied them to safeguard digital currency." Thus, the argument continues, such developers made cryptocurrencies vulnerable to erosive

---

36 Frederic Boissay et al, *Blockchain scalability and the fragmentation of crypto* (Bulletin No 56, Bank for International Settlements 2022), online: https://www.bis.org/publ/bisbull56.pdf, accessed 18 June 2024.

37 Gideon Samid, "A LeVeL Paying Field: Cryptographic Solutions towards Social Accountability and Financial Inclusion" (Research Gate, February 2022), online: https://www.researchgate. net/publication/358479911_A_LeVeL_Paying_Field_Cryptographic_Solutions_towards_Social_Accountability_and_Financial_Inclusion, accessed 28 May 2024.

38 For the two main technology archetypes, Quantum versus Crypto see Amnon Samid, "Automated Embedded Payment Systems" (2022) 12 *International Journal of Embedded Systems and Applications* 1, online: https://www.researchgate.net/publication/367014225_Automated_Embedded_Payment_Systems, accessed 28 May 2024; for BitMint Money see "BitMintMoney," online: https://www.bitmintcash.com/, accessed 18 July 2024; for the superior protection of randomness premised on "a cipher which use[s] no mathematical complexity but instead call[s] for large amounts of randomness," see e.g., Carsten Stöcker, "Randomness: The Fix for Today's Broken Security" (*Medium*, 9 November 2017), online: cstoecker.medium.com /randomness-the-fix-for-todays-broken-security-39ea7dc3a89b, accessed 18 June 2024; for BitMint being considered in China see "Q-Pay could mark the next sea change in finance" (*DigFin*, 8 January 2019), online: https://www.digfingroup.com/bitmint-q-pay, accessed 18 June 2024.

cryptographic intractability.[39] Moreover, "some of the most widespread cryptographic methods currently used in cybersecurity" are likely to become exposed to successful attacks by quantum computers.[40] This will undoubtedly undermine the integrity of cryptocurrencies. In the ongoing fight against counterfeiters and fraudulent copiers, centralized schemes are better positioned to apply superior defence measures to protect the integrity of the database as well as enhanced security procedures in both coin and identity verification upon redemption and in trade.[41]

As discussed in chapter 4, quantum-resistant currency has been proposed as a solution to these drawbacks. Unlike cryptocurrencies, quantum-resistant currency is not hinged on algorithm complexity – that is, a mathematical riddle that even as it cannot be solved at present may be solved in the future. Rather, quantum-resistant currency, while utilized under protocols that employ crypto tools for messaging and storage, is based on randomness premised on unpredictability. It is neither based on algorithm complexity nor generated by a non-random computer program, and as such is known as quantum or pure randomness.[42]

Relevant technological issues ought to be addressed by experts and examined in proofs of concept and pilots. The above is general information as appearing in the literature with the view of guiding the exploration process.

---

39 Samid, *Tethered Money*, above note 23 at 26, meaning unmanageable cryptographic complexity that *is eroded over time*, usually by more effective computer machines and/or deeper mathematical insight.

40 Sara Castellanos, "Visa, JPMorgan Are Already Preparing for Potential Quantum Cyberattacks" (*The Wall Street Journal*, 9 October 2020), online: https://www.wsj.com/articles /visa-jpmorgan-are-already-preparing-for-potential-quantum-cyberattacks-11602255213, accessed 18 June 2024); quantum computing facilitates more powerful calculations. Briefly stated, rather than using long strings of "bits," a quantum computer uses "qbits," so that "whereas a classical computer works with ones and zeros, a quantum computer will have the advantage of using ones, zeros, and 'superpositions' of ones and zeros. Certain difficult tasks that have long been thought impossible (or 'intractable') for classical computers will be achieved quickly and efficiently by a quantum computer." See Institute for Quantum Computing, "Quantum Computing 101" (*University of Waterloo*), online: https://uwaterloo.ca /institute-for-quantum-computing/quantum-computing-101#What-is-quantum-computing, accessed June 18 2024.

41 See e.g., Samid, *Tethered Money*, above note 23 at 92–94 and *cf* 125–27 as well as 25, 98–100, albeit focusing on the advantage of paying with digital coins over that of paying in scriptural money, which may expose account data to hackers.

42 For the superior protection of randomness premised on "a cipher which use[s] no mathematical complexity but instead call[s] for large amounts of randomness" see Stöcker, above note 38.

III. THE BANK OF CANADA'S POWER TO ISSUE RCBDC AND EQUIP IT WITH LEGAL TENDER STATUS

The Preamble to the *Bank of Canada Act*,[43] from its inception in the mid-1930s of the previous century,[44] reads as follows:

> WHEREAS it is desirable to establish a central bank in Canada *to regulate credit and currency in the best interests of the economic life of the nation, to control and protect the external value of the national monetary unit* and to mitigate by its influence fluctuations in the general level of production, trade, prices and employment, so far as may be possible within the scope of monetary action, and generally to promote the economic and financial welfare of Canada.

Currency regulation ought to be read to include (albeit not to be necessarily limited to) currency issuance and yet there is no specific provision in the Act implementing the task of currency regulation. The closest we have in the statute is the power to issue circulating notes. Thus, as discussed in chapter 2, under section 25(1) of the *Bank of Canada Act*,[45] the Bank of Canada "has the sole right to issue notes and those notes shall be a first charge on the assets of the Bank." "Notes" are defined in section 1 to mean "notes intended for circulation in Canada." Under section 25(6), "Notes of the Bank of Canada are neither promissory notes nor bills of exchange within the meaning of the *Bills of Exchange Act*."[46] Section 25(2) goes on to require the Bank of Canada to make adequate arrangements for the issue into and removal out of circulation of notes. Under section 25(3), "[n]otes of the Bank shall be in such denominations and shall be printed and signed or otherwise executed as the Governor in Council by regulation determines." Form and material of the notes shall be subject to the minister's approval, "but each note shall be printed in both the English and French languages,"[47] that is, on that point there is no discretion.

A common view appears to be that a digital coin is not a note, i.e., as it is not a tangible object.[48] This is based on a strictly literal interpretation of monetary laws that does not consider the adaptation of their meaning to meet evolving technological changes. As set out in chapter 6, I do not share this perspective and the resulting conclusion. To clarify, I do not argue against the passage of a specific statute authorizing the Bank of Canada to issue rCBDC and regulating its features. Nor do I argue that in any statute "banknote" and

---

43 RSC 1985, c B-2.

44 *Bank of Canada Act*, SC 1934, c 34 (emphasis added). See chapter 2.

45 *Bank of Canada Act*, above note 43.

46 *Ibid*, s 25(6)

47 *Ibid*, s 25(4).

48 Bossu et al, above note 6 at 36–37.

"note" are *automatically* to be interpreted as including an electronic version. Rather, context and purpose are to be taken into account, and even application of rules may be selective and/or by analogy. My point is thus that broadly speaking, DBI- rCBDC issuance falls within the banknote issuance power of a central bank and hence within the broad currency issuance power of the Bank of Canada. A specific statutory treatment is nevertheless recommended, if only to eliminate challenges and to set out features of the rCBDC, even as such features derive from the tangible banknote. As a matter of interpreting the *Bank of Canada Act*, the starting point on providing for the rCBDC is that:

1. A "digital coin" is an e-note – so as to fall within the Bank of Canada's note-issuing power under section 25 of the *Bank of Canada Act*. As explained below, it also serves as "legal tender" under the *Currency Act*;[49]

2. The reference to "printing" (e.g., in the *Bank of Canada Act* section 25(3)) has a strong connotation of "paper." Similarly, on its own, "executed" may be taken to envision the delivery of a tangible item. As well, "material" in section 25(6) brings to mind something physical. At the same time, monetary law has universally been subject to liberal interpretation taking into account market conditions and technological developments. More on this in chapter 6(V).

This analysis facilitates the issuance of a DBI-based rCBDC by the Bank of Canada.

Equally, it facilitates the duty of the Bank of Canada "to make adequate arrangements for" the issue, supply, and removal of such digital coins under section 25(2). Strictly speaking, the removal duty under section 25(2)(b) is for non-current notes as well as those which are "worn or mutilated." As in connection with "printing," the immediate association of "worn or mutilated" is with tangible items, and yet a liberal and creative interpretation may read the provision to refer to any "defective" note, be it on paper or in a digital form.

As for an account-based CBDC, the starting point is that under section 18 of the *Bank of Canada Act*, so far as deposit-taking is concerned, the Bank of Canada may:

(1) accept deposits from the Government of Canada and pay interest on those deposits;

(1.1) accept deposits from any bank, authorized foreign bank that is not subject to the restrictions and requirements referred to in subsection 524(2) of the *Bank Act* or other member of the Canadian Payments Association;

---

49   RSC 1985, c C-52.

> (**l.2**) pay interest on the deposits referred to in paragraph (l.1) if the money deposited is to be used for the purpose of making loans or advances referred to in paragraph (h);
>
> (**l.3**) accept deposits from the government of any province or from any corporation or agency of the Government of Canada;
>
> ...
>
> (**m**) accept deposits from central banks in other countries, the Bank for International Settlements, the International Monetary Fund, the International Bank for Reconstruction and Development and any other official international financial organization, act as agent or mandatary, or depository or correspondent for any of those banks or organizations, and pay interest on any of those deposits;
>
> ...
>
> (**o**) accept deposits of money that are authorized or required by an Act of Parliament to be transferred to the Bank, and, in accordance with that Act, pay interest on money so deposited and pay out money to any person entitled to it under that Act; and
>
> (**p**) carry on any business activity that is incidental to or consequential on something the Bank is allowed or required to do by this Act.

Deposit taking from the public at large is thus precluded. At the same time, arguably, nothing including section 18(l.1) precludes a commercial bank from assigning to its customers' specifically designated accounts funds deposited with the Bank of Canada thereby effectively creating an account-based rCBDC.

However, the Bank of Canada does not have the power to confer a "legal tender" status on any monetary or other object. Rather, its notes are "legal tender" by virtue of the provisions of the *Currency Act*.[50] Accordingly, unless the digital coins issued by the Bank of Canada are considered to be "notes" under the present wording of the *Bank of Canada Act*,[51] specific provisions in the *Currency Act* (or elsewhere) will be required to confer on the "legal tender" status.

To clarify: as discussed in chapter 2, under section 3(1) of the *Currency Act*,[52] "[t]he monetary unit of Canada is the dollar." The dollar must be taken to be "the currency of Canada" under which coins and notes are to be issued.[53] Subject to limitations as to what denominations can be used in payment of various sizes, under section 8(1), "a tender of payment of money is a legal tender if made" in

---

50 *Ibid.*

51 *Bank of Canada Act*, above note 43.

52 *Currency Act*, above note 49.

53 Respectively, under ss 7(1), 7.1 of the *Currency Act, ibid.*

coins and notes "that are current." Current coins and notes are those respectively issued by the Royal Canadian Mint and the Bank of Canada.[54] The Governor in Council's power to authorize the issue, characteristics, and design of circulating coins is governed by sections 6.4–6.6 of the *Royal Canadian Mint Act*.[55]

There is nowhere in Canada a statutory provision defining "legal tender." As explained in chapter 1, in principle, a medium of exchange that a creditor is not privileged to refuse if it is tendered by a debtor in payment of their debt is "legal tender."[56] A more detailed elaboration on the scope and effects of legal tender banknotes and coins addresses the creditor's duty to accept (unless otherwise agreed), the acceptance by the creditor of full face value, and a legal recognition as a means of discharge from payment obligation.[57]

Vesting in an rCBDC a legal tender status is thus problematic if only because paying and getting paid by rCBDC requires some equipment. While an rCBDC law ought to address accessibility and inclusiveness there may always be those who will be excluded even if only by choice. To that end I set out below the legal tender provisions of the Proposed Digital Euro Regulation.[58] Particularly note the exceptions and the prohibition of unilateral exclusion. As for the former, under article 9, in addition to small enterprises, non-profit legal entities, tender of the digital euro may be refused "where a refusal is made in good faith and where such refusal is based on legitimate and temporary grounds ... " as well as "where the payee is a natural person acting in the course of a purely personal or household activity."

The provisions of the Proposed Digital Euro Regulation set out below may be considered for adoption in Canada with necessary modifications:

CHAPTER III
LEGAL TENDER

Article 7
Legal tender status

1. The digital euro shall have legal tender status.
2. The legal tender status of the digital euro shall entail its mandatory acceptance, at full face value, with the power to discharge from a payment obligation.

---

54   *Ibid*, ss 7, 7.1.
55   RSC 1985, c R-9.
56   Arthur Nusbaum, *Money in the Law: National and International* (The Foundation Press, 1950) at 45, s 4.
57   See e.g., European Legal Tender Expert Group (ELTEG), "Report on the definition, scope and effects of legal tender of euro banknotes and coins" (ELTEG, 21 January 2009) at 4.
58   COM (2023) 369 final, above note 18.

3. In accordance with the mandatory acceptance of the digital euro, the payee shall not refuse digital euro tendered in payment to comply with that obligation.

4. In accordance with the acceptance at full face value of the digital euro, the monetary value of digital euro tendered in payment of a debt shall be equal to the value of the monetary debt. Surcharges on the payment of debt with the digital euro shall be prohibited.

5. In accordance with the power of the digital euro to discharge from a payment obligation, a payer shall be able to discharge himself from a payment obligation by tendering digital euro to the payee.

Article 8
Territorial scope of legal tender status

1. The digital euro shall have legal tender status for offline payments of a monetary debt denominated in euro that take place within the euro area.

2. The digital euro shall have legal tender status for online payments of a monetary debt denominated in euro to a payee residing or established in the euro area.

Article 9
Exceptions to the obligation to accept the digital euro

By way of derogation from Article 7(3) and Article 8, a payee shall be entitled to refuse digital euro in any of the following cases:

(a) where the payee is an enterprise which employs fewer than 10 persons or whose annual turnover or annual balance sheet total does not exceed EUR 2 million, or is a non-profit legal entity ... unless it accepts comparable digital means of payment;

(b) where a refusal is made in good faith and where such refusal is based on legitimate and temporary grounds in line with the principle of proportionality in view of concrete circumstances beyond the control of the payee;

(c) where the payee is a natural person acting in the course of a purely personal or household activity;

(d) where, prior to the payment, the payee has agreed with the payer on a different means of payment, subject to Article 10.

For the purposes of point (b), the burden of proof to establish that legitimate and temporary grounds existed in a particular case and that the refusal was proportionate shall be on the payee.

Article 10
Prohibition of the unilateral exclusion of payments in the digital euro

Payees subject to the obligation to accept the digital euro shall not use contractual terms that have not been individually negotiated or commercial practices which have the object or the effect to exclude the use of the digital euro by the payers of monetary debts denominated in euro. Such contractual terms or commercial practices shall not be binding on the payer. A contractual term shall be regarded as not individually negotiated where it has been drafted in advance and where the payer has therefore not been able to influence the substance of the term, particularly in the context of a pre-formulated standard contract.

Article 11
Additional exceptions of a monetary law nature

The Commission is empowered to adopt delegated acts[59] ... to supplement this Regulation by identifying additional exceptions of a monetary law nature to the principle of mandatory acceptance. Those exceptions shall be justified by an objective of public interest and proportionate to that aim, shall not undermine the effectiveness of the legal tender status of the digital euro, and shall only be permitted provided that other means for the payment of monetary debts are available. When preparing those delegated acts, the Commission shall consult the European Central Bank.

Article 12
Interaction between the digital euro and euro banknotes and coins

1. The digital euro shall be convertible with euro banknotes and coins at par.
2. Payees of a monetary debt denominated in euro shall accept payments in digital euro according to the provisions of this Regulation, irrespective of whether they accept payments in euro banknotes and coins. ... Where the acceptance of euro banknotes and coins and of the digital euro is mandatory. ... the payer is entitled to choose the means of payment.

---

59 Being non-legislative acts adopted by the European Commission that serve to amend or supplement the non-essential elements of the legislation. See art 290 Treaty on the Functioning of the European Union, Consolidated Version, art 128(1), 26 October 2012, OJ C 326/47 [TFEU]

Per Article 7, once accepted, acceptance must be at full face value. This is not controversial. For its part, the mandatory acceptance *per se* is in line with Article 2 of the Commission Recommendation of 22 March 2010, *On the Scope and Effects of Legal Tender of Euro Banknotes and Coin*[60] providing for the obligatory acceptance of payments in euro banknotes and coins in retail transactions. However, there may not be a corresponding obligation to accept cash in Canada, and hence an obligation to get a digital coin appears to be problematic.

There may be a few ways to resolve this contradiction. First, the lack of an obligation to accept cash in retail transactions may be re-examined. Second, the obligation to accept digital currency may be fastened only on those retailers accepting cash. Third, only those retailers accepting electronic payments – such as by credit or debit card – may be required to accept digital currency.

Christian Pfister claims that the concept of "legal tender" is in any event obsolete – or at least of a limited use – particularly in the context of payment by rCBDC.[61] Indeed, for the use of any currency, acceptability is more important than "legal tender" status. There is at least one monetary system of which I am aware where a currency was selected to be the deemed money of both account and payment on the basis of being "widely accepted" without being conferred a "legal tender" status.[62] At the same time, it cannot be denied that a "legal tender" status promotes acceptability. Hence, it is recommended to examine the options set out above with the view of selecting an optimal solution to the issue.

IV. DBI-BASED RCBDC – THE OPTIMAL DESIGN

As an e-banknote, the rCBDC ought better be legal tender, even if within limits as discussed above. As well, it ought not bear interest.[63] Similarly to the

---

60 "Commission Recommendation 2010/191/EU of 22 March 2010 on the scope and effects of legal tender of euro banknotes and coins" 2010/191/EU [2010] OJ L 83/70, online: https:// eur-lex.europa.eu/legal-content/EN/TXT/?uri=uriserv%3AOJ.L_.2010.083.01.0070.01.ENG& toc=OJ%3AL%3A2010%3A083%3ATOC, accessed 19 June 2024; a proposal was made based on the recommendation, see European Commission, "Proposal for a Regulation of The European Parliament and of The Council on the Legal Tender of Euro Banknotes and Coins" COM (2023) at 364 final, online: https://eur-lex.europa.eu/legal-content/EN/TXT/?uri= CELEX%3A52023PC0364, accessed 19 June 2024.

61 Christian Pfister "Digital Euro: The Case Against Legal Tender" (*SUERF*, SUERF Policy Brief No 799, 15 February 2024, online: https://www.suerf.org/publications/suerf-policy-notes-and -briefs/digital-euro-the-case-against-legal-tender/, accessed 19 June 2024.

62 UN Administration in Kosovo, "REGULATION NO.1999/4 ON THE CURRENCY PERMITTED TO BE USED IN KOSOVO" (UNMIK Regulation No 1999/4, 2 September 1999), online: https:// www.bqk-kos.org/repository/docs/2010/UNMIK_REG_1999_4.pdf, accessed 19 June 2024.

63 Corinne Zellweger-Gutknecht, "Digital Euro," above note 17; see also Bossu et al, above note 6 at 37.

paper banknote, rCBDC ought to be distributed to the public through banks. Payment in it ought to be comparable to that of payment in a tangible note.

Payment in cash is expected to be simple, universally available 24/7/365 anywhere, confidential as desired, and as soon as it is made to fully discharge a debt. This Part will set out the essential features needed to be met by the optimal DBI. Whether these requirements ought to be included in the call to industry for proposals – as recommended here – is something to be discussed. Regardless, it will be for technical experts to assess the achievability of the recommended features as well as to verify the technological claims of proposed systems by running pilots and other methods as, for example, has extensively been carried out in China[64] and is mandated to be done by statutory proposal in the United States for stablecoins.[65]

Essential criteria to be addressed include:

1. A selection between a currency premised on cryptography or quantum resistance (based on vulnerable to erosive cryptographic intractability) – with the latter allegedly[66] providing enhanced protection against risks such as quantum computing, hacking, and vulnerable to erosive cryptographic intractability;[67]

2. The choice between a centralized or decentralized system for transfer – whether or not operating on a blockchain;

3. Online and offline validation – with the view of achieving full finality even in a full offline setting;

4. Security/Safety (see number 1, above, as well as the relationship between the private and public keys);

5. Universal accessibility and resilience [availability] – including by simple mobile (and not necessarily smart) phone as well as off-line;

6. Risk of compromising access particularly upon loss or theft of a "loaded" device;

---

64   See e.g., Thomas W Pauken II, "China Leaps Far Ahead into Central Bank Digital Currencies Development" (*China Focus*, 2 June 2023), online: http://www.cnfocus.com/china-leaps-far-ahead-into-central-bank-digital-currencies/, accessed 19 June 2024.

65   United States HR Draft Bill, "To provide requirements for payment stablecoin issuers, research on a digital dollar, and for other purposes" (118 Cong 2023), ss 101(16), 201, online: https://docs.house.gov/meetings/BA/BA21/20230419/115753/BILLS-118pih-Toproviderequirements forpaymentstablecoinissuersresearchonadigitaldollarandforotherpurposes.pdf, accessed 19 June 2024; see also, Clarity for Payment Stablecoins Act of 2023, HR 4766, 118 Cong, s 2(13). The bill is addressed in chapter 4 of this study.

66   To that end see, *Project Polaris Part 1: A handbook for offline payments with CBDC* (Bank for International Settlements Innovation Hub, May 2023), online: https://www.bis.org/publ /othp64.pdf, accessed 19 June 2024.

67   See Amnon Samid, above note 39.

7. Balancing privacy (vis-à-vis the outside world, operator(s) and parties to the payment transaction), and law enforcement; and

8. Efficiency (saving on intermediaries; bypassing peer-dependent validation; availability of coin splitting without resorting to network validation; speed, lower fees).

9. Which system is more environmentally friendly, increases accessibility, is more user friendly?

10. Will the public at large – consumers and business end-users – receive a higher add-value?

V. WHOLESALE CBDC

Wholesale CBDC (wCBDC) is designed to facilitate settlement in the interbank domain. A few experiments in it have been carried out.[68]

As a proof of concept (PoC) both Bank of Canada under the Jasper Project[69] and Monetary Authority of Singapore under the Ubin Project[70] experiment with a DLT (distributed ledger technology) based wholesale payment settlement premised on the use of a blockchain for interbank settlement in central bank money. Thereunder, the central bank issues to each participating bank digital depository receipts against the security of funds withdrawn from the reserve account of that bank. For each payment order processed, interbank settlement continuously takes place by transacting with these

68 See also Phoebus L Athanassiou, "Wholesale central bank digital currencies: an overview of recent central bank initiatives and lessons learned" in *ESCB Legal Conference 2020: 11 September–2 November 2020* (European Central Bank 2020) at 191.

69 See James Chapman et al, "Project Jasper: Are Distributed Wholesale Payment Systems Feasible Yet?" (Bank of Canada Financial System Review, June 2017), online: http://www.bankofcanada.ca/wp-content/uploads/2017/05/fsr-june-2017-chapman.pdf, accessed 19 June 2024; for the earlier stage of the project see Rod Garratt, "CAD-coin versus Fedcoin" (R3 Report May 2017), online: https://www.finextra.com/finextra-downloads/newsdocs/cad-coin-versus.pdf, accessed 19 June 2024; see also, Laura Shin, "Canada Has Been Experimenting With A Digital Fiat Currency Called CAD-COIN" (*Forbes*, 16 June 2016), online: http://www.forbes.com/sites/laurashin/2016/06/16/canada-has-been-experimenting-with-a-digital-fiat-currency-called-cad-coin/#536fabe91b0c, accessed 19 June 2024; Pete Rizzo, "Bank of Canada Demos Blockchain-Based Digital Dollar" (*CoinDesk.com*, 16 June 2016), online: http://www.coindesk.com/bank-canada-demos-blockchain-based-digital-dollar/, accessed 19 June 2024; see also Claire Brownell, "No cryptocurrency anytime soon, Bank of Canada says: 'We're very far off'" (*Financial Post*, 17 June 2016), online: http://business.financialpost.com/news/fp-street/no-cryptocurrency-anytime-soon-bank-of-canada-says-were-very-far-off, accessed 19 June 2024.

70 See Deloitte and Monetary Authority of Singapore, "The future is here – Project Ubin: SGD on Distributed Ledger" (Deloitte Consulting Ltd 2017), online: https://www2.deloitte.com/content/dam/Deloitte/sg/Documents/financial-services/sg-fsi-project-ubin-report.pdf or https://www.mas.gov.sg/-/media/Jasper-Ubin-Design-Paper.pdf, accessed 19 June 2024.

digital receipts over the blockchain. Both entered a collaboration to test and develop a cross-border solution using crypto tokens issued by the two central banks.[71]

In Jasper, Digital Depository Receipts (DDRs) issued by the Bank of Canada are secured by an omnibus account in which each participating bank deposits central bank money withdrawn from its settlement account. In Ubin, Depository Receipts (DRs) are issued by the Monetary Authority of Singapore (MAS) to each participating bank against central bank money deposited by the latter in an individual cash custody account held with the former. In Ubin participating banks may hold deposit receipt balances on the blockchain overnight and have greater flexibility in pledging and redeeming DRs during operating hours. In Jasper DDRs are created and destroyed upon redemption on a daily basis.

Ubin uses a system built on the Ethereum platform. This was true for the first phase of Jasper (Jasper 1). This platform uses Proof of Work (PoW) consensus protocol, requiring expensive computations to validate transactions and update the ledger. For that reason, the second phase of Jasper (Jasper II) switched to the Corda platform in which a notary function replaces that of the PoW.[72] The notary role in Jasper II is assigned to the Bank of Canada. As such it has access to the entire ledger and is able to verify that the funds involved in a transaction are available.

Jasper II improved on both Jasper 1 and Ubin in facilitating a liquidity-saving mechanism (LSM) in the form of a payment queue with periodic multilateral payment netting for payments designated as "non-urgent."

Both Jasper and Ubin have been successful as a proof of concept for a DLT-based interbank settlement system that has the potential of replacing the traditional Real-time Gross Settlement (RTGS). However, in assessing Jasper, it was concluded that:[73]

- For critical financial market infrastructures, such as wholesale payment systems, current versions of DLT may not provide an overall net benefit relative to current centralized systems. Recent versions of DLT have, however, made advances compared with initial cryptocurrency applications of DLT.

---

71   Speech by Ravi Menon, Managing Director Monetary Authority of Singapore, at Money20/20 (15 March 2018), online: https://www.bis.org/review/r180321c.htm, accessed 16 November 2024.

72   James Chapman et al, above note 69 at 5.

73   *Ibid* at 1.

- Benefits for the financial system of a DLT-based wholesale payment system could likely arise from its interaction with a larger DLT ecosystem of financial market infrastructures, potentially including cross-border transactions.

Ultimately, blockchain technology may supplement and be integrated into existing financial infrastructure, and yet does not appear to replace it altogether. Advantages may be incurred in the form of the development of tokenized financial markets in which DLT synchronized processing and settlement in central bank money facilitates securities and cross-currency/forex transactions.[74] Progress of projects in this direction and specific legal issues concerning them are outside the scope of this study.[75] A distinct example to be noted is Project mBridge experimenting with a multi-CBDC common platform for wholesale cross-border payments focusing on the use case of international trade. The project has the potential to connect central banks and commercial banks around the world as a public good.[76]

Phoebus Athanassiou enumerates four legal concerns with regard to wholesale CBDC:[77]

1. The legal competence of central banks to launch alternative to fiat money;
2. Finality of transfer;
3. The legal characterization, namely, the fundamental legal nature, of the tokens on which all of the wholesale CBDC experiments rely; and

---

74   See Christian Pfister, "Issuing a Wholesale Central Bank Digital Currency: Why and How" (2024) 59 *Intereconomics* 35.

75   See e.g., Committee on Payment and Market Infrastructures, *Central bank digital currencies for cross-border payments: Report to the G20* (Bank for International Settlements 2021), online: https://www.bis.org/publ/othp38.pdf, accessed 19 June 2024; see also Committee on Payment and Market Infrastructures (2022), *Options for access to and interoperability of CBDCs for cross-border payments: Report to the G20* (Bank for International Settlements 2022), online: https://www.bis.org/publ/othp52.pdf, accessed 19 June 2024.

76   BIS Innovation Hub, *Project mBridge Update: Experimenting with a multi-CBDC platform for cross-border payments* (Bank for International Settlements October 2023), online: https://www.bis.org/innovation_hub/projects/mbridge_brochure_2311.pdf, accessed 19 June 2024. The project reached the minimum viable product (MVP) stage in mid-2024. See online: https://www.bis.org/about/bisih/topics/cbdc/mcbdc_bridge.htm, accessed 16 November 2024.
      The Bank for International Settlement (BIS) left the project on 31 October 2024, apparently against the background of "growing geopolitical scrutiny of global transfers." See online: https://www.reuters.com/business/finance/bis-leave-cross-border-payments-platform-project-mbridge-2024-10-31/, accessed 16 November 2024.

77   Athanassiou, above note 68 at 195–96.

4. The outsourcing of central bank settlement accounts necessitated by the use of distributed ledgers for the processing and validation of transactions involving tokenized CBDCs would be permissible.

Regarding the first question, by reference to Canada, as recalled, under section 25(1) of the *Bank of Canada Act*,[78] "[t]he Bank has the sole right to issue notes and those notes shall be a first charge on the assets of the Bank." Under section 2, "notes" are defined to mean "notes intended for circulation in Canada." Even if the DDR is an e-note, it is not "intended for circulation in Canada." Accordingly, section 25(1) does not confer on the Bank of Canada to issue something like the DDR, as the latter are not intended for circulation in Canada. Similarly, section 18 of the *Bank of Canada Act* does not appear to enumerate directly any power from which the DDR issuance could be justified. This is so unless one reads the power under section 18 (1.1) to "accept deposits from any bank, authorized foreign bank ... or other member of the Canadian Payments Association" to include the settlement of interbank payments among such deposits. In fact this must be a correct interpretation for section 18(1.1); in its absence, without any statutory provision directly authorizing the Bank of Canada to provide on its books settlement for interbank payments, the Bank of Canada could not be said to have the power to carry out such settlement!

Accordingly, if the Bank of Canada has the power to provide interbank settlement, which indeed must be the case, it is possible to see the DDR issuance as a "business activity that is incidental to or consequential on something the Bank is allowed or required to do by [the Bank of Canada] Act" under section 18(p). In the alternative, the power under section 18(1.1) to accept deposits must be taken to include the issuance of certificates of indebtedness, such as DDRs, at least under section 18(p), as a "business activity that is incidental to or consequential on" the acceptance of such deposits.

The second question, as to the finality of payment, is in fact the same as in relation to all blockchain payments and is discussed in both chapter 4 and elsewhere in this chapter. More in general, finality of payment is a matter to be addressed by settlement system rules.

The third question concerns the determination of the DDR characterization. The answer depends on the particular features of the instrument selected. It could thus be an e-note, even if not under section 25(1) of the *Bank of Canada Act*. In the alternative, in could be a simple e-IOU instrument.

---

78 *Bank of Canada Act*, above note 43.

The answer to the fourth question, regarding the outsourcing of the settlement activity, requires further examination of the powers of the Bank of Canada. No direct answer is given in section 18. I should add that such a practice exists both universally and globally.

VI. ARCHITECTURE AND ISSUANCE MODELS

a. Introduction

In the ensuing discussion I assume for some of the rCBDC models that the Bank of Canada's power to issue digital currency – particularly DBIs – includes the power to both distribute them to, and operate the system for transferring them among, members of the public.

For their part, rCBDC models are often divided into direct, hybrid, and indirect.[79] In the direct model, the central bank issues the digital coins and runs its transfer system.[80] In a hybrid system, the central bank issues its digital coins to the public, but the distribution and transfer system is run by intermediaries.[81] Under the indirect model, the central bank issues the currency to intermediaries, which then issue to the public their own currency, fully backed by the central bank-issued currency. Those intermediaries also run the inter-customer transfer system.

I do not fully adopt this classification, together with its terminology. In my view, it is not sufficiently fine-tuned as to take into account all reasonable scenarios. In particular, it focuses strongly on the transfer of digital coins while addressing their distribution to the public in a rather rudimentary way. It also fails to take into account the option of having commercial banks act on behalf of the central bank in issuing digital coins. Further, especially concerning hybrid models, a distinction between intermediated and direct distribution to end-users is missing. A more-fine-tuned architecture purporting to take into account such concerns is set out below.

b. Issuance (and Redemption) Options

Under the first four scenarios outlined here, a member of the public holding an e-banknote has a direct claim against the central bank.

---

79 See e.g., European Central Bank, "Report on a Digital Euro" (October 2020) at 39–41; Raphael Auer and Rainer Böhme, "The Technology of Retail Central Bank Digital Currency" [March 2020] *BIS Quarterly Review* 88, 88–93, online: https://www.bis.org/publ/qtrpdf/r_qt2003j.pdf, accessed 19 June 2024.

80 ECB, "Digital Euro Report," *ibid* at 40, Figure 3; no corresponding model in Auer and Böhme, above note 79.

81 *Ibid* at 41, Figure 4 and "intermediated" model in Auer and Böhme, above note 79 at 20.

i. Full direct option

Both the distribution and transfer systems are run by the central bank.

In this scenario, the central bank deals directly with digital coin holders.[82] Holders purchase digital coins directly from the central bank, typically paying out of bank accounts or, in theory, in paper banknotes. The central bank runs a comprehensive network linking all digital coin holders. As with any other system set out below, this option does not require that members of the public open or use accounts in central banks.

ii. Limited direct option

Distribution is run by commercial banks, while the central bank operates the transfer system.

As far as distribution is concerned, this scenario mimics the current system for paper banknotes.[83] Commercial banks buy digital coins from the central bank, paying out of their reserve accounts. Commercial bank customers purchase digital coins (issued by the central bank) from their own commercial banks and typically pay for them by having their respective accounts with their commercial bank debited. As in (i), a holder of a digital coin has a direct relationship with the issuing central bank. Moreover, the central bank operates a comprehensive network linking all digital coin holders.

iii. Hybrid-intermediated option

Both the distribution and transfer systems are operated by commercial banks.

This option replicates the scenario discussed in (ii), with the exception that the inter-customer transfer system is also run by commercial banks (rather than the central bank).[84] As noted in (ii), commercial banks buy digital coins from the central bank. Upon the issuance of a digital coin to the commercial bank, the commercial bank's reserve account at the central bank is debited. Commercial bank customers purchase digital coins (issued by a central bank) from their own commercial banks and typically pay by having their respective accounts with their commercial banks debited.

iv. Hybrid-direct option

Both the distribution and transfer systems are operated by commercial banks.

Unlike in the scenario set out in (iii), commercial banks issue the digital coins as agents for the central bank. Upon the issuance of a digital coin to the

---

82   As it does not involve intermediaries, this model has no corresponding model in ECB, "Digital Euro Report," *ibid* at 39–41.

83   This model is comparable to that used in ECB, "Digital Euro Report," *ibid* at 41, Figure 3.

84   This model is comparable to that used in ECB, "Digital Euro Report," *ibid* at 41, Figure 4 (the latter, however, does not distinguish between intermediated and direct distribution).

holder, the reserve account of the ("issuing") commercial bank at the central bank is debited. This scenario differs from the option addressed in (iii) in facilitating the issuance of digital coins by one or more commercial banks on behalf of the central bank. The task delegated to a commercial bank is purely ministerial and does not involve policy choices. Instead, the issuing commercial bank acts strictly as instructed by the delegating central bank.

v. Backed option

Both the distribution and transfer systems are operated by commercial banks.

In contrast to the four scenarios above, the holder of a digital coin does not have a direct claim against the central bank. At the same time, as long as the system operates as intended, the holder has the security of full backing by the central bank, as if the digital coin had been issued by the central bank itself. While I assume that a digital coin issued by a commercial bank is not legal tender, it is redeemable (i.e., payable) in legal tender – namely, banknotes (whether in paper or electronic form) issued by the central bank.

In this scenario, authorized commercial banks issue digital coins in their own names so that each commercial bank has a direct relationship under each digital coin with the respective holder. The latter will not be in privity with the central bank. However, to the extent that the digital coins are fully backed by Central Bank money, they are likely to freely circulate as monetary objects in discharge of payment obligations. The scenario does not envisage a system of private issuance of fiduciary digital currencies.[85] Hence, issues identified in the old system, under which paper banknotes were issued by commercial banks as a form of commercial bank money,[86] are not anticipated.

In fact, this model mimics the issuance of written banknotes in the United Kingdom by several designated banks in Scotland and Northern Ireland.[87] Such banknotes are not accorded legal tender status but are accepted in practice as

85 With regard to which, I recognize the need for government intervention, as in Ben Fung, Scott Hendry, and Warren E Webber, "Swedish Riksbank Notes and Enskilda Bank Notes: Lessons for Digital Currencies" (2018) Bank of Canada Staff Working Paper 2018-27, online: https://www.bankofcanada.ca/2018/06/staff-working-paper-2018-27/, accessed 19 June 2024.

86 The experience with the old system is discussed by Ben Fung, Scott Hendry, and Warren E Weber, "Canadian Bank Notes and Dominion Notes: Lessons for Digital Currencies" (2017) Bank of Canada Staff Working Paper 2017-5, online: https://www.bankofcanada.ca/2017/02/staff-working-paper-2017-5/, accessed 19 June 2024.

87 See *Banking Act, 2009* pt 6, particularly s 213; for HM Treasury Consultation Document see HM Treasury, *Banknote issue arrangements in Scotland and Northern Ireland: A Consultation Document* (Her Majesty's Stationary Office 2005), online: https://webarchive.nationalarchives.gov.uk/+/http:/www.hm-treasury.gov.uk/media/7/0/banknote_issue_arrangements_210705.pdf, accessed 19 June 2024. For the legal nature of such banknotes, as promissory notes and otherwise, see *Clydesdale Bank v The Commissioners for Her Majesty's Revenue & Customs* [2019] UKFTT 0419 (TC).

payment.[88] By law, these banknotes are required to be fully backed by earmarked sterling obligations of the Bank of England.[89] Similarly, in the scenario envisaged under this option, commercial banks may be authorized to issue digital coins, fully backed by Central Bank money.

Effectively, this is the "Synthetic CDBC," known as "sCBDC," model – discussed in chapter 8(V). Under that model, stablecoins fully backed by central bank money are issued by commercial banks. Strictly speaking, not bearing a direct obligation of the central bank, such coins are not CBDC, and yet may practically be treated as such.[90]

c. **Final Observations**

1. In all scenarios, the Central Bank retains its position as a facilitator or catalyst as well as an overseer (or even regulator) of the digital coin system.[91] Only in the scenarios set out in subparts (i) and (ii), where the Central Bank is involved to one degree or another in distribution and transfer, will it also be an operator or direct provider.

2. Operationally, the scenarios described in (iv) and (v) may be the same. In each case, a commercial bank earmarks funds from its reserve account with its central bank, against which it issues the digital coins. However, in each such scenario, the legal implications of the central bank's liability and legal tender status are substantially different.

3. While in the scenarios discussed in (iv) and (v), commercial banks' funds in their reserve account are earmarked, in the scenarios addressed in (ii) and (iii), a commercial bank uses such funds to pay its central bank for the digital coins to be purchased. The difference appears to be that in the scenarios described in (iv) and (v), funds are debited from the reserve account only upon the redemption of each digital coin, while in the scenarios discussed in (ii) and (iii), funds are debited to the commercial bank's reserve account as soon as the digital coins are purchased.

88 See e.g., Northern Ireland Assembly, "The Status of Scottish and Northern Irish Banknotes" (Research And Library Services Briefing Note 122/08, 2008), online: http://archive.niassembly.gov.uk/io/research/2008/12208.pdf, accessed 19 June 2024.

89 Scottish and Northern Ireland Banknote Regulations 2009, SI 2009/3056 issued by the Treasury under ss 215–220 of the *Banking Act, 2009*.

90 See Anna Maria Bracio and Jonas Gross, "Synthetic central bank digital currency (sCBDC) – Public private CBDC collaboration" (Medium, 15 July 2020), online: https://jonasgross.medium.com /synthetic-central-bank-digital-currency-scbdc-public-private-cbdc-collaboration-46a3f4eb9808, accessed 5 July 2024.

91 For these central bank functions in the payment system, see in general, Ben Fung, Miguel Molico, and Gerald Stuber, "Electronic Money and Payments: Recent Developments and Issue" (2014) Bank of Canada Staff Discussion Paper 2014-2 at 19, online: https://www.bankofcanada.ca/wp-content/uploads/2014/04/dp2014-2.pdf, accessed 19 June 2024.

4. Commercial banks' reserve funds at the Central Bank are not involved in the scenario addressed in (i). In that scenario, a holder "purchases" the digital coin directly from the issuing commercial bank.

5. The scenarios addressed in (iv) and (v) involve the actual issuance of digital coins by commercial banks and thus require effective monitoring and – where needed – enforcement by regulatory authorities, including the Central Bank.

6. Prima facie, the scenario addressed in (iii) – that of the hybrid-intermediated option, under which both distribution and transfers of a digital coin issued by the Central Bank are run by commercial banks – appears to be the most advantageous. This is because it maintains an optimal balance between a visible holder's claim against the central bank and the maximum operational role for commercial banks. At the same time, as discussed in chapter 8(V), to enhance competition in an environment within which stablecoins may be heavily used, and under the proper regulation, the scenario addressed in (v), that of the backed option or sCBDC, may well be superior.

VII. MOVING FORWARD – PROPOSED DRAFT LEGISLATION

This chapter concludes that the Bank of Canada may issue wCBDC – without the need for further statutory authority. See Part VI.

Regarding rCBDC, by way of summary, the Bank of Canada's power to issue CBDC serving as legal tender requires:

1. In the case of a DBI-based CBDC, the interpretation of "note" in the *Bank of Canada Act* to cover a DBI coin. As indicated, I am supportive of this interpretation and yet acknowledge it is imaginative and creative so as possibly not to be universally shared;

2. In the case of an account-based CBDC, bypassing the conferment of "legal tender" by statute only to notes and coins. As indicated, "legal tender" is a desired feature for something to be considered as "money" and yet not indispensable; and

3. The regulation of CBDC maximal amounts to be stored and paid. While I avoid proposing specific limits to CBDC holding and anonymous payments may I mention as an indirect precedent the reporting requirements under the *Proceeds of Crime (Money Laundering) and Terrorist Financing Act (PCMLTFA)*[92] and the regulation passed thereunder.[93] As

92 SC 2000, c 17.

93 Regulations Amending the Proceeds of Crime (Money Laundering) and Terrorist Financing Regulations and the Proceeds of Crime (Money Laundering) and Terrorist Financing Administrative Monetary Penalties Regulations, SOR/2022-76 ("PCMLTFA Regulations").

discussed in chapter 4, reporting is required for receipts of $10,000 or more of cash as well as virtual currency in any twenty-four hour period.

Taking into account these difficulties, this chapter recommends legislation as the better route for implementing rCBDC in Canada. The basis of the following rough draft is a bill titled *Electronic Currency and Secure Hardware (ECASH) Act*,[94] incorporating a part modelled on the EU Proposed CBDC Regulation,[95] and modified to reflect the optimal CBDC as presented in this chapter.

Two preliminary points are in place:

1. The proposed statute is not a final proposed text but rather a basis for discussion;
2. If subject to all the uncertainties set out in this chapter the decision is to pursue a CBDC program based on existing powers of the Bank of Canada, the proposed Act could serve as a basis for a regulation to be issued by the Bank of Canada.

THE DIGITAL CANADIAN DOLLAR ACT

SECTION 1: THE DIGITAL CANADIAN DOLLAR

(a) **ESTABLISHMENT** – *The* BANK OF CANADA *shall promote and facilitate the development and deployment of a digital version of the Canadian Dollar for use by the general public that replicates and preserves the privacy, anonymity-respecting, and minimal transactional data-generating properties of tangible coins and notes to the greatest extent technically and practically possible.*

(b) **DIGITAL CANADIAN DOLLAR REQUIREMENTS**[96] – *Subject to this Act and necessary modifications, the Digital Canadian Dollar described under subsection (a) shall be deemed to be and treated as a note under the Bank of Canada Act Section 2. It shall be:*

(1) *issued by* THE BANK OF CANADA *as a digital note under its authority under* THE BANK OF CANADA ACT *Section 25(1);*

(2) *a distinct entity consisting of data in the form of a unique string of bits that cannot be forged and compromised by strong computers, and that has a distinct unique identity, that cannot be separated from the string of bits that represent the value (like a banknote's serial number and value) so*

---

94 *Electronic Currency and Secure Hardware (ECASH) Act*, HR 7231, 117 Cong (introduced by Mr. Lynch (for himself, Mr. García of Illinois, Ms. Pressley, Ms. Adams, and Ms. Tlaib on 28 March 2022, and was referred to the Committee on Financial Services).

95 EC, "Digital Euro Proposal," above note 19.

96 This provision assumes the adoption of a DBI-based CBDC and will require changes if this will not be the case.

that while there are tokens with same value, there are no two tokens with same identity and value;

(3) *payable to bearer on demand and capable of fully, irrevocably and unconditionally discharging a monetary debt, by the transfer of control from one person to another with no need to connect to any network, in a manner functionally equivalent to the transfer of possession of a tangible coin or note;*

(4) *as provided in Section 2, legal tender.*

(5) *created and issued into circulation by THE BANK OF CANADA, either directly or through one or more entities commanding public trust ("trustful Mint") that will be authorized and regulated by THE BANK OF CANADA, in such quantities, denominations and technical forms as, subject to the monetary policy, THE BANK OF CANADA determines to be appropriate;*

(6) *capable of being distributed directly or through intermediaries such as banks to, and being owned, held, and used directly by members of the general public, stored in users' device, granting users control on their privacy, enabling moving the Digital Canadian Dollar freely with free liquidity 24/7/365.*

(7) *available directly and inclusively to members of the general public, used for instantaneous, final, direct, peer-to-peer cash like transactions even in the absence of a bank account, using a protocol to detect counterfeits and prevent double spending, having all features of physical cash, with no trace of value and identities of payer and payee, securing cash-like payment, that is, a payer and a payee are able to execute a payment such that no one besides said parties can retrieve information regarding the transaction, reconciling with the public interest in countering illegal activities. To better serve users' privacy only a warrant will enable exposing transactions history through chain of custody written on the token and/or via the flow of changed private keys that are connected to the token flow between users.*

(8) *available for off-line payments, so that also in circumstances under which there is neither Internet nor access to electricity, the payer and payee should be able to validate that the locally stored Digital Canadian Dollars are genuine, and execute a transaction within seconds, making the payment irrevocable, unconditional, and final. To that end the issuer will provide to members of the general public a low-cost device ("Wallet"), which is a closed enclosure containing the Digital Canadian Dollar and a payment software. The secure software erases all money paid out to prevent double spending in a system under which one Wallet is paid from another Wallet, thereby creating a trusted off-line payment regi-*

men should the Internet and electricity be compromised, up to a period prescribed by regulations [at least a six-consecutive-months period?] without the need to provide electricity to the Wallet. The payer's Wallet authentication by payee's Wallet and the payment are executed in a simplified and fast process that does not require technical capabilities, apart from indicating the value to be transferred, while achieving payment finality in the offline mode. The Wallet is protected against all possible attacks, and any tampering attempt of the Wallet will fail and erase all the e-cash tokens stored in the Wallet.

(9) *operate in a system that to the possible extent is inter-operable with existing financial institution and payment provider systems, and generally accepted payments standards and network protocols, as well as other public payments programs,*

(10) *classified and regulated in a manner similar to physical currency for the purposes of anti-money laundering, know-your-customer, counter-terrorism, and transaction reporting laws, and thus subject to third-party exemptions to a reasonable expectation of privacy only by warrant that order to unveil the chain of custody of the token; low-value payments, which are usually low risk in terms of money laundering, terrorism financing and violations of relevant laws should be excluded even from this warrant option;*

(11) *designed, issued, and administered to be consistent with –*
   (A) *the statutory objectives articulated in subsection (c), as well as any rules, standards, and criteria enacted to further those objectives;*
   (B) *the consumer protections articulated in subsection (d), as well as any rules standards, and criteria enacted to further those protections; and*
   (C) *any and all other technical and policy criteria established by this Act or by the Secretary or Director under the authority granted to them under this Act;*

(12) *fully convertible and interchangeable among themselves and with tangible coins and notes of the same value,*

(13) *as prescribed by regulations issued by* THE BANK OF CANADA *redeemable on demand with tangible notes and coins and to a balance in an account where such account is available to the holder;*

(14) *operated in a system of which effectiveness meets high standards, regulations and rules, prescribed by the Secretary as to ubiquity, efficiency, safety and security, speed, certainty and predictability of governing legal rules, and effective and inclusive governance; and*

(15) *as prescribed by regulations issued by* THE BANK OF CANADA *available subject to necessary modification for use in interbank payments including for interbank settlement.*

(c) **STATUTORY OBJECTIVES** – THE BANK OF CANADA *shall promulgate and enforce regulations, rules, standards, and criteria pertaining to the development and implementation of Digital Canadian Dollar notes, devices, technologies, platforms, and supporting and enabling infrastructure, as well as the issuance, dissemination, circulation, storage, and use of Digital Canadian Dollar notes including use in transactions, and rights and obligations of participants buying, selling, paying and receiving payments in the Digital Canadian Dollar, in such a manner and to such an extent as* THE BANK OF CANADA *determines to be necessary or appropriate to achieve the objectives of this Act, subject to the following conditions:*

(1) OWNERSHIP – THE BANK OF CANADA *shall own and operate or authorize several technology vendors to own and operate a Mint or several Mints, which are the heart of the Digital Canadian Dollar system. It is where the Digital Canadian Dollar bit-string claim checks are being minted. It includes a high-security database, designed to withstand the most aggressive hackers' attacks.* THE BANK OF CANADA *shall require that any and all Digital Canadian Dollar notes are capable of being owned, held, and used directly by the general public via widely available hardware devices, including mobile phones, tablets, laptops and dedicated Wallets, without the necessary involvement of third-party custodial or payment processing intermediaries.*

(2) PRIVACY – THE BANK OF CANADA *shall require users to identify themselves when they first receive Digital Canadian Dollars and when they redeem it in tangible coins and notes. In between, when paying peer-to-peer, users will be able to control the level of privacy they wish to maintain. Users will be provided with appropriate technology protocols that are not based on hackable primary cryptography, in order that they shall not being subject to any surveillance, personal identification or transactional data-gathering, or censorship-enabling backdoor features.*

(3) UNIVERSALITY – THE BANK OF CANADA *shall prioritize wherever possible technologies, practices, and programs that promote universal access and usability, particularly for –*
(A) individuals with disabilities, including visual impairment;
(B) low-income individuals; and

(C) *communities with limited access to the internet or telecommunications networks.*

(4) INCLUSION – THE BANK OF CANADA *shall take into consideration the unique needs and circumstances of marginalized communities and populations that have historically been excluded from or otherwise prevented from taking full advantage of traditional and current financial institutions and payment services.*

(5) TRANSPARENCY – THE BANK OF CANADA *shall seek out and encourage Digital Canadian Dollar notes distribution via real time market multiple settlement methods, including practically feasible use of hardware and software technologies issued under open-source licenses, and shall further require that all publicly funded research and technology be released under a suitable open-source license and made available for study and review by the scientific community and the general public.*

(d) CONSUMER PROTECTIONS –

(1) FEES – THE BANK OF CANADA *will provide free software-based applications (mobile and web applications) to the public, that will enable storing them on users' mobile or personal computers ("PC"), splitting tokens without network connections, and transferring Digital Canadian Dollar notes in any resolution from one device to another for making payments.* THE BANK OF CANADA *may charge reasonable prices when selling Digital Canadian Dollar notes–compatible hardware for offline use (henceforth "Digital Canadian Dollar devices" or "Wallets") directly to the public, provided such prices are proportionate to, and not unduly in excess of, actual production and administration costs, but may in no instance impose fees or other charges for holding, receiving, sending, or otherwise transacting with e-cash balances using such devices.*

(2) SOLICITED ISSUANCE OF Digital Canadian Dollar HARD-WARE DEVICES –THE BANK OF CANADA *or authorized Wallets distributors may sell Wallets to a member of the public only in response to an oral or written request for such device.*

(3) SOLICITED ISSUANCE OF DIGITAL CANADIAN DOLLAR NOTES – THE BANK OF CANADA *or an authorized Digital Canadian Dollar Mint may issue Digital Canadian Dollar notes to a user only in response to an oral or written request to receive funds in the form of Digital Canadian Dollar.*

(4) FEES BY MERCHANTS – *It shall be unlawful to impose a service fee or an interchange fee, or other processing fee or surcharge, for the use of Digital Canadian Dollar in payments or purchases.*

(5) TRANSACTIONAL REPORTING – *Under no circumstance, regardless of the particular technology involved, shall any transaction data generated by Digital Canadian Dollar payments be collected, monitored, or retained by* THE BANK OF CANADA, *the Government, an authorized e-cash distributor, or any other counterparty except via the exemptions provided by this Act.*

(e) **REQUIREMENT TO ACCEPT** *Digital Canadian Dollar notes –*
  (1) GOVERNMENT – *The Government shall –*
    (A) *accept Digital Canadian Dollar notes, for any payment to the Federal Government, including payments for taxes, fines, and fees; and*
    (B) *upon request, provide any Government benefit in the form of Digital Canadian Dollar.*

(f) **ILLICIT FLOWS** –PRESUMPTION OF LEGITIMATE USE – *Under no condition shall the acquisition, possession, or use of Digital Canadian Dollar devices and notes under the parameters established by this Act be treated as prima facie or intrinsic evidence of criminal activity or intent, nor be established as a predicate offence or factor in crimes not specified in or under the authority established by this Act.*

(g) **SYSTEMIC LIQUIDITY** – THE BANK OF CANADA *shall take appropriate measures to ensure that the implementation and adoption of Digital Canadian Dollar does not disrupt or substantially impact, the general availability or cost of liquidity for banks or their capacity to extend credit and other financial services*

(h) **SUPPLY AND REMOVAL** – THE BANK OF CANADA *shall have the duty to make adequate arrangements for*
  (1) *the issue in Canada, the supply and distribution of Digital Canadian Dollar notes as required for circulation in Canada; and*
  (2) *the removal from circulation in Canada of defective and insecure Digital Canadian Dollar notes and those withdrawn from circulation.*

SECTION 2: LEGAL TENDER

(a) **LEGAL TENDER STATUS**
  (1) *The Digital Canadian Dollar shall have legal tender status.*
  (2) *The legal tender status of the Digital Canadian Dollar shall entail its mandatory acceptance, at full face value, with the power to discharge from a payment obligation.*

(3) *In accordance with the mandatory acceptance of the Digital Canadian Dollar, the payee shall not refuse Digital Canadian Dollar tendered in payment to comply with that obligation.*

(4) *In accordance with the acceptance at full face value of the Digital Canadian Dollar, the monetary value of the Digital Canadian Dollar tendered in payment of a debt shall be equal to the value of the monetary debt. Surcharges on the payment of debt with the Digital Canadian Dollar shall be prohibited.*

(5) *In accordance with the power of the Digital Canadian Dollar to discharge from a payment obligation, a payer shall be able to discharge himself from a payment obligation by tendering Digital Canadian Dollar to the payee.*

(B) TERRITORIAL SCOPE OF LEGAL TENDER STATUS

(1) *The Digital Canadian Dollar shall have legal tender status for offline payments of a monetary debt denominated in Canadian Dollar that take place within Canada.*

(2) *The Digital Canadian Dollar shall have legal tender status for online payments of a monetary debt denominated in Canadian Dollar to a payee residing or established in Canada.*

(C) EXCEPTIONS TO THE OBLIGATION TO ACCEPT THE DIGITAL CANADIAN DOLLAR

By way of derogation from paragraphs (a) (3) and (b), a payee shall be entitled to refuse Digital Canadian Dollar in any of the following cases:

(i) *where the payee is a an enterprise which employs fewer than 10 persons or whose annual turnover or annual balance sheet total does not exceed [XXX], or is a non-profit legal entity, unless it accepts comparable digital means of payments;*

(ii) *where a refusal is made in good faith and where such refusal is based on legitimate and temporary grounds in line with the principle of proportionality in view of concrete circumstances beyond the control of the payee;*

(iii) *where the payee is a natural person acting in the course of a purely personal or household activity;*

> *[Alternative to (iii) where the payee is a natural person who does not make payments over the Internet or at a terminal]*

(iv) *where, prior to the payment, the payee has expressly agreed with the payer on a different means of payment.*

For the purposes of point (ii), the burden of proof to establish that legitimate and temporary grounds existed in a particular case and that the refusal was proportionate shall be on the payee.

(D) PROHIBITION OF THE UNILATERAL EXCLUSION OF PAYMENTS IN THE DIGITAL CANADIAN DOLLAR

Payees subject to the obligation to accept the Digital Canadian Dollar shall not use contractual terms that have not been individually negotiated, or any other procedures, offers or other means that have not been individually negotiated and drafted in advance and that aim at a contractual agreement for the purpose of not accepting the Digital Canadian Dollar by the payers of monetary debts denominated in Canadian Dollar.

(E) ADDITIONAL EXCEPTIONS OF A MANDATORY ACCEPTANCE

THE BANK OF CANADA is empowered to adopt regulations identifying additional exceptions to the principle of mandatory acceptance. Those exceptions shall be justified by an objective of public interest and proportionate to that aim, shall not undermine the effectiveness of the legal tender status of the Digital Canadian Dollar, and shall only be permitted provided that other means for the payment of monetary debts are available.

SECTION 3: DIGITAL CURRENCY INNOVATION PROGRAM

(a) *IN GENERAL THE BANK OF CANADA shall establish the Digital Currency Innovation Program to direct, oversee, coordinate, and harmonize the development, implementation, maintenance, and regulation of Digital Canadian Dollar notes, devices, technologies, platforms, and supporting and enabling infrastructure in accordance with the technical and policy criteria established by this Act.*

(b) PILOT PROGRAMS –
    (1) ESTABLISHMENT –
        (A) *IN GENERAL – Not later than 90 days after the enactment of this Act, THE BANK OF CANADA shall initiate a two-phase Digital Canadian Dollar pilot program in anticipation of general deployment of Digital Canadian Dollar to the public not later than forty-eight months after the date of enactment of this Act, designing and testing pilots (MVP - Minimal Viable Projects), including those based on one of two different archytypes: One – quantum-generated digital CANADIAN DOLLAR coins, and a transaction protocol based on a centrally governed distributed public ledger, that is not based on nodes, peers and validators, and is combined with algorithmic mutation to achieve con-*

trolled privacy and quantum-resistance; and Two – crypto-generated CANADIAN DOLLAR and a permissioned-DLT.

(B) PHASE 1 – *Phase 1 of the pilot program shall consist of not less than three distinct pilots (in this section referred to as "Proof-of-Concept Pilots"), each of which shall launch no later than 180 days after the date of enactment of this Act, and run for no longer than 360 days thereafter.*

(C) PHASE 2 – *Phase 2 of the pilot program shall consist of at least one large-scale deployment to a segment of the public (in this section referred to as "Field Test Pilots"), which shall launch no later than 2 years after the enactment of this Act, and run for no longer than 2 years thereafter.*

(D) EXTENSION OF TIMELINES FOR PILOT PROGRAMS – *The timelines for the implementation of the two phases of the Digital Canadian Dollar pilot program described in this paragraph may be extended upon a determination by the Director that such an extension is necessary to ensure the security and integrity of the technologies to be piloted in the program.*

(E) ADMINISTRATION – *The pilot programs shall be administered by* THE BANK OF CANADA.

(2) OBJECTIVES – *The objectives of the pilot programs are to test the viability and capacity of various forms of Digital Canadian Dollar technologies to –*

   (A) *preserve the privacy, anonymity-respecting, and minimal transactional data-generating properties of tangible coins and notes to the greatest extent technically and practically possible;*

   (B) *enforce total balance and transactional activity limits on a per-device basis without rendering such devices vulnerable to surveillance or censorship by third parties including the Government;*

   (C) *deploy rapidly, securely, and efficiently on a mass scale; and*

   (D) *maintain ease of use and interoperability with existing financial institution and payment provider systems, as well as any other digital dollar products.*

(4) PARAMETERS AND CONSTRAINTS –

   (A) *All technologies selected for Proof-of-Concept Pilots and Field Test Pilots shall be –*

      (i) *designed as bearer instruments;*

      (ii) *capable of instantaneous, final, direct, peer-to-peer, offline transactions; and*

(6) REPORTING – *Not later than 180 days after the date on which each phase of the pilot programs terminates, the Secretary shall submit to Congress a report regarding that phase of the pilot programs, which shall –*

(A) *include –*

(i) *a description of which elements of the pilot programs were successful and which were unsuccessful;*

(ii) *recommendations regarding legislative changes to the pilot programs and related authority under this Act and elsewhere; and*

(iii) *recommendations for additional pilots and revisions to the pilot program; and*

(B) *make the non sensitive analytical data available for public review and comment.*

chapter six

IS THE DIGITAL COIN AN E-BANKNOTE?

SYNOPSIS

A digital coin containing an unconditional promise, made and authenticated by its issuer, engaging to pay to bearer on demand a sum certain in money is an e-bearer note payable on demand. Where it is made and authenticated by a bank and circulates as a medium of exchange it is an e-banknote. This conclusion derives from a liberal interpretation of Canadian statutes governing promissory notes and banknotes. It is supported by an analysis of both monetary law principles, and international and United States law reform projects governing digital assets. Legislation along such lines is recommended for Canada with the view of supporting and reinforcing the conclusion. "Custody" of digital currencies is distinguished from "banking" and yet it is stressed that the distinction does not flow from inherent different features of paper and electronic banknotes.

SUMMARY OF CONTENTS

I. INTRODUCTION

This chapter endeavours to establish that, as in fact argued in chapter 5(III), a digital coin containing an unconditional promise, made and authenticated by a bank, engaging to pay to bearer on demand a sum certain in money, and circulating as a medium of exchange – hereafter referred to in this chapter as "digital coin" – is an e-banknote. The discussion covers digital coins whether they are issued by commercial banks (in which case they are stablecoins) or a central bank (in which case they form a Central Bank Digital Currency (CBDC).

As discussed in chapter 3, in its form a banknote is a promissory note made by a bank, payable to bearer on demand, and intended to circulate as money.[1] This is true even where it is merely denominated in a specific sum of money without an express promise to pay it.[2] As a rule, it neither bears interest[3] nor states a due date, and certainly is never made payable to a particular person or order. It is transferrable from one person to another by delivery; as such the banknote is a negotiable instrument,[4] passing from hand to hand free from claims and defences.

For its part, any instrument payable to bearer on demand that is intended to circulate as money, whether it is issued by a bank or another type of issuer, including the government, is a currency note. Currency note is thus a broader term that includes but is not limited to the banknote, which nevertheless is the primary category of the currency note.

This chapter examines whether a digital coin which is either a CBDC or stablecoin could be a bank or currency note, as the case may be, whether under present Canadian law, or under (or with the assistance of) a law

---

1   Jonathan M Phillips, Richard Hanke, and Ian Higgins (eds), *Byles on Bills of Exchange*, 30th ed (Sweet & Maxwell, 2020) at 394.

2   *Banco de Portugal v Waterlow and Sons, Ltd* [1932] AC 452 (HL) 487.

3   As such its holder "makes haste to part with it" so that it circulates better than the interest bearing bill of exchange payable in a specific future date, see Henry Thornton, *An Enquiry into the Nature and Effects of the Paper Credit of Great Britain* (1802) (Friedrich Hayek ed) (AM Kelley, 1962) at 93.

4   See e.g., David AL Smout, *Chalmers on Bills of Exchange*, 13th ed (Stevens & Sons, 1964) at 274; Arthur W Rogers, *Falconbridge on Banking and Bills of Exchange*, 7th ed (Canada Law Book, 1969) at 127; Charles Proctor, *Mann and Proctor on the Law of Money*, 8th ed (Oxford University Press, 2022) at 24–25; subsequent editions of *Chalmers* and *Falconbridge*, which are in fact successors rather than new editions of the above works, do not have parallel discussions; a leading case is *Banco de Portugal*, above note 2 at 483, 487 (and as to the promise, see also 478, 480).

reform project inspired by developments elsewhere. The question is whether a digital coin, which contains information complying with the statutory requirements for a promissory note payable to bearer, is a "promissory note" payable to bearer – as well as whether being issued by a bank – with the intention that it will circulate as money – it is a "banknote," or more specifically, an e-banknote. The discussion will focus on the banknote, issued by a bank (whether commercial or central), being the most common type of a currency note, and yet, with obvious necessary modifications, it applies to any type of a currency note, regardless of its issuer.

Part II examines whether existing Canadian law accommodates an electronic or digital promissory note. **Part III** addresses the legal nature of the digital coin as a transferrable or controllable electronic record. **Part IV** discusses whether a digital coin fulfils the function of a banknote. **Part V** endeavours to reinterpret existing law by reference to the way monetary law has been interpreted elsewhere in accepting the legitimacy of tangible banknotes issued without a specific statutory backing. **Part VI** analyzes control over a digital coin and payment by its transfer. **Part VII** addresses business models relating to custody of digital coins. **Part VIII** discusses legal aspects of custody. Both Parts **VI** and **VII** point at the fundamental difference between the safekeeping of money by banks and that of digital coins by custodians. These differences emerge from different practices that require a different legal analysis. Differences are not the result of any conceptual difference between paper banknotes and e-banknotes.

Concluding **Part IX** calls for a legislative reform in Canada. The discussion points at various options and addresses the constitutional issue of legislative competence. The chapter concludes with an **Appendix** containing a proposed Electronic Promissory Note statute that may be either a standalone Act or a new chapter in the *Bills of Exchange Act*.

In the absence of direct legislation in Canada as well as most countries, the discussion in Parts III, VI, VII, and VIII focuses on the framework emerging from the *Electronic Trade Documents Act 2023*[5] in the United Kingdom (ETDA), uniform state legislation and one federal statute in the United States as well as the *UNIDROIT Principles on Digital Assets and Private Law*, 2023[6] (*UNIDROIT Principles*) and *UNCITRAL Model Law on Electronic Transferable*

---

5 2023, c 38.

6 UNIDROIT International Institute for the Unification of Private Law, UNIDROIT *Principles on Digital Assets And Private Law* (UNIDROIT 2023), online: https://www.unidroit.org/wp-content/uploads/2024/01/Principles-on-Digital-Assets-and-Private-Law-linked.pdf, accessed 25 June 2024.

Records (2017)[7] (*MLETR*). The American uniform state laws are *Uniform Commercial Code Article 12 – Controllable Electronic Records, 2022*[8] (UCC Article 12); the *Uniform Electronic Transactions Act, 1999*[9] (UETA), *Uniform Regulation of the Virtual-Currency Businesses Act, 2017*[10] (URVCBA), and *Uniform Supplemental Commercial Law for the Uniform Regulation of Virtual Currency Business Act, 2018*[11] (SCLURVCBA). A United States federal statute to be addressed is *Electronic Signatures in Global and National Commerce Act*[12] (ESGNCA).

II. PRESENT LAW IN CANADA

Under section 176(1) of the *Bills of Exchange Act (BEA)*,[13]

A promissory note is an unconditional promise in writing made by one person to another person, signed by the maker, engaging to pay, on demand or

---

7   United Nations, *UNCITRAL Model Law on Electronic Transferable Records* (United Nations Publication 2017), online: uncitral.un.org/sites/uncitral.un.org/files/media-documents/uncitral/en/mletr_ebook_e.pdf, accessed 25 June 2024.

8   The Uniform Law Commission then approved and recommended it for enactment in all the States at its 131st annual meeting in Philadelphia on 8–13 July 2022. It was enacted in nineteen jurisdictions and introduced in ten. See Uniform Law Commission, "2022 Amendments to UCC" (2022), online: https://www.uniformlaws.org/committees/community-home?communitykey=1457c422-ddb7-40b0-8c76-39a1991651ac, accessed 25 June 2024. Wide adoption is anticipated. The author was an observer in the drafting process and yet all views and errors are his.

9   National Conference of Commissioners on Uniform State Laws, "Uniform Electronic Transactions Act" (NCCUSL 1999).

10 URVCBA was drafted by the National Conference of Commissioners on Uniform State Law (NCCUSL) and approved and recommended by it for enactment in all the states in the United States at its Annual Conference Meeting in its 126th year in San Diego, California on 14–20 July 2017. It was enacted in three states and introduced in one. See Uniform Law Commission, "Regulation of Virtual Currency Businesses Act" (NCCUSL 2017, online: https://www.uniformlaws.org/committees/community-home?CommunityKey=e104aaa8-c10f-45a7-a34a-0423c2106778, accessed 25 June 2024. Commercial law rules for transactions covered by URVCBA are provided by the *Uniform Supplemental Commercial Law for the Uniform Regulation of Virtual Currency Business Act*.

11 Drafted by the National Conference of Commissioners on Uniform State Laws and by it approved and recommended for enactment in all the states in its Annual Conference Meeting in its 127th year, in Louisville, Kentucky, 20–26 July 2018. So far it has only been adopted in Rhode Island and is being considered in Nevada: see Uniform Law Commission, "Supplemental Commercial Law for the Uniform Regulation of Virtual-Currency Businesses Act" (NCCUSL 2018), online: https://www.uniformlaws.org/committees/community-home?CommunityKey=fc398fb5-2885-4efb-a3bb-508650106f95, accessed 25 June 2024.

12 15 USC section 7021(a)(1) [as amended].

13 RSC 1985 c B-4.

at a fixed or determinable future time, a sum certain in money to, or to the order of, a specified person or to bearer

Not only must the "promissory note" be "in writing;" *BEA* section 4 indicates that the signature it bears ought to be either by the "own hand" of the person to be liable on the instrument or "written" under that person's authority. In turn, under section 35(1) of the *Interpretation Act*,[14] in every enactment:

> *writing*, or any term of like import, includes words printed, typewritten, painted, engraved, lithographed, photographed or represented or reproduced by any mode of representing or reproducing words in visible form.

For their part, notes intended for circulation in Canada issued by the Bank of Canada are not "promissory notes" within the meaning of the *BEA*.[15] While this exempts these banknotes from complying with the formal requirements fastened on a "promissory note," they are nevertheless to be "printed and signed or otherwise executed."[16] No "signature" requirements are set out. For its part, "execution" is usually taken to mean "signed and delivered."

Thus, under *BEA* section 176(1), a promissory note must be "in writing" and "signed." For its part, under section 35(1) of the *Interpretation Act*, "writing" includes words "printed, typewritten, painted, engraved, lithographed, photographed or represented or reproduced by any mode of representing or reproducing words in visible form." It does not take much stretching (if at all) to interpret "words" in section 35(1) of the *Interpretation Act* to include "figures." Furthermore, "reproducing words in visible form" under the same provision can arguably be stretched to cover visibility on a computer screen. At the same time, at least as a starting point, the written signature requirement for a promissory note under *BEA* section 4 may still stand in the way of envisioning a digital promissory note.

In turn, a Bank of Canada note ought to be "printed and signed or otherwise executed." There is no statutory definition to "printing" and it is not required that the banknote necessarily be signed manually. Regardless, other than under a strict statutory interpretation, and ignoring the "material" the minister needs to approve for the notes under section 25(4) of the *Bank of Canada Act*, it is possible to envisage an electronic execution, and hence, an

---

14   RSC 1985, c I-21.

15   *Bank of Canada Act*, RSC 1985, c B-2, s 25(6) (in conjunction with s 2).

16   *Ibid*, s 25(3). See also s 25(4).

electronic Bank of Canada note. A creative interpretation may thus accommodate an electronic Bank of Canada note under the *Bank of Canada Act*.

No assistance in confirming these conclusions can be drawn from general legislation addressing digitalization. Thus, in principle, under section 41 of the *Personal Information Protection and Electronic Documents Act (PIPEDA)*,[17] a requirement under a provision of a federal law for a document to be in writing is satisfied by an electronic document. Similarly, in principle, under *PIPEDA* section 43, a requirement under a provision of a federal law for a signature is satisfied by an electronic signature. For its part, "electronic signature" is defined in *PIPEDA* section 31(1) to mean,

> a signature that consists of one or more letters, characters, numbers or other symbols in digital form incorporated in, attached to or associated with an electronic document.

However, both *PIPEDA* sections 41(a) and 43(a) are stated to apply, inter alia, only where "the federal law or the provision is listed in Schedule 2 or 3." Neither the *BEA* nor *Bank of Canada Act* is listed in these Schedules.

In any event, neither the legislative framework of the *BEA*, nor the concept of the banknote as discussed in chapter 3 may be satisfied by the mere existence of an electronic note, including by listing both statutes in *PIPEDA* Schedules 2 or 3. This is so because the laws governing promissory notes and banknotes build around concepts of possession and delivery of the note, thereby assuming it to be a tangible item of property.

Nonetheless, in the spirit of the discussion in chapter 5(III), it can be noted that the tangibility feature derives from the "writing" requirement as envisioned prior to the electronic age. At that time, there was no way of "writing" on an intangible media; writing in the air was (and is) meaningless. However, with new technologies, it has become possible to write on something intangible. We write an email much the same as we write a postcard or a letter. What paper or any other tangible medium gives to writing is permanence – which technologically can now be accorded via an intangible record in the cyberspace. Accordingly, I argue, notwithstanding the fact that it is a uniquely generated item of information and as such, an intangible, the digital coin may nevertheless be seen as "written."

Similarly, in principle, a "signature" may be written, lithographed, facsimiled, or stamped on a document (or anything else tangible) with the intent of authenticating liability on a contract.[18] The key is, however, a permanent record for

---

17   SC 2000, c 5.
18   See e.g., Rogers, above note 4 at 440–41, 443, 444.

the authentication of liability. Accordingly, the electronic authentication of an electronic record that substitutes writing will satisfy the signature requirement.

Observations to such ends were already made in the common law.[19] In one case, the court did not doubt that "if a party creates and sends an electronically created document then he will be treated as having signed it to the same extent that he would in law be treated as having signed a hard copy of the same document."[20] In another case, the court considered an email as written.[21]

Accordingly, as long as the signing issuer is unconditionally liable to pay to the bearer on demand a sum certain in the stated fiat money, a claim-check digital coin (a stablecoin), being a claim to a specified "quantity" denominated in the official unit of account, appears to fall into the definition of a "promissory note" in an electronic form under the *BEA* so as to be an e-note. When it is intended for circulation and is issued either by a commercial bank or under the *Bank of Canada Act* it appears to be a "note" (or in effect a currency note or banknote) in an electronic form so as to be an e-banknote. For our purposes, we speak of an e-note governed by the *BEA* and an e-banknote issued under the *Bank of Canada Act* – and as such not governed by the *BEA*.

Nonetheless, for this conclusion to work it ought to be anchored in a framework addressing the legal nature of the digital asset, both in general and as monetary instrument. The ensuing parts of this chapter will thus discuss this legal framework from several perspectives. First, Part III analyzes the treatment of the digital coin in contemporary international and United States law reform projects. The discussion is designed to point at the emergence of universal norms that could serve as a basis of law reform in Canada. Next, Part IV discusses whether as an e-banknote the digital coin fulfils in payment the function of a banknote. Thereafter, Part V draws a lesson from the legal history of the banknote whose acceptance as money preceded the legal recognition of this function. Finally on this point, Part VI examines the electronic functional equivalence for "possession" and "delivery" which are essential as a legal basis for the use of digital coin in payment.

III. THE DIGITAL COIN AS A TRANSFERABLE OR CONTROLLABLE ELECTRONIC RECORD: LEGAL ASPECTS

As discussed in chapter 1, a digital coin consists of encrypted data expressed in strings of bits. As "an entity that amounts to a string of bits," a coin has

19   Simon Gleeson, *The Legal Concept of Money* (Oxford University Press, 2018) at 176 para 9.47.
20   *Pereira Fernandes v Mehta* [2006] 1 All ER (Comm) 885 [28].
21   *Golden Ocean Group v Salgocar Mining Industries* [2012] EWCA Civ 265.

a numerical value as well as a unique identity.[22] This part will address definitions from legislative projects addressing transactions in digital coins, frequently referred to as "assets." Such transactions include payments.

Whether under general law a digital coin can be treated as an object of property or asset will first be addressed. For its part, the common law recognizes proprietary features of an intangible right even where it is not a chose in action, as long as the right is "definable, identifiable by third parties[,] capable in its nature of assumption by third parties and [has] some degree of permanence or stability."[23] Accordingly, it was held that cryptocurrencies are to be treated as property.[24] A bill confirming this conclusion, as further addressed by the UK Law Commission,[25] is now before Parliament.[26]

22   Gideon Samid, *Tethered Money: Managing Digital Currency Transactions* (Elsevier, 2015) at 105–06; for a legal perspective on the unique identity of a digital coin see David Fox, "Cryptocurrencies in the Common Law of Property" in David Fox and Sarah Green (eds), *Cryptocurrencies in Public and Private Law* (Oxford University Press, 2019) at 142–45 paras 6.11–19, 147 para 6.25.

23   *National Provincial Bank v Ainsworth* [1965] AC 1175 (HL) [1247]–[1248], [1965] 2 All ER 472 (HL) [494] (Lord Wilberforce).

24   First in *B2C2 Limited v Quoine PTE Ltd* [2019] SGHC(I) 03 [142]; followed in *AA v Persons* [2019] EWHC 3556 (Comm) [61]. In reaching its conclusion, *AA v Persons* also treated the UK Jurisdiction Taskforce [UKJT], "Legal Statement on Cryptoassets and Smart Contracts" (LawTech Delivery Panel, 2019) as persuasive and yet not being an authoritative statement of the law, see *AA v Persons* [27]. For a full discussion see *AA v Persons* at [35]–[85] (and, to a lesser extent, also [86]–[99]); for mostly earlier scholarly discussion see David Fox, "Cryptocurrencies in the Common Law of Property" in Fox and Green, above note 22 at 139, 152–54 paras 6.38–6.41; see also Christopher Hare, "Cryptocurrencies and Banking Law: Are There Lessons to Learn?" in Fox and Green, above note 22 at 229, 237 footnote 53; see also Gleeson, above note 19) at 166 para 9.10. Another discussion is by George Walker, "Financial Technology Law – A New Beginning and a New Future" (2017) 50 *The International Lawyer* 137. For another perspective, see Sarah Jane Hughes, "Property, Agency, and the Blockchain: New Technology and Longstanding Legal Paradigms" (2019) 65 *Wayne Law Review* 57. In Canada *Re Quadriga Fintech Solutions Corp et al* (24 March 2020) Toronto, ONSC CV-19-627184-00CL (31-2560674), CV-19-627185-00CL (31-2560984), and CV-19-627186-00CL (31-2560986), stands for the proposition that cryptocurrency owned by a bankrupt debtor is "property" forming part of the estate divisible among the bankrupt's creditors.

25   (UK) Law Commission, *Digital assets: Final Report*, Law Com No 412 (27 June 2023), online: https://webarchive.nationalarchives.gov.uk/ukgwa/20250109172211mp_/https:/s3-eu-west-2.amazonaws.com/cloud-platform-e218f50a4812967ba1215eaecede923f/uploads/sites/30/2023/06/Final-digital-assets-report-FOR-WEBSITE-2.pdf, archived website, visited 4 June 2025; (UK) Law Commission, *Digital Assets as Personal Property: Supplemental report and Draft Bill* (Law Commission, 2023) online: https://webarchive.nationalarchives.gov.uk/ukgwa/20250109095350mp_/https:/cloud-platform-e218f50a4812967ba1215eaecede923f.s3.amazonaws.com/uploads/sites/30/2024/07/Digital-assets-as-personal-property-supplemental-report-and-draft-Bill-web-version.pdf, archived website, visited 4 June 2025. Note that contrary to the Law Commission I don't see a third category which is neither a thing in possession nor a thing in action. Rather, I see assets falling into two broad categories, *viz*, tangibles (things in possession) and intangibles, with the latter category consisting primarily (but not only) of things in actions and digital assets forming two sub-categories.

26   *Property (Digital Assets etc) Bill [HL]* HL Bill 67, February 2025, a bill to make provision about the types of things that are capable of being objects of personal property rights, passes. Under its s 1:

Civilians may have been more dogmatic.[27] In turn, drawing on Gaius' distinction between *res corporales* and *res incorporales*, Nicholas maintains the existence of "abstract things, such as a debt or *a right of way*" that cannot be possessed and yet can be owned.[28] He concludes that the "the law of things includes all those rights which are capable of being evaluated in money terms."[29] From this perspective, treating the digital coin or asset as an object of property is in line with general principles of law.

A universally agreed definition for a digital asset or coin as an item of property is still work in progress. In its Final *Digital Assets* Report, the UK Law Commission cited its original proposed definition that a thing should be recognized as a "digital asset" to which personal property rights can relate if:

(1) it is composed of data represented in an electronic medium, including in the form of computer code, electronic, digital or analogue signals;
(2) it exists independently of persons and exists independently of the legal system; and
(3) it is rivalrous.

With the latter feature meaning that "the use or consumption of the thing by one person, or a specific group of persons, necessarily prejudices the use or consumption of that thing by one or more other persons."[30]

For his part, Fox observed that to see a digital asset "as mere data would ignore its larger functionality, just as we would fail to appreciate the full economic or legal significance of a coin by treating it as a mere metal disc." Rather he went on to describe a digital asset as "an ideational construct," of which:

A full understanding ... requires us to see it as a set of transactional functionalities which the law can recognise through its own specialist categories of analysis, such as ownership, title and transfer. The most important of

---

A thing (including a thing that is digital or electronic in nature) is not prevented from being the object of personal property rights merely because it is neither –
(a) a thing in possession, nor
(b) a thing in action.

27   See in detail e.g., Daniel Carr, "Cryptocurrencies as Property in Civilian and Mixed Legal Systems" in Fox and Green, above note 22 at 177.

28   Barry Nicholas, *An Introduction to Roman Law* (Clarendon Press, 1962) at 106 (emphasis added). Indeed, "incorporeal things" are recognized by the Institutes: *The Institutes* (Book II Title II) translation reproduced in RW Lee, *The Elements of Roman Law*, 4th ed (Sweet & Maxwell, 1956) at 114 and discussion at 110.

29   Nicholas *ibid* at 98.

30   (UK) Law Commission, *Digital assets: Final Report* (n25) para 4.5 p 56 note 217.

these functionalities is the capacity of the person who holds the private key to effect new transactions on the ledger, each of which is specifically attributed to unique data in the system. The practical movement of a specific transactional power over unique data entries can be understood as the transfer of the asset from one holder to another. The programming features which protect the holder's exclusive control over transactions with the data protect the value of the asset and any rights, such as securities, which may be associated with it.[31]

Before discussing legislative pieces governing digital assets at the outset, I will address statutes covering digital equivalents of paper documents. First, I examine the *MLETR*[32] as a legislative framework for treating the digital coin as a functional equivalent for a paper banknote.

The *MLETR* governs the circumstances under which an "Electronic transferable record" satisfied the statutory requirements for "a transferable document or instrument." Under *MLETR* Article 2, "Transferable document or instrument" is defined to mean:

[A] document or instrument issued on paper that entitles the holder to claim the performance of the obligation indicated in the document or instrument and to transfer the right to performance of the obligation indicated in the document or instrument through the transfer of that document or instrument.

For its part, "Electronic record" is defined in MLETR Article 2 to mean:

[I]nformation generated, communicated, received or stored by electronic means, including, where appropriate, all information logically associated with or otherwise linked together so as to become part of the record, whether generated contemporaneously or not.

And "Electronic transferable record" (being the functional equivalent of "transferable documents or instruments") is defined under the *MLETR* to mean "an electronic record that complies with the requirements of Article 10." Under the latter:

---

31   D Fox, "Digital Assets as Transactional Power" (2022) 1 *Journal of International Banking and Financial Law* 3.

32   *UNCITRAL MLETR*, above note 7.

1. Where the law requires a transferable document or instrument, that requirement is met by an electronic record if:

    (a) The electronic record contains the information that would be required to be contained in a transferable document or instrument; and

    (b) A reliable method is used:

        (i)   To identify that electronic record as the electronic transferable record;

        (ii) To render that electronic record capable of being subject to control from its creation until it ceases to have any effect or validity; and

        (iii) To retain the integrity of that electronic record.

2. The criterion for assessing integrity shall be whether information contained in the electronic transferable record, including any authorized change that arises from its creation until it ceases to have any effect or validity, has remained complete and unaltered apart from any change which arises in the normal course of communication, storage and display.

Electronic functional equivalent is further provided in MLETR Article 8 under which

> Where the law requires that information should be in writing, that requirement is met with respect to an electronic transferable record if the information contained therein is accessible so as to be usable for subsequent reference.

As well as under *MLETR* Article 9:

> Where the law requires or permits a signature of a person, that requirement is met by an electronic transferable record if a reliable method is used to identify that person and to indicate that person's intention in respect of the information contained in the electronic transferable record.

In this framework, a digital coin complying with the requirements of *MLETR* Article 10 is the functional equivalent of a paper bearer note.

A second statute to a similar effect is the *ETDA*[33] in the United Kingdom. Under circumstances set out in section 2(1), it treats the "electronic trade document" as the functional equivalent of a "paper trade document," the latter being under section 1(1), a document which

---

33   Above note 5.

(a) ... is in paper form,

(b) ... is a document of a type commonly used in at least one part of the United Kingdom in connection with –

(i)   trade in or transport of goods, or

(ii) financing such trade or transport, and

(c) [its] possession ... is required as a matter of law or commercial custom, usage or practice for a person to claim performance of an obligation.

ETDA section 1(2)(a) and (b) points at a a bill or exchange and a promissory note as "examples of documents that are commonly used as mentioned in subsection (1)(b)."

Under *ETDA* Section 2(1), an "electronic trade document" exists "where information in electronic form ... that if contained in a document in paper form, would lead to the document being a paper trade document." Under *ETDA* section 2(2), this information, together with any other information with which it is logically associated that is also in electronic form, constitutes an "electronic trade document" ... [only] if a reliable system is used to –

(a) identify the document so that it can be distinguished from any copies,

(b) protect the document against unauthorised alteration,

(c) secure that it is not possible for more than one person to exercise control of the document at any one time,

(d) allow any person who is able to exercise control of the document to demonstrate that the person is able to do so, and

(e) secure that a transfer of the document has effect to deprive any person who was able to exercise control of the document immediately before the transfer of the ability to do so (unless the person is able to exercise control by virtue of being a transferee).

The key is thus the reliability of the system. Under *ETDA* section 2(5), the following matters are included in those that may be taken into account in determining whether a system is reliable:

(a) any rules of the system that apply to its operation;

(b) any measures taken to secure the integrity of information held on the system;

(c) any measures taken to prevent unauthorised access to and use of the system;

(d) the security of the hardware and software used by the system;

(e) the regularity of and extent of any audit of the system by an independent body;

(f) any assessment of the reliability of the system made by a body with supervisory or regulatory functions;

(g) the provisions of any voluntary scheme or industry standard that apply in relation to the system.

Under *ETDA* section 3,

...

(2) An electronic trade document has the same effect as an equivalent paper trade document.

(3) Anything done in relation to an electronic trade document has the same effect (if any) in relation to the document as it would have in relation to an equivalent paper trade document.

Effectively then, the *ETDA* introduces an electronic bill of exchange and promissory note.[34]

While both the *MLETR* and the *ETDA* govern a digital asset standing for something already established by law in a paper form, UCC Article 12, *UNCITRAL Principles* as well as *URVCBA* govern digital assets standing on their own without purporting to meet the statutory requirements for a paper instrument or document.

UCC Article 12 deals with controllable electronic records (CERs), "often ... referred to as digital assets."[35] It is a major part of an effort to adapt the UCC to emerging technologies as they might affect electronic commerce. It was introduced in 2022. It was drafted, in partnership with the American Law Institute, by the Uniform Law Commission, and approved and recommended by it for enactment in all the states at its meeting in its 131st year in Philadelphia on 8–13 July 2022.[36]

According to the Preface, Article 12 is designed to provide legal rules governing the transfer – both outright and for security – of interests in CERs. More in general, the Preface states:

---

34 ITFA: International Trade and Forfaiting Association, 2023 *Addendum to the ITFA DIGITAL NEGOTIABLE INSTRUMENTS INITIATIVE Handbook*, online: https://itfa.org/wp-content /uploads/2023/11/The-ITFA-DNI-Addendum-final_v3.pdf, accessed 21 January 2025.

35 Prefatory note to UCC Article 12, above note 8.

36 By 14 October 2023, it was enacted by eleven jurisdictions and introduced in seventeen. For a full list see Uniform Law Commission, "2022 Amendments to UCC," *ibid*. Wide adoption is anticipated. The author was an observer in the drafting process and yet all views and errors are his.

Article 12 creates a legal regime that is meant to apply more broadly than to electronic (intangible) assets that are created using existing technologies such as distributed ledger technology (DLT), including blockchain technology, which records transactions in bitcoin and other digital assets. It also aspires to apply to electronic assets that may be created using technologies that have yet to be developed, or even imagined.

Under UCC section 12-102(a)(1), "controllable electronic record" (CER) means a record stored in an electronic medium that can be subjected to control under Section 12-105. ... " Electronic is defined in UCC section 1-201(b)(16A) to mean "relating to technology having electrical, digital, magnetic, wireless, optical, electromagnetic, or similar capabilities." For its part, "record" is defined in UCC section 1-201(b)(31) to mean "information that is inscribed on a tangible medium or that is stored in an electronic or other medium and is retrievable in perceivable form." Article 12 is technology neutral; as such it is meant to cover presently known technology and also technologies which might be invented in the future.

Exceptions to the scope of UCC Article 12 are stated in section 12-102(a)(1). One relevant exception is "electronic money," defined in UCC section 9-102(a)(31A) to mean "money in an electronic form"; for its part, "money" is defined in UCC section 1-204(a)(24) to mean "a medium of exchange currently authorized or adopted by a domestic or foreign government. ... " This excludes CBDC.

A second relevant exception is that of a "transferable record" as defined in *UETA* § 16(a) or ESGNCA section 7021(a)(1).[37] Under each of these provisions, "transferable record" is defined to mean an electronic record[38] that "would be a note under [UCC Article 3] ... if the electronic record were in writing."[39] Such an electronic record is referred to below as an "electronic note."

---

37 See above notes 9 and 12.

38 "Electronic record" is defined in *UETA*, above note 9, § 2(7) to mean "a record created, generated, sent, communicated, received, or stored by electronic means." For its part, "record" is defined in *UETA* § 2(13) to mean "information that is inscribed on a tangible medium or that is stored in an electronic or other medium and is retrievable in perceivable form." Finally, "electronic" is defined in *UETA* § 2(5) to mean "relating to technology having electrical, digital, magnetic, wireless, optical, electromagnetic, or similar capabilities."

39 Under UCC s 1-201(b)(43), "writing" requires the reduction to tangible form. Information inscribed on a tangible medium (i.e., written information) is distinguished from information stored in an electronic medium which is retrievable in a perceivable form in UCC s 1-201(b)(31). Hence, under the UCC, an electronic record is not written.

UCC Article 3 governs negotiable instruments, one of which is the promissory note ("note"). Under UCC section 3-104, the note is a negotiable instrument in the form of an unconditional written and signed[40] promise[41] to pay to bearer or to order a fixed amount of money payable on demand or at a definite time. A note that does not state a payee is payable to bearer.[42] In passing, UCC Article 3 corresponds to the *Bills of Exchange Act*.[43] Under its section 176(1):

> A promissory note is an unconditional promise in writing made by one person to another person, signed by the maker, engaging to pay, on demand or at a fixed or determinable future time, a sum certain in money to, or to the order of, a specified person or to bearer.

To be a "note" under *UETA* or *ESGNCA*, a "transferable record" must contain this information in an electronic record as well as be electronically signed.[44] Each statute contains its own qualification to the basic definition of a "transferable record" as an electronic note. Under ESGNCA section 7021(a)(1)(C), only an electronic note relating "to a loan secured by real property" is a "transferable record." For its part, *UETA* section 16 (a)(2) provides that an electronic note is covered by *UETA* only where "the issuer of the electronic record expressly has agreed [that it] is a transferable record."[45] Arguably, where the respective qualification does not exist, the electronic note remains covered under UCC Article 12.

Under *UNIDROIT*[46] *Principle* 2(2), "'Digital asset' means an electronic record which is capable of being subject to control." For its part, under *UNIDROIT Principle* 2(1), "'Electronic record' means information which is (i) stored in an electronic medium and (ii) capable of being retrieved."

Under *URVCBA* section 102(23) "Virtual currency":

---

40   Under UCC s 1-201(b)(37) "signed" includes using any symbol executed or adopted with present intention to adopt or accept a writing.

41   UCC s 3-103(12). For its part, the promise to pay may be implicit. *Cf Banco de Portugal v Waterlow and Sons, Ltd* [1932] AC 452 (HL) 483, 487, a non-UCC case addressing the issuer's implicit promise to pay the sum appearing on a banknote.

42   UCC s 3-109(a).

43   *Bills of Exchange Act*, above note 13.

44   Under *UETA* s 2(8) as well *ESGNCA*, above note 12, § 7006(5) (made applicable under § 7021(2)) "electronic signature" is defined to mean "an electronic sound, symbol, or process, attached to or logically associated with a contract or other record and executed or adopted by a person with the intent to sign the record."

45   Query why the mere issuance of the "transferable record" should not suffice to signal the issuer's agreement.

46   *UNIDROIT Principles*, above note 6.

(A) means a digital representation of value that:

  (i) is used as a medium of exchange, unit of account, or store of value; and

  (ii) is not legal tender, whether or not denominated in legal tender.

The definition goes on to exclude certain merchants' affinity or rewards programs and the equivalent sorts of value in online games and online game platforms. This exclusion applies only "if the same game or platform publisher is involved to the extent that the accounting units cannot be converted into cash, bank credit, or other virtual currencies."[47]

In excluding legal tender,[48] the definition purports to exclude any official currency; as such it excludes CBDC. The definition envisages monetary use for a "virtual currency," albeit quite awkwardly. Thus, there is a consensus that a medium of exchange, unit of account, and store of value, constitute monetary features as (A)(i) appears to acknowledge. However, the consensus is that for an item to be "money" it must have *all* of these three features, even if not to a perfect degree.[49] At the same time, under (A)(i), for "a digital representation of value" to be "virtual currency," suffice it to be used "as a medium of exchange, unit of account, *or* store of value" (emphasis added); that is, suffice it to meet only one requirement, such as "unit of account."

Most problematic, however, is the lack of any definition of "digital." On its own "digital representation of value" may be quite broad, so as to include the representation of value in a bank account on the screen of a digital device. Endeavouring to explain the purpose of the Act, the Prefatory Note adds to the confusion. Thus, the drafters state, "Virtual currencies are a subset of cryptocurrencies." However, they make no attempt to define cryptocurrencies as well as to explain how virtual currencies are a subset of cryptocurrencies. The inescapable conclusion is that under *URVCBA* "virtual currency" is to be taken to mean digital coin or currency privately issued. It may or may not be cryptocurrency.

By way of partial summary, Central Bank Digital Currency (CBDC) is governed by *UNIDROIT Principles*.[50] It is not excluded from the *MLETR*. As already pointed out, CBDC is excluded from the scope of both UCC Article

---

47   *URVCBA*, above note 10, s 102(23)(B) and Comment. Quote is from Comment.

48   Defined in *URVCBA*, s 102(8) to mean:
    [A] medium of exchange or unit of value, including the coin or paper money of the United States, issued by the United States or by another government.

49   Nigel Dodd, *The Sociology of Money: Economic, Reason & Contemporary Society* (Continuum, 1994) at xv.

50   *UNIDROIT Principles* at 16 para 2.11.

12 and *URVCBA*. Since paper banknotes are excluded from legislation governing promissory notes,[51] CBDC is excluded from both *UETA* and *ESGNCA*. Nonetheless, so far as the inherent features of the asset is concerned, "CER" under UCC Article 12, "digital asset" under *UNIDROIT Principles*, e-note under *UETA* and *ESGNCA*, and "virtual currency" under *URVCBA* are all interchangeable. Covering digital currencies and their underlying principles ought to be taken to cover stablecoins as well as CBDCs.

IV. DOES THE DIGITAL COIN FULFIL THE FUNCTION OF A BANKNOTE?

The functionality of the digital coin to serve as a banknote is addressed here from two perspectives. First, the embodiment in a medium of which transferability (or its functional equivalence) discharges a monetary debt. Second, the attribution of functions inherent in the use of the paper banknote, such as privacy, availability, and accessibility.

a. The Embodiment in a "Transferable Medium"

The obligation on a banknote (sterile as it is nowadays when it is issued by a central bank) is embodied in the chattel, so as to inure to the benefit of the holder of the chattel.

Indeed, the transfer of possession is a requirement to the transfer of title to – and hence payment in – money.[52] Accordingly, for the digital coin to function as a written banknote, it must not only be "signed" and "written," but also embodied in an object of property, capable of being moved from the exclusive control of one person to that of another.

The feature of a digital coin as an object of property was established in Part III. The fulfilment of the second characteristic, that of transferability from hand to hand, requires, first, an exploration of the mechanics of payment in digital currency. Second, it requires an assessment of the legal treatment of the mechanism. Focusing on the functionality of the banknote, this sub-part will consider only the first feature. The discussion of the second feature is deferred to Part VI, addressing the legal aspects of control and its transfer.

---

51 UCC s 3-102 states that Article 3 "does not apply to money." For the position in Canada see chapter 3.

52 David Fox, *Property Rights in Money* (Oxford University Press, 2008) at paras 3.32–3.42.

For its part, the mechanics of payment in a digital coin depends on the specific design of the coin and its underlying scheme. A common denominator for all mechanisms is the use of a telecommunication network and the availability of a validating intermediary, designed to prevent double payment. To both such ends, several scenarios are available:

1. Being in control of a digital coin "affixed" to a single internet domain, for which it attorns to the payer, a "bailee"[53] complies with the payer's instructions and executes them by attorning to the payee, thereby causing "possession" – or in fact control – in the coin to be transferred from the payer to the payee. Alternatively, such a system may be viewed as run by a central switch operator which, at the instruction of the payer, transfers the control of the coin from the payer to that of the payee;[54]

2. A "coin" in the form of an unspent transaction output (UTXO)[55] in the payer's wallet, reflecting earlier transactions, is transformed into a new UTXO in the payee's wallet. Where the payer does not use up the entire UTXO, payment is carried out by splitting the payer's UTXO into two UTXO's: one in the sum of payment going to the payee's wallet, and the second in the amount of the balance of the UTXO remaining in the payer's wallet.[56]

....

53   We agree with the UKJT, "Cryptoassets and Smart Contracts," above note 24 at paras 87–88 that strictly speaking no "bailment" can exist with respect to a "digital banknote," except that we address below the option of "control" as a functional equivalent to "possession."

54   This method of payment is put forward by WingCash, now Open Payment Network (OPN). See online: https://wingcash.com/ and https://openpaymentnetwork.us/, both accessed 25 June 2024.

55   The term is explained in e.g., Delton Rhodes, "What's a UTXO? A Guide to Unspent Transaction Output (UTXO)" (*Komodo*, 26 July 2018), online: https://komodoplatform.com/whats-utxo, accessed 25 June 2024.

56   This is e.g., Satoshi Nakamoto, "Bitcoin: A Peer-to-Peer Electronic Cash System" (Bitcoin.org, 2008) at 2, online: https://bitcoin.org/bitcoin.pdf, accessed 8 May 2024; see also e.g., Stuart Hoegner et al, *The Law of Bitcoin* (iUniverse 2015) at 1; Neil Guthrie, "The End of Cash? Bitcoin, the Regulators and the Courts" (2014) 29 *Banking and Finance Law Review* 355; for its mechanics, see Jonathan Levin, "Bitcoin: New Plumbing for Financial Services" (*Coindesk*, 29 November 2014), online: http://www.coindesk.com/bitcoin-new-plumbing-financial-services/, accessed 8 May 2024; see also Nicholas Wenker, "Online Currencies, Real-World Chaos: The Struggle to Regulate the Rise of Bitcoin" (2015) 19 *Texas Rev L & Politics* 145; Jacob Hamburger, "Bitcoins vs. State Money Transmission Laws: Protecting Consumers or Hindering Innovation?" (2015) 11 *J L Economics & Policy* 229; see also, Wikipedia, "Bitcoin," online: https://en.wikipedia.org/wiki/Bitcoin, accessed 8 May 2024; Andrey Sergeenkov, "What is Bitcoin?" (*Coindesk*, 26 January 2022), online: http://www.coindesk.com/information/what-is-bitcoin/, accessed 8 May 2024; Benjamin Wallace, "The Rise and Fall of Bitcoin" (*Wired*, 23 November 2011), online: http://www.wired.com/2011/11/mf_bitcoin/, accessed 8 May 2024; and *The*

3. The payer sends from their device to the payee's device a "coin" or any split of it. The payee may (but is not required to) validate the coin authenticity with the "mint."[57]

Payment under each scheme is premised on the transfer of control of the digital coin. The functional equivalence with the transfer of possession of a paper banknote is obvious. For example, in a case of digital coins accessed by keys, Fox speaks of a presumption in favour of control by the public key holder as the "intangible analogue of the familiar (...) presumption that possession is evidence of title."[58]

b. Inherent Features: Privacy, Availability, and Accessibility

Cash payments (namely in banknotes and coins) can be carried out and instantly discharge a debt in full privacy, 24/7/365, and by everybody (who has it). This section will examine to existence of these inherent features for payment in digital currency.

Interestingly, the predominant motive in the search for a digital currency was the quest for privacy, or more specifically in this context, confidentiality and intractability of payment transactions, as part of a libertarian vision. Endeavouring to mimic the features of the paper banknote, the digital coin follows suit so that preservation of privacy, albeit within limits, is a highly desired objective of its designers as well.[59]

For the purpose of the ensuing discussion, "privacy" may be broken down to the following elements:

- *Secrecy* exists where payment information is not available to third-party outsiders, including government authorities. It is, however,

---

Economist, "The Great Chain of Being Sure About Things" (*The Economist*, 31 October 2015); see also Bitcoin Wiki, "How Bitcoin Works," online: https://en.bitcoin.it/wiki/How_bitcoin_works, accessed 8 May 2024.

57 This is BitMint. See e.g., online: http://www.bitmint.com/, accessed 28 May 2024; see also "BitMint Overview" (*Startup Nation Central*, 16 February 2022), online: http://finder.startupnationcentral.org/company_page/bitmint/, accessed 28 May 2024, and sites and videos accessible through it; see also "BitMint: AI Powered Cyber Innovation" (*Medium*), online: https://medium.com/@bitmintnews, accessed 28 May 2024, and associated articles.

58 David Fox, "Cryptocurrencies in the Common Law of Property' in Fox and Green, above note 22 at 157 para 6.50.

59 See e.g., Digital Euro Association Public Digital Euro Working Group, "Privacy and Central Bank Digital Currencies" (Digital Euro Association 2023), online: https://7869715.fs1.hubspotusercontent-na1.net/hubfs/7869715/Privacy%20and%20CBDCs%20-%20Digital%20Euro%20Association%20Working%20Group.pdf, accessed 25 June 2024.

available to the payer and the payee as well as, where applicable, to an intermediary such as the account-holding bank;

- *Anonymity* exists where payer's identity is not available to payee;
- *Confidentiality* exists where identity of payer and payee is not known to intermediaries such as banks involved in the payment.

Nowadays, prior to the advent of digital currency,

- Secrecy is available in cash as well as bank money payments. It is, however, subject to the rights of authorized third parties, such as the government under AML/ATF legislation.
- Anonymity may exist in a cash payment. In may exist (at least in part) even in the typical case of a face-to-face cash payment where the payer and the payee see each other but at least one of them is not necessarily identified. In a face-to-face cash payment, under prescribed circumstances, it may be contrary to legislation as in respect to secrecy.
- Confidentiality is relevant only in bank money payments except that it does not exist there.

In relation to digital currencies validation focuses on the identification of the coin and not its payer. Confidentiality is irrelevant in a direct payment between payer and payee. It does not exist in a payment involving a custodian. Otherwise, the ultimate level of privacy may depend on the technology used. In principle, both secrecy and anonymity are undermined in a payment by cryptocurrency and appear to be preserved in payments in BitMint. Both technology's archetypes are presented in chapter 1(VI).

Here is a brief comparison in relation in regard to privacy preservation under each:[60]

- For **cryptocurrencies**, the chain of custody of the coin is written on a distributed ledger and is thus exposed. Verification of coin will identify payer's public key and payment will be publicized to the entire

---

60 Gideon Samid, Bitcoin.BitMint, "Reconciling Bitcoin with Central Banks – Volatility: No; Anonymity: Yes – Optimal Balance between Privacy and Law Enforcement" (2014), online: https://eprint.iacr.org/2014/244.pdf, accessed 25 June 2024; Amnon Samid, "Automated Embedded Payment Systems" (2022) 12 *International Journal of Embedded Systems and Applications* 1, ss 2.2, 2.3, 2.4, online: https://www.researchgate.net/publication/367014225_Automated_Embedded_Payment_Systems, accessed 28 May 2024; Amnon Samid, "Gaining trust for self-referential CBDC (practical solutions)" (*The Paypers*, 9 January 2024), online: https://thepaypers.com/thought-leader-insights/gaining-trust-for-self-referential-cbdc-practical-solutions--1266139, accessed 25 June 2024.

community. The bit sequence represents the value of the coin, and it is exposed on the blockchain.

- In **BitMint currency** chain of custody can be written on the coin itself. While it can be exposed by court order it is not public so that cash-like secrecy is preserved and illicit activities are not enabled even as the network of validators and intermediaries are eliminated. Furthermore, a coin that is used in a transaction which raises suspicion can be singled out by law enforcement and posted on a "Hold" ledger, indicating that this particular coin is temporarily unredeemable. Such posting will instantly render this coin unto "non-payable" status. It is up to that owner to approach the posting authority (law enforcement), identify themselves, and prove to the authorities that they have received this coin in a bona fide transaction. Once they clear themselves, the coin returns to "redeemable" status and business continues. As in cash payments, in payments over a specified threshold participants may be required to identify themselves but otherwise a cash-like anonymity is preserved. This is so since the payment process does not require the payee to identify the payer – who just prior to payment may cancel tethering; for their part, the payee needs to verify only validity of coin and that it was not double spent. The fully random bit sequence defines only the unique identity of the coin (like the serial number in a banknote), while value function defines the value. Accordingly, where the coin is delivered through a blockchain (which is not essential) only the coin's identity but not the value will be exposed. The BitMint's LeVeL transaction protocol[61] requires the payer to prove ownership only to the payee and not the community at large. It thus preserves the privacy of all parties, without enabling illicit activities, consistent with oversight accountability and law enforcement.

So far as ongoing availability and universal accessibility:

- **Cryptocurrency** requires a smartphone and is internet dependent. Off-line payments, carried out in an environment devoid of internet as well as electricity become final, so as to discharge the debt paid by them, only upon the restoration of internet connection;

---

61   For which see Gideon Samid, "A LeVeL Paying Field: Cryptographic Solutions towards Social Accountability and Financial Inclusion" (Research Gate, February 2022), online: https://www.researchgate.net/publication/358479911_A_LeVeL_Paying_Field_Cryptographic _Solution s_towards_Social_Accountability_and_Financial_Inclusion, accessed 28 May 2024.

- While **"Bitmint'ed" currency** functionality is best when a smartphone is used over the internet, payment can also be carried out with a simple mobile phone over cellular network as well as in a complete off-line environment. Particularly, for proximity payments, a "hard wallet," which can store and be used for payment in coins other than "bitmint'ed," is available. Off-line validation is designed to ensure that the coins inside the payer's hardware wallet are genuine and that coins have not already been spent. It operates by a "quick touch," and only for genuine freshly minted coins. It may be an independent device, serving unbanked or underbanked people as well as people without mobile phones, or a chip embedded in a smartphone that can work offline – that is, in an environment devoid of internet as well as electricity – providing finality under such conditions.[62]

V. THE DIGITAL COIN AS AN E-BANKNOTE: MONETARY LAW AND THE HISTORY OF THE BANKNOTE

Throughout its history, the written banknote transformed in substance in response to ongoing advancing technological conditions, changing market demand, and evolving institutional frameworks. With technology facilitating the change in the media, the move to digital is just another step in the same process.

The role of statutory law in the evolution of the banknote was not to lead, but rather to facilitate developments for societal benefit. Hence, statutes and constitutional powers in relation to money ought to be interpreted in the spirit of accommodating new developments, harnessing them for the protection of the public, but not hindering them.

In England, for example, the law followed the emergence of banknotes, originally issued in the course of the seventeenth century by goldsmiths as receipts for moneys deposited with them.[63] Even in the absence of an explicit note issuing power under its establishing statute,[64] the Bank of England began, shortly after its establishment, to issue to depositors, "probably to a

---

62   Gideon Samid, "BitMint Hard Wallet: Digital Payment without Network Communication: No Internet, yet Sustained Payment Regimen between Randomness –Verifiable Hard Wallets" (IOT, Electronics and Mechatronics Conference, Institute of Electrical and Electronics Engineers 2020) at 1–7.
63   For the goldsmith banking system see chapters 1(IV) and 3(II) and (III).
64   *Bank of England Act, 1694* (UK), 5 & 6 Will & Mary, c 20, s XIX.

very considerable extent,"[65] notes payable to the bearer.[66] These were characterized by Lord Mansfield as "as much money, as guineas themselves are; or any other current coin, that is used in common payments, as money or cash."[67] The Bank of England notes were made legal tender by statute as late as under section 6 of the *Bank of England Act, 1833*.[68]

For its part, the issuance of the banknote in the United States, first by practice then by statute, bypassed a rigid interpretation of a federal constitutional power under Article 1 section 8 of the US Constitution "to coin money,"[69] which has been taken to give the power to issue only full-bodied metallic money.[70] Market (and government) demands were met by the issuance of banknotes, originally by state chartered banks with no statutory basis, later by national banks, and finally by the Federal Reserve – first by its regional Reserve Banks and subsequently by the Board of Governors of the Federal Reserve System.[71] All such banknotes have served as money, even as only the latter are accorded legal tender status. All were held not to be in violation of the United States Constitution.

Reflecting on this history, Khan observed that:

> Money is a living creature of the market and its form changes to facilitate commercial transactions in an ever more efficient, convenient, safe manner. As such, most innovations in monetary practices are attributable to the decisions of the market.[72]

65　*Bank of England v Anderson* (1837) 3 Bing 589, 654; 132 ER 538, 562 (Tindal CJ).

66　James M Holden, *The History of Negotiable Instruments in English Law* (Gaunt & Sons, 1993) at 89–90.

67　*Miller v Race* (1758) 1 Burr 452, 97 ER 398.

68　*Bank of England Act, 1833* (UK), 3 & 4 Will IV, c 98.

69　For constitutional aspects of money issuance in the United States, see e.g., Thomas Wilson, *The Power "to Coin" Money: The Exercise of Monetary Powers by the Congress* (M.E. Sharp, 1991); Ali Khan, "The Evolution of Money: A Story of Constitutional Nullification" (1999) 67 *U Cin L Rev* 393; the full text of the US Constitution is at e.g., online: https://www.archives.gov /founding-docs/constitution-transcript, accessed 25 June 2024.

70　Khan, above note 69 at 393.

71　For a succinct summary see e.g., Warren E Weber (formerly of the Federal Reserve Bank of Minneapolis), "Government and Private E-Money Like Systems: Federal Reserve Notes and National Bank Notes" (2015) Bank of Canada Working Paper 2015-18, at 3, online: https:// www.bankofcanada.ca/wp-content/uploads/2015/06/wp2015-18.pdf, accessed 25 June 2024: "Throughout most of U.S. history, bank notes have been issued either solely by private banks or solely by the government through the Federal Reserve System, the central bank."

72　Khan, above note 69 at 396, quoting Cyril James, "International Cooperation in the Field of Money: A Strand of Economic History in Money and the Law 1" (1945) at 1–2.

Accordingly, as far as the banknote is concerned, "entrenchment in the legal system was the affirmation of a simple monetary tradition: the market creates, modifies, and recreates the concept of money. The law simply recognises and changes, often *ex post facto*."[73] An obvious takeaway from this is that "no legal text, not even the most authoritative, such as the United States Constitution can fully predict how the future will discard some of the most obvious paradigms."[74]

These observations are confirmed by the shifting nature of the banknote – first in substance, and ultimately, I argue, in form. Principles of law that recognized the paper banknote, even in the absence of a statute, are good to recognize the e-banknote as a matter of statutory interpretation of any statute conferring banknote issuing power.

VI. CONTROL OVER A DIGITAL COIN AND PAYMENT BY ITS TRANSFER

"Payment" may be carried out by the physical delivery of cash, that is, currency, consisting of banknotes and coins. Delivery is the transfer of possession from one person to another.[75] For its part, possession is confined to tangible items of property.[76] As well, unless contextualized within a specific statutory pronouncement,[77] as matter of jurisprudence 101, possession, whose essence is "physical control" is confined to tangible items of property.[78]

An imaginative court may find ways to overcome this conceptual obstacle and apply "possession" to intangibles.[79] Nonetheless if only for certainty, specific legislation ought to be adopted. Indeed, the functional equivalence of (i) control and its transfer, by reference to an intangible to possession, and (ii) delivery, by reference to a tangible item, is the key to the application of

---

73   Khan, above note 69 at 414.

74   *Ibid* at 397.

75   As codified e.g., in the *Ontario Sale of Goods Act*, RSO 1990, c S.1, s 1(1).

76   *OBG Ltd v Allan* [2007] UKHL 21, [2008] 1 AC 1; notwithstanding *Li v Li*, 2017 BCSC 1312 and *Nelson v Gokturk*, 2021 BCSC 813 to the contrary. See chapter 4(III).

77   As was *In the matter of Lehman Brothers International (Europe) (in administration)* [2012] EWHC 2997 (Ch) at para 131 (see also para 136), interpreting *Financial Collateral Arrangements (No 2) Regulations 2003* (SI 2003/3226) (FCARs), implementing an EU Directive.

78   *Your Response Ltd v Datateam Business Media Ltd* [2014] 4 All ER 928 at para 18 (CA); *OBG Ltd v Allan* [2007] UKHL 21 at para 222; notwithstanding *Li v Li* 2017 BCSC 1312 at paras [213]–[218] and *Nelson v Gokturk* 2021 BCSC 813 at paras [36]–[42], assuming (with no discussion) to the contrary.

79   I take that this is the position of Fox. See Fox, in Fox and Green, above note 22 at 155–62 paras 6.45–66.

the models discussed earlier. The treatment of this functional equivalence by the various sources – together with its legal impact – is addressed in this Part.

Under *ETDA* section 3(1), "A person may possess, indorse and part with possession of an electronic trade document." The use of "possession" by reference to intangible is unorthodox and not in line with other legislative models. At the same time, *ETDA* section 2(2) speaks of the existence of a person who is able "to exercise control" – as a requirement for a complying "electronic trade document."[80] In turn, under *ETDA* section 2(3),

> (a) a person exercises control of a document when the person uses, transfers or otherwise disposes of the document (whether or not the person has a legal right to do so), and
>
> (b) persons acting jointly are to be treated as one person.

As well, under section 2(4):

> Reading or viewing a document is not, of itself, sufficient to amount to use of the document for the purposes of subsection (3)(a).

In the view of the UK Law Commission,

> In order to qualify as an electronic trade document, a trade document in electronic form must be divestible; that is, after the document is transferred, any person who before the transfer was able to exercise control of the document is no longer able to do so.[81]

"Divestibility" is tantamount to a transfer of control, which might necessarily include a different process to a physical transfer of a paper trade document. In particular, a transfer might include replacing, modifying, destroying, cancelling, or eliminating at least the data structure element of that electronic trade document, and the resulting and corresponding derivative creation of a new electronic trade document (a derivative electronic trade document).[82]

Accordingly, a transfer of control will generally be effected by the transferor using their private key to send the electronic trade document to the account of the transferee, thereby divesting themselves of the electronic trade document. On a central registry system, it will be similar: once the transfer is effected, only the transferee's security credentials (that is,

---

80 ETDA section 2(2) is discussed at length in Part III. For an extensive discussion on possession of electronic trade documents see (UK) Law Commission, *Electronic Trade Documents: Report and Bill*, Law Com No 405 (15 March 2022) chapter 7.

81 *Ibid* para 6.125 at 126.

82 *Ibid.*

login details) will provide the ability to transfer or otherwise exercise control over the document.[83]

In sum, ETDA speaks of the "possession" of an "electronic trade document."[84] At the same time it effectively requires "control" as an indication of that "possession."[85] Accordingly, in substance though not in form, it is in line with legislation elsewhere.

MLETR Article 11(1) treats "exclusive control of [an] electronic transferable record" as a functional equivalent to "the possession of a transferable document or instrument."[86] Under *MLETR* Article 11(2), the transfer of control over an electronic transferable record is the equivalent to the transfer of possession of a transferable document or instrument.[87] At the same time, being "the functional equivalent of … 'possession', which in turn, may vary in each jurisdiction" "control," is not defined in the *MLETR*.[88]

Under the *URVCBA*, "control of virtual currency" is central to the three "core concepts animating what constitutes 'virtual-currency business activity,'"[89] namely exchange, transfer, and storage,[90] all of which will be addressed further below. Under *URVCBA* section 102(3):

"Control" means:

(A) when used in reference to a transaction or relationship involving virtual currency, power to execute unilaterally or prevent indefinitely a virtual-currency transaction.

According to the Prefatory Note to UCC Article 12, the following general functions, all of which have been established by the experience with

---

83   *Ibid* para 7.105 at 159.
84   ETDA section 2(2).
85   ETDA section 2(3).
86   "Transferable document or instrument" is defined in Article 2 of the MLETR, above note 7 as follows:

   [A] document or instrument issued on paper that entitles the holder to claim the performance of the obligation indicated in the document or instrument and to transfer the right to performance of the obligation indicated in the document or instrument through the transfer of that document or instrument.

87   In this context, Article 15 of the *MLETR*, provides the following: "Where the law requires or permits the endorsement in any form of a transferable document or instrument, that requirement is met with respect to an electronic transferable record if the information required for the endorsement is included in the electronic transferable record and that information is compliant with the requirements set forth in Articles 8 and 9."
88   Explanatory Note to UNCITRAL MLETR para 106.
89   Comment 2 "Virtual-currency Business Activity" to *URVCBA*, above note 10, s 102.
90   *URVCBA*, s 102(5), (21), (20).

"record-management systems," form the basis of the control[91] concept, so as to facilitate the use of electronic records as effective and reliable means of transferring economic value:

- The electronic record must have some ... benefit that one person can enjoy and can exclude all others from enjoying ...
- A person must be able to transfer to another person this exclusive power to use and the exclusive power to transfer the electronic record. To remain exclusive, the transfer must divest the transferor of the power to use the electronic record.
- A person must be able to demonstrate to others that the person has the power to use and transfer control of the electronic record.

To that end, under section 12-105(a), for the purposes of UCC Article 12:

A person has control of a controllable electronic record if the electronic re-cord, a record attached to or logically associated with the electronic record, or a system in which the electronic record is recorded:

(1) gives the person:
    (A) power to avail itself of substantially all the benefit from the electronic record; and
    (B) exclusive power,[92] subject to subsection (b), to:
        (i) prevent others from availing themselves of substantially all the benefit from the electronic record; and
        (ii) transfer control of the electronic record to another person or cause another person to obtain control of another controllable electron-ic record as a result of the transfer of the electronic record; and

---

91 According to the Prefatory Note to UCC Article 12, above note 8, the meaning of control in the UCC depends on the type of property involved. See ss 7–106 (electronic documents of title): ss 8–106 (four different types of investment property, each with a different definition of "control"): ss 9–104 (deposit accounts): ss 9–105 (chattel paper): ss 9–105A (electronic money). The comments to s 12–105 explain the requirements for obtaining control of a controllable electronic record. For present purposes of exposition, it is sufficient to think of Bitcoin and other virtual currencies as prototypical controllable electronic records. The pro-visions under other laws that govern control and other matters for other types of electronic records (some of which are modified by these amendments) are not addressed by Article 12.

92 Under UCC s 12-105(b), power is exclusive even if (i) the electronic record or its system "limits the use of the electronic record or has a protocol programmed to cause a change" or (ii) "the power is shared with another person," except that under UCC s 12-105(c), each one of them is authorized to exercise the power alone.

(2) enables the person readily to identify itself in any way, including by name, identifying number, cryptographic key, [public][93] office, or account number, as having the powers specified in paragraph (1).

According to Official Comment (7) to the section, subsection (a)(2), requiring "control" to enable "a person to identify itself in any way, including by ... cryptographic key," does not obligate a person to identify itself as having control. "However, to prove that it has control, a person would need to prove that the relevant records or any system in which the controllable electronic record is recorded readily identifies the person as such." Stated otherwise, the relevant records or system, rather than the person itself, ought to identify the person in control. For its part, under UCC section 12-105(e), "control" can be exercised indirectly, that is, through another person (other than a transferor on behalf of a transferee) who has actual control, whether with or without an acknowledgment of the agency.

Under section 12-104(c), "law other than [Article 12] determines whether a person acquires a right in a controllable electronic record and the right the person acquires." This appears to suggest that Article 12 governs neither rights in "controllable electronic records" nor the rights that such a record confers. Indeed, the UCC does not purport to harmonize properties laws of the various states. Rather, it is designed to secure that rights in electronic assets are recognized in each adopting jurisdiction.

To that end, under the shelter principle of section 12-104(d),[94] "A purchaser of a controllable electronic record acquires all rights in the controllable electronic record that the transferor had or had power to transfer." "Purchaser" is broadly defined as a person that takes by "any ... voluntary transaction creating an interest in property" and thus includes a buyer, secured party, or even recipient of gift;[95] hence, to benefit from the shelter principle a "purchaser" is not even required to take the CER by control.

Even better, under prescribed circumstances, which include the taking by control, a bona fide purchaser for value gets a better title than that of the transferor.[96] Thus, under UCC section 12-104(e), "A qualifying purchaser acquires its rights in the controllable electronic record free of a claim of a property right in the controllable electronic record." For its part, under UCC section 12-102(a)(2), a "qualified purchaser" must have obtained control of the CER for value, in good faith, and without notice of a claim of a property

---

93 See UCC Official Comment 7 referring to "Section 3-110, Comment 3."
94 The corresponding principle in the *UNIDROIT Principles*, above note 6 is *Principle 9.*
95 UCC, above note 8, s 1-201(30) and (31).
96 The corresponding principle in the *UNIDROIT Principles*, above note 6 is *Principle 8.*

right in it. In turn, "value" is defined in UCC section 12-102(4), to incorporate (with necessary modifications) the definition under UCC section 3-303(a), under which an executory consideration – namely, a promise that has not been performed, is excluded.

As under UCC Article 12, the key to having and exercising rights on a transferable record is control. *UETA*[97] section 16(b) and *ESGNCA*[98] section 7021(b)) require "control" to be evidenced by a reliable system establishing an issuance or transfer to the claimant. *UETA* section 16(c) and *ESGNCA* section 7021(c)) go on to require such a system to be premised on a uniquely identifiable, unalterable single authoritative copy of the transferable record. According to the comment, the control requirements may be satisfied by the use of a trusted third-party registry system, such as those existing for the transfer of securities entitlements under UCC Article 8[99] and for the transfer of cotton warehouse receipts.

UNIDROIT Principles[100] 6–9 govern control and transfer. Under *UNIDROIT Principle* 6(1):
A person has "control" of a digital asset if,

(a)   ... the digital asset, or the relevant protocol or system, confers on that person:
    (i)   the exclusive ability to prevent others from obtaining substantially all of the benefit from the digital asset;
    (ii) the ability to obtain substantially all the benefit from the digital asset; and
    (iii) the exclusive ability to transfer the abilities in sub-paragraphs (a)(i), (a)(ii) and (a)(iii) to another person; and
(b) the digital asset, or the relevant protocols or system, allows that person to identify itself as having the abilities set out in sub-paragraph (a).

Paragraph (1)(a) is stated to be subject to paragraphs (2) and (3). As for paragraph (2), it addresses two aspects of a change of control over a digital asset. First, a transfer of control does not necessarily transfer the proprietary right in the digital asset. Two qualifications exist. First, transfer of control

97   *UETA*, above note 9.
98   *ESGNCA*, above note 12.
99   Uniform Law Conference of Canada, "Uniform Securities Transfer Act (USTA)" (2004), online: https://ulcc-chlc.ca/ULCC/media/EN-Uniform-Acts/Uniform-Securities-Transfer-Act.pdf, accessed 25 June 2024 – adopted in Ontario as *Securities Transfers Act*, SO 2008, c 8; Bill 41 (*OSTA*) is modelled after UCC Article 8.
100 *UNIDROIT Principles*, above note 6.

may be to an agent, as for example, as discussed further below, to a custodian. In such a case the transferor retains the title while the agent or custodian is equipped with the power to transact with the asset, albeit for the benefit of the transferor. To a similar end, even in a proprietary transaction, a transfer of control may be for the creation of a security interest rather than transfer full ownership. Second, depending on the nature of the digital asset, "transfer" may well be transformation. For example, as discussed in Part II, such is the case in Bitcoin, where the transaction destroys the original asset held by the transferor and creates a new replacing asset in the transferee's hands. Both aspects are addressed by *UNIDROIT Principle* 6(2), providing that:

> A "change of control" means a transfer of the abilities in sub-paragraph (1) (a) [*UNIDROIT Principle* 6(1)] to another person, and includes the replacement, modification, destruction, cancellation, or elimination of a digital asset, and the resulting and corresponding derivative creation of a new digital asset (a "resulting digital asset") which is subject to the control of another person.

For its part, paragraph (3) of *UNIDROIT Principle* 6(1) provides that the ability under paragraph 1(a) "need not be exclusive," either due to "the inherent attributes of a digital asset or the system in which it resides,"[101] or where "the person in control has agreed, consented to, or acquiesced in sharing that ability with one or more other person."[102] The latter point will be further discussed in connection with custody agreements.

As for the identification of a person in control of a digital asset, under *UNIDROIT Principle* 7(2):

> The identification mentioned in Principle 6(1)(b) may be by a reasonable means, including (but not limited to) an identifying number, a cryptographic key, an office, or an account number, even if the means of identification does not indicate the name or identity of the person to be identified.

The transferee's proprietary rights are governed by *UNIDROIT Principle* 9. Thereunder, in principle:

> (1)   ... a person can transfer only the proprietary rights that it has in a digital asset, if any, and no greater proprietary rights.
>
> (2) A transferee of proprietary rights in a digital asset acquires all of the proprietary rights that its transferor had or had the power to transfer,

---

101 *UNIDROIT Principle* 56 para 6.11.
102 *UNIDROIT Principle* 6(3)(b).

except that the transferee acquires rights only to the extent of the rights that were transferred.

As explained by the Commentary, while "Principle 9(1) states the familiar rule *of nemo dat quod non habet* (one cannot give what one does not have)," "Principle 9(2) states the shelter principle: a transferee acquires all the proprietary rights of the transferor that were transferred or that the transferor had the power to transfer," and yet "if a transferor transfers less than all of its proprietary rights in the digital asset, the transferee acquires only the proprietary rights that were transferred."[103]

However, *UNIDROIT Principle* 9 is stated to be subject to *Principle* 8 governing "Innocent acquisition." Under *Principle* 8(1):

In order to qualify as an innocent acquirer, a transferee must:

(a) obtain control of a digital asset; and

(b) comply with requirements equivalent to those found in the relevant good faith acquisition and take-free rules as specified by the relevant State.

Stated otherwise, *UNIDROIT Principle* 8 assumes the existence in the adopting state of a "good faith acquisition" rule that allows under certain circumstances and for identified assets a transferee to take the asset free at least for some restrictions and limitations that affected the transferor's title. In the absence of such rule in a given state, *Principle* 8(5) goes on to provide "default set of requirements for a transferee to be an innocent acquirer."[104] Thereunder:

[I]n addition to the requirement in subparagraph (1)(a), the following requirements for a transferee to be an innocent acquirer apply with respect to a digital asset:

(a) A transferee of a digital asset is an innocent acquirer of a digital asset unless, at the time the transferee takes control of the digital asset, the transferee actually knows or ought to know that another person has an interest in the digital asset and that the acquisition violates the rights of that other person in relation to its interest;

(b) In determining whether a person ought to know of an interest or fact:

(i) the determination must take into account the characteristics and requirements of the relevant market for the digital asset; and

(ii) the person is under no general duty of inquiry or investigation;

---

103 *UNIDROIT Principle* 66 para 9.2.

104 *UNIDROIT Principle* 65 para 8.10.

(c) An organization actually knows or ought to know of an interest or fact from the time when the interest or fact is or ought reasonably to have been brought to the attention of the individual responsible for the matter to which the interest or fact is relevant; and

(d) A transferee of a digital asset is not an innocent acquirer if the transfer of the digital asset is made by way of gift or otherwise gratuitously and is not the grant of a security right.

Effectively paragraph (d) adds a taking for "value" requirement, which in the context of the better title given to an innocent acquirer is quite natural. Unfortunately, however, paragraph (d) does not exclude executory consideration, that is, a promise the innocent acquirer has not performed subsequent to acquiring a damaging knowledge.

Upon compliance with the innocent requirement requirements, under *Principle* 8(2):

An innocent acquirer takes a digital asset free of conflicting proprietary rights ("proprietary claims").

So that under *Principle* 8(3):

No rights based on a proprietary claim relating to a digital asset can be successfully asserted against an innocent acquirer of that digital asset.

In turn, *UNIDROIT Principle* 9(4) appears to me to be redundant. It states that the "innocent acquirer" can defeat a proprietary right in a digital asset even when the innocent acquirer acquired from a transferor "who is acting wrongfully and has no proprietary right in the digital asset."

Under *UNIDROIT Principle* 12(1), where a custodian maintains a digital asset under a custody agreement,[105] "no rights based on a proprietary claim to that asset may be successfully asserted against the client." Under *Principle* 12(2), this is so unless "the client, at the time from which the custodian maintains the digital asset for that client, actually knows or ought to know that another person has an interest in the digital asset and that the acquisition violates the rights of that other person in relation to its interest." Where the assets are maintained by the custodian for more than one client as an undivided pool, "paragraphs (1) and (2) apply to each client for whom the digital assets are maintained."[106]

---

105 As defined in *UNIDROIT Principle* 10(3) and (4) discussed in Part VI.
106 *UNIDROIT Principle* 12(3).

UNIDROIT Principle 12 is an adaptation of the innocent acquisition rule tailored for the circumstances of custody. It applies where a custodian maintains a digital asset pursuant to a custody agreement. It provides that unless the client knows or ought to have known of a third person's violation of rights, the client cannot be subject to a successful claim to the digital asset where the claim is brought by a person whose rights are violated by the change of control to the custodian. The standard of "innocence" is stated to be that set out in *Principle* 8(5)(a), "although, in accordance with Principle 8(1)(b), a State has flexibility to adapt this standard to be consistent with its own good faith purchase and take free rules."[107]

VII.   CUSTODY AND RELATED SERVICES: BUSINESS MODELS

Digital currencies may be controlled by keys held in "crypto wallets." For their part, crypto wallets may be classified in several way: software-based versus paper- or hardware-based; hot versus cold; custodial versus non- (or self-) custodial.[108] Hot (software-based) wallets are connected to the internet, while cold (paper- or hardware-based) wallets are kept off-line.

In **hot wallets**, private keys are stored and encrypted on the app itself, which is kept online. More specifically, hot wallets securely store and manage the private key on a server, a mobile device, or a computer hard drive. They are thus respectively classified as *web-based, mobile,* and *desktop wallets.* A combined web-based and desktop wallet is a *browser wallet.*

For its part, a **cold wallet** is off-line. The main types of cold crypto wallets include *paper wallets,* where the private key is written on a physical medium, usually paper, stored in a safe place, as well as *hardware wallets,* where the private key is stored in a thumb-drive device that is kept in a safe place and only connected to a computer when one wants to use one's crypto. Either way, a cold wallet requires a tangible external storage such as a piece of paper or a device –which stores the private key. In practice, third-party exchangers maintain 80 percent of their assets in custodial cold storage.

---

107   *UNIDROIT Principle* 86 para 12.1.

108   There are numerous websites addressing this subject. See e.g., Sean Michael Kerner, "Definition: Crypto Wallet" (*TechTarget*), online: https://www.techtarget.com/searchsecurity/definition /crypto-wallet-cryptocurrency-wallet, accessed 25 June 2024. My Torys colleague Mohammed Muraj helped me to make sense of much of the information which is not always consistent. All errors are mine. For the wallet as a storage mechanism see e.g., Christopher Hare, "Cryptocurrencies and Banking Law: Are there Lessons to Learn?" in Fox and Green, above note 22 at 229, 233–40 paras 9.05–12.

Keys "stored" in a paper wallet may be the safest to guard but the hardest to use. In turn, keys stored in online wallets are the most convenient to use and yet they are the most exposed to security risk. This makes hardware wallets optimal in balancing between security and convenience.

With a custodial wallet, the custodian has control over the client's private keys (and hence the client's digital assets). In effect, the custodian's clients transfer their digital assets to addresses or private keys controlled by that custodian, or the custodian acquires digital assets which it controls for the client.[109]

Conversely, with a non- (or self-) custodial wallet, the client has exclusive access to the private key and therefore to the digital assets. Briefly stated, the non-custodial wallet gives the client direct control at the cost of less security. In turn, a custodial wallet gives the client more security at the cost of less control.

A non-custodial wallet may be browser-based. This is a software application in which the private key is saved on an internet browser. It allows its user to securely store, manage, and transfer *cryptocurrencies directly from* their web browser.

Non-custodial wallets may also be paper-based but are mostly hardware-based resembling a USB thumb drive. Non-custodial wallets are kept off-line.[110] They are only online when connected to a computer or mobile device, typically as needed for a transaction. The signing of transactions using the private key happens within the hardware device itself and is only sent to be confirmed by the blockchain once it is back online. The client is exclusively responsible for "signing" and ensuring that the transaction is correctly completed.

In securing access to digital value, a custodial wallet arrangement bears a superficial similarity with a bank account. At the same time, strictly speaking, having been considered as a "custodian ... of the customer's money" providing a "safe place of deposit,"[111] a bank is nevertheless obligated to its customer on a bank deposit as a debtor on a loan.[112] A bank does not segregate deposits

---

109 *UNIDROIT Principles*, above note 6 at 76 para 10.18.

110 This makes non-custodial hardware wallets virtually inaccessible to hackers. And yet, if a user loses the paper or device storing the private key (and doesn't memorize it) there is virtually no way to access the digital assets associated with it. While many non-custodial wallet providers give users a recovery phrase or "seed phrase," consisting of twelve to twenty-four random words, serving as a sort of backup password recovery method, even if a wallet is lost, deleted, or destroyed, this phrase should be guarded just as carefully as the private key.

111 *National Bank of Virginia v Nolting* (1897) 26 SE 825 (Va SC) 828 (Harrison J).

112 *Foley v Hill* (1848) 2 HLC 28, 9 ER 1002 (HL).

and in fact uses them by way of lending to others for its own account rather than keeping them. On demand it pays the amount deposited – but not the same banknotes and coins originally deposited. At the same time, wallet-custodians do not take "possession" of the funds; rather, they take control of the private keys accessing the coins associated with them. Their rights to the coins and whether they can nevertheless lend them will be discussed further below in Part VIII. At this point it is sufficient to say that as is the case with funds held at a bank, access to cryptocurrencies held at a custodial wallet requires intermediation.

Regardless, transactions in digital assets need the support of service providers. This is true in conjunction with both custodial and self/non-custodial arrangements.

Commentary to UNIDROIT Principle 10 *sets out several business models for self-custody arrangements:*

a. Self-custody by Wallet Software[113]

An open-source software is developed by a global community of developers and designers. It is compatible with a variety of hardware wallets. Its user creates a wallet password and a secret recovery phrase, which are stored, together with the private keys, in an encrypted format on the mobile phone or computer on which the open-source software is installed. Transactions conducted through wallets using the open-source software are broadcasted on-chain.

b. Self-custody by Cloud-based Software-as-a-Service[114]

In this business model a service provider (SP), provides a non-custodial wallet for users. A user creates an account, and creates a password, which gives the user access to an encrypted file kept by the SP on the blockchain containing a "seed" (a secret private key recovery phrase), the users' private keys, and addresses of digital assets. The password is not stored by the SP and must be kept safe and confidential by the user. The SP has no access to the user's private keys, seed, or password. When a password or seed phrase is used correctly, the file containing private keys is decrypted locally on the user's computer or mobile phone, and the user can carry out transactions,

---

113 *UNIDROIT Principles,* above note 6 at 75 para 10.16.
114 *UNIDROIT Principles* 75–76 para 10.17.

which are conducted directly on-chain. The SP stores the encrypted file in the cloud.

This is in contrast to the previous business model (of the open-source software) under which the encrypted file is stored locally on the user's computer or mobile phone.[115] Users of the software-as-a-service model, therefore, could find themselves in difficulty should the SP ever decide to stop providing the wallet services.

c. Safeguarding of Private Keys[116]

In this business model a service provider (SP) safeguards its client's private keys or provides software or hardware to facilitate the client's safeguarding its private keys. Depending on the features, the SP may (or may not) have the ability to use the client's private keys and thus take control of the client's digital assets. However, this is not the purpose of this type of arrangement. The SP will be prohibited from using the client's private keys for any purpose that has not been agreed to by the client. The client still has control of the digital asset and has the ability to change the control of the asset. Strictly speaking, this business model is therefore not a custody service though it is frequently referred to as such.

In turn, Commentary to UNIDROIT Principle *10 sets out the following business models for custodial business arrangements:*

(i) Custodial or hosted wallet[117]
Under this business model, users transfer digital assets to the wallets of a custodian who holds the private keys of the wallet to which the digital asset is thereafter connected.

(ii) Trading account[118]
An account offered by a custodian is a functionality within a wallet that enables a user to buy and hold all digital assets purchased with fiat currency through the custodian. The contract between the custodian and its client does not transfer the digital assets to the custodian. Rather, the contract expressly provides that title to the digital assets in the trading account is held by the user. The contract goes on and emphasizes that these digital assets neither belong nor even loaned to the custodian.

---

115 *Ibid.*
116 UNIDROIT *Principle* 76 para 10.18.
117 UNIDROIT *Principle* 73 para 10.11.
118 UNIDROIT *Principle* 74 para 10.12.

d. Agreement for Delivery of Digital Assets[119]

A "custodian" maintains an account (similar to a bank account, as opposed to the "bailment" or custody of assets belonging to the client) on which credits and debits of a particular digital asset are recorded from time to time. The account balance evidences at any time the quantity of such digital asset the "custodian" is obliged to deliver to the client (or, as the case may be, may claim from the client) on demand. The "custodian" effectively operates like a bank on a bank account and unless agreed otherwise does not have to hold a 100 percent reserve. Rather, for each digital asset, such an account operates in the same way as a current account in a national currency. The client does not have control of digital assets; they merely have an unsecured personal claim against the custodian.[120]

VIII.   CUSTODY: LEGAL ASPECTS

In the absence of any direct statutory provision in Canada, it is tempting to examine whether the custodian can be viewed as holding the digital assets in trust for the client. However, a good reason to reject this perspective at the outset is that an equitable right is weaker than legal title and is exposed to additional risk. Hence proposed statutory solutions will be examined.

The relationship between a client and a service provider in a self-custody arrangement is governed exclusively by contract law. For its part, UCC Article 12 does not address the holding of digital assets by a third party. Conversely, *UNIDROIT Principles* 10–13, contained in section IV, govern custody agreements. Proprietary aspects of custodial arrangements are addressed in the *URVCBA* and are more fully covered in the *SCLURVCBA*.

UNIDROIT Principle 10 speaks of a custodian maintaining a digital asset for a client by *controlling* the digital asset in a way that "the client does not have the exclusive ability to change the control of the digital asset." Control lies with the custodian, yet the custodian exercises it for the client. Inasmuch as it preserves a direct relationship between the client and the digital currency maintained by the custodian, this sounds like a quasi-bailment[121] arrangement coupled with agency and not like a bank account. As pointed out in Part

---

119   *UNIDROIT Principles* 76–77 para 10.20.
120   Customers may be disadvantaged by misunderstanding the nature of this arrangement. See Dan Awrey, *Beyond Banks: Technology, Regulation, and the Future of Money* (Princeton, NJ: Princeton University Press, 2024) at 177–83.
121   It is a quasi-bailment and not strictly a bailment only because traditionally bailment is associated with chattels and not intangibles. See text, below note 128.

V, between a bank and customer, property to the money on deposit passes to the bank that remains a mere debtor to the customer.[122] By way of further elaboration, under *Principle* 11(2), "[u]nless prohibited by the custody agreement or by other law, a custodian may maintain fungible digital assets of two or more of its clients in an undivided pool." In this case, each client holds an undivided share in a stock of digital assets.

"Custody" is not defined by *UNIDROIT Principles*. The Commentary to *Principle* 10 explains that broadly speaking, "custody" is a situation where a person maintains a digital asset on behalf of and for the benefit of another, called a "client." The custodian is "usually a legal person, which may be a regulated entity," and the manner in which the digital asset is maintained is such "that gives the client special protection against unauthorized dispositions of the asset and against the insolvency of the custodian who maintains the digital asset."[123] This explanation is derived from definitions set out in *Principle* 10. Thus, under *Principle* 10(1)(a), "custodian" is defined to mean a person who provides services to a client pursuant to a "custody agreement." In turn, under *Principle* 10(1)(c), a "client" is a person to whom a custodian provides services under such an agreement.[124] Under *Principle* 10(3), an agreement for services to a client in relation to a digital asset is a "custody agreement"[125] if:

(a) the service is provided in the ordinary course of the service provider's business;

(b) the service provider is obliged to obtain (if this is not yet the case) and to maintain the digital asset for the client; and

(c) the client does not have the exclusive ability to change the control of the digital asset within the meaning of Principle 6(2).[126]

---

122 *Foley*, above note 112.

123 Commentary in *UNIDROIT Principles*, above note 6 at 69 para 10.1. Note however, that protection from an unauthorized disposition by the custodian is quite limited as the latter may have an apparent authority.

124 In turn, though, under *UNIDROIT Principle* 10(5), "the client may be acting in any capacity on behalf of a third party in relation to the digital asset."

125 Unless, under *UNIDROIT Principle* 10(4), "[I]t is clear from the agreement that, if the service provider enters into an insolvency-related proceeding, the digital asset would be part of the service provider's assets available for distribution to its creditors."
    Stated otherwise, the arrangement is not a "custody agreement" where "it is made clear that the assets controlled by the service provider form part of the service provider's assets available for distribution to its creditors if it enters into an insolvency-related proceeding." *UNIDROIT Principle* 73 para 10.10.

126 See also *UNIDROIT Principle* 6(3)(a).

According to the Commentary, together with *UNIDROIT Principle* 11(4) contemplating authorized sub-custody agreements, *Principle* 10(3)(b) "sets out the core duty of a custodian."[127] It covers the acquisition, control, and where applicable, use of sub-custodial services.[128]

Under *Principle* 10(2):

(2) A custodian "maintains" a digital asset for a client if:
   (a) that custodian has control of the digital asset; or
   (b) that custodian enters into a custody agreement, as defined in paragraph (3), with a sub-custodian with respect to the digital asset in the circumstances set out in Principle 11(4).

Under *UNIDROIT Principle* 10(1)(b), "sub-custodian" is a custodian providing services to another custodian under a custody agreement. Vis-à-vis the sub-custodian, the custodian is thus a client. The circumstances set out in *Principle* 11(4) are where the sub-custody is authorized either by the client or "other law."

For its part, the *URVCBA* envisages a broad range of activities, beyond mere custody, by a service provider in control, namely a custodian, of a virtual currency. Thus, under *URVCBA* section 102(25)(A) "Virtual-currency business activity" is defined to include exchanging, transferring, or storing virtual currency.[129] According to the Comment, each of these three covers the core concepts animating what constitutes "virtual-currency business activity." Section 102 goes on to explain of the meaning of these "core concepts" as follows:

(5) "Exchange," ... means to assume control of virtual currency from or on behalf of a [client], at least momentarily, to sell, trade, or convert:
(A) virtual currency for legal tender, bank credit, or one or more forms of virtual currency; or
(B) legal tender or bank credit for one or more forms of virtual currency.
(21) "Transfer" means to assume control of virtual currency from or on behalf of a [client] and to:
(A) credit the virtual currency to the account of another person;
(B) move the virtual currency from one account of a [client] to another account of the same [client]; or
(C) relinquish control of virtual currency to another person.

----

127 *UNIDROIT Principle* 71 para 10.6.
128 *Ibid.*
129 URVCBA, above note 10.

> (20) "Store," means to maintain control of virtual currency on behalf of a [client] by a person other than the [client].

In relation to "Store" the comment confusingly states that the term "is analogous to deposit-taking and holding or to safe deposit business" as if these two activities are the same. It goes on to explain that "storage is similar to placing a deposit of funds with a bank" or else "on an 'electronic wallet.'" It is thus not clear whether for the storage activity the *URVCBA* envisages "custody," namely "bailment," or whether it envisages ownership passing to the storer, so that it owes a debt. Even if the latter is the case, it is not clear whether the debt is under a fractional reserve as that of a commercial bank on a bank deposit, or under what is known under Roman law as "irregular deposit," which requires a 100 percent non-fractional reserve.[130]

However, the issue is resolved by *URVCBA* section 502 providing for the position of a virtual-currency business which has "control" of virtual currency for another person. For its part, as indicated in the paragraphs quoted above, "control" may be acquired in any virtual-currency business activity, including an exchange, transfer, and storage transaction. Effectively section 502 confers on the one for whom control of virtual currency is held by a virtual currency business an *"entitlement to virtual currency."* This right is modelled on Part V of the American UCC Article 8 governing "indirect holding" of securities and providing for an investor a "security entitlement" to securities held by the securities intermediary for that investor. The investor's claim is thus fully backed by securities held by the securities intermediary which are beyond the reach of the latter's creditors. Thus, under *URVCBA* section 502:

> (a) A [custodian][131] that has control of virtual currency for one or more persons shall maintain in its control an amount of each type of virtual currency sufficient to satisfy the aggregate entitlements of the persons to the type of virtual currency.
>
> (b) If a [custodian] violates subsection (a), the property interests of the persons in the virtual currency are pro rata property interests in the type of virtual currency to which the persons are entitled, without regard to the time the

---

130 For the irregular deposit see in general Robert W Lee, *The Elements of Roman Law with a Translation of the Institutes of Justinian*, 4th ed (Sweet & Maxwell, 1956) at 295; see also Reinhard Zimmermann, *The Law of Obligations – Roman Foundations of the Civilian Tradition* (Cape Town Juta, 1990) at 215–19.

131 That is, "licensee or registrant" in the original throughout.

persons became entitled to the virtual currency or the licensee or registrant obtained control of the virtual currency.

(c) The virtual currency referred to in this section is:

(1) held for the persons entitled to the virtual currency;

(2) not property of the [custodian]; and

(3) not subject to the claims of creditors of the [custodian].

According to the Comment to *URVCBA* section 502:

1. This section is based on [UCC] Sections 8-503 and 8-504[132] and protects the owner of virtual currency that is entrusted to a [custodian] for a purpose governed by this act. … In essence, this section takes the virtual currency under the control of a [custodian] off the balance sheet of the virtual currency business and beyond the business' right to deal with it as their own property. …

2. This section favors the interests of persons who place virtual currency under the control of a [custodian] over the interests of a [custodian]'s creditors. … To clarify the rights of persons that place their virtual currency under the control of virtual currency business and of the virtual-currency the virtual-currency businesses themselves, the Uniform Law Commission is developing an act that will provide … a substitute for Section 502 of this act that instead adopts UCC Article 8's more balanced approach to the matter. The act is expected to be ready … in 2018.

Comment (1) refers to the one who relinquishes control of virtual-currency to a virtual-currency business as "the owner of virtual currency." However, in fact, by giving "control," this person will have ownership of virtual currency replaced by an "entitlement to virtual currency." The latter is in effect a personal claim against the virtual-currency business in "control," albeit fully backed by the virtual-currency that become owned by that business, and subject to the claim of that person. The terminology is thus imprecise and yet the drafters' intention is clear.

The application of a UCC Article 8 regime to virtual-currency business is, however, quite controversial. Katherine Cooper quotes Coinbase to be of the view that "a simpler full-backing, permissible investment obligations regime is preferable" as well as to argue that incorporating UCC Article 8 would invoke:

---

132 In Canada UCC ss 8-503 and 8-504 correspond to *USTA*, above note 99, ss 108 and 109 respectively.

> [A] distinct body of law not well-developed in our field, will complicate future application of prevailing consumer financial protection laws that may come to bear on retail virtual currency businesses and does not appear to enhance the fundamental obligations Coinbase and similar [custodians] already owe to their customers.[133]

With the view to address Coinbase's concerns, the drafters supported a "compromise" in the form of "a separate stand-alone commercial-law uniform act that mandates the application of Article 8 law."[134] Indeed, if the Article 8 route is the preferable policy choice, a dedicated statute is preferable to *URVCBA* section 502 for two reasons. First, a comprehensive statute will allow adjustments to be considered and made where necessary so as to ensure suitability for the virtual currency business activity. Second, a commercial law statute will give an opportunity to consider the application of its regime also to persons excluded from the coverage of the *URVCBA* and/or exempted from its provisions. In the final analysis, whether or not the Article 8 route is selected, the nature of the obligations of a custodian in "control" of a virtual currency to its client is a matter of commercial or private – and not regulatory – law – as *URVCBA* is.

To implement the proposal for a comprehensive statute the drafters promulgated *SCLURVCBA*.[135] Thereunder, a custodian who expressly agrees with its clients to treat virtual currency maintained for them as financial assets credited to the clients' securities accounts, incurs the following UCC Article 8 duties:[136]

- The duty to maintain sufficient financial assets to satisfy all security entitlements to the financial assets ...

---

133 See Katherine Cooper, "Uniform Regulation for Virtual Currency Businesses: Coming to a State Near You" (*CoinDesk*, 2 July 2017, online: https://www.coindesk.com/markets/2017/07/02/uniform-regulation-for-virtual-currency-businesses-coming-to-a-state-near-you/, accessed on 25 June 2024. For a stiffer opposition (citing earlier opposition to the *URVCBA* itself) see e.g., Bitcoin Foundation, "Letter to Liza Karzai, Executive Director, The National Conference of Commissioners on Uniform State Laws" (*The Bitcoin Foundation*, 30 April 2018), archived website: https://web.archive.org/web/20180512224900/https://bitcoinfoundation.org/wp-content/uploads/2018/05/Letter-to-ULC-05-30-2018-final.pdf, accessed 25 June 2024; see e.g., The Bitcoin Foundation "The Foundation strongly opposes Article 8 Companion Act to the Uniform Regulation of Virtual Currency" (*The Bitcoin Foundation*, 3 May 2018), archived website: https://web.archive.org/web/20210306075955/https://bitcoinfoundation.org/the-foundation-strongly-opposes-article-8-companion-act-to-the-uniform-regulation-of-virtual-currency/, accessed 25 June 2024.

134 *Ibid.* Whether this is a true compromise is of course in the eye of the beholder.

135 *SCLURVCBA*, above note 11.

136 See the extensive commentary to *SCLURVCBA*, s 4.

- The duty to comply with the entitlement holder's entitlement orders to transfer or redeem a financial asset ... [and]
- The duty to change the entitlement holder's security entitlement to another form of holding for which the entitlement holder is eligible, or to deliver out a financial asset, at the request of the entitlement holder ... [137]

For its part, a custodian who transfers virtual currency as instructed by the client, in principle, cannot be held liable to an adverse claimant to the virtual currency.[138] As well, virtual currency of which a custodian has control for a client would generally not be subject to claims of creditors of the custodian.

At a minimum, under the *SCLURVCBA*, the custodian must act in respect of its duties with "due care in accordance with reasonable commercial standards," the latter being the default standard under UCC Article 8.[139]

Not addressing the juridical basis of the custodian-client relationship, *UNIDROIT Principle* 11 nevertheless provides for the custodian's duties owed to its client. In the view of the drafters, "[t]hese are basic duties and a State should not permit them to be excluded by the terms of the custody agreement."[140] Under *Principle* 11(1):

(1) A custodian owes the following duties to its client in relation to a digital asset it maintains for that client:

(a) the custodian is not authorised to transfer the digital asset, or use it for its own benefit, except to the extent permitted by the client and by other law;[141]

(b) the custodian is obliged to comply with an instruction given by the client to transfer the digital asset, unless:

(i) the custodian is prohibited from complying with the instruction by other law or by any agreement between the custodian and a third party to which the client is a party or has consented;

(ii) the custodian is not obliged, by other law or by an agreement with the client, under certain circumstances, to comply with the instruction;

---

137 Respectively under UCC, above note 8, ss 8-504(a), 8-507, and 8-508 (corresponding in Canada to *USTA*, above note 99, ss 109(1) & (2), 112, and 113 respectively.)

138 Exceptions enumerated in UCC s 8-115 (corresponding in Canada to *USTA*, above note 99, s 63) cover the violation of an injunction properly served, collusion, and knowledge of theft.

139 See UCC, ss 8-504(c)(2), 8-505(a)(2), 8-506(2), 8-507(a)(2), and 8-508(2) (corresponding in Canada to *USTA*, above note 99, ss 109(4)(b), 110(2)b), 111(2)(b), 112(2)(b), and 113 (2)(b) respectively).

140 *UNIDROIT Principles*, above note 6 at 80 para 11.1.

141 Defined in *UNIDROIT Principle* 2(4) to mean "a State's law to the extent that it is not Principles law."

(c) the custodian is obliged to safeguard the digital asset.

In the view of the drafters, details of "safeguarding" under *UNIDROIT Principle* 11(1)(c), are to be elucidated in the custody agreement, but in any event the safeguarding duty "includes the attainment of the result set out in Principle 13(2) (that the assets safeguarded are not to be part of the assets available for distribution to the custodian's creditors if it enters into an insolvency-related proceeding)."[142] More in general:[143]

> The language of Principle 11(1) is intended to be functional and neutral between legal cultures. In some jurisdictions, the relationship between custodian and client will be legally characterized as a trust while in other jurisdictions it may be characterized as a contractual or other type of legal relationship.

While appreciating the drafters' reluctance to get into details separating among legal systems, I am inclined to think of the custody arrangement as classified as a bailment of an intangible. "Bailment" is known to all legal systems and while the consensus around it has envisioned it as limited to tangible items,[144] its extension by analogy to intangibles subject to control would have been a decisive step in the modernization of universal legal concepts. For sure, the position of a custodian of an intangible item under their control is quite analogous to that of a bailee of a tangible item. In this context, a reference to a client's account is in effect a reference to the value of digital assets of the same description held for the client either separately or as a portion of a bulk as it keeps changing from one transaction to another. It is not a reference of a mere debt owed in the value of these digital assets.

UNIDROIT Principle 11(3) goes on to list duties that may be owed by the custodian to the client. These are:

(a) the duty to keep a record of the digital assets it maintains for each client;

(b) the duty at all times to securely and effectively maintain digital assets in accordance with the records it keeps for its clients;

(c) the duty to acquire digital assets promptly if this is necessary to satisfy the duty under sub-paragraph (b);

---

142 *UNIDROIT Principle* 81 para 11.4. *Principle* 13 addresses the exclusion of clients' assets from the custodian's estate upon the custodian's bankruptcy.

143 *UNIDROIT Principles* 81 para 11.5.

144 Daniel Greenberg (ed), *Stroud's Judicial Dictionary of Words and Phrases*, 11th ed (Sweet & Maxwell, 2023), vol 1 at 264. See also FH Lawson and Bernard Rudden, *Law of Property*, 3d ed (Oxford University Press, 2002) at 81.

(d) the duty to separate the digital assets maintained for clients from the digital assets maintained for its own account;

(e) subject to any right granted to the custodian or to another person, the duty to pass the benefits arising from digital assets to the client for whom it maintains those assets

For its part, the record to be kept separately under *UNIDROIT Principle* 11(3)(a), "may either be kept separately from the distributed ledgers which record the respective digital assets or, if technology allows, be part of the information stored in the distributed ledger."[145]

While strictly speaking not a banker, the custodian ought to be fastened with duties to the client analogous to that of a bank to the customer. In this context Christopher Hare enumerates the duty to act within mandate, the duty of secrecy, the duty to act with reasonable skill and care, and in some cases fiduciary duties.[146] He further addresses countermand and unauthorized instructions where the usual banking rules apply.[147]

UNIDROIT Principle 11(4) permits a custodian to fulfill its duties under *Principle* 11 "by entering into a custody agreement with a sub-custodian" provided this is authorized by either the client or "other law" and only where "the sub-custodian is bound by the duties set out in … Principle [11]."

UNIDROIT Principles 11(2) and (5) address custodian's obligation regarding proprietary aspects. Under *Principle* 11(2), as long as it is not contrary to the custody agreement or other law, "a custodian may maintain digital assets of the same description for two or more of its clients as an undivided pool." Stated otherwise, while under *Principle* 11(3)(d) a custodian is under a duty to separate between digital assets of *all* clients from those of the custodian there is no duty to segregate fungible assets of *each* client.[148] As for the quantity of assets to be held for each client, as discussed, under *Principle* 10(2), the maintenance of a digital asset requires its control, either directly or through a sub-custodian, so that effectively a fractional reserve, as for a bank in regard to money, is precluded. Rather, 100 percent reserve is required. Note, however, that parties may contract out of the *Principle* 11(2) scheme, albeit, prima facie only by agreeing to have the digital assets in custody segregated for each client. Conversely, an agreement for a fractional reserve is not explicitly envisioned. It remains to be seen whether such an agreement is to be

---

145   *UNIDROIT Principle*, above note 6 at 83 para 11.9.
146   Hare, in Fox and Green, above note 22 at 240–48 paras 9.13–20.
147   *Ibid* at 248–53 paras 9.21–25.
148   *UNIDROIT Principles*, above note 6 at 84 para 11.13.

considered void or whether the arrangement will simply be reclassified into something else other than custody.

In turn, *UNIDROIT Principle* 11(5) takes into account that a digital asset maintained by a custodian for a client may be subject to a security interest:[149]

   (a) granted to that custodian by the client;
   (b) in favour of that custodian arising by operation of other law; or
   (c) granted to a third party by the client.

IX. CONCLUSION: LEGISLATIVE OPTIONS FOR CANADA

This chapter endeavours to establish that, as in fact argued in chapter 5(III), a digital coin containing an unconditional promise, made and authenticated by a bank, engaging to pay to bearer on demand a sum certain in money, and circulating as a medium of exchange, is an e-banknote.

The chapter does not argue that every statutory reference to a banknote automatically applies to the e-banknote; rather, in each case, the context ought to be considered and where applicable adjustments in statutory interpretations are to be made. However, the banknote issuance power and principles of law applicable to it fully apply to a digital coin serving as an e-banknote.

This conclusion derives from a liberal interpretation of Canadian statutes governing promissory notes and banknotes supported by an analysis of both monetary law principles, and international and United States law reform projects governing digital assets. Legislation along such lines is recommended for Canada with the view of supporting and reinforcing the conclusion.

It was noted in this chapter that custody arrangements for digital currencies are different than deposit taking by banks. Hence a choice has to be made on the appropriate legal framework and back it by legislation. In this context the proprietary aspects of holding and keeping in custody digital coins have to be addressed. Nonetheless, it was stressed that the difference between custody of digital currency and safekeeping of money on deposit result from different business practices and not from any conceptual difference between a digital coin and a paper banknote.

So far, the United States leads the pack in domestic legislation addressing relevant issues. Due to domestic political reasons the US legislation suffers from duplication, overlaps, and definitional inconsistencies; yet in bringing

---

149 For Secured Transactions under *UNIDROIT Principles* see s V containing *Principles* 14–17.

forward the right concepts it is a model worth watching. UNCITRAL and *UNIDROIT* projects merit equal attention. All projects and statutes discussed in this chapter provide adequate basis for a rational comprehensive legislative agenda for Canada.

For sure, law reform also requires the regulation and licensing of entities involving in the provision of services, particularly but not only custody. This aspect is, however, outside the scope of this study.

Launching a legislative project in Canada focusing on private law governing transfer of and payment in digital currencies requires a determination as to the competent body to do it under the Constitution.

As discussed in chapter 2, establishing Confederation, the *British North America Act, 1867*[150] conferred in section 91 on the Parliament of Canada exclusive legislative power in relation to "Matters coming within [enumerated] Classes of Subjects." They include "Currency and Coinage"; "Banking, Incorporation of Banks, and the Issue of Paper Money"; "Bills of Exchange and Promissory Notes"; and "Legal Tender."[151]

Full and exclusive competence relating to money and the monetary system was thus given to the federal Parliament.[152] Listed powers included not only currency, coinage, paper money, and legal tender, all of which dealing exclusively with money; rather they also included scriptural money insofar as it falls under banking. They also included banknotes and other currency notes insofar as they are promissory notes. In line with the prevailing understanding at that time, currency was linked to coinage and paper money to banking. Nonetheless, over the years, currency has not been limited to coinage and paper money has not been restricted to banking.

It is thus quite clear that the issuance and regulation of digital currencies as money is in the hands of Parliament. Nonetheless, so far as digital currencies are not strictly speaking "money," as well as when it comes to the transfer of digital assets in general, the provincial legislative power in relation to "Property and Civil Rights in the Province" as well as "Generally all Matters of a merely local or private Nature in the Province"[153] enter into the picture. Nonetheless, even as overlap of jurisdictions is recognized under

---

150 *British North America Act, 1867* (UK), 30 & 31 Vict, c 3; *Constitution Act, 1867* (UK), 30 & 31 Vict, c 3, reprinted in RSC 1985, Appendix II, No 5.

151 *Ibid* at s 91(14), (15), (18), and (20), respectively.

152 Emilio S Binavince and H Scott Fairley, "Banking and the Constitution: Untested Limits of Federal Jurisdiction" (1986) 65 *Canadian Bar Review* 228 at 333–37, albeit focusing on the banking jurisdiction.

153 *Constitution Act, 1867*, above note 150, s 92(13) and (16), respectively.

the "double aspect doctrine,"[154] under what came to be known as "federal paramountcy," "where there are inconsistent (or conflicting) [competent] federal and provincial laws, it is the federal law which prevails."[155] Federal paramountcy may arise from either the impossibility of dual compliance or the frustration of a federal purpose (or its "intention").[156]

A first step in required legislative reform is the establishment of the e-note as a functional equivalent of the paper promissory note so as to lead to the conclusion that the e-banknote is treated as a paper banknote. To that end a draft proposal is appended to this chapter. Such legislation ought to be accompanied by a comprehensive examination on the federal level of all aspects of digitalization of money and the monetary system. In parallel, it is recommended that a provincial law project on proprietary aspects of digital assets is to be launched, ideally by the Uniform Law Conference of Canada. Elements to be addressed and options to be taken in such a project are discussed in the chapter in the context of proprietary aspects of digital coins. However, as a whole, such a project is outside the scope of this study.

154 *Hodge v The Queen* (1883) 9 App Cas 117 (PC) 130.

155 Peter W Hogg and Wade K Wright, *Constitutional Law of Canada*, 5th ed (Thomson Reuters, 2023) §§ 16:1, 16:2.

156 *Quebec (AG) v Canadian Owners and Pilots Association* 2010 SCC 39 at paras 25–61, 64.

Appendix

DRAFT PROPOSAL FOR ELECTRONIC PROMISSORY NOTES ACT [OR BILLS OF EXCHANGE ACT/BEA PART VI]

I. PREFATORY NOTE

Proposal particularly draws from Section 16 of the *US UNIFORM ELEC-TRONIC TRANSACTIONS ACT* (1999) (*UETA*) and to a much less extent from the US UCC Article 12 – CONTROLLABLE ELECTRONIC RECORDS (2022), *UNCITRAL Model Law on Electronic Transferable Records* (2018), and UNIDROIT Principles on Digital Assets and Private Law.

It is proposed to have the draft statute apply with necessary modifications to notes intended for circulation in Canada issued by the Bank of Canada under Section 25(6) of the *Bank of Canada Act* RSC 1985 c. B-2.

II. TEXT

Article 1: Definitions
In this Act [BEA PART]:

(a) *"Electronic promissory note" means an electronic record that would be a promissory note under [the BEA], if it were in writing.*
(b) *"Electronic record" means information generated, communicated, received or stored by electronic means, including, where appropriate, all information logically associated with or otherwise linked together so as to become part of the record, whether generated contemporaneously or not;*
(c) *"Electronic signature" means electronic information that a person creates or adopts in order to sign a document and that is in, attached to or associated with the electronic promissory note.*

Article 2: Application of the BEA
The provisions of the BEA apply with the necessary modifications, to electronic promissory notes. In particular:

(a) *Any signature requirement is met by an electronic signature which is reliable for the purpose of identifying the person, and where its association with the relevant electronic document is reliable.*
(b) *Any possession requirement is met where a reliable method is used to establish control;*
(c) *Any delivery or transfer of possession is met by where a reliable method is used to establish transfer of control over the electronic promissory note;*

(*d*) *Any requirement that information should be in writing is met with respect to an electronic promissory note if the information contained therein is accessible so as to be usable for subsequent reference;*

(*e*) *Any presentment requirement is met by displaying the electronic promissory note as to be visible in full to the person to whom it is presented;*

Article 3: Control-Alternative A

(*a*) *A person has control of an electronic promissory note if a system reliably establishes that person as the person to which the electronic promissory note was issued or transferred so that this person has the exclusive power to enforce or transfer the electronic promissory note,*

(*b*) *Subject to paragraph (c), a person has the exclusive power under paragraph (a) even where the power is shared with another person.*

(*c*) *A power of a person is not shared with another person under paragraph (b) and the person's power is not exclusive under paragraph (a) if:*

    (1) *the person can exercise the power only if the power also is exercised by the other person: and*

    (2) *the other person:*

        (A) *can exercise the power without exercise of the power by the person or*

        (B) *is the transferor to the person of the electronic promissory note.*

(*d*) *A person that has control under this section is not required to acknowledge that it has control on behalf of another person.*

(*e*) *If a person acknowledges that it has or will obtain control on behalf of another person, unless the person otherwise agrees or law other than this chapter otherwise provides, the person does not owe any duty to the other person and is not required to confirm the acknowledgement to any other person.*

(*f*) *A system satisfies paragraph (a), and a person is deemed to have control of an electronic promissory note, if the electronic promissory note is created, stored, and assigned in such a manner that:*

    (1) *a single authoritative copy of the electronic promissory note exists which is unique, identifiable, and, except as otherwise provided in paragraphs (4), (5), and (6), unalterable;*

    (2) *the authoritative copy identifies the person asserting control as:*

        (A) *the person to which the electronic promissory note was issued; or*

        (B) *if the authoritative copy indicates that the electronic promissory note has been transferred, the person to which the electronic promissory note was most recently transferred;*

    (3) *the authoritative copy is communicated to and maintained by the person asserting control or its designated custodian;*

    (4) *copies or revisions that add or change an identified assignee of the authoritative copy can be made only with the consent of the person asserting control;*

> (5) each copy of the authoritative copy and any copy of a copy is readily iden-
> tifiable as a copy that is not the authoritative copy; and
> (6) any revision of the authoritative copy is readily identifiable as authorized
> or unauthorized.

==

Article 3: Control-Alternative B

(1) A person has "control" of an electronic promissory note if:
  (a) subject to paragraphs (2) and (3), the electronic promissory note, or the relevant protocol or system, confers on that person:
    (i) the exclusive ability to prevent others from obtaining substantially all of the benefit from the electronic promissory note;
    (ii) the ability to obtain substantially all of the benefit from the electronic promissory note; and
    (iii) the exclusive ability to transfer the abilities in sub-paragraphs (a)(i), (a)(ii) and (a)(iii) to another person; and
  (b) the electronic promissory note, or the relevant protocols or system, allows that person to identify itself as having the abilities set out in sub-paragraph (a).
(2) A "change of control" means a transfer of the abilities in sub-paragraph (1)(a) to another person, and includes the replacement, modification, destruction, cancellation, or elimination of an electronic promissory note, and the resulting and corresponding derivative creation of a new electronic promissory note (a "resulting electronic promissory note") which is subject to the control of another person.
(3) An ability for the purposes of sub-paragraph (1)(a) need not be exclusive if and to the extent that:
  (a) the electronic promissory note, or the relevant protocol or system, limits the use of, or is programmed to make changes to, the electronic promissory note, including change or loss of control of the electronic promissory note; or
  (b) the person in control has agreed, consented to, or acquiesced in sharing that ability with one or more other persons.
(4) In any proceeding in which a person's control of an electronic promissory note is at issue:
  (a) it is sufficient for that person to demonstrate that the identification requirement in Article 3(1)(b) is satisfied in respect of the abilities specified in Article 3(1)(a);
  (b) if that person demonstrates that it has the abilities specified in Article 3(1)(a)(i) and 3(1)(a)(iii), those abilities are presumed to be exclusive.
(5) The identification mentioned in Article 3(1)(b) may be by a reasonable means, including (but not limited to) an identifying number, a cryptographic key, an office, or an account number, even if the means of identification does not indicate.

==

Article 4: Proof of Control

If requested by a person against which enforcement is sought, the person seeking to enforce the electronic promissory note shall provide reasonable proof that the person is in control of the electronic promissory note. Proof may include access to the authoritative copy of the electronic promissory note and related business records sufficient to review the terms of the electronic promissory note and to establish the identity of the person having control of the electronic promissory note.

Article 5: Proof of Reliability

For the purposes of this Law, the method to prove reliability or otherwise referred to shall be:

(a) *As reliable as appropriate for the fulfilment of the function for which the method is being used, in the light of all relevant circumstances, which may include:*
   (i) *Any operational rules relevant to the assessment of reliability;*
   (ii) *The assurance of data integrity;*
   (iii) *The ability to prevent unauthorized access to and use of the system;*
   (iv) *The security of hardware and software;*
   (v) *The regularity and extent of audit by an independent body;*
   (vi) *The existence of a declaration by a supervisory body, an accreditation body or a voluntary scheme regarding the reliability of the method;*
   (vii) *Any applicable industry standard; or*
(b) *Proven in fact to have fulfilled the function by itself or together with further evidence.*

Article 6: Notice

With regard to electronic promissory notes notices may be sent in any format allowed under [the BEA] as well as in an electronic record capable of retention by the recipient at the time of receipt. An electronic record is not capable of retention by the recipient if the sender or its information processor inhibits the ability of the recipient to print or store the electronic record

Article 7: Application to Bank of Canada Notes[157]

Notwithstanding Section 25(6) of the Bank of Canada Act RSC 1985 c. B-2 this Law applies to notes as defined in Section 2 of that Act, [and unless the context requires otherwise,] except that the Governor as defined in Section 2 of that Act may issue directives exempting such notes from BEA provisions specified by the directive.

---

157 Alternative approaches could be either to designate in advance which BEA provisions will not apply or to specify that only selected provisions of this law will apply to Bank of Canada notes.

chapter seven

NON-STATE COMMUNITY CURRENCIES

SYNOPSIS

A "community currency" is a non-bank privately issued currency. Alongside the state issued currency it is used in a particular community, whether defined by geography or otherwise. Historically, its use often arose due to the scarcity of state issued monetary objects. The digitalization of currency has resulted in the formation of new monetary communities, whose widespread acceptance of a particular digital currency is sufficient to make it a community currency. A community currency is money despite not being legal tender, since money under the common law is that which passes freely between members of society and is widely accepted (even under economic duress) as payment in final discharge of debts. While caselaw focused on banknotes, its broad principles apply to community scrips and privately issued digital currencies. Community money need not be fitted with perfect monetary features, and in any event the common law is not entirely clear regarding the ability of privately issued money to function as an absolute payment in every case. While privately issued currencies may continue to function as less-than-perfect monetary objects, the use of digital currency in business activities ought to be regulated in an effort to promote financial stability.

SUMMARY OF CONTENTS

I. INTRODUCTION

This chapter addresses non-bank privately issued currencies in both paper and digital forms. **Part II** is an introductory explanation to the meaning and scope of "community currency" as a non-bank privately issued currency. It needs not necessarily be backed by 100 percent reserve of fiat currency or any other asset so as to be in its digital form a stablecoin (discussed in chapter 4). **Part III** reminds the reader that money is not necessarily "legal tender" and hence need not be exclusively issued by the state. **Part IV** addresses the relationship between "acceptance" and "community." **Part V** outlines the origins of community money highlighting the point of "acceptance." **Part VI** proceeds to address the possible impact of digitalization, particularly in the form of permissionless digital access, on "monetary community." The chapter goes on to address the legal history of the banknote (**Part VII**), the application of its lessons to the community paper-based money (**Part VIII**), and subsequently to digital currencies (**Part IX**). The discussion is designed to demonstrate the convergence between the socio-historical and legal approaches and thus confirms the broad meaning of "money" covering community currency in general and in relation to digital currencies in particular. Benefits of community currencies are briefly discussed in **Part X**. The conclusion in **Part XI** is that the law is flexible so as to accord monetary status to anything accepted as money. As well, concerns with financial stability and the protection of the public justify some form of regulation of business activity in relation to digital community currencies. In the final analysis, particularly with the broader perspective digitalization gave to the meaning of "community," "community money" does not distinguish itself as a separate category of "private money."

II. WHAT IS A COMMUNITY CURRENCY?

Broadly speaking, community currencies are non-bank privately issued currencies. They are means of payment issued other than by the state. They are designed to be voluntarily used, side by side with state-issued (that is, national) currency, either in a particular geographical area or by a group of users. This chapter deals with them as their media has been transforming from paper to digital. Discussing the legal aspects of digital community currencies as monetary objects, this chapter combines two perspectives. The first is an analysis general to the law of community currencies regardless of the media in which they are embodied. The second is an analysis of the general law governing digital currencies as applied to community currencies. In their digital form, community currencies may also be stablecoins discussed in chapter 4.

Community currencies may be issued by an individual, non-profit association, business, or a public, regional, or local authority. Where the community is geographically defined the currency is said to be local or regional. Otherwise, the community currency is spoken of as being parallel or complementary.[1] By reference to their availability for use side by side with national currencies, community currencies may be referred to as alternative currencies.[2] Literature is not precise on terminology and all such terms are often used interchangeably. Since local currencies may be the largest category of community currencies, these two terms are frequently used indiscriminately, a point to be kept in mind throughout this chapter.

The group using the currency, whether or not it is geographically based, may be referred to as a "monetary community." Its governance may be democratic or hierarchical. It may be formed either for-profit, for the mutual benefit of its members, or for the enhancement of a cause to which the participants adhere.

A community currency may take diverse forms. It may evolve from barter into the use of a unit of account reflecting the value of a given product or amount of labour,[3] which may be evaluated in the national currency. Such a system may operate as an exchange of mutual or reciprocal credit system.

---

1   For this classification see Stephen DeMeulenaere, "An Overview of Parallel, and Community Currency Systems" (1998), online: http://www.appropriate-economics.org/materials/overview_of_Parallel_Local_and_Community_Currencies.pdf, accessed 30 June 2024; for even more extensive information of complementary currencies see Wikipedia, "Complementary Currency," online: https://en.wikipedia.org/wiki/Complementary_currency, accessed 30 June 2024.

2   Caroline Kenny, "Alternative Currencies" (POST Note No 475, Houses of Parliament: Parliamentary Office of Science and Technology 2014), online: http://researchbriefings.parliament.uk/ResearchBriefing/Summary/POST-PN-475#fullreport, accessed 30 June 2024.

3   According to Jérôme Blanc, "Local Currencies in European History: an Analytical Framework" (2006) HAL Open Science, online: https://ideas.repec.org/p/hal/journl/halshs-00102974.html, accessed 30 June 2024, the first local currency was envisioned and executed by Robert Owen,

Among such systems, Local Exchange Trading Systems (LETS) are denominated in the national currency while Time Banks systems are denominated in service hours. As well, to the extent they can be used to buy goods or services from third parties, reward miles extended by airlines to their customers constitute a form of money.[4] Alternatively, a community currency could be a scrip, namely a circulating document reflecting its issuer's IOU obligation to pay the bearer, denominated, either at its own unit of account, such as service hours,[5] or in the unit of account of the national currency.[6] As an alternative mode of financing, scrips (as well as credits) may be issued at discounted value by retail business to consumers for future purchases at their full face value. Or else scrips and credits may be issued as promotional tools.[7] Retailers and suppliers may also purchase community currency directly from the issuer.[8] Scrips may circulate in the community until they are redeemed, at which point, they may be re-issued. To achieve success, scrip circulation must occur "in a circle," "forming a closed loop, that involves only participants in the system, both with respect to exchanges of the ... currency for goods and services, and exchanges of goods and services for the ... currency."[9]

Historically, some non-bank private money was a response to the scarcity of monetary objects sanctioned by the state particularly for low

in the form of "labour notes" exchanged first in Indiana (US) in 1824 and then in a "National Labour Exchange" in England in 1832–34.

4   See Bradley Crawford, "Reward Miles: An Important New Medium of Payment" (2013) 28 *Banking and Finance Law Review* 213.

5   Lewis D Solomon, "Local Currency: A legal policy Analysis" (1995) 5 *Kansas J of L & Policy* 59, 74–76.

6   It is distinguished from trading stamps which were mostly outlawed in the United States and Canada at the turn of the twentieth century that were given as a discount to a purchaser against the promise to redeem them of someone other than the seller (who typically overcharged). See Bradley Crawford, "New Methods of Payment and New Forms of Money" (2004–05) 20 *Banking and Finance Law Review* 393 at 398–402.

7   See Gregory A Krohn and Alan M Snyder, "An Economic Analysis of Contemporary Local Currencies in the United States" (2008) 12 *International Journal of Community Currency Research* 53 at 55–56, online: https://ijccr.files.wordpress.com/2012/05/ijccrvol122008krohn.pdf, accessed 30 June 2024; and in greater detail see Solomon, above note 5 at 74–81.

8   Mona Naqvi and James Southgate, "Banknotes, local currencies and central bank objectives" (*Bank of England*, Quarterly Bulletin 2013 Q4) at 322 Figure 2, online: https://www.bankofengland.co.uk/quarterly-bulletin/2013/q4/banknotes-local-currencies-and-central-bank-objectives, accessed 30 June 2024.

9   For this expression see Marussa V Freire, "Social Economy and Central Bank: Legal and Regulatory Issues on Social Currency (Social Money) as a Public Policy Instrument Consistent with Monetary Policy" (2009) 13 *International Journal of Community Currency Research* 76 at 84, online: https://ijccr.files.wordpress.com/2012/05/ijccrvol132009pp76-94freire.pdf, accessed 30 June 2024.

denomination. Scarcity resulted from logistical reasons as well as lack of interest by the state in the needs of poor people who heavily used "tokens" issued by traders as well as local authorities. Use of such tokens has not been sanctioned and yet is tolerated by the state.[10]

By way of example, between 1649–1672, more than 10,000 issuers issued 13,000+ known types of tokens in 1,566 locations all over England and Wales. The majority of the tokens stated the issuer's identity (by an inscription of their name or initials), their location, and occupation (by an inscription or iconography, such as the coat of arms of a particular livery company), and the year of issue. Issuers were among many professions: butchers, bakers, candlestick makers, and coffee shop and inn owners, which explains why the tokens are known as "trade tokens," "traders," or "tradesmen's token."[11] On the debate of whether tokens were made in one place or were localized, it was argued that they were semi-centralized, with manufacturing in London and dies for the tokens created for different locations. Furthermore, it is believed that the Royal Mint's personnel used the mint to create private tokens as a side job, though issuing also existed outside the mint as well.

This meant that the tokens declared in 1672 by King Charles II to be a crime were at least partly issued by the same people who issued King Charles II's own official coinage. There was no evidence that those involved in creating dies, working the presses, or distributing the tokens were prosecuted in any way. This suggests that although the tokens were seen as a trade nuisance and a problem relating to the poor, they were not regarded as a threat to the sovereign or state.[12]

The disappearance of privately issued tokens can partly be explained by the great recoinage of 1816, which reformed the value of silver and copper to be redefined as representative of gold coinage, rather than having an intrinsic value of their own. This signaled the beginning of the gold standard. The fact that silver and copper acquired a symbolic value in relation to gold meant that the ongoing problem of maintaining sufficient metallic content in small change was officially solved.[13] However, in Ben-Or's view, the resolution of the "small change" problem and the resulting disappearance of private coins

10   For a comprehensive study see Idit Ben-Or, "Non-governmental Monies in Early Modern England: A Social, Political and Material Culture Analysis" (Thesis for the degree of "Doctor of Philosophy" submitted to the senate of the Hebrew University of Jerusalem, January 2021).

11   *Ibid* at 34.

12   *Ibid* at 90–93.

13   *Ibid* at 181, 193–94. More specifically, the author speaks at 194 of silver and *gold* having a symbolic relation to gold. From the context, I take this to be a typo so that I read the author to say silver and *copper* had symbolic value in relation to gold.

cannot be understood without the enhanced aspiration of the state to control the financial sphere.[14]

Canada has a rich history of non-bank private money, consisting of "coins and paper scrip produced by individuals and companies, which commanded sufficient confidence within a community that they circulated freely."[15] As pointed out in chapter 2, both in New France and for the first decades after the British takeover, well into early nineteenth century, paper scrips not backed by specie were issued by merchants as "bons" and tokens, to be used to buy goods in the issuer's stores. These were IOUs – that quickly began to change hands as money, with their value and the extent of the circulation depended on the reputation of the issuer. Similarly, brass and copper tokens, issued either privately or by authorities (albeit without legal backing), circulated and served in payment of small amounts. In fact, trade tokens remained popular into the 1930s even as most colonial tokens were taken out of circulation shortly after confederation. The "prosperity certificates," issued by Alberta's Social Credit government during the Great Depression of the 1930s and further discussed below, is another example to that end.[16]

So far as Canada is concerned, Powell distinguishes between such "alternative money"[17] and "community money." He restricts the latter to "scrip or alternative currencies that could be used locally to buy goods and services" in "typically" isolated communities.[18] He gives a few examples, namely, notes issued by William Lyon Mackenzie following his abortive 1837 rebellion; during the second half of the nineteenth century by Calvin & Son – a family owned firm on Garden Island located in Lake Ontario near Kingston; and since 2001 by Salt Spring Island, British Columbia.[19] While not circulating in an isolated community, broadly speaking, the now defunct Toronto Dollar can be added to this list.[20]

For two reasons I do not find Powell's distinction between "alternative money" and "community money" to be persuasive. First, there is no exact borderline between "limited" and "wide" use on which his distinction lies.

---

14   *Ibid* at 201.

15   James Powell, *A History of the Canadian Dollar* (Bank of Canada 1999) at 92, online: https://www.bankofcanada.ca/wp-content/uploads/2010/07/dollar_book.pdf, accessed 15 July 2024.

16   *Ibid* at 92–94. Note, however, that he includes Canadian Tire "money," which to the best of my knowledge does not circulate but is rather strictly used for redemption of goods sold by the issuer.

17   *Ibid.*

18   *Ibid* at 95.

19   *Ibid* at 95–96.

20   For an overview visit Wikipedia, "Toronto Dollar," online: https://en.wikipedia.org/wiki/Toronto_dollar, accessed 30 June 2024.

Second, which is more important, there is no conceptual difference between money used in a vast territory (whatever its size is) and a small community (whatever its size is). Such a difference may concern the economist – in terms of impact on monetary policy – but is of no interest to the lawyer. On another level, there may be a distinction between money effectively *imposed* on a community – and one *created* by a community (that is, "top-down" versus "down-top"). Such a distinction is of no concern in the present study that focuses on the *acceptance* of private money by a community. Accordingly, this chapter uses "alternative money" and "community currency" interchangeably.

At present scrips may be substituted by digital currencies. Throughout this chapter "digital currency" is taken to mean "virtual currency." It consists of privately issued digital coins of which each is "an entity that amounts to a string of bits" which must have a numerical value and a unique identity.[21] For its part, a "cryptocurrency" is a digital currency in which encryption techniques are used to regulate the generation of units of currency and verify the execution of payment transactions[22] on a decentralized network. Where it does not have an issuer, it is likely to have founders or promoters of its technology. Present digital community currencies are overwhelmingly cryptocurrencies.

Participants in a digital currency scheme may use a centralized network or permissioned decentralized one.[23] A permissionless decentralized network[24] such as Bitcoin may not be seen as facilitating a community currency as by definition it is open to all. On the other hand, the voluntary basis of participation in an open permissionless network makes its currency akin to that of a community, the latter being defined by the participation in the network.

---

21   Gideon Samid, *Tethered Money: Managing Digital Currency Transactions* (Academic Press, 2015) at 105–06.

22   This definition slightly modifies that from The Wolf of Crypto, "Basic Cryptocurrency Starter Guide" (*Medium*, 18 September 2017), online: https://medium.com/@Wolfofcrypto /basic-cryptocurrency-starter-guide-8f2071ea85de, accessed 18 June 2024. Specifically, I replaced "transfer of funds" with the "execution of payment transactions" to highlight payment by the transmission of "coins" rather than "generic value" in the forms of funds.

23   For centralized, decentralized, and hybrid models see e.g., Dong He et al, "Virtual Currencies and Beyond: Initial Considerations" (SDN/16/3, International Monetary Fund 2016) at 8–9, online: www.imf.org/external/pubs/ft/sdn/2016/sdn1603.pdf, accessed 28 May 2024.

24   For permissioned and permissionless decentralized schemes see e.g., UK Government Chief Scientific Adviser, "Distributed Ledger Technology: beyond block chain" (UK Government Office for Science 2016) at 17, online: https://www.gov.uk/government/uploads/system /uploads/attachment_data/file/492972/gs-16-1-distributed-ledger-technology.pdf, accessed 28 May 2024.

III. MONEY – NOT NECESSARILY STATE-ISSUED

While "[t]he right of issuing notes for payment of money, as part of the circulating medium" is said to belong to "the supreme power in every State,"[25] there is a solid line of caselaw from which it may be concluded that "money" is not limited to state-issued currency. Thus, in *Miller v Race* (1758), referring to banknotes issued by the Bank of England prior to them becoming eligible for a legal tender, Lord Mansfield observed that they were "treated as money, as cash, in the ordinary course and transactions of business, by the general consent of mankind." He went on to conclude that this "[gave] them the credit and currency of money, to all intents and purposes" so as to be "money,"[26] the latter being "whatever common consent has fixed upon as a sign denoting a certain value."[27]

Subsequently, albeit dealing with a coin, Darling J expressed his view in *Moss v Hancock* (1899)[28] that "money" is,

> that which passes freely from hand to hand throughout the community in final discharge of debts ... being accepted equally without reference to the character or credit of the person who offers it and without the intention of the person who receives it to consume it.

Along the same lines, Duff CJ said in *Reference Re Alberta Statutes* (1938):[29]

> [M]oney as commonly understood is not necessarily legal tender. Any medium which by practice fulfils the function of money and which everybody will accept in payment of a debt is money in the ordinary sense of the words.

By saying that any medium that "by practice fulfils the function of money" is money (provided "everybody will accept [it] in payment of a debt in money"), Duff CJ shifted the focus of the discussion from what money *is* to what money *does*, that is, to the function fulfilled by money, namely, the payment of a debt. Anything that fulfills this task in a given societal point is thus "money" regardless of what it is made of and/or who is its issuer.

Caselaw in the United States has been to a similar end. Thus, the US Constitution[30] confers on Congress the power "To coin Money [and] regulate the

---

25   *The Emperor of Austria v Day* (1861) 3 De G F&J 217, 234; 45 ER 861 at 868, per Lord Campbell.

26   *Miller v Race* (1758) 1 Burr 452 at 457; 97 ER 398 at 401.

27   (1758) 2 Keny 189 at 199; 96 ER 1151 at 1154 [Notes of Cases in KB].

28   *Moss v Hancock* [1899] 2 QB 111 at 116.

29   [1938] SCR 100 at 116.

30   US Const art I, § 8; for constitutional aspects of money issuance in the US, see e.g., Thomas Wilson, *The Power "to Coin" Money: The Exercise of Monetary Powers by the Congress* (ME Sharp,

Value thereof." Under other provisions of the Constitution, states are precluded from coining money and emitting "bills of credit."[31] As well, there is a long history of federal legislation restricting private coinage. However, both the legitimation of the use of any "current money," even a prohibited one, and the issue and use of non-legal tender non-coined money have generally been recognized.[32]

To that end, as a generic term, "money" was said to be "any circulating medium in general use as the representative of value,"[33] or "anything that circulates as the ordinary medium of exchange in buying and selling property."[34] Accordingly, "money" is:

> [E]verything which by consent is made to represent property, and passes as such currently from hand to hand, whether it be the iron of the Spartans, the cowrie of the African, the gold and silver of the world, or the paper of modern Europe and America[35]

However, the presence of "consent" must be by reference to "acceptance" in and by a "community." True, in any given transaction, parties may bilaterally agree on what is to be accepted as money. Nonetheless, on its own, a bilateral agreement will not elevate an item into "money." For its part, acceptance in the community must lead to "consent" to receive the item without any concern over the payer's credentials, as long as it is made in good faith and without suspicion of the payer's title.[36]

IV. EXCHANGE, COMMUNITY, AND MONEY – CHICKEN AND EGG? (Written by Dorit Geva)

Whether something is "money" thus depends on its *acceptance in the community as a medium of exchange for the discharge of debts.* There is no obligation to accept as money something which is not "legal tender." However, arguably, acceptance in a community of something as money may give rise in each case

---

1991); see also Ali Khan, "The Evolution of Money: A Story of Constitutional Nullification" (1999) 67 *University of Cincinnati Law Review* 393.

31   US Const art I, §10.

32   There may, however, be restrictions by a few states. For the legal position in the United States, see discussion by Solomon, above note 5 at 81–86.

33   *Johnson v State* 52 So 652 (Ala 1910).

34   *State v Finnegan* 103 NW 155 (Iowa 1905).

35   *Ibid, cf Rhodes v Lindly,* 3 Ohio 51 (OH 1827), where payment "in good merchantable whisky" was held not to be payment in money presumably in the absence of proof as to its acceptability as such.

36   *Cf London Joint Stock Bank v Simmon* [1892] AC 201 (HL).

to a rebuttable presumption of consent or advance agreement by a member of that community to accept that thing as money, at least when tendered in payment by a member of that community.[37] Given this, are "acceptance" and "community" two distinct factors courts should consider in assessing whether something is "money"?

From the perspective of economic sociology, the answer is negative. For any practice to be accepted, it must already be organized within the boundaries of a community. Therefore, as a norm, "acceptance" implies an already-existing community. Émile Durkheim argued that morals and norms which bind a community are continuously reproduced through everyday practices, and that there is no proverbial chicken preceding the egg, or egg preceding the chicken, when it comes to norms and society.[38] Norms create society, while society creates norms.

Marcell Mauss extended some of Durkheim's insights to his analysis of economic exchange. Mauss argued that exchange relations are by definition social relations, which operate through formal and informal rules, with collective symbolic, and moral dimensions, and that exchange *creates* social relations.[39] Mauss's own analysis compared the gift economy in multiple "primitive" societies, and how giving and receiving gifts ought not to be seen as acts of generous benevolence, but rather as cultivating relations of obligation and networks of reciprocity.[40] Exchange relations, in line with the chicken and egg, are postulated to create social bonds, and are organized by the social bonds. Communities are the product of exchange, and networks of exchange constantly reproduce communities.

Money, in this tradition, has some unique features, but is not that unique in the framework of exchange analyzed by economic sociology and economic anthropology. Emphasizing the unique aspect of capitalist money, sociologist Georg Simmel claimed that capitalist money is distinct because it is an

---

37   For a statutory recognition of this principle, albeit probably only in connection with the use of foreign currency, see e.g., Section 1 UN Administration in Kosovo, "REGULATION NO.1999/4 ON THE CURRENCY PERMITTED TO BE USED IN KOSOVO" (UNMIK Regulation No 1999/4, 2 September 1999), online: https://www.bqk-kos.org/repository/docs/2010/UNMIK_REG_1999_4.pdf, accessed 19 June 2024, providing that "Parties to a contract or any other voluntary transaction may denominate such transaction in any currency agreed upon by the parties. Unless proven otherwise, such an agreement shall be deemed to exist with regard to any foreign currency that is widely accepted in the territory of Kosovo."

38   Emile Durkheim and Karen E Fields, *The Elementary Forms of Religious Life* (Free Press, 1995).

39   Bill Maurer, "The Anthropology of Money" (2006) 35 *Annual Review of Anthropology* 15.

40   Marcel Mauss and WD Halls, *The Gift: The Form and Reason for Exchange in Archaic Societies* (WW Norton, 1990).

abstract unit of value, which emphasizes "quantity" over "quality."[41] Inspired by some of Karl Marx's analysis of the capitalist commodity form, Simmel argued that capitalist money transformed qualitatively specific objects, and the qualitatively specific social relations and individuals who produced them, into goods and services to be exchanged in the abstract and impersonal capitalist market.[42] Simmel thus argued that the capitalist money economy tended to flatten and homogenize social relations.

However, others since Simmel, especially the sociologist Viviana Zelizer, have shown that despite the features of capitalist money identified by Simmel, like Mauss's gift exchange, money still creates relations of reciprocity, and is morally bounded.[43] Like all systems of exchange, money can only be exchanged for other units of money, or exchanged for other goods and services, if there is social acceptance regarding its legitimacy. This legitimacy has multiple dimensions. It needs to be accepted as a store of value, and of equal importance, the exchange is made possible only if those engaging in the exchange agree that the goods and services are operating within the boundaries of what is socially permitted.

Whether or not there is a sovereign state conferring this legitimacy is not central to this sociological view of money. The currency issued by the sovereign state is but one variant of money, albeit a historically prominent one which became central to the modern "political economy" described by

---

41   Georg Simmel, *The Philosophy of Money* (David Frisby (ed and tr), Tom Bottomore (tr)) (Routledge, 2004).

42   Karl Marx's monumental three-volume *Capital* begins with his analysis of the peculiarity of the capitalist commodity form. In the first pages of volume I he identifies what he views as the essential features of the commodity form. Here he makes his famous distinction between "use-value" and "exchange-value." Use-value is what is qualitatively specific about a commodity; specific labour skills, specific people in a specific place, specifics materials, and hence, creating a very specific object with a particular use. This use-value is a necessary feature of the capitalist commodity form, and not in itself unique to capitalist commodities. But what is peculiar to the capitalist commodity form, according to Marx, is the extreme manner by which use-values are transformed into exchange-values. Exchange-value is how value is identified in a commodity, which in capitalism entails erasing, even denying, the socially specific labour relations, labour skills, and labour time that goes into the production of a commodity – which he claimed was the source of surplus value, or profit – and then in determining its exchange-value. Hence, the twofold nature of the commodity form, according to Marx, lies in this combination of its specificity as a use-value, and then its transformation into a generic exchange-value through the historic creation of "abstract labour" made possible by capitalist relations of production; in Karl Marx, *Capital: A Critique of Political Economy; Volume I* (Lawrence & Wishart, 1983). See also Moishe Postone, *Time, Labor, and Social Domination: A Reinterpretation of Marx's Critical Theory* (Cambridge University Press, 1995).

43   *Cf* Viviana Zelizer, *The Social Meaning of Money* (Basic Books, 1994), and Viviana Zelizer, *The Purchase of Intimacy* (Princeton University Press, 2007).

economic historian Karl Polanyi.[44] Furthermore, on its own, currency issued by the state may fail to become "money." More generally, if an individual, group, or a unit of government tries to introduce a new money or scrip into circulation, but no one accepts that it represents value, and no one is willing to therefore engage in the "magic," which converts one specific use-value (e.g., goods) into an abstract exchange-value, this is not *de facto* money. This is the "magic" of money, sometimes called "commensurability" by some sociologists, in reference to the social codes that enable making commensurable, or equivalent, one thing to another.[45] An everyday transaction, made so banal by the capitalist money economy, in which one exchanges, for example, a single dollar coin for a package of chewing gum at a local corner store, contains a complex world of trust, social solidarity, communal ties, legitimacy, and moral boundaries. This is as true for a community currency as it is for state-issued currencies.

This sociological view converges with the legal view that money cannot operate where there is not sufficient consent around its legitimacy and its representation of value. In *Moss v Hancock* (1899)[46] there is specific reference to circulation which is "accepted" within "the community." In *Reference Re Alberta Statutes* (1938),[47] there is recognition of the *de facto* "practice" of accepting money as payment of debt, and where "everybody," although not explicitly identified as such in the judgment, ought to be understood as "everybody in the community."

As well, in the sociological perspective taken here, controversies are also telling markers of whether or not a community exists.[48] Debates over boundaries of appropriate rules and norms suggest that a group of individuals are relationally oriented around a shared project. In that shared project individuals who might have distinct interests also have a stake in defining the boundaries of appropriate behaviour and membership in a community. For example, refusal to accept state-issued paper money with one of its corners torn off does not in itself undermine the legitimacy of the money in general. On the contrary, it reproduces the boundaries of acceptable money. Or,

---

44 Karl Polanyi, *The Great Transformation* (Beacon Press, 1957). This work is a social and intellectual history of the development of the capitalist market economy and the development of the modern state's management of the crises of capitalism.

45 Bruce G Carruthers and Wendy Nelson Espeland, "Money, meaning, and morality" (1998) 41 *American Behavioural Scientist* 1384.

46 Above note 28.

47 Above note 29.

48 See Luc Boltanski and Laurent Thévenot, *On Justification: Economies of Worth* (Princeton University Press, 2006).

as another example, the moral claim that a child cannot be sold as a commodity,[49] that is, that a human being is not commensurable to units of exchange-value represented by money, also does not undermine the legitimacy of money. Here there is a possible divergence between the legal and sociological views. The legal view of money emphasizes practical consensus within a community. The economic sociologist agrees that practical consensus is likewise essential to money, but also sees contestation over appropriate use of money as defining a community of users and the practical viability and acceptance of money.

With this view of money exchange as constituting a community and vice versa, community currencies unquestionably constitute communities. Whether they entail an exchange of goods, services, or paper money, they are privately issued systems of money, accruing credit and discharging debt between actors who adhere to the formal and informal rules of the currency framework. While community currencies are often designed to serve a small, pre-existing group, they can also be used as schemes to foster civic engagement and collective solidarities.[50] They are therefore explicitly relational, not only reflecting pre-existing community relations, but sometimes organized to strengthen a community. To the extent that they take on a money form, token form, or any unit which represents a unit of credit or exchange, they must retain the feature of being a means of accounting for exchange-value. They cannot, and often do not, survive if they do not meet some minimal level of economic viability as a means of measuring and exchanging value.[51] And if there are debates among its users, this is often a good sign of an active and engaged community.

V. HOW FAR OUGHT ACCEPTANCE BE FREE? LESSONS FROM HISTORY

History proves the crucial importance of "acceptance" of a circulating medium for the characterization and success of an item of property as "money." History also teaches us that suffice it for economic conditions and selfish motives to generate the societal acceptance of something as money.

---

49   *Cf* Viviana Zelizer, *Pricing the Priceless Child: The Changing Social Value of Children* (Basic Books, 1985).

50   Jérôme Blanc, *"Penser la pluralité des monnaies à partir de Polanyi: un essai de typologie"* dans *Socioéconomie et démocratie: L'actualité de Karl Polanyi* [2013] ERES 241.

51   Michael S Evans, "Zelizer's Theory of Money and the Case of Local Currencies" (2009) 41 *Environment and Planning* 1026.

Thus, during the nineteenth century in the United States, tokens issued by transportation companies and fractional paper currencies issued by municipal bodies, were designed to meet shortages in legal tender.[52] Scrips issued in the United States by mining companies between 1820 and 1940, serving as advance payments of wages[53] are said to be the forerunners of community currency.[54] However, such scrips were designed to facilitate payment for goods and services provided by the issuer.[55]

Subsequently experimentation took place in small towns on both sides of the Atlantic amidst the pre-Second World War Great Depression.[56] An uncontested milestone came to be known as the "Miracle of Woergl" or the "Woergl Experiment." It took place in the small Tyrolese town of Woergl (Wörgl) in Austria in the early 1930s.[57] To fight unemployment and enhance economic activity, Mayor Michael Unterguggenberger put a small amount on deposit with a local savings bank. Against the security of the deposit *stamp scrip* was issued in the amount of the deposit. There was no final redemption, but the town treasury and local banks would redeem each bill against a 2 percent stamp fee.

Stamp scrip is a medium of exchange for which the holder pays a small monthly "user fee," which is effectively a "negative interest" charge. In Woergl a "Relief Contribution Stamp" was needed to be applied each month at 1 percent of face value. This user fee gave the bearer the incentive not to hoard the bills as each month they depreciated. It thus encouraged spending and enhanced economic activity in a deflationary environment. Moreover, the disadvantages of redemption at 2 percent were at any given moment greater than the probable disadvantages of deferring payments at the cost of 1 percent so that the redemption privilege could not hurt circulation.

The mayor used the stamp scrip to pay for a municipal project. For lack of any real alternative, workers, contractors, and merchants in the town were prepared to be paid by stamp scrip. Also municipal taxes were promptly paid

---

52 Richard H Timberlake, "The Significance of Unaccounted Currencies" (1981) 41 *Journal of Economic History* 853.

53 Richard H Timberlake, "Private Production of Scrip-Money in the Isolated Community" (1987) 19 *Journal of Money, Credit and Banking* 437.

54 Krohn and Snyder, above note 7 at 53, 55.

55 Timberlake, above note 53 at 440.

56 Krohn and Snyder, above note 7 at 55, and further below in this Part.

57 Earlier experimentation in a similar scheme took place in 1932 in the little town of Schanenkirchen in Germany. See Blanc, above note 3. However, this experimentation "did not leave much trace behind." See Fritz Schwarz, "The story of Wörgl" in *The Experiment in Worgl* (Verlags-Genossenschaft Freies Volk, 1951), online: https://www.hanseisenkolb.de /woergl.htm, accessed 30 June 2024.

with the scrips, and were promptly used by the town if only to avoid depreciation.[58] Transactions velocity had thus gained tremendous momentum. The
economy quickly turned around, and the mayor successfully accomplished
a long list of municipal projects. The 1 percent anti-hoarding fee proved extremely effective to generate work, as "[i]n fact, every one of the schillings
in stamp scrip created between 12 and 14 times more employment than the
normal schillings circulating in parallel."[59]

A more ambitious Great Depression project, albeit less successful, and
yet to the same end, was launched in the province of Alberta in Canada by
Premier William Alberhart as part of implementing a social credit vision.[60]
Under section 2 of *The Prosperity Certificates Act* of 1936,[61] the provincial
treasurer of Alberta was "authorized to issue and reissue credit certificates to
any persons who may be willing to accept them." Acceptance ought to have
been in connection with public works undertaken by the provincial government, existing government services, agreements with municipalities relating
to unemployment relief projects, and designated public expenditures. Such
certificates were stated under section 3 to "be known as Alberta Prosperity Certificates."[62] They were to be redeemable after two years at their face
value provided that upon redemption they bear 104 stamps, each reflecting a
1 percent weekly "user fee"[63] designed to discourage hoarding and encourage
spending. Provisions were also made for early redemption, payment of certain taxes,[64] and subsequently, upon the discontinuance of issuance.[65]

The program designers certainly contemplated that driven by economic
difficulties the unemployed would "willingly" accept this certificate (as an
alternative to staying unemployed) knowing very well that local merchants –
starving for business will equally be "willing" to accept them – as they were

---

58 Effectively, however, only about a third of the issue was re-issued by the municipal administration to avoid depreciation by reference to the regular Schilling.

59 Bernard Lietaer, "The Wörgl Experiment: Austria (1932–1933)" (*Currency Solutions for a Wiser
World*, 27 March 2010), online: https://web.archive.org/web/20180702021420/https://www.
lietaer.com/2010/03/the-worgl-experiment/, accessed 30 June 2024 (archived webpage).

60 For a brief historical outline of social credit in Alberta visit e.g., "Bible Bill – About
Social Credit in Alberta" (*MAA & PAA Theatre*), online: https://web.archive.org/
web/20180722030638/http://www.maapaa.ca/past-productions/bible-bill-the-gospel-musical
/bible-bill-about-social-credit-in-alberta/, accessed 30 June 2024 (archived webpage).

61 *An Act Respecting Prosperity Certificates*, SA 1936, c 4.

62 *Ibid*, s 3; various relevant documents are available online: https://www.gosling.ca/apc
/AlbertaProsperityCertificates.pdf, accessed 30 June 2024.

63 *Ibid*, ss 5, 6, and 8.

64 *Ibid*, s 10.

65 *Ibid*, s 10a added under *The Prosperity Certificate Act Amendment Act*, 1937 SA, c 83, s 2.

the only "game in town" so to speak. The project nevertheless failed precisely on the key element of acceptability: "the hassle and expense of the stamps made the certificates unpopular with the public." Inconvenience was caused also by "the tiny postage-style stamps (smaller than 1 cm² (0.16 sq in)) [that] were prone to falling off" and the program was cancelled after about a year.[66]

This early history of community currency proves that "acceptance" may be motivated by necessity and still be effective to turn the scrip into "money." If so agreed in advance, the unemployed will work even for an "inferior" money, particularly as they know that local merchants will accept it for a lack of or inadequate availability of any better means of payments circulating in an impoverished town such as Woergl. Accordingly, the acceptance of a community scrip money as well as of that of digital currency may be motivated by lack of confidence in the state-issued money, something which is not inconceivable particularly in a failing state. At the other extreme, and yet to the same end, participation in a digital currency scheme could be motivated by benefits from its underlying technology. In short, neither "economic duress" nor even greed will disqualify the acceptance of the privately issued "money" driven by it.

VI. DOES DIGITALIZATION CHANGE THE MEANING OF A "MONETARY" COMMUNITY?

Does digitalization change the relationship between money, community, and the meaning of a monetary community? Is a group defined strictly by the use of a currency constituted a "monetary community"? This issue has arisen with digitalization. Heretofore, a community adopted a currency so as to turn it into a community currency. But has digitalization itself – or the participation in a digital currency scheme – turned participants into community members? To what extent, for example, do permissionless cryptocurrencies as subtypes of digital currencies share the same features as community currencies? More specifically, do those users constitute a community in any conventional sense of "community"?

One implication for a positive answer to each question is that the characterization of "digital currency" as "money" squarely falls within the theory under which a community currency is "money." Hence, it is important to

---

66   Wikipedia, "Prosperity Certificate" (*Wikipedia*), online: https://en.wikipedia.org/wiki
      /Prosperity_certificate, accessed 30 June 2024; see also Powell, above note 15 at 94–95.

determine whether the mere existence of a community within which the use of something as "money" is accepted, renders that something "community money." On the other side of the coin, and this may only be a matter of classification, if digitalization does not create a "community," is the currency it uses – assuming it is "money" – a community currency?

At first glance, blockchain users might not appear to constitute a community. They are de-territorialized so as to be distributed geographically and socially in networks of exchange. They accrue credits and discharge debts in applying the blockchains highly formalized distributed network, which looks to be free of moral and social boundaries. They might, therefore, appear to be the highest expression of money's capacity to abstract market relations of exchange from grounded social relations.

The reality, however, is quite different. As economic sociologist Nigel Dodd argued, Bitcoin (a blockchain-utilizing currency), for example, has a thriving social life.[67] The social organization of Bitcoin is not that of a distributed network that mimics its formal characteristics, but rather a community with hierarchy, inequality, and other attributes rife with dispute. The disputes cannot be clearly separated as either normative or technical. Controversies over reforms, updates, and resultant forks, reveal that the technical *is* the normative. Satoshi Nakomoto's white paper is treated like a constitution around which the foundational mission of the coin is debated and interpreted.[68] The Bitcoin Foundation, founded in 2012, was established by a group trying to establish an authoritative claim to leading the community, and mediating between the technical and the normative. Yet its role is also disputed. Such disputes do not indicate dysfunctionality; rather, they indicate sociologically a community of users who care about the use and design of Bitcoin, and its socio-political organization.

Given that blockchain currencies are not just money, but also *technologies*, they cannot be freed of human contestations over the use, reform, and vision of their technology. Even privately controlled coins, such as Ethereum, cannot escape the dynamics of jockeying for control over the coin's destiny. The community around Ethereum actively debates its purpose and technical specifications, sometimes wrestling control away from its founders. This jockeying is perhaps magnified by added functionalities such as smart contracts, which could be seen as use-values integrated into exchange-values.

----

67 Nigel Dodd, "The Social Life of Bitcoin" (2017) 35 *Theory, Culture, and Society* 3 at 35–56.
68 Satoshi Nakamoto, "Bitcoin: A Peer-to-Peer Electronic Cash System" (Bitcoin.org, 2008) at, online: 2 https://bitcoin.org/bitcoin.pdf, accessed 28 May 2024.

Ethereum's founders try to maintain a balance by heading research and design, and taking in community input, but cannot exert absolute control on the coin's technical fate. If enough users mobilize to effect and adopt a reform, creating a definitive and applied fork, then a new sub-community has formed. Digitalization therefore de-territorializes and expands users geographically. It also potentially increases numerically the volume of actors participating in a monetary community. However, digitalization does not fundamentally change the essential sociological features of a monetary community. These features include the *de facto* pre-condition of consent without which no monetary exchange can successfully operate; a sufficiently high degree of trust and normative boundaries enabling actors to agree that one unit of value is commensurate to another; organizational hierarchy and sets of rules of behaviour which are binding such that most actors abide by them; and at the same time, a degree of debate about what constitutes right or wrong behaviour, illustrating a moral investment in the collective project.

Nonetheless, even as participation in a digital currency network may be taken to create a "community" it does not follow that every digital currency is "money." Simply stated, as explained below, not every digital currency is "money" even where it is envisaged as such. This is true for both permissionless networks and permissioned schemes. This is so notwithstanding the fact that "community" indicates "acceptance." The reason is that to be money the digital currency ought to be "accepted" *as money*. The reality, however, is that notwithstanding its "currency" characterization, digital currency may be accepted other than for payment for goods and services but rather for other purposes such as media of investment or else as tokens accessing new technologies.[69] Indeed, as discussed, motivation for acceptance is a non-issue; and yet, acceptance itself, regardless of what motivates it, ought to be as "money."

True, participants in a centralized network or permissionless decentralized scheme may be required to formally agree to accept the relevant digital currency as "money." Nevertheless, the existence of such an agreement may not be conclusive as to its enforcement or the actual use of the digital currency. Stated otherwise, an advance agreement to "accept" something as money will not suffice to turn that something into money; rather, actual acceptance as money is required. An actual advance agreement to accept may be a helpful building block but otherwise is neither a required nor sufficient element in the characterization of something as money.

---

69   See Part VIII below.

A broader issue to be explored is whether, or to what extent, the socio-historic approach is accepted by the law. This issue is addressed in the ensuing three parts of this chapter.

VII. PRIVATELY ISSUED MONEY: DOES LAW CONVERGE WITH ECONOMIC SOCIOLOGY?

Broad judicial statements effectively defining "money" as anything accepted in a community as a medium of exchange were not made in cases involving privately issued currency. Nor were these statements addressed specifically to privately issued money. Hence statements in that regard may well be considered obiter. In short, while the principle pronounced in these cases was broad enough to cover privately issued money, this coverage was not an essential element in the *ratio* of each case. For example, *Moss v Hancock* (1899)[70] was concerned with a state-issued coin used as a collector's item rather than money. *Reference Re Alberta Statutes* (1938)[71] dealt with, among other matters, the power of a Canadian province to issue circulating debt instruments.

There is, however, one exception concerning privately issued banknotes. Thus, echoing *Miller v Race* (1758),[72] for their part, *State v Finnegan* (1905),[73] and *Johnson v State* (1910)[74] dealt with the extension of the definition of "money" to non-legal tender banknotes issued by private banks. Certainly, with respect to non-legal tender banknotes the law has converged with economic sociology.

Thus, in post-Medieval England, goldsmiths, the forerunners of modern commercial bankers, issued notes either against the deposit of coined money or by way of loans.[75] Toward the end of the seventeenth century, it was already judicially acknowledged in England that "[t]he notes of goldsmiths ... are always accounted among merchants as ready cash."[76] However, a creditor could refuse a tender of goldsmith's notes and insist on payment in metallic money.[77] Underlying the latter rule was apparently the risk of the goldsmith's default. Indeed, insofar as a goldsmith was authorized to lend

---

70   Above note 28.

71   Above note 29.

72   Above note 26.

73   Above note 34.

74   Above note 33.

75   The ensuing discussion on the goldsmiths' system and banknotes draws on Benjamin Geva, *The Payment Order of Antiquity and the Middle Ages: A Legal History* (Hart Publishing, 2011) at 467–84.

76   *Tassell and Lee v Lewis* (1695) 1 Ld Raym 743 at 744; 91 ER 1397 at 1398.

77   *Ibid.*

money deposited with him,[78] the risk of his failure to meet his obligations to repay deposited money, leading to his insolvency, could not be overlooked, irrespective of his good reputation.

As discussed in chapter 3, the prevailing mercantile view nevertheless was that an accepted payment in goldsmith notes was absolute. In in an open defiance to that view,[79] the payment in goldsmith notes was held to be conditional on payment in coin if not by the goldsmith then by the payer.[80] This principle, as pronounced by Lord Holt in *Ward v Evans* (1702),[81] was stated to be limited to the taking of a goldsmith note for a *precedent* debt.[82] It was premised on the view that, in the absence of agreement to the contrary, "paper is no payment where there is a precedent debt," so that "the acceptance [by a creditor] of … a [goldsmith's] note is not actual payment."[83] Rather, under the conditional payment principle, "when such a note is given in payment, it is always intended to be taken under this condition, to be [absolute] payment [only] if the money be paid thereon. … "[84] Where the condition was broken, the paying debtor's liability was resurrected. The condition was dispensed with, so that the paying debtor was discharged, upon the creditor's failure to demand payment from the goldsmith "in convenient time."[85]

Privately issued banknotes are not widespread anymore and yet are not extinct. At present banknotes are issued in the United Kingdom by a few designated banks in Scotland and Northern Ireland.[86] Such banknotes are not

----

78 *Ibid.*

79 See *Ward v Evans* (1702) 2 Ld Raym 928 at 930; 92 ER 120 at 121, where Lord Holt CJ stated the rule "notwithstanding the noise and cry, that it is the use of Lombard-Street, as if the contrary opinion would blow up Lombard-Street. … "

80 See in general, James M Holden, *The History of Negotiable Instruments in English Law* (Gaunt & Sons, 1993) at 85–86, 109–11 (who nevertheless appears to overlook the distinction, set out below, between the situation where goldsmith note was taken for an antecedent and when it was taken for a present debt).

81 *Ward v Evans*, above note 79.

82 *Ibid.*

83 *Ibid.*

84 *Ibid.*

85 *Ibid*; compare *Tassell and Lee v Lewis*, above note 76 at 744 (Ld Raym), 1398 (ER) where the report cites *Hopkins v Geary* (1702) Hil 1 Ann BR Guildhall; see also *Hill & Al v Lewis* (1693) 1 Salk 132 at 133; 91 ER 124 at 125, where Lord Holt CJ instructed the jury that "what should be thought convenient time, ought to be according to the usage among traders. … On payment by banknote, see in general chapter 3.

86 See *Banking Act, 2009*, pt 6, particularly s 213; for HM Treasury Consultation Document see HM Treasury, *Banknote issue arrangements in Scotland and Northern Ireland: A Consultation Document* (Her Majesty's Stationary Office 2005), online: https://webarchive.nationalarchives. gov.uk/+/http:/www.hm-treasury.gov.uk/media/7/0/banknote_issue_arrangements_210705. pdf, accessed 19 June 2024. For the legal nature of such banknotes, as promissory notes and

accorded a legal tender status but are accepted as payment as a matter of practice.[87] They are required to be backed by earmarked sterling obligations of the Bank of England.[88] Hence the holder of such banknotes is protected against the risk of default by an issuing bank so that their use as money does not raise the question as to the application of the authorized "conditional payment" principle. In any event, arguably, nowadays, whether a note is given for a precedent debt or contemporaneous consideration is unlikely to play a role is determining whether it is given in conditional or absolute payment. Taking into account the likely anonymity of the transaction, not to mention reliance on the issuer and the possible availability of earmarked backing assets, the chance is that a court will find the parties intended absolute payment by banknote.[89]

For our purposes it is relevant to note that whether or not they conferred final discharge, goldsmith notes and their successors, private banknotes, circulated and were accepted in payment of debts, so as to have strong distinctive monetary features. A tentative conclusion is thus that in treating an item of property circulating as a means of payment as "money" – courts may not insist on it being accepted in absolute payment. More in general, even less than perfect monetary objects can be "money."

VIII. IS THE BANKNOTE UNIQUE? THE REACH OF ITS LEGAL HISTORY

There appears thus to be a tension between the broad judicial statements – which are in accord with the sociological perspective as confirmed by history regarding private money – and actual holdings focusing on private banknotes so as to arguably restrict private money to what is generated by the banking system. Is there truly a conflict between sociology and history on one hand and legal history on the other, and if so, are courts' powers restricted by legal history?

Prima facie, a few hurdles exist in relying on the ongoing legal history of the banknote as a basis for recognizing community currencies, and digital currencies in particular, as money in general. Community and digital currencies may be distinguished from the private banknotes in a couple of ways.

---

otherwise, see *Clydesdale Bank v The Commissioners for her Majesty's Revenue & Customs* [2019] UKFTT 0419 (TC).

87   See e.g., Northern Ireland Assembly, "The Status of Scottish and Northern Irish Banknotes" (Research and Library Services Briefing Note 122/08, 2008), online: http://archive.niassembly.gov.uk/io/research/2008/12208.pdf, accessed 19 June 2024.

88   Scottish and Northern Ireland Banknote Regulations 2009, SI 2009/3056 issued by the Treasury under ss 215–220 of the *Banking Act, 2009*.

89   For such factors see *Re Charge Card Services Ltd* (1988) 3 All ER 702 (CA).

First, at its inception, the banknote was a receipt for the deposit of coined money. True, its evolution into "money" in its own right paralleled its transformation into a credit obligation of the banker. However, it is uncontested that the banknote has retained its image, of being a claim to a deposit for safekeeping of coined money, even if as a matter of law it is certainly baseless.[90] To put it differently, the history of the banknote as a credit obligation goes hand in hand with the evolution of the view that funds on deposit with a commercial bank constitute "commercial bank" money. In more general terms, the view of the bank as an issuer of money evolved from its perceived position as a guardian of money.

Second, historically, in both the United States and Canada, non-legal tender banknotes issued by private banks circulated parallel to those of the state – so as to be "money" – albeit not without difficulty, and only with public authorities providing safety nets to the public using them.[91] For their part, as indicated in Part VII, Scottish and Irish banknotes are fully backed by earmarked sterling obligations of the Bank of England which appear to be crucial for their acceptance as money. It is thus tempting to argue that not all banknotes – but only those supported to one degree or another by the state – may qualify as money.

For their part, like banknotes, community scrips are typically denominated in the official unit of currency and frequently backed by an earmarked fund albeit possibly of commercial bank money. However, this is not universal. In any event, where available, the earmarked fund backing community scrips is not supported by the state in any way. As well, the earmarked fund is neither regulated by legislation nor covered by deposit insurance. Accordingly, the argument continues, whether or not they are denominated in the official currency unit and backed by an earmarked fund, community scrips may be considered one step removed from banknotes and thus the banknotes precedent cannot be used as a basis for conferring monetary features on community scrips.

Such a strict view on the law that sanctioned the monetary nature of the banknote ought to be rejected, and both objections should be dismissed. Rather, while earmarked funds, and state support, help to achieve acceptance, they are not required on their own. In principle, a scrip accepted as

---

90 The classical case for the banker mere debt obligation on a deposit is *Foley v Hill* (1848) 2 HLC 28, 9 ER 1002 (HL).

91 See e.g., Ben Fung, Scott Hendry, and Warren E Weber, "Canadian Bank Notes and Dominion Notes: Lessons for Digital Currencies" (2017) Bank of Canada Staff Working Paper 2017-5, online: https://www.bankofcanada.ca/2017/02/staff-working-paper-2017-5/, accessed 19 June 2024. See discussion in chapter 8.

money, notwithstanding a lack of connection to a coined money or to a full reserve, and without a state support, is nevertheless "money." More in general, a reliable safety net to users is a strong factor that is likely to lead to public acceptance in the relevant community; nevertheless, neither its absence nor its weakness is determinative in denying a scrip the status of "money" – if its issuer is trusted so that the scrip is nevertheless accepted in the discharge of debts in the community. As a matter of "jurisprudence 101," in the landmark case of *Miller v Race*,[92] Lord Mansfield's reasoning was premised on the broad perspective regarding the acceptability of private money in the marketplace, as applied to banknotes, but was by no means restricted to either them or their specific features. There was nothing in his judgment that relied on the fact that banknotes are products of banking operation.

Accordingly, there is no basis in caselaw to defy history and sociology. True, modern literature emphasizes that for an item to qualify as "money," its acceptance must be as a medium of exchange, a store of value,[93] and a unit of account.[94] For sure, the banknote has met these requirements. Nevertheless, "the iron of the Spartans, the cowrie of the African, the gold and silver of the world" were accepted as "money"[95] without necessarily having in full all monetary features enumerated by the literature. Literature requiring such high standard ought to be taken to focus on the qualities of "good money" rather than on what "money" *is*. Another way to put it is that having in full all such features will enhance the chances of an item to be accepted as "money" and thus to be "money" but their absence does not disqualify it in advance from so being. Rather, "money" is "something generally accepted as a medium of exchange, a measure of value, *or* a means of payment";[96] it does not even have to embody *all* such features.

---

92   See above note 26 and text discussion there.

93   William Stanley Jevons, *Money and the Mechanism of Exchange* (Henry S. King & Co, 1875) at 13 does not include this element in the definition. Indeed, money is a store of value only in the sense of being a "surplus" liquid resource of stable value available in one's hands for acquiring new commodities as may be needed and wished.

94   Nigel Dodd, *The Sociology of Money: Economic, Reason & Contemporary Society* (Continuum, 1994) at xv. For Geoffrey Ingham, *The Nature of Money* (Polity Press, 2004) at 198, "money" is effectively something that, "[r]egardless of [its] particular form and substance," answers the promise and description provided (and measured) by the unit of account.

95   *Ibid. Cf Rhodes v Lindly*, 3 Ohio 51 (OH 1827), where payment "in good merchantable whisky" was held not to be payment in money presumably in the absence of proof as to its acceptability as such.

96   See the definition of "money" (*Merriam Webster*), online: http://www.merriam-webster.com/dictionary/money, accessed 30 June 2024 (emphasis added).

In the final analysis the lesson from the legal history of the banknote is not strictly limited to the banknote. Rather, it can be stretched all the way to be a mere example to the broad principle put forward in *Miller v Race* (1758)[97] and subsequently pronounced in *Moss v Hancock* (1899)[98] and *Reference Re Alberta Statutes* (1938).[99] In this context it may be worthwhile to recall, as already pointed out at the end of Part VII, that insofar as it may have conferred only conditional payment, even the goldsmith note itself did not have perfect monetary qualities and nevertheless was taken to be "money."

IX. DO DIGITAL CURRENCIES CONSTITUTE "MONEY"?

Caselaw in the United States has treated Bitcoin as money,[100] but also considered it to have "a long way before it is the equivalent of money."[101] Such caselaw was context-driven and thus cannot be used as a basis for a general principle. Accordingly, this part will examine in general terms the modifying conditions for the application of the preceding analysis to digital currencies. Since it has already been established that whether something serves as money depends on acceptance, which is a question of fact, there is no preclusion for digital currencies to be "money" if they are so accepted. Hence, this part will address specific factors that may affect the monetary use of digital currencies, namely their acceptance as money.

As already pointed out, centralized schemes and permissioned decentralized ones could be used as substitutes for scrips in "traditional" access-restricted community currency schemes. As well, participants in a permissionless decentralized scheme can also be viewed as a community. Either way, for now, unlike banknotes but like scrips, community digital currencies are issued outside the banking system. Unlike banknotes and scrips, digital currencies may use a unit of account different from that of the national currency and may not have an issuer. Do these modifying conditions affect the application of the previous analysis?

There is no inherent limitation for a centralized self-anchored or claim-check digital currency to be money as it is not conceptually different from a scrip-based community currency. The difficulty is with digital

---

97   Above note 26.
98   Above note 28 at 116.
99   Above note 29.
100   *United States of America v Faiella*, 39 F Supp 3d 544 (SD Ny 2014).
101   *State of Florida v Espinoza*, Case No F14-2923 (Fla 11th Cir, July 22, 2016); see article by Lalita Clozel, "Bitcoin Not Money, Fla. Judge Says, Tossing AML Charges" (*American Banker*, 25 July 2016).

currencies, which are self-anchored mathematical creatures.[102] They hinge on cryptographic algorithms, each being "a procedure or formula for solving a problem,"[103] not only for protection against hacking but also to control the creation of new units and facilitate payments. Not being anchored to a specific tradeable asset, such as a commodity or a fiat currency, a self-anchored digital currency such as a cryptocurrency is inherently unstable, volatile, and easily amenable for speculation.[104]

The provision of an unstable unit of account is an obstacle for the monetary use of digital currencies. This weakness is, however, not without a solution. For example, blockchains generating digital currencies denominated in the national currency have been floating in the form of a few proposed central bank cryptocurrency schemes.[105] In the United States, proposals have been made for Fedcoin, being a central bank-issued centrally created cryptocurrency, to be available to the public at large.[106] Digital coins are to be centrally issued on a blockchain-style decentralized ledger, but nevertheless with the central bank being in full control of quantity, timing, and fixed value in denominations of the national fiat currency unit of account. Effectively, transactions will be validated by an independent notary nominated by the central bank. A similar proposal was made in the United Kingdom for RSCoin.[107] Another proposal is for a NationCoin, being a Regulated and

---

102   Samid, above note 21 at 14.

103   See definition of "algorithim" in Alexander S Gillis, 'What is an Algorithm?" (*TechTarget WhatIs*, July 2023), online: http://whatis.techtarget.com/definition/algorithm, accessed 30 June 2024.

104   See e.g., Samid, above note 21 at 14–15 (on the concept of self-anchored money), and 109–110 (on self-anchoring in bitcoins). While by definition, a fiat currency is a mere abstract obligation of a central bank and its value is not anchored in a commodity, the stability of its value hinges on the powers and obligations of the drivers of that economy, which is obviously not the case for self-anchored virtual currency.

105   See Morten Bech and Rodney Garratt, "Central bank cryptocurrencies" (Bank for International Settlements Quarterly Review, September 2017) at 55, online: https://www.bis.org/publ/qtrpdf/r_qt1709f.pdf, accessed 28 May 2024; see also Katrik Hegadekatti, "Towards Regional Monetary Unions through Blockchain Networks" (2017) Munich Personal RePEc Archive Paper No 82838, online: https://mpra.ub.uni-muenchen.de/82838/, accessed 28 May 2024; see also Heike Mai, "Why Would We Use Crypto Euros? Central bank-issued digital cash: a user perspective" (Deutsche Bank Reports, EU Monitor Global Financial Markets, 15 February 2018), online: https://www.dbresearch.com/PROD/RPS_EN-PROD/PROD0000000000462095.PDF, accessed 28 May 2024.

106   See e.g., Wendy McElroy, "Fedcoin: The U.S. Will Issue E-Currency That You Will Use" (*Bitcoin.com*, 12 January 2005), online: https://news.bitcoin.com/fedcoin-u-s-issue-e-currency/, accessed 28 May 2024.

107   See George Danezis and Sarah Meiklejohn, *Centrally Banked Cryptocurrencies* (University College London, 2015), online: https://eprint.iacr.org/2015/502.pdf, accessed 28 May 2024, in

Sovereign Backed Cryptocurrency (RSBC). The scheme envisages cryptocurrency coins, which as in Bitcoin, will be created by and transacted over a blockchain. However, upon their creation, the coins will be stored and released to the public by a Digital Asset Reserve, such as RSBC, at the fixed value of the national unit of account. Transactions are to be verified by "miners" who will be paid freshly minted coins.[108]

In principle, such schemes do not require participation by the central bank and may be privately run. Nor do they require that their currency be accorded a legal tender status. Its acceptance will hinge on the trust of participants in the system. The introduction of a potentially distrusted central counterparty to a trusted blockchain system, even if only to ensure a stable unit of account, will undermine the overall confidence in the system and may therefore be a pyrrhic victory. After all, if a central counterparty is trusted to keep the unit of account stable, why would it not be allowed to do the settlement and avoid the blockchain altogether?

Indeed, in the absence of an issuer, confidence in cryptocurrencies hinges on trust in the system or technology, or more specifically, in the generation of digital coins in its blockchain in a way that will keep them secure and valuable. As for the basis of this trust, pointing at Bitcoin, Ammous explains that it is the high processing power threshold which prevents both hacking and the establishment of a manipulative untrusted central control. Both achievements secure neutrality and full benefit of decentral structure, and yet at the cost of a fixed supply of growth that cannot be made to adjust to satisfy a purely market-determined demand and hence results in price instability. At the same time, he observes, attempts in other cryptocurrencies to bypass the expensive, inefficient, and wasteful Proof of Work (PoW), by other settlement mechanisms such as Proof of Stake,[109] consensus, or a trusted notary, compromise the neutrality of the system, enhance the control of the issuer, and/or require a third party verifier. Hence, he concludes, Bitcoin

---

part this article is too technical to the uninitiated in computer science and related subjects (including myself). "RSCoin is the core of a system of scalable and auditable transactions, not a full product" which thus could be used as a basis for either a retail or wholesale product. Email message to the author from George Danezis dated 4 December 2017.

108 Kartik Hegadekatti and Yatish S G, "Generation, Security and Distribution of NationCoins by a Sovereign Authority" (SSRN, 7 January 2017), online: https://papers.ssrn.com/sol3/papers.cfm?abstract_id=2888347, accessed 28 May 2024.

109 For the difference between proof of work and proof of stake see e.g., Mike Antolin, "Proof-of-Work vs Proof-of-Stake: What is the Difference?" (*CoinDesk*, 18 July 2022), online: https://www.coindesk.com/learn/proof-of-work-vs-proof-of-stake-what-is-the-difference/, accessed 28 May 2024.

could be no more than a store of value,[110] while other cryptocurrencies cannot fulfill any monetary feature. Rather, they are mere tokens for designated applications.[111]

At present,[112] the blockchain also suffers from poor scalability. For example, Bitcoin can handle at most seven transactions per second.[113] All this militates against a wide-scale monetary use of cryptocurrencies in retail transactions since everyday economic activity requires a robust, quick, and efficient processing and settlement of payments.

X. DOES COMMUNITY MONEY BRING NET BENEFITS? A BRIEF OVERVIEW

Community currency advocates are either critics of the centralized monetary system as a whole or reformers who endeavour to point at possible welfare gains realized from the use of community currencies.[114] Either way, community currencies may be used now to direct a specific share of sales proceeds for community projects, a sort of a voluntary local tax earmarked to a common goal.[115] More generally, the use of community currency is rationalized nowadays on a policy purporting to promote the decentralization of

110 Not everybody is in agreement. For considering Bitcoin to be an "imperfect store of value" due to its volatility see Aaron Kumar and Christie Smith, "Crypto-currencies – An introduction to not-so-funny moneys" (2017) Reserve Bank of New Zealand Analytical Note Series AN2017/07 at 2, online: https://www.rbnz.govt.nz/-/media/ReserveBank/Files/Publications /Analytical%20notes/2017/an2017-07.pdf, accessed 28 May 2024.

111 Saifedean Ammous, "Can Cryptocurrencies Fulfill the Functions of Money?" (2016) Columbia University Center on Capitalism and Society Working Paper No 92, online: https://posei-don01.ssrn.com/delivery.php?ID=89803106806902001308410009400111511302400804906803, accessed 28 May 2024.

112 See details at e.g., Christopher Malmo, "Bitcoin is Unsustainable" (*Vice: Motherboard*, 29 June 2015), online: http://motherboard.vice.com/read/bitcoin-is-unsustainable, accessed 28 May 2024; see also e.g., John Quiggin, "Bitcoins are a waste of energy – literally' (*ABC News*, 5 October 2015), online: http://www.abc.net.au/news/2015-10-06/quiggin-bitcoins-are-a-waste-of-energy/6827940, accessed 28 May 2024.

113 See e.g., Bitcoin Wiki, "Scalability FAQ" (*BitcoinWiki*), online: https://en.bitcoin.it/wiki /Scalability_FAQ#What_is_this_Transactions_Per_Second_.28TPS.29_limit.3, accessed 28 May 2024. For a discussion and statistics on blockchain scalability see e.g. chapter I(VI) paragraph containing notes 210–15 and chapter 4(IV) note 71.

114 Ian Schmutte, "A Basic Critique of Economic Argument for Local Currencies" (2002) Monetary Theory and Policy: Economics at 420, online: https://web.archive.org/ web/20200218060902/https://pdfs.semanticscholar.org/d51b/97285539b645d26cf51a3c-5469295cee4180.pdf, accessed 30 June 2024 (archived webpage).

115 A good example is the Toronto Dollar scheme under which merchants redeemed community currency for 90 percent of its value with the rest going to charity. For an overview visit Wikipedia, "Toronto Dollar," online: https://en.wikipedia.org/wiki/Toronto_dollar, accessed 30 June 2024.

economic and political power.[116] Actual use is usually motivated by belief in external benefits.[117] According to Naqvi and Southgate,[118] "[l]ocal currencies are established to support local sustainability by incentivising spending at, and between, participants of the scheme" so "that a greater proportion of consumer spending and retailers' supply chains are kept within the specified geographical area, improving local sustainability."

Be that as it may, a positive view of community currencies is not universally shared. Acknowledging the "initial" success of the Woergl experiment, the German Bundesbank pointed at costs incurred by users, and went on to argue that "[b]y segregating off different regions by means of community currencies, users and enterprises are deliberately opting out of an efficient division of labour across regional borders."[119]

In assessing the relevance of community currency schemes to the Bank of England's monetary and financial stability objectives, Naqvi and Southgate are more equivocal. Their observations can be summarized as follows:[120] Since the aggregate size of the UK schemes relative to the spending in the economy is small, it does not have a significant impact on the price level and hence on monetary stability. At their present size, community currencies do not generate sufficient pressure on the price level as captured by the consumer prices index so as to dramatically boost economic activity. However, they opine, "even if the schemes were large enough to affect spending at the macroeconomic level," it would be within the power of the Bank to adjust

---

116 Solomon, above note 5 at 66–74; see also Robert Swan and Susan Witt, "Local Currencies: Catalysts for Sustainable Regional Economies" (Schumacher Center, 1995), online: https://www.appropriate-economics.org/materials/local_currencies_catalysts.pdf, accessed 30 June 2024; a mutual credit system is said to redress a deficit region drain on liquidity. See Jorim Schraven, "The Economics of Community Currencies: A Theoretical Perspective" (2001), online https://web.archive.org/web/20201029154308/http://www.jorim.nl/economicscommunitycurrencies.pdf, accessed 30 June 2024.

See also Jorim Schraven, "The Economics of Local Exchange and Trading Systems: a Theoretical Perspective" (2000) 4 *International Journal of Community Currency Research* 5, online: https://ijccr.net/wp-content/uploads/2012/05/ijccr-vol-4-2000-5-schraven.pdf, accessed 30 June 2024.

117 Johanna McBurnie, "Investigating the Role of Money: The Case of Salt Spring Dollars" (Thesis, University of Victoria, 2012), online: https://web.archive.org/web/20180712181358/https://www.uvic.ca/socialsciences/economics/assets/docs/honours/McBurnie.pdf, accessed 30 June 2024 (archived webpage).

118 Naqvi, above note 8 at 317, 320–21.

119 Deutsche Bundesbank Eurosystem, "The Cost Behind The Moniker: Local Currencies In Germany" (*Deutsche Bundesbank Eurosystem*, 26 March 2013), online: https://web.archive.org/web/20140612025033/https://www.bundesbank.de/Redaktion/EN/Topics/2013/2013_06_26_the_cost_behind_the_moniker_local_currencies_in_germany.html, accessed 30 June 2024 (archived webpage).

120 Naqvi, above note 8 at 32–24.

its monetary policy. I suppose that to the extent that one-for-one backing for sterling exists for current community-currency schemes the issuance of community currency is not an increase in the amount of money per se but rather an increased circulation.

As well, they mention the risk of counterfeit notes, expressing the fear that is particularly true due to the typical physical similarity in appearance between a community currency voucher and a banknote, "a successful counterfeit attack on a community currency voucher scheme might generate a spillover effect that reduces confidence in other physical instruments, like [Bank of England's] banknotes." Strictly speaking, this fear does not apply to virtual currencies except that by analogy one could be concerned with the risk of hacking and counterfeit digital coins. They also raise the prospect of a "run" on a private scheme adversely affecting financial stability if community currencies were to become a significant part of the payment system. Indeed, in the case of a cryptocurrency, the risk of a "run" is replaced by the risk of massive exchange to national currencies leading to value depreciation.

Finally, Naqvi and Southgate point out that community currencies do not enjoy "legal tender" status. In each case, an issuer of a community currency may not be creditworthy and in any event, it is not as creditworthy as the Bank of England. Moreover, it is typically an unregulated financial institution or entity. Accordingly, in principle, holders of community currencies do not enjoy a high degree of user protection without an assured one-for-one backing for sterling. True, "commercial bank money" equally does not enjoy "legal tender" status. As well, not only is it issued by regulated financial institutions and covered by deposit insurance, but its use also has the advantage of bypassing the risk associated with payment in physical cash, in a context in which both the value of the unit of account and the convertibility to legal tender are automatically guaranteed. Hence, the one-for-one backing for a community banking may well be needed for protection and acceptability.

XI. CONCLUSION AND FINAL OBSERVATIONS

To ensure confidence and safety, community currencies controlled by a private issuer would need to be fully backed. Effectively, this means that digital community currencies are in effect a specie of stablecoins discussed in chapter 4. This applies to digital claim-checked currencies. It does not apply to self-anchored digital currencies such as Bitcoin.

Use of national currency unit of account will enhance acceptance of all community currencies. To incentivize users, restricted access schemes could be bought or earned in a discounted value and be depreciative so as to encourage prompt use. Compared to scrip-based models, not being regionally based, centralized digital schemes as well as permissioned cryptocurrency schemes are likely to be more effective in preventing spillover to other regions or groups.

Indeed, features such as a reserve (or otherwise confidence in the value of the currency) and use of the unit of account of the national currency are likely to enhance acceptance; at the same time, as discussed, the law ought to be taken as according monetary status to anything accepted as money. Stated otherwise, such features are helpful in establishing community acceptance and yet acceptance on its own suffices even in the absence of some of all such conditions.

A remaining question is the need for regulation. Once financial stability is put at risk regulation ought to be unquestionable. However, protection of the public requires regulation well ahead of that point. Regulation ought to be not so much of the currencies but rather of the business activity in relation to them such as exchange, transfer and storage.[121] Certainly, customer protection, at least in terms of requirements addressing full disclosure as to terms and risks, ought to be highlighted in any regulatory scheme. Particularly for digital currencies this is so regardless of whether they are money.

In the final analysis it should however be pointed out that from a legal perspective, community currencies do not appear to distinguish themselves as a separate category of private currencies. This has become more apparent with digitalization, a context in which there is not necessarily a pre-existing community; rather, it is the digitalization which links participants in a virtual currency scheme into a community. At the same time, it is acceptance in the community which renders a candidate for private money, be it a voucher or digital coin, into "money." Both law and sociology fully converge at this point.

---

121 For example, a comprehensive statute for digital currencies is the US *Uniform Regulation of the Virtual-Currency Business Act* (URVCBA), drafted by the National Conference of Commissioners on Uniform State Law (NCCUSL) and approved and recommended by it for enactment in all the states in the United States at its Annual Conference Meeting in its 126th year in San Diego, California on 14–20 July 2017. So far it has been introduced in Connecticut, Hawaii, and Nebraska. See Uniform Law Commission, "Regulation of Virtual Currency Businesses Act" (NCCUSL 2017, online: https://www.uniformlaws.org/committees/community-home?CommunityKey=e104aaa8-c10f-45a7-a34a-0423c2106778, accessed 25 June 2024. Commercial law rules for transactions covered by URVCBA are provided by the *Uniform Supplemental Commercial Law for the Uniform Regulation of Virtual Currency Business Act*.

ENVISIONING A "HUB, SPOKES AND FELLOES" MONETARY SYSTEM: WILL THE WOLF LIVE WITH THE LAMB?[1]

SYNOPSIS

Increased digitalization of private money raises questions as to the interaction with currency issued by the central bank. The principal issue is that of uniformity of currency – required for transacting and crucial for smooth operation of the market. Several Bank of Canada studies have indicated that regulation is required to ensure harmony and full interchangeability. For its part, a diverse array of private digital currencies promotes competition and in turn innovation. The creation of a synthetic Central Bank Digital Currency (sCBDC) can ensure not only the benefit of publicly issued money but also uniformity while leaving room for innovation. Under a proposed scheme, regulated financial institutions will be able to issue digital currencies that will be fully backed by central bank money and interchangeable with other sCBDCs or Central Bank Digital Currency (CBDC) itself. This system will require standards related to interoperability and an evolution in the ways in which currency is regulated in Canada.

SUMMARY OF CONTENTS

---

1   The subtitle of this chapter is inspired by and paraphrases the Bible, Isaiah 11:6.

I. INTRODUCTION

Chapter 2 identified key recurring themes that have arisen throughout the monetary history of Canada. They are the relationship between money and gold; multiplicity of currencies; a quest for the uniformity of money; balancing between the roles of government and private/commercial banks in making and distributing money; and finally, the place and impact, if any, of non-bank private money.

Until not long ago, fundamental issues underlying each of these themes seemed to have been settled. Thus, it has been determined, not only that money should not necessarily be made of gold, money ought also neither necessarily (whether partially or fully) be backed by nor even redeemable in gold. True, the divorce between money and gold was neither smooth nor amical. Nevertheless, in Canada, as elsewhere, the separation happened. Side by side with this divorce it has been established that while private parties may choose a currency for their contract or transaction, the currency issued and denominated in the currency of Canada, that is, the Canadian dollar, is by far the prevailing one. It is issued by the Bank of Canada (and to a lesser extent by the Royal Canadian Mint) and is uniform throughout. It is both physically distributed and scripturally multiplied by the banking system which includes all members of the Canadian Payments Association (Payments Canada). While non-bank private money has been tolerated and may exist it has not had a significant role in the Canadian monetary system.

To some degree or another, the ongoing digital revolution has challenged the prevailing consensus around most of the above themes, though not upsetting or undermining them altogether. Primarily, these themes are the multiplicity of currencies, the uniformity of the money, and the role of the private sector, whether banks or other entities. In effect, only the divorce, or at least the independence, from gold has remained, on the whole, unchallenged.

All challenges have been rooted in the digital revolution introducing new types of money, whether stablecoins, self-anchored cryptocurrencies, and in the future possibly a Central Bank Digital Currency. Can history be a guide as to how to address these challenges?

To begin with, multiplicity of currencies has not been unusual in the Canadian monetary landscape since early settlement. Indeed, as indicated in chapter 2, ratings of French coins were addressed in decrees dated 18 July 1654 and 7 October 1661[2] and French monetary units, *livres, sols and denier*,

---

2   See Adam Shortt (ed), *Documents relating to Canadian Currency, Exchange and Finance During the French Period, Vol I* (Acland, 1925) at 2–4.

were adopted on 20 March 1662 as money of account.[3] "Money madness" taking place in British North America less than 200 years later, prior to the adoption of the dollar as well as Confederation, is described by Powell as follows:[4]

> The diversity of notes and coins in circulation was frustrating, making simple transactions complex. In a letter to the Acadian Recorder in 1820, an irate citizen in Halifax complained that when he bought vegetables costing six pence in the market using a £1 Nova Scotian Treasury note, his change amounted to 93 separate items, including 8 paper notes from four different merchants or groups (ranging in value from 5 shillings to 7 1/2 pence), one silver piece, and 84 copper coins. The letter ended "For God's sake, gentlemen, let us get back our DOLLARS" (Acadian Recorder, 21 October 1820, Martell 1941, 15).

Indeed, a simple and yet essential solution to the multiplicity of money is the establishment of a uniform money of account. The latter is the currency in which an obligation or debt is measured. It is distinguished from the money of payment, relating to the means or object in which the debt is discharged. Accordingly, a specific amount of money of payment discharges a debt of another specific amount in the money of account.[5] Without a uniform money of account it is impossible to effectively compare prices, hence the importance of determining it.

At the same time, the episode described above demonstrates that determining a uniform money of account is only a partial solution to the multiplicity of currencies problem. It may work well in niche markets, such as airport stores, but otherwise it makes transactions awkward. This is so even without considering the possibility that there may be different degrees of acceptability for various currencies circulating in a given market. Multiplicity of currencies should either be abolished or remedied by interchangeability among various currency forms or objects, each denominated in the same unit of account and equally accepted in the relevant market.

---

3   Adam Shortt (ed), *Documents relating to Canadian Currency, Exchange and Finance During the French Period*, Vol 2 (Acland, 1925) at 4–7.

4   James Powell, *A History of the Canadian Dollar* (Bank of Canada, 1999) at 19; see also Pierre Duguay, "The quest for confidence: 400 years of money – from La Nouvelle France to Canada today" (Remarks to students and faculty of Laval University, 10 November 2008) at 4, online: https://www.bankofcanada.ca/2008/11/quest-confidence-400-years-money/, accessed 5 July 2024.

5   *Woodhouse AC Israel Cocoa Ltd SA v Nigerian Product Marketing Co Ltd* (1971) 2 QB 23 at 54 (CA) (Lord Denning).

This chapter addresses the challenge of accommodating various currencies in Canada under various possible scenarios and circumstances. **Parts II and III** address studies from the Bank of Canada. **Part II** focuses on three studies prepared by Warren E. Weber, while he was a visiting scholar at the Bank of Canada's Currency Department, on the experience in the United States with various forms of currency notes that concurrently circulated. **Part III** discusses a study prepared by staff members of the Bank of Canada (including Warren Weber during his tenure as a visiting scholar) led by Ben Fung on the comparable Canadian experience. **Part IV** presents an analysis applying the studies addressed in Parts II and III to the evolving scenario of digital monetary objects. **Part V** concludes that an optimal multi-medium harmonized national monetary system is feasible. Briefly stated, to meet the challenge posed by the ongoing evolution of the monetary system in Canada, uniformity of currency ought to be addressed.

The architecture underlying the envisaged monetary system is that of a "hub, spokes and felloes" monetary system. Thereunder, each spoke (large commercial bank) is linked to the hub (the central bank); in turn, the various spokes are connected not only via the hub but also directly over the felloes. The digital currency itself is issued by either the central bank or each commercial bank against 100 percent reserve central bank money. It is distributed by the commercial banks, each facilitating a transfer system linked to all other transfer systems.

A regime of effective regulation addressing non-bank issuers, and matters such as safety, security, and conformity with monetary policy, must be in place. Systems not denominated in Canadian dollars may operate and be tolerated. On their own they are unlikely to endanger Canadian monetary sovereignty.

II. WEBER'S STUDIES

The three studies by Weber address the experience in the United States with private banknotes during different periods. **The first two studies** discuss lessons relevant to e-money from the experience in the United States, first with state banknotes issued prior to 1863,[6] and second, with national banknotes issued as of 1864.[7] Each paper examines historical evidence on how well the

---

6   Warren E Weber, "The Efficiency of Private E-Money-Like Systems: The US Experience with State Bank Notes" (2014) Bank of Canada Working Paper 2014-15, online: https://www .bankofcanada.ca/2014/04/working-paper-2014-15/, accessed 5 July 2024 [Weber-1].

7   Warren E Weber, "The Efficiency of Private E-Money-Like Systems: The US Experience with National Bank Notes" (2015) Bank of Canada Working Paper 2015-3, online: https://www .bankofcanada.ca/2015/01/working-paper-2015-3/, accessed 5 July 2024 [Weber-2].

banknotes, being privately issued in a currency system with multiple issuers, functioned with respect to ease of transacting, counterfeiting, safety, over-issuance, and par exchange (a uniform currency).

In each case Weber finds that banknotes made transacting easier and were not subject to over-issuance. There was, however, difference as to security and safety. For its part, counterfeiting of state banknotes was widespread; banknotes were not perfectly safe, notes of different banks did not exchange at par, and rates of exchange were volatile. On the other hand, national banknotes were perfectly safe because they were insured by the federal government. Further, national banknotes formed a *uniform currency*. Notes of different banks traded at par with each other and with greenbacks.

Issues related to currency uniformity can rise by reference to different media of exchange. According to Weber, media of exchange can be different because they are of different "kinds" of media of exchange *or* of different "denominations" of the same kind of medium of exchange. By different "kinds" of media of exchange, Weber distinguishes between, for example, coins of different metals, paper currencies of different issuers, deposits in different banks, and so forth. By different "denominations," he distinguishes different numbers (denominations) on the same kind of medium of exchange.[8]

According to Weber, multiple media of exchange issued by different issuers are a uniform currency, if:[9]

1. they are expressed in the same monetary unit,
2. they trade at par (at their face value) in all transactions that involve the non-issuer public, and
3. prices are stated in terms of the monetary unit only.

By reference to this definition, he states:[10]

1. A uniform currency system requires the media of exchange to be expressed in terms of the same monetary unit. Thus, by this definition a set of media of exchange could not be a uniform currency if, for example, some were expressed in dollars and others in pesos;
2. Both privately-issued and governmentally-issued media of exchange ought to be included in the uniform currency system. Thus, different privately-issued media of exchange traded at par with each other, not just with whatever is issued by the government. Consequently, for national banknotes to have

---

8   *Ibid* at 20.
9   *Ibid* at 19.
10   *Ibid* at 20.

been a uniform currency, they would have had to trade at face value against each other and against government currency notes;

3.   The set of agents for whom the media of exchange must trade at par is specified as the non-issuer public, not as all agents; and

4.   Different prices are not quoted for different media of exchange; that is, there would not be such things as "discounts for cash."

Weber cites research concluding that after 1874, national banknotes were a uniform currency: notes of different national banks exchanged at par with each other and with government currency notes.[11]

The mechanism in the *National Banking Act*[12] that led to national banknotes being a uniform currency had five parts.[13] The first three parts of the mechanism were:

- Redeemability in government currency notes on demand at the issuing bank at par;
- Par acceptance by every national bank;
- Federal insurance covering the issuing bank's default.

These first three parts made the general public indifferent in choosing between the notes of individual national banks, and between national banknotes and government currency notes if national banks themselves were indifferent between the notes of other national banks and government currency notes. Such indifference between notes of other national banks and government currency notes on the part of banks is critical; without it, banks would very likely have treated the notes of other banks as distinct from each other, from their own notes, and from government currency notes, when non-issuers were making deposits. For their part, had banks differentiated between notes of individual national banks and government currency notes, discounts or premia on the notes of different banks and on government currency notes could have varied over time and across locations. The result would have been that national banknotes would not have been a uniform currency.

The fourth and fifth parts of the mechanism were:

- Gross clearing facility – located and run by the US Treasury as the National Redemption Agency, to which national banks were required to join by depositing 5 percent of the US circulation; and

---

11   *Ibid.*

12   The National Banking Acts of 1863 (12 Stat. 665) and 1864 (13 Stat. 99) were two United States federal banking acts that established a system of national banks chartered at the federal level, and created the United States National Banking System.

13   Weber-2 above note 7 at 21–27.

- Clearing costs borne by issuers of national banknotes rather than by the users (non-issuer public) of the notes.

These fourth and fifth parts of the mechanism made banks indifferent between notes of other national banks and government currency notes.

In Weber's view, the US experience with both state and national banknotes suggests that a privately issued e-money system can operate efficiently but only with appropriate government intervention, regulation, and supervision first, to minimize counterfeiting and to promote safety and par exchange. It will also require government intervention, regulation, and supervision to provide the mechanism necessary for different media of exchange to exchange at par with each other.

In a **third study** focusing on government and e-money Weber explores the period between 1914 and 1935 in the United States.[14] During that period, privately issued national banknotes and central banknotes, issued by the Federal Reserve, were simultaneously in circulation. He explains that the reason for the issuance of Federal Reserve notes did not hinge on any inherent deficiency in the circulation of the private banknotes, which in fact served well the public demand for circulating media. Rather, the reason for issuing Federal Reserve notes was that national banknotes failed to provide an elastic currency, meaning a currency that automatically increases and decreases in volume with the demands of businesses. Having an elastic money was considered to be important for the US economy at the time.

In Weber's view, there were two respects in which national banknotes were considered inelastic. The first was that the national banking system did not provide a method by which banks could pool their gold resources during periods of financial stress. Stated otherwise, the national banking system did not have a lender of last resort for the system as a whole. Instead, it was up to the individual banks or groups of banks to act on their own in periods of financial stringency.[15] The second respect in which national banknotes were not elastic is that the supply of national banknotes in various parts of the country did not fluctuate in accord with the large seasonal fluctuations in the demand for currency.[16]

In turn, the reason that national banknote currency was "inelastic," was the requirement that national banknotes be backed by US government bonds

14   Warren E Weber, "Government and Private E-Money-Like Systems: Federal Reserve Notes and National Bank Notes" (2015) Bank of Canada Working Paper 2015-18, online: https://www.bankofcanada.ca/2015/06/working-paper-2015-18/, accessed 5 July 2024 [Weber-3].

15   *Ibid* at 11.

16   *Ibid* at 12.

as collateral. It prevented banks from both issuing and retiring notes as freely and promptly as they otherwise would. This inevitably raised a question as to why the backing securities requirement was not eliminated.[17] Weber argues that this was so because the better solution was to establish a central bank authority. Thus, on one hand:[18]

> if any mutualization of redemption liability had been involved at the same time, … then all banks involved would have had to bear the risk of default.

And on the other hand:

> A central bank acting as a lender of last resort and providing currency would take this risk away from banks. … Further, if this central bank were to acquire a large fraction of the nation's gold and had the power to issue notes with only fractional gold backing, as the Federal Reserve banks were allowed to do, it would allow for a larger and more elastic supply of currency in the case of a run on bank deposits.

While this may explain the introduction of Federal Reserve Notes in the United States, it fails to explain the accompanying elimination of the National Bank Notes. According to Weber, it became necessary to eliminate these private notes to allow the Federal Reserve to effectively control the reserves and, in this way, conduct monetary policy with the view of exercising control over the extension of credit in the economy. As Weber explains, if national banks could issue notes, the Federal Reserve System would not have complete control over the reserves of the banking system. This is so since national banks would also have the ability to create reserves for the banking system. This could happen because national banknotes could be deposited with Federal Reserve banks, and these deposits counted as part of reserves that member banks were required to hold against deposits. Thus, a member bank could take national banknotes that it received in the course of business, deposit them at its district Federal Reserve bank, and then make loans on the basis of these reserves.[19]

In his study, Weber endeavours to address the following five questions:[20]

1. Should the central bank issue e-money?
2. If privately-issued e-moneys are already in existence, can the central bank get its e-money into circulation?

---

17   *Ibid* at 13–14.
18   *Ibid* at 15.
19   Weber-3, above note 14 at 15, see also 24.
20   Set out *ibid* at 3.

3. If the central bank should issue e-money, what form should that e-money take?

4. Can privately-issued and centrally-issued e-moneys coexist, or if the central bank issues e-money will it become the sole issuer?

5. Should the central bank be the monopoly issuer?

The following is a summary of his analysis.

The **first question** is whether the central bank should issue e-money.[21] One possible argument in favour, Weber states, could be that the central bank would save on the costs of providing coins and paper currency. Nonetheless, Weber dismisses this argument, reasoning that the cost savings do not appear to be large, given the recent innovations in providing coins and paper currency. Another argument is that issuing e-money would increase the central bank's seigniorage because it would increase the demand for central bank currency, which is the chief source of central bank seigniorage. However, that might not be the case, since it is possible that central bank e-money would only be a substitute for the central bank's paper currency. Either way, he maintains, the strongest argument for a central bank to issue e-money is that it would be a way for the central bank to continue to have a significant source of seigniorage revenue if its seigniorage revenue were being threatened by a reduced public demand for central bank currency. This could be caused by a shift of public demand to privately issued e-moneys. Of course, there could be other threats as well. The importance of a central bank having a stable source of a significant amount of seigniorage is that it gives the central bank operational independence to conduct monetary policy as it sees fit.

Next, Weber explores the **second question**, *viz* whether the government can get its e-money into circulation in an environment in which privately issued e-moneys already exist.[22] On the basis of the United States 1914–1934 experience, he gives a resounding affirmative answer to the question. He cites several ways in which the *Federal Reserve Act*[23] made the introduction of the Federal Reserve notes a success story:

(i) It provided Federal Reserve notes with federal government insurance; Federal Reserve notes were obligations of the US government;

---

21 *Ibid* at 22 (into 23).

22 *Ibid* at 23.

23 The *Federal Reserve Act*, c 6, 38 Stat 251, passed in 1913, created a national currency and a monetary system that could respond effectively to the stresses in the banking system and create a stable financial system.

(ii) It made Federal Reserve notes acceptable as reserves for banks. Banks could deposit Federal Reserve notes with district banks, and these deposits counted as part of the reserves that banks had to hold against their demand deposits;

(iii) Federal Reserve notes were receivable for "taxes, customs, and other public dues;" (section 16)

(iv) The fact that the US was on the gold standard and Federal Reserve notes had to be 40 percent backed by gold meant there was a limit to how many notes could be issued.

Weber goes on to argue that these same methods are mostly available to a central bank today:

(i) Because all central bank currencies today are fiat, safety, in the sense of redeemability, is not an issue;

(ii) Even though most countries do not impose reserve requirements, most banks choose to hold reserves at the central bank for clearing reasons. A central bank could accept its e-money for bank reserves;

(iii) A central bank's e-money could be made legal tender by the government; and

(iv) Modern monetary theory argues that the supply of a fiat money has to be limited if the fiat money is to be valued. The central banks in most developed countries have at least the implicit commitment to do this as evidenced by the concerns to keep inflation within some low target range. Thus, unless the issuance of e-money by the central bank puts this commitment in doubt, there should not be a problem getting central bank e-money into circulation.

At the end of the study[24] he highlights the role of government issued e-money as insurance against the possibility of large amounts of privately issued e-money being withdrawn, which would severely disrupt exchanges.

The next issue, that is, the **third question**, explored by Weber addresses the form central bank issued e-money will take, assuming of course that e-money is to be issued by the central bank.[25] In his view, the answer depends on the reason for the issuance of central bank e-money, and the media of exchange already in existence:

Federal Reserve notes were issued because the central bank needed to be able to issue currency in order to act as a lender of last resort. Privately-issued

----

24   Weber-3, above note 14 at 25.
25   *Ibid* at 23–24.

media of exchange, national bank notes, were already in existence, and the public was accustomed to using a paper currency. Hence, it was logical that Federal Reserve notes would also be in the form of a bank note. In fact, in terms of size and color, the design of the Federal Reserve note was quite similar to that of the national bank note.

Today, Weber argues, if the rationale for issuing central bank e-money is to regain seigniorage revenue being lost because privately issued e-moneys are replacing central bank currency, the e-money to be provided by the central bank ought to be superior to the privately issued one. For example, a central bank-issued e-money might capture market share by committing not to engage in discriminatory practices by private issuers giving favourable treatment to holders of their own-issued notes.

Next, moving to the **fourth question**, Weber discusses whether privately issued and central bank-issued e-moneys may coexist, or whether e-money issued by the central bank will necessarily drive out privately issued e-moneys.[26] He starts the discussion by pointing out that national banknotes did not go out of circulation until more than twenty years after the *Federal Reserve Act*,[27] and it is likely that they would have continued to circulate if their continued circulation had not been made legally impossible. Accordingly, he speculates, the non-bank public will continue to use an old, existing medium of exchange after a new one is introduced, especially if the new one does not offer many advantages over the old one.

The final issue raised by Weber as the **fifth question** is whether the government should be the monopoly issuer.[28] He first points out that the critical factor in the ability of national banks to create reserves, prior to the issuance of Federal Reserve notes, was that Federal Reserve banks were required to credit the account of national bank A with notes of national bank B deposited by national bank A to national bank A's account. Federal Reserve banks were required to do so without debiting the reserve account of national bank B. The ability of national banks to increase the supply of reserves ultimately led to the elimination of national banknotes. Weber goes on to argue that this need not be necessarily the case for privately issued e-money:

> Presumably a central bank would not accept privately-issued e-money as a deposit from a financial institution unless the issuer of that e-money had an account with the central bank. In that case, the account of the financial

---

26 *Ibid* at 24.
27 Above note 23.
28 *Ibid* at 24–25 (by reference to an earlier discussion at 15).

institution depositing the privately-issued e-money would be credited and the deposit of the issuer would be debited. The result: no net creation of reserves.[29]

Nonetheless, Weber argues, there are circumstances under which the issue of private e-money may be prohibited. Such would be the case if privately issued e-moneys were driving central bank currency out of circulation and thereby threatening the central bank's seigniorage revenue so as to undermine the independence of the central bank.

III. BANK OF CANADA'S STUDY

Weber's three studies set the stage for a subsequent 2017 Bank of Canada Staff Working paper by Ben Fung, Scott Hendry, and Warren Weber.[30] This study examines the historical Canadian evidence on privately issued banknotes and publicly issued Dominion notes from the early 1800s until the introduction of the Bank of Canada in 1934. From this experience with competing public and private currencies, the authors endeavour to derive lessons regarding what might happen in the future as various groups attempt to introduce private digital currencies.

As the basis for studying the Canadian experience with notes and for drawing lessons about that experience, the authors discuss banknotes and government notes in terms of five desirable characteristics of a medium of exchange. These characteristics are:[31]

(i) ease of transacting – a financial asset will be more desirable as a medium of exchange the easier it is to transport and the less often it either requires a seller to make change or requires the buyer to pay a higher price because of a lack of divisibility;

(ii) minimal counterfeiting – an extremely low level of counterfeiting or easy detection of counterfeits permits sellers to be relatively certain that they are receiving an authentic asset in exchange for their products or services;

(iii) high degree of safety – holders of a medium of exchange would like to be relatively certain that the financial instrument they are holding will store

---

29 Weber-3, above note 14 at 25.

30 Ben Fung, Scott Hendry, and Warren E Weber, "Canadian Bank Notes and Dominion Notes: Lessons for Digital Currencies" (2017) Bank of Canada Staff Working Paper 2017-5, online: https://www.bankofcanada.ca/2017/02/staff-working-paper-2017-5/, accessed 5 July 2024 (Fung et al).

31 *Ibid* at 3–4.

value and be acceptable in exchange when they want to use it to make purchases;

(iv) scarcity – limitations on the growth of the supply of a medium of exchange are essential if it is to be valued or if it is to maintain its value over time; and

(v) uniform currency – when there is more than one medium of exchange in a country issued using the same monetary unit, it is desirable that each can be exchanged one-for-one with any other regardless of the identity of the issuer, the location of the issuer, the location of the other issuer, the location in which the exchange is to take place, and the time at which the exchange is to take place. In other words, when there is more than one medium of exchange in a country issued using the same monetary unit, it will be desirable if a dollar issued by A exchanges one-for-one with a dollar issued by B always and everywhere.

The paper draws the following four lessons for digital currencies based on the evidence from Canada and the United States with banknotes and government issued notes:[32]

- Digital currencies will likely be counterfeited;
- Digital currencies likely will not be inflationary;
- Private digital currencies will not be safe and will not be a uniform currency without government intervention; and
- A central bank can always get its digital currency into circulation, but its digital currency will not necessarily drive out existing private digital currencies.

In Section 6 of the paper[33] the authors use the historical experience with private and government notes in Canada, and also in the United States, to provide five lessons[34] about what might be the Canadian experience with digital currencies qua currency:

Lesson 1: Digital currencies will be counterfeited
In effect, this lesson applies to digital currencies in general, whether they are virtual or CBDCs. Having mentioned past experience with note counterfeiting albeit without asserting a difference between Dominion and banknotes,

---

32   *Ibid* at 2; for a study on pre-1863 notes issued by state banks in the United States see Weber-1, above note 6.

33   *Ibid* at 27–32.

34   As seen below, by reference to the four lessons listed above, five lessons are discussed. This is so because the discussion of the third listed lesson listed above was split below to two, respectively lessons 3 and 4.

Fung et al appear to say in effect that the impact of counterfeiting digital currency is likely to surpass that of counterfeiting paper currency. This is because of factors such as cyberattacks which may generate a large number of fake digital coins. They also mention the double spending possibility for a digital coin that does not exist for a paper banknote. Nonetheless, they concede that "[i]n the case of decentralized digital currencies that use a distributed ledger, this problem has been solved by requiring 'proof of work' or 'proof of stake' before a block of transactions can be added to the blockchain."[35] In the final analysis, this lesson does not relate to the nature of multi-currency system.

Lesson 2: Digital currencies likely will be scarce

The risk addressed here by Fung et al is that of the inflationary effect of flooding the market with an uncontrolled quantity of digital coins. They argue that "[p]rivate digital currencies are likely to be scarce only when subject to strong government regulation or when there are rules for issuance hard coded from the beginning and not subject to any changes."[36] As an example for the latter they cite "the algorithm that determines the rate at which new bitcoin is created [that] cannot be altered."[37]

This lesson does not appear to apply to stablecoins as well as to virtual currencies created by the same or similar mechanism underlying the creation of "commercial bank money" in the present system.

Lesson 3: Digital currencies will not be safe, although government intervention can help

In this context, Fung et al first consider fractionally backed digital currencies redeemable on demand. Acknowledging that "[n]o fractionally backed financial instrument that is redeemable on demand, whether issued by a private entity or the government, can ever be perfectly safe,"[38] they conclude that "the historical experience with Canadian and United States bank notes also shows that private digital currencies can be made perfectly safe with government intervention, although it cannot be achieved solely through regulation."[39] On the top of regulation, such as a first lien or a requirement to back notes issued by public bonds, some type of insurance is needed. In the United States such insurance was provided by the government. In Canada, the insurance was provided by the banks themselves, that is, the note issuers,

---

35   Fung et al, above note 30 at 27.

36   *Ibid* at 28.

37   *Ibid.*

38   *Ibid.*

39   *Ibid* at 29.

albeit they were required to do so by law. Thus, the *Bank Act* of 1890[40] provided for the Bank Circulation Redemption Fund, to which bank contributed. As well, under that Act, notes holders were paid interest from the date of suspension to the date of redemption. This prevented notes of a failed bank from going upon suspension at a discount.

Lesson 4: Digital currencies will not be a uniform currency without government intervention

Currency or money uniformity means that all versions of the same denomination must have the same purchasing power. Practically speaking, all versions of the same denomination circulate at the same value, typically the denominated one, without any discount, and irrespective of issuer, location, media, place of redemption, or any other factor.

Fung et al's stated starting point in regard to the fourth lesson is that "[w]hen there are multiple media of exchange, some type of mechanism is generally required for them to be a uniform currency."[41] Moreover, they say, the mechanism to achieve currency uniformity requires some intervention by a government. They acknowledge the success of one privately operated interbank clearing arrangement in the United States to eliminate discounts[42] but treat it as an exception. They thus go on and point out that in Canada, in the absence of an interbank clearing mechanism until the *Bank Act* of 1890,[43] notes of sound banks from geographically distant locations typically went at a discount.

A similar phenomenon was also documented in the United States. In Canada, the intervention was the requirement in the *Bank Act* of 1890[44] that banks establish redemption agencies in the country's major financial centres. In the United States, the intervention was the establishment of a note clearing facility run by the United States Treasury.

Fung et al go on to say that nonetheless, "having the government intervene to establish a clearing mechanism is not enough to achieve uniformity in and of itself." Rather, "[w]hat is also required is that the cost of clearing or redeeming notes be borne by the issuer of the note rather than by the holder."[45] Accordingly, banks in Canada were required to establish and run

---

40 *An Act Respecting Banks and Banking, 1890* (UK), 53 Vict, c 31.

41 Fung et al, above note 30 at 30.

42 This was the Suffolk Banking System in New England, which operated from the 1820s to 1858. The Suffolk Banking System was a private clearing arrangement that led to the elimination of discounts on the notes of New England banks during the period in which it operated. *Ibid* at 30.

43 *An Act Respecting Banks and Banking, 1890* (UK), 53 Vict, c 31.

44 *Ibid.*

45 Fung et al, above note 30 at 30.

redemption agencies in commercial centres or nominate other institutions to act for them in such centres. But it was not only banknotes issued by diverse banks that failed to function as a uniform money:

> It may seem obvious that a government digital currency would be a uniform currency. No mechanism would be needed. And we would agree that is the case when there is only one government digital currency. However, the Canadian experience shows that if there is more than one government issued media of exchange that may not be the case. Between 1868 and 1880, Canada had several government issued media of exchange ... the Dominion notes payable at Receiver General offices in Montreal, Toronto and Halifax were distinct media of exchange. And, there is evidence that the Dominion notes that were payable in Montreal did not always exchange at par in Toronto and vice versa. Dominion notes became a uniform currency only when they were made payable at all Receiver General offices; that is, when the system was changed so that there was only one government issued medium of exchange. Thus, in a sense Canada established a mechanism by eliminating the need for one.[46]

Accordingly, bank and Dominion notes were a uniform currency only after Dominion notes were made redeemable at all Receiver General offices and the *Bank Act* of 1890[47] went into effect.

Finally, regarding currency uniformity, Fung et al raise a point regarding virtual currencies that did not exist at the time when banknotes and Dominion notes co-existed, namely that of the unit of account. Thus, during their co-existence, both bank and Dominion notes were denominated in the same unit of account, being the Canadian dollar. This is of course not necessarily the case with virtual currencies that may be issued in other units of account, which is universally the case for self-anchored virtual currencies, such as Bitcoin.[48]

Under such circumstances, Fung et al believe that for three reasons uniformity of currencies among all digital currencies will not be achieved:

- **First,** they opine, no government would be willing to establish the clearing mechanism required for those currencies to have fixed price with its currency.
- **Second,** no private entity will be able to establish the required mechanism as it would eventually run out of the government or virtual

---

46   *Ibid* at 31.
47   *An Act Respecting Banks and Banking*, 1890 (UK), 53 Vict, c 31.
48   Fung et al, above note 30 at 31.

currency necessary to intervene in the market to keep the exchange rate fixed.

- **Third,** it would not be in the interest of any virtual currency issuer to establish such a mechanism as it may undermine some of the competitive advantage that the issuer of any such a currency is attempting to achieve.

Lesson 5: A central bank can always get its digital currency into circulation, but its digital currency will not necessarily drive out private digital currencies

This lesson addresses the impact of a CBDC on virtual currencies and vice versa. The starting point is that "[h]istorical experience indicates that designating an instrument to be legal tender might not be enough to get it into circulation."[49] To that end Fung et al argue that the restrictions on banknote issue in the mid-nineteenth century were motivated by the policy of anchoring the then newly issued government money. Indeed, a well-accepted private or foreign currency may neither be uprooted nor uproot a publicly issued currency even where only the latter is legal tender. After all, unless the use of an alternative currency is successfully outlawed, to the point of effective enforcement of the prohibition of its use, it cannot be forced out. On their own, legal tender laws have not precluded parties from agreeing on payment in another currency. In a free market, a democratic country can insist on payment of taxes in legal tender, but not on more than that.

From this Fung et al conclude that "the historical evidence also suggests that if a central bank were to issue a digital currency, this currency would not drive out existing private digital currencies."[50] Rather, both the Canadian and US experience with private banknotes and public currency notes "suggests that if a private digital currency is in existence and the central bank begins to issue a digital currency, the two currencies will co-exist."[51] And yet, both in the United States and Canada, the historical experience suggests that changes in government regulation affecting the banknote issuance, and not the introduction of government-issued notes, triggered an improvement in the way banknotes functioned as media of exchange so as to "qualify" them to co-exist with the government-issued notes.

The authors then raise the question as to whether a virtual currency can gain wide acceptance if a government has the monopoly on issuing paper

---

49   *Ibid* at 32.
50   *Ibid.*
51   *Ibid.*

currency or coins denominated in a country's monetary unit. The answer they give is that:

> Octopus cards in Hong Kong, M-PESA in Kenya, PayPal prepaid balances and Visa/Master Card prepaid cards show that digital currencies denominated in a country's monetary unit can arise. Further, bitcoin shows that it is also possible for a digital currency with its own monetary unit can arise. That bitcoin's acceptance appears to be growing would seem to indicate that such an alternative digital currency can became widely accepted.[52]

They however go on to acknowledge that:

> [N]o government has yet issued a digital currency and so we don't know if people will still be using Octopus cards, M-PESA, prepaid cards, or bitcoin when there is a central bank digital currency.[53]

They end up speculating that:

> It is possible that people may find it more beneficial to use the central bank digital currency than these other digital currencies. Further, it is unlikely that bitcoin, or any other private digital currency that has it own monetary unit, will drive out central bank issued digital currencies.[54]

The ultimate conclusions of the study are that:

- **First**, privately issued digital currencies will not be perfectly safe without government intervention,
- **Second,** government-issued digital currency will not drive out existing private digital currencies, and
- **Third** government intervention will be required for privately issued and government-issued digital currencies to be a uniform currency.

IV. ANALYSIS

Multiplicity of currencies has been common in both global and Canadian monetary history. In fact, as long as the environment is competitive, treating "money" as it is a type of "goods" like any other "goods" available in a market, libertarians are likely to welcome the proliferation of currencies even to the

---

52   *Ibid.*
53   *Ibid.*
54   *Ibid.*

exclusion of a national one in all its forms.[55] And yet as already pointed out, a uniform unit of account appears to be essential to the smooth operation of transactions and hence markets. As for the interchangeability among various media, in each of his three studies[56] Weber presented the following characteristics that would make potential media of exchange more desirable for the non-issuer public. These characteristics were that they:

- provide ease of transacting;
- are subject to only minimal counterfeiting;
- provide a high degree of safety;
- are not subject to over issuance; and
- in the case of multiple media of exchange, provide a uniform currency.

In turn, according to Weber,[57] as for the last (fifth) element, multiple media of exchange of different issuers constitute a uniform currency, where:

1. they are expressed in the same monetary unit;
2. they trade at par (at their face value) in all transactions that involve the non-issuer public; and
3. prices are stated in terms of the monetary unit only, which means that different prices are not quoted for different media of exchange
   For its part, uniformity has been achieved by:[58]

- Redeemability in government currency notes on demand at the issuing bank at par;
- Par acceptance by every bank;
- Insurance covering the issuing bank's default;
- Gross clearing facility; and
- Clearing costs borne by issuers of banknotes.

The conclusion of all four studies discussed in this chapter has been that the achievement of a model complying with each of the above requires governmental intervention in the form of regulation and supervision. Such a model will be referred to hereafter in this chapter as an *optimal multi-media harmonized national monetary system*. Outside of such model, interchangeability and

---

55   For an exposition of this idea see Friedrich A Hayek, *Denationalisation of Money – The Argument Refined*, 3d ed (The Institute of Economic Affairs, 1990). For example, at 32–33 he argues that" universally, government's exclusive right to issue and regulate money" has not served the citizens but only those who rule them.

56   Weber-3, above note 14 at 8; see also Weber-1, above note 6 at 3; Weber-2, above note 7 at 4.

57   Weber-3, above note 14 at 9; see also Weber 2, above note 7 at 19.

58   Weber-2, above note 7 at 21–27.

smooth transferability are unlikely to be achieved. According to these studies, both the United States and Canadian experiences, each with banknotes issued by commercial banks side by side with government-issued currency notes, confirmed this conclusion.

Nonetheless, there are two obvious differences between the present situation and the one addressed by the studies discussed in this chapter. First, there is the point of historical direction. The studies addressed a scenario in which the movement was toward the take-over by the government of the monetary landscape. That is, privately issued media have been superseded by government-issued media with the period of multiplicity of currencies being transitional. Conversely, the present situation is an introduction of new currencies, predominantly privately issued, with a view of challenging the hegemony of the public system, and staying side by side with it indefinitely.

Second, there is a difference with regard to the media involved. As indicated earlier in this chapter, according to Weber,[59] media of exchange can be different either because they are of different "kinds" of media of exchange or of different "denominations" of the same "kind" of medium of exchange. By different "kinds" of media of exchange, Weber distinguishes between, for example, coins of different metals, paper currencies of different issuers, deposits in different banks, and so forth. By different "denominations," he distinguishes different numbers (denominations) on the same kind of medium of exchange. Technically, this is broad enough to cover electronic/digital media, except that the scenarios discussed in the earlier studies all involved tangible media. It is thus necessary to examine the conclusion of the earlier studies by reference to each of the media introduced by the new technologies.

The following digital assets may function as money once they exist and are so used:

1. Self-anchored cryptocurrencies (such as Bitcoin);
2. Electronic currency notes – unbacked by a full reserve – whether or not they are issued by banks;
3. Stablecoins purporting to maintain stable value by referencing the value of the Canadian dollar (and backed by a full reserve);
4. Stablecoins purporting to maintain stable value by referencing the value of a foreign official currency (and backed by a full reserve);
5. Stablecoins purporting to maintain a stable value by referencing the value of an asset (such as gold) or basket of assets (including official currencies) (and backed by a full reserve); and
6. CBDC.

59   *Ibid* at 20.

It is obvious that self-anchored cryptocurrencies such as Bitcoin will not be part of an optimal multi-medium harmonized national monetary system. This is so if only because it will not meet the uniformity of money requirement. Indeed, nothing should prevent people from making and receiving Bitcoin payments if they wish to do so. Furthermore, if demand justifies it, such people may establish a cold-storage facility maintaining bitcoin accounts through which they can make payments as envisaged by Ammous and discussed in chapter 1(VI). Legislative and regulatory intervention will be required to protect users and at least monitor and/or supervise the exchange with Canadian dollars. Otherwise, such system will not be linked in any way to the main Canadian monetary and payment system. Short of the occurrence of an extreme inflationary condition of the Canadian dollar, I see such a system bringing neither a risk to nor upheaval in the Canadian monetary system.

When it comes to a commercial bank's obligations serving as money in whatever form, it is useful to review some basics underlying the past experience with banknotes issued by them. As analyzed particularly in chapter 2, note issuing has historically been a banking function. In that respect, a bank's liability on a banknote bears no more risk than a bank's liability on a deposit. The problem is that a customer of Bank A, who accepts the risk (whatever it is) of the default of Bank A on its obligation, may not be ready to accept the risk of a default by Bank B on its obligation and thus may be reluctant to accept payment by means of Bank B's banknote. However, as pointed out, the solution lies in the establishment of an optimal multi-medium harmonized national monetary system – as existed both in Canada and the United States for paper currency notes. In that respect the electronic dimension does not provide any modifier. Strict controls preventing over-issuance will preclude the undermining of monetary policy.

Non-banks ought not to be allowed to issue circulating notes other than stablecoins. For their part, stablecoins ought to be fully backed and their issuers strictly regulated as discussed in chapter 4. In this framework they will provide protection to their holders. When they are denominated in (and backed by) Canadian dollar financial assets they will not undermine monetary policy. At the same time, saving on intermediation costs, their use is likely to adversely affect the use of existing payment systems.

Stablecoins denominated in and backed by financial assets other than the Canadian dollar – including a foreign currency – may risk monetary policy in the case of an extreme inflationary condition of the Canadian dollar but not otherwise. Under normal conditions they will provide a niche for those who require such payments.

Use of self-anchored cryptocurrencies and stablecoins not denominated in Canadian dollars may be restricted or otherwise controlled when such use may undermine monetary policy. However, such a power may be sparsely used – when a collapse of the Canadian dollar is seen to be imminent.

At present, stablecoins are mainly used to facilitate trading, borrowing, and lending of other crypto-assets. Nonetheless, they also hold the potential to compete as a broader medium of exchange for goods and services. Furthermore, they may become adopted across geographic areas and demographic groups, along with the digitalization trend of the global economy. The design and use of stablecoins could give rise to various risks in the financial system, particularly if the regulation of stablecoin issuers alone propels the growth of DeFi, which could exacerbate vulnerabilities in the overall sector if not appropriately regulated. For example, as discussed in chapter 4, stablecoins facilitate the creation of collateral chains and maturity/liquidity transformation in DeFi.

Just like bank deposits, stablecoins are vulnerable to confidence runs if token holders no longer believe a stablecoin can be redeemed or converted to another form of money on a one-to-one basis. However, the risk of runs on stablecoins can be mitigated by regulations to ensure that reserve assets are invested only in highly liquid and risk-free instruments or that it otherwise employs features of the safety net that currently exists for commercial bank deposits.

Finally, under a possible scenario where stablecoins prove to be a more efficient and low-cost payment instrument than existing alternatives, there could be wide-ranging implications for the supply of credit, the banking sector, and monetary policy.[60]

Zelmer and Kronick argue[61] that the Bank of Canada should adopt a CBDC as a way to facilitate the emergence of stablecoins that are tightly linked to the Canadian dollar. In their view, Canadian-dollar-linked stablecoins could become attractive to Canadians if they are convertible into cash issued by the Bank of Canada and are well designed and well regulated. Bank of Canada issued CBDC could also encourage the private sector to introduce

---

60 Cameron MacDonald and Laura Zhao, "Stablecoins and Their Risks to Financial Stability" (2022) Bank of Canada Staff Discussion Paper 2022-20, particularly concluding remarks at 24–25, online: https://www.bankofcanada.ca/wp-content/uploads/2022/11/sdp2022-20.pdf, accessed 5 July 2024.

61 Mark Zelmer and Jeremy Kronick, *Two Sides of the Same Coin: Why Stablecoins and a Central Bank Digital Currency Have a Future Together* (Commentary No 613, CD Howe Institute, 2021), online: https://www.cdhowe.org/sites/default/files/2021-12/Commentary_613.pdf, accessed 5 July 2024.

Canadian-dollar-linked stablecoins by enabling convertibility to take place digitally without having to rely on physical banknotes. Stablecoin platforms could also be given access to central bank liquidity facilities to ensure that transactions settle in a timely manner, and access to deposit insurance to help mitigate the risk of runs. That way, the Canadian dollar would continue to serve as the unit of account for most transactions in a crypto world, and Canadians would be able to reap the benefits of stablecoins without ceding control over key macroeconomic and financial stability policy levers.

The successful use case of retail CBDC (rCBDC) may well be in cross-border retail payments.[62] This, however, may not be enough to generate adequate demand for rCBDC. Unmet payment needs are typically those of the disempowered members of society. In turn, for an rCBDC to successfully address unmet payment needs, the main consumer groups – who already have access to a range of payment options – would have to widely adopt the CBDC and use it at scale. This is essential to encourage widespread merchant acceptance of CBDC, which would, in turn, encourage further consumer adoption and use.[63] A study by the Bank of Canada is skeptical about rCBDC penetration. It concludes that, "consumers face few payment gaps or frictions and therefore might have relatively weak incentives to adopt and – especially – to use CBDC at scale. If that were the case, widespread merchant acceptance also would be unlikely."[64] This may either overlook or underestimate merchants incentive in a CBDC setting to avoid or at least minimize card acceptance (including interchange) fees and suggests that addressing unmet payment needs for a minority of consumers by issuing a CBDC could be challenging. The minority of consumers with unmet payment needs will only be able to benefit from a CBDC if the majority of consumers experience material benefits and therefore drive its use.[65]

Nor is CBDC fundamental in defending monetary sovereignty by fending off "dollarization," namely, the displacement of the domestic national currency, in our case the Canadian dollar, by attractive foreign money.

----

62   See e.g., Project Icebreaker, *Breaking New Paths in Cross-border Retail CBDC Payments* (Bank for International Settlements Innovations Hub 2023), online: https://www.bis.org/publ/othp61.pdf, accessed 5 July 2024.

63   Christopher Henry et al, "Unmet Payment Needs and a Central Bank Digital Currency" (2023) Bank of Canada Staff Discussion Paper 2023-15, online: https://www.bankofcanada.ca/2023/08/staff-discussion-paper-2023-15/, accessed 5 July 2024.

64   PYMNTS, "CBDCs' Relevance Questioned After Canada Casts Skepticism" (*PYMNTS*, 11 August 2023), online: https://www.pymnts.com/cbdc/2023/cbdcs-relevance-questioned-after-canada-casts-skepticism/, accessed 5 July 2024.

65   Henry et al, above note 63.

True, emerging CBDC and global stablecoins (GSCs) in an attractive foreign currency will make access to that foreign currency significantly easier. Nevertheless, "the ['dollarization'] risk is greatest for countries with high or persistent monetary instability. Even the emergence of foreign CBDCs and GSCs will not fundamentally change this."[66] Accordingly, "foreign CBDCs or GSCs do not pose a threat to a state's monetary sovereignty per se; however, they may impede the attainment of monetary policy objectives when unfavourable economic conditions prompt residents to adopt substitute monies."[67]

Even prior to President Trump's Executive Order effectively prohibiting the issuance of CBDC (other than when required by law), several states in the United States had been in the process of disallowing its introduction, even if (in my view) not out of thoughtful consideration of the relevant factors.[68] And yet I am persuaded that full implementation should wait for further scientific advances. According to Amnon and Gideon Samid,[69]

> To come to its full power CBDC will need a dedicated financial language; universalisation, and standardisation. The tethered content will be written into the transactable coin, as well as to the accounting ledgers tracking that coin – all that must be part of the future CBDC, and it must be carefully designed. It takes time. If we rush to define the new sparkling CBDC as a payment scheme running on Ethereum then we botch this historic opportunity to come forth with a CBDC capable of delivering the historic impact one envisions.

Similarly, Corinne Zellweger-Gutknecht speaks of features such as "programmability [and] purpose-bound payment functionalities" as essential features to ensure CBDC superiority.[70] In that context, while stablecoins

---

66   Corinne Zellweger-Gutknecht, "CBDC and Monetary Sovereignty" in ECB Eurosystem, *Treading softly: How central banks are addressing current global challenges: ECB Legal Conference 2023* (European Central Bank, 2023) at 165, 175.

67   *Ibid* at 181.

68   Ledger Insights, "11 states have pending anti-CBDC legislation. South Dakota votes in favor" (*Ledger Insights*, 2 February 2024), online: https://www.ledgerinsights.com/11-states-have-pending-anti-cbdc-legislation-south-dakota-votes-in-favor/, accessed 5 July 2024. For President Trump's EO, that is, United States President, *Strengthening American Leadership in Digital Financial Technology* (Executive Order 14178), 90 Fed Reg 8647, see chapter 5(II).

69   Amnon Samid and Gideon Samid, "Central Bank Digital Currency (CBDC) – Why Go Slow" (*Fintech Future: North American Edition* 6 July 2022), online: https://www.fintechfutures.com/2022/07/central-bank-digital-currency-cbdc-why-go-slow/, accessed 5 July 2024.

70   Zellweger-Gutknecht, above note 66 at 175. "Tethering" and "programmability" refer to the ability to restrict the use of money to designated purposes.

are being improved, Christian Pfister criticizes a premature CBDC as "the introduction of subsidized means of payment into a competitive environment that has encouraged innovation."[71]

Accordingly, to a large extent, the global focus is now on small-scale special-purpose CBDC, not necessarily "retail" or "general purpose," but rather those aimed at niche applications, such as business-to-business or business-to-government platforms. Projects involve central banks of Australia,[72] Brazil,[73] Hong Kong,[74] and Hungary[75] exemplify this trend.

V. GOING FORWARD

So far as I can tell, tangible banknotes and commercial bank money, with the latter includes e-money fully backed by commercial bank money, are going to stay with us as retail payment means. Digital currencies, whether virtual or CBDC, are going to join as available options. Their appearance will affect the relative use of the other means – and give rise to questions particularly relating to the uniformity of money.

While diversity of currencies as means of payment as well as of units of account may accommodate specific economic and financial niches or pockets, it goes without saying that a uniform unit of account is essential for the operation of the national economic and financial system as a whole. However, at stake is the existence of diverse means of payment issued by diverse issuers, even when each adheres to the national or any other uniform unit of account. In that regard, it was pointed out in chapter 2(VI) that in recommending in 1933 to take away the power to issue circulating banknotes from commercial banks, the Macmillan commission was of the view that the exclusive right to issue legal tender notes would enable the central bank to

71   Christian Pfister, "Digital Euro: The Case Against Legal Tender" (*SUERF*, SUERF Policy Brief No 799, 15 Feb 2024), online: https://www.suerf.org/publications/suerf-policy-notes-and-briefs/digital-euro-the-case-against-legal-tender/, accessed 19 June 2024.

72   Reserve Bank of Australia, *Australian CBDC Pilot for Digital Finance Innovation* (Reserve Bank of Australia 2023), online: https://dfcrc.com.au/wp-content/uploads/2023/08/australian-cbdc-pilot-for-digital-finance-innovation-project-report.pdf, accessed 5 July 2024.

73   Banco Central do Brasil, "Drex: Digital Brazilian Real," online: https://www.bcb.gov.br/en/financialstability/drex_en, accessed 5 July 2024.

74   Hong Kong Monetary Authority, "Central Bank Digital Currency (CBDC)," online: <https://www.hkma.gov.hk/eng/key-functions/international-financial-centre/fintech/research-and-applications/central-bank-digital-currency/, accessed 5 July 2024.

75   Gloria Methri, "Central Bank of Hungary launches first live CBDC project with Perfinal" (*IBS Intelligence*, 18 August 2023), online: https://ibsintelligence.com/ibsi-news/central-bank-of-hungary-launches-first-live-cbdc-project-with-perfinal/, accessed 5 July 2024.

discharge its essential functions such as the regulation of credit and currency, keeping cash reserves for commercial banks, mobilizing gold reserves, managing the national debt, controlling exchange rates, and advising the federal Government. Accordingly, it opined, side by side with being a financial adviser to the Government, holding its accounts, and carrying out on its behalf all major financial transactions, a central bank "should have the sole right to issue legal tender notes" for its "full and satisfactory working" as such.[76]

I do not question the need to make central bank money, or its equivalent, available to the public at large, in one way or another. Indeed, parties who do not wish to take commercial bank risk – particularly the risk of failure of a bank other than theirs – may be given the opportunity to do so, at least as long as this goal does not conflict with policies underlying the prevention of crime, terrorist activity, money laundering, and tax evasion. Nevertheless, with respect, I do not find the Macmillan commission's reasoning to be persuasive, at least under present circumstances. Nor did Weber and Fung et al go so far. Granted, for successfully conducting monetary policy and perhaps to supplement other essential powers, a central bank ought to be given the ability to control the amount of commercial bank money available to the public; the latter being a derivative, or subject to the multiplier effect, of the amount of the central bank money available to commercial banks.[77] The composition of commercial bank money ought not to matter. Historically, it consisted of bank deposits and tangible banknotes. At present it consists exclusively of bank deposits. In the future it may consist of bank deposits and virtual currency.

To put it in simple terms, if virtual currency is issued by commercial banks, everything being equal, there will be no change in the amount of commercial bank money except that it will consist of demand deposits and digital coins issued by banks instead of only demand deposits as today. For their parts, virtual currencies issued other than by commercial banks ought to be stablecoins, fully backed by commercial bank money. True, as discussed in chapter 4, systematically important stablecoin arrangements may give rise to risks, except that those can be contained by proper regulation.

Nevertheless, the picture is more complex. The starting point is a broader context rooted in the five lessons proposed by Fung et al and addressed in Part III of this chapter. As discussed, they argued that the desired characteristics of

---

76 *Report of the Royal Commission on Banking and Currency in Canada* (Ottawa: Privy Council Office, 1933) at 65 para 218.

77 For the relationship among money supply, central bank money, commercial bank money, and the role of the multiplier effect, see e.g., Benjamin M Friedman, "The Future of Monetary Policy: The Central Bank as an Army with Only a Signal Corps?" (1999) 2 *International Finance* 261.

currency notes, whether issued privately or by a public authority, are ease of transaction, minimal counterfeiting, high degree of safety, scarcity so as to ensure the maintenance of stable value, and uniformity. Being skeptical, to say the least, as to the monetary utility of virtual currencies, the authors concluded that digital currencies will be counterfeited, inflationary, and unsafe; left on, that is without government intervention, they will be non-uniform currency. Nevertheless, they observed, virtual currencies are unlikely to be driven out by CBDC.

Accepting their observations as to the desired characteristics of currency note, I nevertheless do not share the gist, and primarily the spirit, of their analysis, other than the need for government intervention. In my view, so far as minimizing counterfeiting and enhancing security, there is no reason to preclude the existence, side by side with CBDC, of virtual currencies, equally meeting these requirements. If needed, regulation to that end will reinforce this conclusion. So far as the necessity for a medium of exchange to be scarce in order to maintain its value, the restriction to commercial bank money ought to meet this concern. As indicated, commercial bank money will be digital currency either issued by commercial banks or 100 percent reserve of commercial bank money to digital currency issued by other private (non-bank) entities.

The stumbling block is, however, the uniformity of money. Indeed, as discussed in this chapter, Weber and Fung et al envisaged co-existence of diverse media of payments in Canada. They further concluded that to meet the challenge posed by the ongoing evolution of the monetary system in Canada, uniformity of currency ought to be addressed. For its part, uniformity of currency consists of expression in the national unit of account, trading at par, uniform adherence to the national unit of account in prices, redeemability to government money on demand, acceptance at par, insurance against default, effective harmonized clearing, and clearing costs not being borne by users. A regime of effective regulation addressing non-bank issuers, and matters such as safety, security, and conformity with monetary policy, must be in place.

Uniformity of money is not undermined where alternative monetary objects are issued for circulation by the same issuer. For example, this is the case for the paper currency of Bosnia and Herzegovina, where most KM banknote are issued in two versions of design per each denomination, one for Federation of Bosnia and Herzegovina and the other for Republika Srpska (being the two Entities of which the State of Bosnia and Herzegovina consists).[78] By reference to other circumstances, on the basis of their study of the past, Fung et al mentioned a few reasons as to why uniformity of money cannot be

78   Centralna Banka Bosne I Hercegovine "KM Banknotes," online: https://cbbh.ba/Content/ Read/19, accessed 5 July 2024.

achieved in a system consisting of diverse issuers of virtual currencies. Their reasoning is premised on the lack of any incentive on the part of government, competing issuers, and any private entity to establish conditions toward the uniformity of money. I tend to agree with them on that point.

A recent Discussion Paper from the Bank of Canada[79] highlights the role of retail public money, at present in the form of cash, as being "essential to a well-functioning monetary system" if not as its cornerstone.[80] Particularly, it helps to ensure that money remains uniform.[81] In the authors' view:

> Retail public money has two key features. Due to its non-profit motive, it can be designed to be universally accessible and non-exclusionary. These features, together with the other regulatory elements of the monetary system, allow public money ... to interlink the different forms of private money defined in the official unit of account, making them convertible and uniform. Since no private issuer has the same incentives as the public sector, a monetary system without retail public money complementing the regulatory frameworks would be prone to fragmentation and market failures arising from the network effects of payment platforms.

Taking account digitalization, and thus the reduced use of cash, the authors thus propose that:[82]

> [T]o maintain a well-functioning monetary system during the transition to a more digital economy, the safer policy response seems to be to complement regulatory changes with the issuance of a digital equivalent to cash – a CBDC. In a future without a digital form of retail public money providing the disciplining channel for customers, the capacity of the regulatory framework to adapt would be weakened because all retail money in the economy would be privately issued. Private issuers would then be in a stronger position to shape the regulatory framework to their advantage.

Indeed, uniformity of money will be enhanced where the central bank issues rCBDC. Considering an earlier study that did not find public appetite for rCBDC,[83] the conclusion to issue it is, however, startling. At the same time, a variation premised on public currency as an anchor and yet offering an enhanced role to the public sector will now be put forward.

---

79   Francisco Rivadeneyra, Scott Hendry, and Alejandro García, "The Role of Public Money in the Digital Age" (2024) Bank of Canada Staff Discussion Paper 2024-11, online: https://www.bankofcanada.ca/wp-content/uploads/2024/07/sdp2024-11.pdf, accessed 26 July 2024.
80   *Ibid* at 1–2.
81   *Ibid* 19.
82   *Ibid* at 6.
83   Henry et al, above note 63.

One option is to have the central bank issue a generic no-frills CBDC allowing commercial banks to compete among themselves by clothing it with add-on features available only to their customers. Alternatively, and yet to the same end, uniformity will be enhanced once means of payment in central bank money equivalents are issued by private players and are fully interchangeable – among themselves – and CBDC – if available. Fully backed by central bank money, such equivalents are known as "synthetic CBDC" or sCBDC. Effectively these are stablecoins fully backed by central bank money. Strictly speaking, not bearing a direct obligation of the central bank, such coins are not CBDC, and yet may practically be treated as such.[84]

Interestingly, such a proposal is a variation on a precedent in the paper money world. As pointed out in chapter 3, banknotes are issued in Hong Kong by designated commercial banks against Certificates of Indebtedness denominated in foreign currency issued to those banks by a Currency Board against payment of the amount in the foreign currency.[85] Similarly, what is offered here, is CBDC issued to a commercial bank against payment in central bank money in their settlement account.

To enhance the feature of sCBDC as a uniform money, a smooth clearing and settlement system ought to exist, something which is arguably possible to a much higher degree in the digital age for digital objects than for tangible objects in any previous era. For its part the central bank would ensure universal access either by regulation and/or by issuing its own "no-frill" CBDC in such diversified environment.

The sCBDC design herein presented is that of digital coins issued by private players against central bank money purchased by them from the central bank. Such a scheme mimics the issuance of written banknotes in the United Kingdom by several designated banks in Scotland and Northern Ireland.[86] In its digital expression under the model envisioned here, the digital coins are

<hr>

84 See Anna Maria Bracio and Jonas Gross, "Synthetic central bank digital currency (sCBDC) – Public private CBDC collaboration" (*Medium*, 15 July 2020), online: https://jonasgross. medium.com/synthetic-central-bank-digital-currency-scbdc-public-private-cbdc-collaboration-46a3f4eb9808, accessed 5 July 2024.

85 Chapter 2, above note 10, citing Joseph Yam, "Review of Currency Board Arrangements in Hong Kong" (Monetary Authority of Hong Kong, 5 December 1998) at 30, online: https://www.hkma.gov.hk/media/eng/publication-and-research/reference-materials/monetary/rcbahke.pdf, accessed 7 June 2024.

86 See *Banking Act*, 2009 pt 6, particularly s 213; for HM Treasury Consultation Document see HM Treasury, *Banknote issue arrangements in Scotland and Northern Ireland: A Consultation Document* (Her Majesty's Stationary Office 2005), online: https://webarchive.nationalarchives. gov.uk/+/http:/www.hm-treasury.gov.uk/media/7/0/banknote_issue_arrangements_210705. pdf, accessed 19 June 2024. For the legal nature of such banknotes, as promissory notes and otherwise, see *Clydesdale Bank v The Commissioners for her Majesty's Revenue & Customs* [2019] UKFTT 0419 (TC).

central bank money equivalents, so that no control will be accorded to private players on the amount of digital currency in circulation.

Such a design will reflect the public interest in promoting competition among issuers of digital currencies that will enhance innovation, something that will not happen if all aspects of digital currency will be handled exclusively by the central bank. Competition may relate to storage, exchange, transfer system, and possibly side-benefits, such as programmability, as well as others, similar to Air Mile points provided by credit card issuers. Hence, contrary to past experience relating to multiple issuers of paper money, the present digital era gives rise to a public interest in promoting the uniformity of money that is either issued or backed by the central bank and yet handled in proprietary systems of competing private sector players.

A key for successful necessary regulation is the establishment of standards for interoperability of the various systems. To that end, attention is to be given to a Canton Network Pilot, a most extensive blockchain project that connected forty-five leading financial institutions, asset managers, and service providers.[87]

With respect to such design three questions arise:

- First, who will be qualified to issue, distribute, and facilitate payments in either rCBDC or the so-called sCBDC?
- Second, will coins so issued be legal tender? and
- Third, to what extent if at all will virtual currencies survive in this environment?

The answer to the **first** question is simple. Under one scenario, only the central bank will issue the currency which will thus be CBDC. Alternatively, or even concurrently, whoever has an account with the central bank may issue a digital equivalent. Whether it is rCBDC or sCBDC, only such account holders will distribute and facilitate transfers of the digital currency. At the moment, only the large banks fall into that category. As for the **second** question, the starting point is that, sCBDC should have the same status as that of rCBDC directly issued by the central bank. This is because in a well-regulated and supervised system, as envisaged here, there is no reason why the central bank would not guarantee liability on digital coins fully backed by central bank money. In fact, such coins could well be legal tender, even without a direct liability of the central bank. Regardless, as pointed out in chapter 5(III), in the digital age, legal tender may not be a critical element in the acceptance

---

87 Canton, "Connected Capital Markets Take Flight: Insights From The Canton Network Pilot," online: https://www.canton.network/insights-from-the-canton-network-pilot, accessed 25 May 2024.

of any type of money. In any event, to enhance uniformity of money, it will suffice to require all banks to accept such currencies at par.

What is envisaged is a "hub, spokes and felloes" monetary system. Thereunder, each spoke (large commercial bank) is linked to the hub (the central bank); in turn, the various spokes are connected not only via the hub but also directly over the felloes. The digital currency itself is issued by either the central bank or each commercial bank against 100 percent reserve central bank money. It is distributed by the commercial banks, each facilitating a transfer system linked to all other transfer systems possibly under the auspices of the Canadian Payments Association (Payments Canada)[88] or a new interbank entity such as Interac. Those transfer systems are interconnected, interoperable, and may become integrated. The enhanced role given to commercial banks ("lambs") vis-à-vis the central bank (the "wolf") in the envisaged system requires a harmonious regulatory regime, with the central bank not overstepping in what would be better handled by the market.

As for the **third** question, that concerning virtual currencies, a distinction ought first to be made between stablecoins issued by non-banks (e.g., Fintech companies) and backed by commercial bank money and virtual currencies issued by commercial banks. The former are effectively secured by commercial bank money. At the same time, the latter, being themselves commercial bank money, carry the obligations of the issuing commercial banks which are not different from those on their deposit obligations. As discussed, and in fact pointed out by Fung et al, achieving uniformity of money for this kind of assortment of digital coins may be a challenging task. Even maximal interoperability facilitated by the most advanced Canton Network may not overcome variation in issuers' credit worthiness, which is bound to undermine the uniformity of money. For sure, they will be overshadowed by CBDC or sCBDC. On top of this, a landscape consisting of rCBDC/sCBDC circulating side by side with stablecoins and virtual coins, all of which are denominated in the Canadian currency is bound to be confusing. It will thus be a difficult regulatory decision how far to accommodate such a diverse system, universally, in selected niches, or even at all.

Either way, it is obvious that the emerging environment will be different from the one that gave rise to multiple currencies in the previous centuries. During those periods a uniform unit of account connected multiple tangible monetary objects. Compared to the era of concurrent use of Dominion and bank currency notes, the forthcoming digital environment will be more

---

88   Under the *Canadian Payments Act*, RSC 1985, c C-21.

complex – if only because distribution and transfer (namely payment) are integral parts of the monetary system itself. As pointed out, the emerging system will not necessarily gravitate to a single homogenous system – as the one out of which we are now exiting. At the same time, the treatment of the situation at the time of the past concurrency among multiple tangible monetary objects provides a good basis for devising measures to address the evolving conditions of the forthcoming environment.

To complicate matters, technological innovation may facilitate the use of digital currencies operating on their own in payments in which the Canadian dollar is neither the money of payment nor the money of account. Schemes operating such systems are unlikely to undermine the Canadian dollar or more in general, the monetary sovereignty of Canada. However, in turn, they are bound to require legislative or regulatory interference with the view of protecting the public.

As pointed out in chapter 2, full and exclusive competence relating to money and the monetary system was thus given to the federal Parliament.[89] It was also indicated there that the Preamble to the *Bank of Canada Act, 1934*[90] envisioned the assignment to the Bank of Canada the powers "to regulate credit and currency ... [and] to control and protect the external value of the national monetary unit ... ." However, insofar as the domestic currency regulation power is concerned, only the power to issue currency notes was explicitly given to the Bank of Canada.[91] Furthermore, as further indicated in chapter 2, the power – which may not be delegated – "to aid the control and protection of the external value of the monetary unit of Canada" was given under section 17(2) of the *Currency Act*[92] to the minister in whose name the Exchange Fund Account is run. Finally, the *Bank of Canada Act* equips the Bank with the means of conducting "monetary policy or promoting the stability of the Canadian financial system."[93] However, on monetary policy the statute fastens on the minister of finance and the governor of the Bank of Canada a duty to "consult regularly." In a case of "a difference of opinion" the minister is accorded the power to overrule the governor, albeit not without

<hr>

89 Emilio S Binavince and H Scott Fairley, "Banking and the Constitution: Untested Limits of Federal Jurisdiction" (1986) 65 *Canadian Bar Review* 228 at 333–37, albeit focusing on the banking jurisdiction.

90 *Bank of Canada Act*, SC 1934, c 43.

91 Originally in s 24(1) *ibid*; at present *Bank of Canada Act*, RSC 1985, c B-2, s 25(1).

92 *Currency Act*, RSC 1985, c C-52.

93 *Bank of Canada Act* 1985, above note 91, s 18(g).

taking required formal specified steps.[94] Stated otherwise, even in matters of monetary policy the Bank of Canada is not given an exclusive power.

All this appears to have worked very well in the current centralized system. However, the system I envision will be less centralized and yet, if only to ensure an effective monetary policy and uniform currency, not be decentralized. In a nutshell, tangible banknotes and coins issued by the Bank of Canada and the Royal Mint are likely to stay with us in the digital age. They may be needed in emergencies and perhaps for some vulnerable members of the public. Meeting adequate demand where and when they are needed may well present a logistical challenge.

Nonetheless in the final analysis, I envision the monetary system in Canada to become overwhelmingly digital. It will be dominated by either a no-frill CBDC issued by the Bank of Canada – supplanted by add-on features of each commercial bank – or a series of linked interoperable sCBDC – each issued against full central bank money and bearing its own competitive improvement.

To that end, against the background of potential emergence of new currencies, it is recommended to go back to the drawing board and design a scheme clearly dividing powers relating to the regulation of currency in Canada. Arguably, the leadership already held by the Bank of Canada in terms of currency issuance as well as the regulation of payment system risk, together with its leadership in affecting monetary policy, ought to accord the Bank of Canada a primary role in shaping the forthcoming evolution of the required legislative scheme.

94   *Ibid*, s 14.

ABOUT THE AUTHOR

Benjamin Geva, LLB (cum laude) (1970), Jerusalem; LLM, and SJD (commercial law area) Harvard Law School; member of the Law Society of Ontario; specializing in monetary and payment law, commercial banking, negotiable instruments, funds transfers, digital currencies, payment and settlement systems, and documents of title.

Professor of Law, Osgoode Hall Law School of York University, Toronto, Canada (faculty member since 1977); Research Fellow, University of Vienna, Department of European, International, and Comparative Law Team (2024–); counsel (part-time), payments and cards group in Torys LLP, Toronto (since 2012);

Founding Editor of the *Banking and Finance Law Review*; author of *Financing Consumer Sales and Product Defences*; *The Law of Electronic Funds Transfers*; *Bank Collections and Payment Transactions: Comparative Study of Legal Aspects*; and *The Payment Order of Antiquity and the Middle Ages: A Legal History*. Co-author of *International negotiable Instruments*.

Under the International Monetary Fund technical assistance program he advised and drafted key financial sector legislation, particularly payment laws, in several developing and post-conflict countries (particularly in the former Yugoslavia, Cambodia, Sri Lanka, and Timor-Leste). For the World Bank he has been advising on banking transactions code for Ethiopia; for the Asian Development Bank he advised on CBDC in Bhutan.

Writer of numerous articles particularly on funds transfers, negotiable instruments, and digital currencies; held numerous visiting positions in United States universities (Chicago, Illinois, Northwestern, Duke program in Hong Kong, and Utah), Australia (Melbourne, Monash, Deakin, and Sydney),

Israel (Tel Aviv), Singapore (National University of Singapore), as well as in France (Aix-en-Provence), and Germany (Hamburg); also held research fellowships at Oxford University, Cambridge University, Max-Planck Institute for Comparative and Private International Law (Hamburg), New York University, University of Vienna, and UNCITRAL; member of MOCOMILA (Monetary Law Committee of the International Law Association); participant in projects and working groups working on and drafting domestic and international legislation on personal property security, securities transfers, letters of credit, payment systems, documents of title (transport documents and warehouse receipts), and banking transactions.